HARALAMBOS *and* HOLBORN

Sociology
Themes and Perspectives

AS- and A-level

STUDENT HANDBOOK

Martin Holborn Peter Langley

Published by HarperCollins *Publishers* Limited
77–85 Fulham Palace Road
Hammersmith
London W6 8JB

www.**Collins**Education.com
On-line Support for Schools and Colleges

British Library Cataloguing in Publication Data
A catalogue record for this publication
is available from the British Library

ISBN 0 00 712901 7

10 9 8 7 6 5 4 3 2

Commissioned by Thomas Allain-Chapman
Edited by Sarah Pearsall
Text and cover design by Patricia Briggs
Typesetting by Ken Vail Graphic Design
Printed and bound in the UK by Scotprint

Additional editorial support by Sam Richardson.

You might also like to visit:

www.**fireandwater**.com
The book lover's website

Contents

Acknowledgements

The Publisher and authors would particularly like to thank
Pam Law, Ruth Moores and Steve Chapman for their
substantial and invaluable contribution to this book.
The AQA-style questions were written by Pam Law and Ruth
Moores, and the OCR-style questions by Steve Chapman.

Using this Study Guide

Each chapter of the *Study Guide* consists of five elements.

1 Specification map

Simple grids show you how each chapter relates to the AQA and OCR specifications and assessment.

2 Essential notes

These summarize key issues, arguments and studies in an accessible and simple way. The material included has been selected from the main book because of its relevance to the A-level specifications. The Essential Notes can be used as a record of your course, for revision or as a reminder of the content of the main book.

3 Test your knowledge and understanding

A series of carefully chosen multiple-choice questions at the end of each chapter aims to make you think, as well as simply testing your knowledge. Try answering a few after you have covered each part of a chapter or work through them all as a form of revision. Correct answers are provided at the end of the book.

4 Develop your analysis and evaluation skills

You are given a number of statements that reflect key debates in each chapter. Find out which sociologists agree and which disagree with the views expressed. Why do these differences of opinion exist and what do they tell us about different sociological perspectives? These exercises aim to develop your analytical skills and there are detailed notes on each in the answer section of the study guide (see p. 214).

5 Practice exam questions

Each chapter ends with sample exam questions written by senior examiners from AQA and OCR. The questions are annotated to show how you can use each chapter in the AS or A2 exams, provide guidance on exam technique and give you a clear idea of what will be expected of you in the exams.

Using Sociology Themes and Perspectives

A guide for AS- and A-level students

The table below should give you a quick idea of the relationship between chapters of Sociology: Themes and Perspectives and the OCR and AQA A level specifications. A more detailed 'map' is provided at the start of each chapter of this Study Guide. In practice there is much overlap between different areas of Sociology and the book reflects this. Issues of class, ethnicity and gender, for example, are considered in most chapters and in most parts of both specifications. Similarly, an awareness of sociological perspectives is necessary to follow the key debates in most topics, especially at A2 level. Your ability to see the links between different parts of the course will be tested in the A2 'synoptic' module.

Chapter	AQA
1 Sociological perspectives	Relevant throughout course
2 Social stratification	A2 module: Stratification and differentiation (one option - synoptic)
3 Sex and gender	A2 module: Stratification and differentiation (one option - synoptic)
4 Race, ethnicity and nationality	A2 module: Stratification and differentiation (one option - synoptic)
5 Poverty and social exclusion	AS module: Wealth, poverty and welfare (one option)
6 Crime and deviance	A2 module: Crime and deviance (one option - synoptic)
7 Religion	A2 module: Religion (one option)
8 Families and households	AS module: Families and households (one option)
9 Power, politics and the state	A2 module: Power and politics (one option)
10 Work, unemployment and leisure	AS module: Work and leisure (one option)
11 Education	AS module: Education (one option)
12 Culture and identity	Theme runs through the whole specification
13 Communication and the media	AS module: Mass media
14 Methodology	AS module: Sociological methods
15 Sociological theory	A2 module: Theory and methods Relevant throughout course

OCR

Relevant throughout course, especially at A2

A2 module: Social inequality and difference (synoptic)

A2 module: Social inequality and difference (synoptic)
AS module: Individual and society

A2 module: Social inequality and difference (synoptic)
AS module: Individual and society

A2 module: Social inequality and difference (synoptic)

A2 module: Power and control (Crime and deviance option)

AS module: Culture and socialization (Religion option)

AS module: Culture and socialization (Family option)

A2 module: Power and control (Protest and social movements option)

A2 module: Social inequality and difference (synoptic)

A2 module: Power and control (Education option)

AS module: Individual and society
AS module: Culture and socialization (Youth and culture option)
A2 module: Power and control (Popular culture option)

AS module: Culture and socialization (Mass media option)
A2 module: Power and control (Popular culture option)

AS module: Sociological research skills/Research report
A2 module: Applied research skills/Personal study

Relevant throughout course, especially A2

Chapter 1

Sociological perspectives

Textbook pp. 2–21

Specifications

Specification	Relevant module title	Place in module	Level	Assessment	Other relevant modules
AQA	5: **Sociological theory** and Methods	Main topic of module.	A2	*Either:* One compulsory data-response question **and** one essay question from a choice of two *or:* sociological study (coursework).	This chapter gives a basic introduction to the sociological theory that underpins every module in the AS/A2 specification. See also Chapter 15.
OCR	There is no module on this topic in the OCR specification.	n/a	n/a	n/a	This chapter gives a basic introduction to the sociological theory that underpins every module in the AS/A2 specification but which is given greater emphasis in A2. See also Chapter 15.

Sociological perspectives: essential notes

Culture and society

Ralph Linton (1945) sees culture as the way of life shared by members of a society. It is learned and is a vital part of human society

Cultures vary from society to society. For example, some societies have practised geronticide (the killing of old people). Tasmanian Aboriginals, for example, sometimes left the old to die.

- Socialization is the process through which you learn a culture, and it continues throughout life.
- Primary socialization is the first phase, often taking place in the family.
- Peer groups (groups of a similar age and status), the education system and occupations are important agents of secondary socialization.
- Socialization is essential for participation in human society; humans who have not been socialized – e.g. the wolf-children of Midnapore (see p. 4) – find it very difficult to adapt to human society.
- Values are general guidelines about what is considered good and desirable or bad and undesirable in a society. In contemporary Britain, widely held values include acquiring material possessions, honesty, and so on. In Sioux society, generosity was a key value.
- Norms are specific guides to action which derive from general values. Norms define when, for

example, it is acceptable to remove clothes. Norms are regulated by negative sanctions (punishments) and positive sanctions (rewards).
- Statuses are social positions, such as doctor, teacher, student, wife, man, member of an ethnic group, teenager and so on. Some statuses are ascribed (given to you and largely fixed), e.g. statuses of male and female; others are achieved (they result from your own actions), e.g. different job statuses.
- Each status has social roles attached to it which specify appropriate behaviour for the status (e.g. the roles of teacher and pupil). Roles make behaviour reasonably predictable, though people do not always conform to them.

The development of human societies

Some sociologists see societies as having gone through broad developmental stages, such as premodern, modern and postmodern.

Premodern societies

Anthony Giddens (1997) distinguishes three types:
- Hunting-and-gathering societies based on hunting animals and gathering fruit and vegetables.
- Pastoral and agrarian societies in which animal herding and settled agriculture have developed.
- Non-industrial civilizations such as the Aztecs, Ancient Egyptians, Greeks and Romans.

Modern industrial societies

These started developing in the late eighteenth and nineteenth centuries. Lee and Newby (1983) identify four key features:

- Industrialism – the Industrial Revolution started in the late eighteenth century. It greatly increased human productive power and reduced the degree to which nature shaped social life.
- Capitalism involved the employment of labour for wages and businesses based upon making profits.
- Urbanism resulted in populations being increasingly concentrated in towns and cities.
- Liberal democracy eventually replaced monarchical rule, giving people a say in how society was run.

The above changes have been seen as creating modernity, which involves a belief in the ability to plan, achieve progress and solve problems using science and technology. Some see sociology as closely involved with modernity.

Postmodernity

Postmodernity is claimed by some sociologists to be replacing modernity.

- Postmodernity tends to involve a loss of faith in science and rationality, a loss of belief in progress and increased scepticism about any theories that claim to be able to produce a better future.
- Some non-rational beliefs (such as New Age beliefs) have become more popular. According to some postmodernists, the changes are linked to a post-industrial (service- or information technology-based) economy.

To some postmodernists, older theories of society have become outdated, but other sociologists question the value of theories of postmodernity.

Theories of society

Functionalism

Leading functionalists include Emile Durkheim (1858–1917) and Talcott Parsons (1902–79).

- Originally functionalists borrowed ideas from biology. They saw each part of society as having a function (a purpose or a job it does) like each part of the body (e.g. the government of a society is like a human's brain).
- Functionalists see society as having a structure, with key institutions performing vital functions, and roles directing people in how to behave.
- They identify the functions of each part of the structure – e.g. the family socializes the young and produces a shared culture.
- Institutions are there to meet the basic needs or functional prerequisites of society – e.g. producing food and shelter for people.
- A value consensus (shared beliefs about right and wrong) helps society to run smoothly and integrate the different parts.

Conflict perspectives

Conflict perspectives argue that there are differences of interest between groups in society (what is good for one group is bad for another). This creates the potential for conflict between groups. There are a range of conflict theories.

Marxism

Marxism is based upon the work of Karl Marx (1818–83), though it has been adapted by later writers.

- Marx argues that societies result from humans getting together to produce food.
- The forces of production (the technology used to produce things) shape social relationships.
- The economic system consisting of the forces and social relationships of production forms the infrastructure of society.
- The infrastructure shapes other parts of society such as the government, family life, the education system and religion, which collectively are known as the superstructure.
- Most societies are based upon exploitation of some groups by others. Those who own the means of production (such as the land, factories, raw materials or capital) exploit those who work for them, who lack the means to produce things themselves.
- Contemporary societies are seen as capitalist societies in which the owners of capital are dominant.
- Capitalists (the bourgeoisie) exploit their workers (the proletariat) by paying them less in wages than the wealth created by their work. Capitalists accumulate profits (or surplus value) and get richer and richer.
- In capitalist societies, the ruling class owns the means of production. It tries to use the superstructure (e.g. the government, legal system, religion and the mass media) to persuade workers that society is fair and just, in order to prevent workers from rebelling against their exploitation. If it succeeds, ruling class ideology is dominant and creates false class consciousness (a mistaken belief that society is fair) amongst workers.
- Eventually workers will come to realize that they are being exploited and will overthrow capitalism and create a communist society.
- In communism the means of production (land, factories, etc.) will be communally owned, so there will be no ruling class, no exploitation and much less inequality than in capitalism

Feminism

There are different versions of feminism but all see society as divided between men and women.

- Feminists tend to see women as exploited by men, and society as patriarchal or male-dominated.
- Examples of patriarchy include men monopolizing high-status and well-paid jobs, doing less housework than women and holding the most senior positions in politics.
- Most feminists tend to see women as having shared interests, and believe that progress towards ending patriarchy is possible.
- Difference feminists argue that different groups of women may have different interests, and that not all women are equally exploited.

- Many feminists criticize sociology (particularly older sociology) as being malestream: that is, written by men, largely about men and from a masculine viewpoint.

Interactionism

Unlike macro theories (which look at society as a whole, e.g. Marxism and functionalism), interactionism (a micro theory) looks at social behaviour in smaller groups.

- Interactionists stress the importance of meanings – the way people interpret the behaviour of others.
- Meanings develop during interaction as people try to get a feel for the intentions behind other people's actions.
- Humans possess a self-concept, or idea, of what sort of person they are.
- Self-concepts develop in response to the reactions of others. You end up thinking of yourself in the same way as others think of you.
- Like functionalists, interactionists believe that roles exist, but they see them as much more flexible and negotiable. For example, married couples develop their own interpretations of the roles of husband and wife.
- Society is seen as more fluid, less rigidly fixed, than in macro theories.

Postmodernism

Postmodernist perspectives have developed since the 1980s.

- Some versions see important changes taking place in society.
- Other versions question the ability of conventional sociology to produce worthwhile theories of society.
- Some postmodernists argue that social behaviour is no longer shaped by factors such as class, gender, ethnicity and different types of socialization. It is now simply a question of lifestyle choice.
- Some postmodernists argue that sociological theory can never objectively describe the social world.
- Lyotard (1984) criticizes all grand or general theories, and many postmodernists stress that everybody's viewpoint on society is equally valid.

Views of human behaviour

There are three main views of human behaviour, which underlie different approaches to producing sociological data.

Positivism

- Positivists believe that human behaviour can be objectively measured.
- Direct observation can produce objective data, and only that which can be observed should be studied.
- Human behaviour is shaped by external stimuli.

- Sociologists should use natural science methods.
- Statistical data can be produced which can be used to uncover cause-and-effect relationships between two or more things.

Social action perspectives

- Social action perspectives argue that sociology is not like the natural sciences because it involves the study of conscious human beings.
- Humans interpret the meaning of things before reacting and do not react passively to external stimuli.
- In order to explain behaviour, sociologists need to examine what is going on inside people's heads – these internal meanings cannot be directly observed.
- Proponents of social action approaches include Max Weber (1864–1920) and the interactionists.

Phenomenology

- Phenomenologists deny that any objective classification of the social world is possible.
- All categorization is subjective; statistics are simply based upon personal opinions (e.g. whether a death is a suicide).
- Without factual data, causal explanations of human behaviour cannot be produced.
- Sociologists can only really study the factors that influence the way people categorize the world (i.e. what makes them decide that a death is a suicide or that a particular action is a crime).

Sociology and values

Positivists believe that an objective, unbiased, value-free sociology is possible, but many sociologists argue that it is not. They argue that a researcher's values (or personal beliefs about right and wrong) are bound to influence what they study, how they study it and how they interpret the data.

- Functionalism has often been seen as supporting the status quo and opposing change because it views all institutions as having useful functions. It is therefore seen as having a conservative ideology.
- Marxism and feminism both advocate change in order to remove exploitation and oppression. They can therefore be seen as having radical ideologies.

The sociological imagination

Some sociologists, such as Giddens (1977, 1979, 1984), argue that different perspectives should be combined and that both social structure and social action are important for understanding society.

C. Wright Mills (1959) advocates a similar approach. He argues that links should be made between public issues (such as unemployment) and personal troubles (such as the experience of the unemployed individual).

1 Socialization is:
   a Mixing with other people
   b Influencing other people
   c Learning how society expects you to behave
   d Beliefs about right and wrong

2 The first stage of socialization is called:
   a Primary socialization
   b Initial socialization
   c Elementary socialization
   d Baby socialization

3 An example of a value in British society would be:
   a A belief in the superiority of the English football team
   b A belief that honesty is desirable
   c A belief in UFOs
   d A belief in the theory of evolution

4 An example of an ascribed status is:
   a The status of a taxi driver
   b The status of being a good footballer
   c The status of having passed a degree
   d The status of being a woman

5 A norm is:
   a A specific guide to acceptable behaviour in a social situation
   b Being normal
   c A belief in right and wrong
   d A position in society and the behaviour associated with it

6 Which one of the following is not a key feature of modern industrial societies, according to Lee and Newby?
   a Capitalism
   b Urbanism
   c Liberal democracy
   d Freedom

7 The central feature of modernity is:
   a A belief in the ability to achieve rationally planned progress
   b A lack of faith in science
   c A strong belief in religion
   d The key importance of information technology

8 Postmodernity involves which two of the following?
   a The revival of non-rational beliefs
   b The dominance of manufacturing industry
   c Scepticism about theories which claim to be able to create the perfect society
   d Faith in science

9 Which one of the following perspectives is most likely to see institutions in society as being useful?
   a Functionalism
   b Marxism
   c Feminism
   d Interactionism

10 Which one of the following theories sees the exploitation of women as a key feature of society?
    a Functionalism
    b Marxism
    c Feminism
    d Interactionism

11 Which one of the following theories sees the exploitation of the working class as a key feature of society?
    a Functionalism
    b Marxism
    c Feminism
    d Interactionism

12 Which one of the following theories is a micro theory?
    a Functionalism
    b Marxism
    c Feminism
    d Interactionism

13 Which one of the following theories emphasizes lifestyle choice?
    a Functionalism
    b Marxism
    c Feminism
    d Postmodernism

14 Which one of the following theories emphasizes the importance of the self-concept?
    a Marxism
    b Feminism
    c Interactionism
    d Postmodernism

15 Which one of the following theories emphasizes the difficulty of categorizing the social world?
    a Marxism
    b Social action perspectives
    c Positivism
    d Phenomenology

16 Which one of the following theories emphasizes the importance of following objective, scientific methods?
    a Interactionism
    b Positivism
    c Phenomenology
    d Social action perspectives

17 Which one of these sociologists is most associated with a social action approach?
    a Giddens
    b Weber
    c Marx
    d Lyotard

18 Objective means the same as:
    a Value-laden
    b Value-free
    c Valueless
    d Valuable

19 Which one of these perspectives is often seen as having a conservative ideology?
    a Conflict theory
    b Marxism
    c Feminism
    d Functionalism

20 C. Wright Mills argued that sociology should study the relationship between:
    a The news and history
    b Structure and social action
    c Public issues and personal troubles
    d The economy and society

Develop your analysis and evaluation skills (see p. 195 for guidance notes)

For each of the following statements, identify which sociologists would argue in favour of and which against the view expressed. Explain the reasons for their view.

1 In Britain today we live in a modern society.
2 All societies are characterized by a structure in which people cooperate on the basis of shared norms and values.
3 Sociology is a scientific subject which should use scientific methods.

Chapter 2

Social stratification

Specifications
NB 'Social Differentiation, Power and Stratification' is a core theme of both specifications.

Specification	Relevant module title	Place in module	Level	Assessment	Other relevant modules
AQA	6: **Stratification and Differentiation**; Crime and Deviance	One of two options in this module.	A2	One three-part synoptic question.	This module is synoptic. This means that you will have to link your work here to other topics, key sociological theories and concepts and research methods.
OCR	**Social Inequality and Difference**	Sole topic of module.	A2	One from a choice of two multi-part data-response questions.	This module is synoptic (see above).

Social stratification: essential notes

Introduction

Social inequality refers to any differences that result in some people having more socially valued characteristics than others. Degrees of power, prestige and wealth may be significant.

Social stratification refers to a situation in which people are divided into distinct groups ranked at different levels. The Hindu caste system is an example – different castes have different levels of status depending on their supposed degree of religious purity.

Those at different levels in a stratification system may develop a common subculture or way of life.

Social mobility refers to movement between strata.

Status in stratification systems can be ascribed (given at birth, e.g. the caste system) or achieved (resulting from what you do, e.g. class systems).

Life chances are your chances of getting socially desirable things (e.g. money, education, longevity), and are affected by your place in the stratification system.

Stratification systems have sometimes been based on what were thought to be natural inequalities or biological differences (e.g. apartheid in South Africa assumed that whites were superior to blacks). However, sociologists see such views as rationalizations to legitimate the position of powerful groups.

A functionalist perspective

Parsons – stratification and values
- Parsons (1964) sees all societies as having a value consensus – a general agreement about what is desirable and valuable (or undesirable). Whatever these values, individuals will be ranked in accordance with them.

- Stratification is inevitable as all societies have some values and will make judgements.
- In complex industrial societies, planning and organization require some individuals to have more authority than others.
- Stratification unites people because it derives from shared values.

Criticisms
Critics argue that many values are not shared and that stratification can be highly divisive.

Davis and Moore – role allocation and performance
1. Davis and Moore (1967, first published 1945) argue that all societies share certain functional prerequisites. One of these is role allocation – ensuring that roles are filled and performed effectively and conscientiously.
- Some jobs are more functionally important and some people have more ability than others.
- To match the most able to the most important jobs, and to ensure that tedious, unpleasant or dangerous jobs are filled, a rewards system is needed.
- The better-rewarded will form a higher stratum. This process is inevitable, universal (found in all societies) and beneficial because it helps society to function better.

Criticisms
Melvin Tumin (1953) argues that:
1. Many low-paid and even unskilled jobs are just as vital as higher-paid or more skilled jobs.
2. There is a greater pool of talent than Davis and Moore assume.

3 Training is a pleasant experience and does not require extra rewards to persuade people to undertake it.
4 Stratification systems can demotivate those at the bottom.
5 Stratification systems do not provide equality of opportunity and tend to prevent those from lower strata achieving their potential.
6 Stratification systems encourage 'hostility, suspicion and distrust'.

A Marxist perspective

According to Marx:
- All stratified societies have two major classes: a ruling class and a subject class.
- The ruling class owns the means of production (land, capital, machinery, etc.), and the subject class does not.
- The ruling class exploits the subject class.
- The ruling class uses the superstructure (e.g. legal and political systems) to legitimate (justify) its position and prevent protests by the subject class.
- In capitalist societies the main classes are the bourgeoisie (the capitalist class who own the main means of production – capital) and the proletariat (the working class who have to sell their labour to survive).
- The bourgeoisie exploits the working class through the system of wage labour. Capitalists pay wages to workers, but make a profit (surplus value) because they pay workers less than the value of what they produce.
- Capitalism is the newest type of class society but it will also be the last. Eventually it will be replaced by a communist society in which the means of production (land, capital, factories, machinery, etc.) will be communally owned.

The transition to communism will not be straightforward because it requires revolutionary action by the proletariat. However, the bourgeoisie uses the superstructure (e.g. the media, education system, and political and legal systems) to suppress the proletariat by creating false class consciousness (which means that workers do not realize that they are being exploited). Eventually, though, class consciousness will develop – workers will realize that they are being exploited and will rise up to change society.

Class consciousness will develop because:
- There is a basic contradiction in capitalist societies between the interests of workers and capitalists.
- Workers will become concentrated in large factories, making it easier to communicate with one another and organize resistance.
- Workers' wages will decline in relation to the growing wealth of capitalists, in order to maintain profits. There will be a polarization of classes, with the rich getting richer and the poor poorer, making inequalities more obvious.
- Skill divisions between workers will be reduced as new technology is introduced, resulting in a more homogeneous and united working class.

- The petty bourgeoisie (small capitalists such as shopkeepers) will be unable to compete and will sink into the proletariat.
- Capitalist economies are unstable, and economic crises and periods of high unemployment will cause growing resentment.
- Workers will join together to form unions, political parties and revolutionary movements as class consciousness grows, enabling them to overthrow capitalism and replace it with communism.

Criticisms
Many other theories and much of the research we will look at offer evaluation of the Marxist perspective.

A Weberian perspective

Max Weber (1864–1920) accepted some of Marx's ideas but rejected others.

Weber argued that classes develop from people's market situation (their situation in relation to buying and selling things, including their labour power) in market economies. Weber differs from Marx in a number of ways:
- Like Marx he saw a basic division between those who have considerable property (and can live off the proceeds) and those who do not – the propertyless – who have to sell their labour. However, there are also significant differences within the two groups as well as between them.
- Within the propertyless group there are some who can sell their labour for a higher price (those with scarce but sought-after skills such as professionals and managers). They have an advantaged market situation compared to other groups of workers. Unlike Marx, Weber therefore believed that different occupational groupings could form classes.
- Weber saw no evidence of a polarization of classes. Instead he thought that the middle class of white-collar workers in bureaucracies would expand.
- Weber did not believe that a revolution by the proletariat was likely.
- He thought that some, but not all, power came from wealth.
- He argued that class was not the only basis for group formation. Status groups (groups of people who enjoyed similar levels of status or respect in society) could also be formed. Status groups might be based on ethnicity, age, nationality, gender, etc., and tended to share similar lifestyles. Class and status could be closely linked (for example, ethnic minorities might be excluded from highly-paid jobs in a society), but this was not always the case. Status groups often cut across class divisions (e.g. members of the gay community).
- Organized groups which seek to exercise political power or influence those with power are called parties by Weber. Parties may be political parties (e.g. the Labour and Conservative parties) or they may be pressure groups. They may be based on class (e.g. the 'old' Labour Party), status groups (e.g. Gay Rights organizations) or neither (e.g. Greenpeace).

Changes in the occupational structure

- During the twentieth century the proportion of manual workers and personal service workers fell steadily from over three-quarters of all employees to well under a half, while the proportion of non-manual workers rose from under a quarter to over a half.
- Manufacturing industry declined, particularly in the last quarter of the twentieth century, while service industries grew.
- Private sector service jobs have increased rapidly over recent years.
- Women, especially married women, now form a bigger proportion of the workforce, but women are more likely to work part-time and are concentrated in intermediate and junior non-manual jobs.

The changing distribution of income

Income has an important effect on life chances. Official statistics measure income in a variety of ways:

- Original income refers to all income apart from state benefits.
- Gross income includes state benefits.
- Disposable income deducts tax and national insurance.
- Final income includes the value of benefits such as healthcare, which are not given in cash.

Government figures show that the poorest 20% receive less than half the average final income, while the richest 20% receive nearly twice the average. However, taxes and benefits do equalize and redistribute income to some extent.

The Royal Commission on the Distribution of Income found that there was some redistribution of income away from the richest groups between 1949 and 1979, but middle-income groups benefited most.

From 1979 to 1997 changes in taxation and benefits under Conservative governments generally benefited the well-off at the expense of the poor.

Since 1997 government policies have tended to favour those in low-paid work.

Overall, income inequalities declined in the twentieth century but not enough to eradicate class differences.

The changing distribution of wealth

- There are no direct measures of the distribution of wealth, but surveys and data on the value of the estates of those who have died give some indication of wealth distribution.
- Wealth can be defined in different ways: marketable wealth includes only things that can be sold; non-marketable wealth includes the value of pensions, etc.
- Available figures suggest that wealth inequalities narrowed from 1900 to the early 1990s, but started widening in the 1990s.
- Wealth remains quite highly concentrated: in 1994 the richest 1% of the population owned 19% of all marketable wealth, and the richest 10% owned 51%.
- The proportion of people in Britain owning shares has increased in recent years, but shares make up a declining proportion of personal wealth (15% in 1995), and most people only have small shareholdings.

Westergaard and Resler – a Marxist view

In 1975 Westergaard and Resler (1976) put forward a Marxist view that there was a ruling class in Britain consisting of the richest 5–10% of the population, whose position came from the ownership of capital. Private share ownership was highly concentrated in this minority group.

The ruling class was made up of company directors, top managers, higher professionals and senior civil servants, many of whom were big shareholders.

Saunders – a New Right view

Peter Saunders (1990) puts forward a New Right view of the upper class. He agrees with much of what Westergaard and Resler say about the concentration of wealth, but he sees this group as an influential economic elite rather than a ruling class.

Most big companies are run by managers with only small shareholdings in the company. Much wealth is not privately held but is in pension schemes, insurance policies, etc., meaning that most people have a stake in capitalism.

Saunders claims that the economic elite do not have most of the power – power is decentralized. Class divisions have weakened and a ruling class no longer exists.

Scott – Who Rules Britain?

John Scott (1982, 1991) is influenced by Marxism, elite theory and Weber.

Scott sees Britain as retaining an upper/ruling class but it is much changed since the nineteenth century.

- The upper class evolved from nineteenth-century interlocking networks of landowners, financiers and manufacturers.
- During the twentieth century, family-controlled companies became less common (though important ones remain) and joint stock companies developed. Furthermore, professional managers took a greater role in running companies.
- A capitalist class persists. The ownership of property for use (e.g. housing) has become more widespread, but the ownership of property for power (e.g. stocks and shares, privately owned businesses, etc.) remains highly concentrated.
- The decisions of big companies and big financial institutions are controlled by a network of managers and directors who often have directorships in many companies (interlocking directorships). This capitalist class comprises around 0.1% of the adult population.
- The policies of all governments (even Labour ones) are strongly influenced by the interests of the capitalist class, and governments cannot go against the interests of capitalists without risking grave economic problems.

Sklair – the global system and the transnational capitalist class

Leslie Sklair (1995) argues that globalization and the global system have produced a transnational capitalist class associated with major transnational corporations. Members of this class are not loyal to particular countries; they see their interests in terms of the capitalist system as a whole.

Criticisms

Sklair underestimates the importance of finance capitalists and the continuing power of nation-states, but he may be right to add a transnational dimension to ruling-class theory.

Elite theory and pluralism provide alternative views (see Chapter 9, pp. 101–2).

The middle classes

Marx's ideas on the middle class have influenced later research.

Marx argued that classes would be increasingly polarized between the bourgeoisie and the proletariat. The small business people/self-employed (the petty bourgeoisie) would sink into the proletariat.

Marx recognized the growing number of white-collar workers but said little about their significance. Many critics of Marx argue that there is a growing middle class which undermines his theory of two polarizing classes.

Weber, however, believed that there was a middle class, with superior life chances to the working class and a more advantaged market situation (they had skills and qualifications which were in demand, which allowed them to command higher wages than the working class).

The conventional way to distinguish the middle class and working class is to equate them with non-manual and manual workers. However, the idea that non-manual workers make up the middle class can be criticized:

1 Unlike Marxist and Weberian theories, it has little theoretical basis.
2 Non-manual workers are a diverse group which may overlap with other classes.

The upper middle class

Until the 1980s the petty bourgeoisie of self-employed and small employers declined in line with Marx's theory. However, from the 1980s it increased.

The professions

- The professions grew from around 4% of those employed in 1900 to over 10% by the 1990s.
- Professionals are employed both in growing private businesses and in the welfare state.
- They can be divided into lower professions (e.g. teachers, social workers, nurses) and higher professions (doctors, lawyers, accountants, etc.).
- Savage *et al.* distinguish between professions and welfare professions.
- Professionals generally have above-average incomes, but higher professionals/non-welfare professionals are particularly well paid. Both tend to have greater security and more fringe benefits than most other workers.

The functionalist perspective on the professions

Functionalists such as Bernard Barber (1963) see professional jobs as having distinctive attributes:

- Possession of a body of specialist knowledge.
- Concern for the interests of the community.
- Control of behaviour through a code of ethics.
- High rewards and prestige, reflecting their contribution to society.

Criticisms of functionalism

1 Many have criticized the professions – e.g. lawyers have been accused of mystifying the law; teachers have been attacked for allowing underachievement. Illich (1975) accuses doctors of hiding the damaging effects of the environment.
2 Weberians and Marxists provide alternative views.

The Weberian perspective on the professions

Parry and Parry (1976) believe that professions serve their own interests rather than community interests.

- They restrict entry to the profession in order to limit the supply of qualified workers so as to ensure they get high wages.
- Professional associations tend to protect and defend the image of the profession rather than protecting the public.
- Professional associations ensure that their members have a monopoly, thus protecting their interests.
- Professionalism is seen as a market strategy designed to maximize the security and rewards of a particular job, not as a characteristic of particular types of work.
- Higher professions get paid more than lower professions simply because they have achieved monopoly status (e.g. doctors and the BMA compared to teachers and their unions).

Macdonald – the professional project

Macdonald (1997) argues that groups of workers undertake what he calls the professional project – they organize to get their work accepted as professional using techniques such as social closure (excluding others), establishing their own jurisdiction and attaining respectability.

Professions as servants of the powerful

C. Wright Mills (1951) suggests that professions increasingly serve the interests of the powerful rather than their own interests. Professionals are largely employed by the rich or by large corporations and have to serve those who pay them.

The deskilling of professions

Braverman (1974) argued that professional work was being deskilled (the skill was being removed from it) as the work was increasingly controlled by the powerful.

The declining independence of the professions

Several sociologists have pointed to the declining independence of professionals – e.g. Johnson (1972) argues that accountants have to be loyal to their company above their profession.

The Ehrenreichs – the professional-managerial class

The Ehrenreichs (1979) do not see professions as a separate group. They put forward a neo-Marxist view that there is a distinct professional-managerial class making up 20–25% of the population.

They see this class as carrying out vital functions for capitalism:
- Organizing production.
- Controlling the working class.
- Promoting ruling-class ideology.
- Developing a consumer goods market.

There is conflict between this group and the working class, because the professional-managerial class serve the interests of the ruling class, and the working class sometimes resist their control.

Criticisms

1 Marxists such as E.O. Wright (1978) do not see this group as a distinctive class but merely as intermediate strata.
2 Weberian theorists see the middle classes in terms of market situation rather than the functions they perform for capitalism.

The lower middle class

This group includes clerical workers, secretaries and shop assistants.

According to the proletarianization thesis (supported by Marxists) this group has been proletarianized – they have become working-class.

Harry Braverman (1974) argues that they have been deskilled – e.g. clerical workers have gone from a virtual managerial role to doing very routine work.

Weberians tend to argue that the lower middle class remains distinct from the working class.

David Lockwood (1958) argues that:
1 They have a better market situation than the working class, with higher wages, job security and promotion prospects.
2 They have a better work situation, working closely with managers and not being closely supervised.
3 They have a superior status situation: their work has more prestige than manual work.

Stewart, Prandy and Blackburn (1980), in a study of large firms, argue that most male clerical workers remain middle-class because their jobs are often stepping-stones to junior management positions.

Crompton and Jones (1984) are critical of the Weberian views above. They argue that:
1 Most clerical workers are female and their promotion prospects are much lower than those of men.
2 Many supposed managerial positions to which clerical workers are promoted are themselves routine.
3 Clerical jobs have been deskilled and are now proletarian, whatever the prospects for individuals holding those positions.

Marshall, Newby, Rose and Vogler (1988), in their survey of 1,770 British people, found no evidence of deskilling or loss of autonomy at work among clerical workers. However, they found that personal service workers (who are largely female) had very little control or autonomy at work, and they could be regarded as working-class.

Middle class or middle classes

Giddens – the middle class

Giddens (1973) uses a Weberian perspective to claim that the middle class form a single group, with educational qualifications and the ability to sell their mental labour power.

Goldthorpe – the service and intermediate classes

Goldthorpe (1980) is also a Weberian but he distinguishes between a service class (larger employers, professionals, managers) and an intermediate class (clerical workers, small proprietors, technicians, etc.). The service class form a higher class of employees, who get increments on their salary and have pension rights and promotion prospects.

In later work Goldthorpe divides the middle class up according to whether they are employed, employers or self-employed.

Criticisms

Goldthorpe has been criticized for:
1 Failing to identify a difference between managers and employers and professionals.
2 Disagreeing with the Marxist view that big employers constitute a ruling class.

Roberts, Cook, Clark and Semeonoff – the fragmented middle class

Roberts et al. (1977) conducted a study of class images amongst 243 white-collar workers and distinguished four groups:
1 Those with middle-range, middle-class incomes had an image of society in which most people were middle-class (middle-mass image).
2 Small employers saw themselves as squeezed between a small upper class and a large mass of ordinary workers (compressed middle-class image).
3 Professionals tended to see society as a finely graded ladder of opportunity.
4 Clerical workers saw themselves as working-class (proletarian image).

Roberts et al. conclude that the middle class is fragmented.

Criticisms

This study is based on a small, all-male sample and includes only the subjective views of individuals rather than objective differences in their positions.

Abercrombie and Urry – the polarizing middle class

Abercrombie and Urry (1983) see the middle class as increasingly polarized between proletarianizing routine white-collar workers and professionals and managers with advantaged market and work situations.

Savage, Barlow, Dickens and Fielding

Savage et al. (1992) claim that the middle class can possess three different types of asset:
1 Property assets, which are owned in particular by the petty bourgeoisie.
2 Organizational assets – held, for example, by managers with jobs in large organizations.

3 Cultural assets – deriving from educational attainment and credentials – which are particularly concentrated amongst professionals.

Members of the middle class use their different types of asset to help their children gain middle-class positions.

These different types of asset can lead to differences of interest and division in the middle class.

In recent years another line of division has opened up between public sector professionals and better-rewarded private sector professionals, managers and the petty bourgeoisie.

Different middle-class groups tend to adopt different lifestyles:

- Public sector professionals tend to have a relatively healthy, ascetic lifestyle.
- Well-paid private sector professionals have a more extravagant postmodern lifestyle.
- Managers and civil servants have an undistinctive lifestyle.

Evaluation

This study may underestimate the power and influence of managers and oversimplify lifestyle differences. However, it does highlight important sources of division and discuss the changing nature of the middle classes.

The working class

The working class tend to receive lower wages, enjoy less job security and receive fewer fringe benefits than the middle class.

They have significantly poorer life chances such as lower life expectancy.

The issue of whether the working class share a distinctive lifestyle has been controversial.

In the 1960s, David Lockwood (1966) identified a group which he called proletarian traditionalists, who lived in close-knit working-class communities (e.g. coal miners) and exemplified traditional working-class culture. The main features of the culture were:

- Loyalty to workmates.
- Spending leisure time with workmates.
- A belief in pursuing goals collectively rather than individually.
- A fatalistic attitude to life (a belief that life chances depend on luck).
- A present-time orientation with an emphasis on immediate gratification (i.e. enjoy yourself now).
- A tendency to see class in terms of a division between 'us' (working people) and 'them' (the rich and powerful).
- Segregated conjugal roles, with men as the main breadwinners and women as home-makers.

These characteristics are diametrically opposed to supposed middle-class values such as individualism, a belief in deferred gratification (planning for the future), an image of society as a status hierarchy with opportunities for individuals, and joint conjugal roles.

Marx predicted an expanding and increasingly homogeneous and class conscious working class, but it can be argued that the working class is becoming smaller, more fragmented and less class conscious.

- Less than half the workforce are now manual workers, and traditional male manual work has declined most rapidly (e.g. shipbuilding, mining, mechanical engineering).
- New technology, the growth of more skilled work in high-technology companies and the increased employment of women may have fragmented the working class.
- The working class may be less likely to see themselves as part of a united working class.

However, Beynon (1992) argues that we are not witnessing the 'end of the industrial worker'. Rather:

- Some manufacturing jobs have shifted abroad.
- Many so-called service sector jobs are actually related to production (e.g. working in McDonald's).
- Subcontracting redefines work such as cleaning factories as service sector work.

Thus, the working class remains bigger than statistics suggest.

Embourgeoisement

This theory, first advocated in the 1950s by Kerr et al. and Bernard, suggested that well-paid affluent workers were becoming middle-class in terms of attitudes and lifestyle. If true this would undermine Marx's theory of an increasingly united and class-conscious working class.

Goldthorpe, Lockwood, Bechhofer and Platt (1968a, 1968b, 1969) investigated the theory in a study of affluent manual workers and white-collar workers in Luton in the 1960s.

They found:

1 Although affluent workers earned as much as routine white-collar workers they had inferior conditions of work and a poorer market situation (e.g. fewer promotion prospects).
2 They retained a collectivist outlook but support for unions was no longer based on unconditional loyalty. Instrumental collectivism (collective action if it would improve wages) had replaced solidaristic collectivism (based on strong loyalty).
3 Both affluent workers and white-collar workers had adopted a privatized, home-centred lifestyle, but the manual workers did not mix socially with the white-collar workers.
4 Most saw society in terms of a pecuniary model, in which position was largely determined by income.
5 They continued to be Labour voters, but for instrumental reasons rather than loyalty.

Goldthorpe et al. concluded that affluent workers made up a new working class of privatized instrumentalists, located between the traditional working class and the middle class.

Fiona Devine (1992) returned to Luton in the late 1980s to see how things had changed. She found that the workers:

1 Continued to support unions but remained instrumental collectivists.
2 Continued to choose largely working-class friends and retained fairly traditional conjugal roles.

3 Still had a pecuniary model of society.
4 Retained fairly left-wing political views, but some were disillusioned with the Labour Party, and some intended to vote Conservative.

Devine concluded that they were less individualistic than the affluent workers in Goldthorpe *et al.*'s study, and she felt that they had retained significant features of traditional working-class attitudes and lifestyle.

Marshall, Newby, Rose and Vogler (1988) conducted a large survey on class in Britain in the 1980s, and found evidence of some sectionalism, instrumentalism and privatism. But they argued that these characteristics were nothing new – they dated back to the nineteenth century – and they therefore denied that there had been any major change in the working class.

Divisions in the working class

Ralph Dahrendorf (1959) in the 1950s argued that the working class was increasingly divided by skill level, with a growing proportion of skilled workers anxious to maintain higher wages and status. He claimed that there had been a 'decomposition' of the working class.

Roger Penn (1983) studied cotton and engineering industries in Rochdale between 1856 and 1964 and found that skill divisions had long existed, and there was no evidence that they were becoming much more significant.

Ivor Crewe (1983), on the other hand, claims that there is an increasing division between a growing new working class and a shrinking old working class. The new working class:

- Live in the south.
- Are not union members.
- Work in private industry.
- Own their own home.
- Tend to vote Conservative.

The old working class, in contrast, live in other areas of the country, are union members and council tenants, work in the public sector, and tend to vote Labour.

However, Marshall *et al.* (1988) found that class continued to have more influence on voting than the sectoral divisions identified by Crewe.

Warwick and Littlejohn (1992) studied mining communities in the 1980s and found some divisions between the more successful workers, who were able to buy their council houses, and the less successful who suffered from unemployment. However, these divisions were based on economic differences not level of skill.

Class consciousness

While Marx predicted growing class consciousness, the evidence suggests that it is not happening.

In Goldthorpe *et al.*'s 1960s study of affluent workers in Luton, and in more recent social surveys, most of the working-class subjects see wage inequality as necessary. The Luton workers saw little direct conflict of interest between themselves and managers. However, this and other studies have found that workers still tend to agree with statements such as 'big business has too much power'.

Thus some sociologists believe that the seeds of class consciousness are still there. Devine found that 1980s Luton workers were conscious of inequality and

injustice and still looked to unions and the Labour Party to tackle such issues, but they had little faith that they could achieve much.

Sociologists such as Blackburn and Mann (1975) argue that the working class show inconsistencies and contradictions in their views. They experience exploitation and subordination at work, which encourage class consciousness, but the mass media and the ideology of the dominant class undermine class consciousness.

Marshall *et al.* also found contradictory beliefs: many of the working class in their sample were aware of injustice and inequality but were ambivalent about taking steps to reduce inequality. Overall Marshall *et al.* found considerable potential for class consciousness, in terms of seeing society as unfair, but they criticized the Labour Party for failing to mobilize and harness this sense of dissatisfaction.

The lower strata

Some sociologists have argued that there is a class underneath the working class. This class is often referred to as the underclass.

Murray – the underclass in America and Britain

Charles Murray (1989) puts forward a cultural view of the underclass.

He argues that, in America and more recently in Britain, there is a growing underclass defined in terms of behaviour and attitudes. It includes:

- Single parents.
- The unemployed who did not want to work.
- Those making a living from crime.

In America, a large proportion of the underclass are black.

The underclass reject values such as honesty and hard work. Welfare payments allow people to become single parents, and children lack the role-model of a hard-working father, thus perpetuating underclass attitudes.

Criticisms

1 This cultural theory neglects economic divisions.
2 It ignores structural factors which might cause lack of economic success – e.g. lack of employment opportunities, the decline of manual work.
3 It blames the disadvantaged for their problems (see p. 47 for further criticisms).

Giddens – the underclass and the dual labour market

Giddens (1973) has a more economic theory of the underclass. He sees them as workers who tend to find jobs in the secondary labour market (low-paid, insecure jobs with few prospects). Employers tend to recruit women and ethnic minorities into such jobs, partly because of discrimination and prejudice.

The underclass have more radical views than the working class who are in secure employment.

Criticisms

Kirk Mann (1982) argues that there is no clear dividing line between the primary (secure, well-paid work) and secondary labour markets.

He claims that Giddens fails to give a convincing explanation of why women and ethnic minorities are in secondary employment (see p. 38 for a discussion of ethnicity and the underclass).

Gallie – the heterogeneity of the underclass

Gallie (1988, 1994) argues that the underclass is too heterogeneous to be seen as a single class. He found big differences in the employment situations of women and members of ethnic minorities and points out that there is a big flow into and out of unemployment.

The underclass also includes diverse age groups, and they often have different interests. They are therefore unlikely to develop shared consciousness.

Gallie found no evidence that the long-term unemployed were resigned to being without work and little evidence of a political split between the working class and the underclass.

However, Gallie does think that the long-term unemployed may form a distinct group

Runciman – the underclass as claimants

W.G. Runciman (1990) sees the underclass as consisting of those reliant upon benefits, with little chance of being able to participate in paid employment. This places them in a different economic situation from even low-paid workers.

Criticisms

1 Dean and Taylor-Gooby (1992) criticize Runciman for failing to take into account the large numbers who escape from reliance upon benefits. This makes any supposed underclass highly unstable.
2 Dean argues that the term underclass is used imprecisely in a variety of ways, often with the implication that the disadvantaged are to blame for their problems. He therefore argues that it should no longer be used.

Social mobility in capitalist society

- Open societies allow social mobility (movement between strata) whereas closed ones do not.
- Achieved status means that your status depends upon what you do.
- Ascribed status means that your status is based upon who you are (e.g. kinship, gender, ethnicity, class background).
- Sociologists such as Parsons see industrial societies as increasingly open and based on achieved status.
- Intragenerational mobility refers to mobility within one generation – e.g. being promoted at work.
- Intergenerational mobility refers to mobility between generations – it is measured by comparing the occupational statuses of parents and children.

Glass – social mobility before 1949

In 1949 Glass did the first British study.

It found low rates of long-range mobility (movement across several strata) and high rates of self-recruitment (recruitment of the children of class members) in the highest class.

Criticisms

Glass's research methods have been criticized for using an unrepresentative sample which failed to reflect the growing number employed in white-collar occupations.

The Oxford Mobility Study

In 1972 the Oxford Mobility Study provided more up-to-date and reliable data.

It divided the class structure into three main groups: the service class (highest), the working class (lowest) and an intermediate class.

It found higher rates of long-range mobility than Glass's study and high rates of absolute mobility (the total amount of social mobility). This was largely due to a considerable expansion of the service class, creating more room at the top of the stratification system. There were high rates of upward mobility.

However, relative mobility chances (the chances of those from different backgrounds achieving particular positions) remained unchanged. Thus children from the service class were much more likely to achieve positions in the service class than children from the working class. Kellner and Wilby (1980) summarize this as the 1:2:4 rule of relative hope – for every child from the working class who ends up in the top class, two achieve this from the intermediate classes and four from the service class.

Trends since the Oxford Mobility Study

Goldthorpe and Payne (1986) used data from British election studies to show that from 1972 to 1983 relative mobility chances stayed about the same, despite further growth of the service class.

At the very top of the stratification system there is evidence that mobility is low. Elite self-recruitment tends to take place, whereby elite positions are filled by the children of those already in the elite.

Gender and mobility

- Most studies of mobility have used the class of the main breadwinner (usually a man) to determine the class of family members.
- Goldthorpe and Payne argue that other ways of determining the class of women (e.g. using their own jobs) make little difference to the overall findings of mobility studies.
- Anthony Heath, however, found that women from service-class backgrounds were more likely to be downwardly mobile than men from this class, while women from working-class backgrounds were more likely to be upwardly mobile than men. Heath believes that overall this disadvantages women rather than men.

The most recent major study of mobility was conducted by Marshall, Newby, Rose and Vogler (the Essex study). This also found that there was more absolute mobility for women, but relative mobility (the chance of moving up as opposed to down) was similar for both sexes.

Is Britain a meritocracy?

A meritocracy is a social system in which life chances are based on merit.

Saunders – Unequal but Fair?

Peter Saunders (1996) argues that Britain is meritocratic.

- There is considerable upward mobility from the working class.
- Differences in the chances of those from different classes being upwardly mobile largely stem from inherited differences in terms of intelligence, talent and motivation.
- Saunders used data from the National Child Development Survey to claim that intergenerational mobility rates were higher than suggested in other studies and that class differences in mobility could be explained in terms of differences in ability and effort.

Criticisms
1 Saunders ignores the unemployed and those in part-time work.
2 Measured intelligence might itself be the result of class differences rather than inherited characteristics. Measures of effort (such as levels of absenteeism) might be related to the effects of labelling, ill-health, etc., which are class-related.
3 Marshall and Swift (1986) argue that Saunders has misinterpreted the figures and that even when factors such as effort and intelligence are taken into account working-class children still do considerably worse than middle-class children.
4 Savage and Egerton (1997) examined the *National Child Development Survey* and found high rates of mobility but big differences in opportunities. For example, in the service class, 75% of high-ability sons and 67% of high-ability daughters ended up in the service class, compared to 45% of high-ability sons and 28% of high-ability daughters from the unskilled working class.

Explanations of mobility rates
Changes in mobility patterns can be explained in terms of:
- The growth of white-collar jobs and the decline of manual work.
- Differences in fertility rates. Higher classes have fewer children generally than lower classes, so some working-class children will need to be upwardly mobile to fill all the positions.
- There may be some move towards meritocracy with increasing educational opportunities.

Gender and social class

The position of women in the class structure was neglected in many early studies – women were often assumed to simply have the same class as their husbands. However, increasingly this has been disputed. There are a number of viewpoints:
1 Frank Parkin (1972) argues that the life chances of women are largely determined by the position of the male breadwinner in a family.
2 Britten and Heath (1983) disagree, pointing out that there are an increasing number of cross-class families in which women have a better-paid, higher-status job than men.
3 Goldthorpe (1983) largely agrees with Parkin, arguing that the family is the unit of class analysis. However, he does concede that the class of the family should

be taken from the head of household. This is usually the man, but it can be a woman – e.g. in single-parent households or where the woman has more commitment to paid employment than the man.
4 Michelle Stanworth (1984) argues that men and women should be placed in classes as individuals according to their jobs, not as members of families.
5 Rose and Marshall (1988) found that class fates (e.g. mobility chances) were more affected by the class of individuals, while class actions (e.g. who you voted for) could be better predicted by the family's class.

Contemporary theories of stratification

The death of class?
The postmodernists Pakulski and Waters (1996) claim that class is losing its significance.
- People no longer feel that they belong to classes, and supposed classes include a big variety of people.
- New cleavages are more important in shaping people's social and political beliefs than class.
- Towards the end of the twentieth century, stratification became based on cultural differences rather than economic ones.
- Lifestyle and identity have become more important than economic differences – e.g. your status is more to do with the décor of your house than the job you have.
- Some low-paid jobs (e.g. in the media) have higher status than better-paid jobs.
- As a result, stratification systems are more fragmented and fluid than previous class systems; it is easier to change status than it once was.

Pakulski and Waters explain the death of class in terms of:
1 The increasing importance of educational qualifications in shaping your status.
2 The declining importance of privately owned property compared to property owned by organizations.
3 A wider distribution of wealth, giving more people greater lifestyle choices and more opportunity to choose what they consume according to their taste.
4 Globalization, which has reduced the importance of class inequalities within countries.
5 The growth of new politics based around non-class issues such as ethnicity and religion.

Criticisms
1 Harriet Bradley (1997) argues that Pakulski and Waters have no consistent definition of class.
2 They ignore the extent to which economic class differences still affect what people can afford and therefore what lifestyle choices they can make.
3 Marshall (1997) argues that they are highly selective in the arguments and evidence they use and tend to neglect evidence that economic class inequalities are still a major factor in shaping people's lives.

Westergaard – the hardening of class inequality
John Westergaard (1995, 1997) argues that, far from disappearing, class inequalities are hardening.

He sees class in Marxist/Weberian terms as determined by your position in the economic order. There is strong evidence of increasing inequality:

- In Britain the highest-paid 10% of white-collar workers had a 40% increase in real wages from 1980 to 1990, while the poorest 10% of manual workers had no rise in pay.
- From the 1970s to the 1980s the share of all income earned by the richest 20% of households increased from 37% to 44%, while the share of the poorest 20% of households fell from 10% to 7%.
- Privately owned wealth was becoming more concentrated in the hands of a few in the 1980s.
- The power of big business has been growing as a result of privatization and the adoption of free-market policies.

Westergaard sees the reasons for these changes as lying in government policies and the growth of transnational corporations.

He accepts that lifestyle and consumption have become increasingly related to identity. However, he sees these as strongly influenced by economic differences such as wage inequality.

Gender divisions tend to reinforce class inequality. Middle-class families often have both the man and the woman in well-paid jobs, whereas few working-class families benefit from one partner's higher white-collar salary.

Ethnic divisions are closely related to class, with some ethnic minorities tending to be concentrated towards the bottom of the stratification system.

Westergaard accepts that class consciousness may have declined but he partly attributes this to the Labour Party's failure to express and mobilize dissatisfaction in society.

Class consciousness has the potential to revive since surveys show continued dissatisfaction with inequality in British society.

1   Which one of these is an example of a stratification system as opposed to simple inequality?
    a   A group of sprinters with different personal best times for the 100 metres
    b   A class of pupils who have different scores in their class tests
    c   A number of football teams divided into different leagues ranked hierarchically
    d   A group of people who receive different wages

2   Which one of these is an example of achieved status?
    a   The high status of whites in South Africa before the abolition of apartheid
    b   The high status of men in some societies
    c   The high status of cabinet ministers in British government
    d   The high status of hereditary peers in Britain

3   Which one of these statements would Talcott Parsons agree with?
    a   Stratification causes division in society
    b   Stratification is an inevitable feature of human societies
    c   Stratification is undesirable
    d   Stratification prevents the coordination of activities

4   Which one of these is not a criticism of Davis and Moore's theory of stratification?
    a   Nearly all jobs involve carrying out a crucial role in society
    b   Many more people have talent than rise to the top
    c   Stratification can cause apathy and resignation in the lower strata
    d   Some people need higher rewards to motivate them to work hard

5   Marx calls groups such as shopkeepers and small business people:
    a   The proletariat   b   The bourgeoisie
    c   The petty bourgeoisie   d   The subject class

6   False class consciousness involves:
    a   Making less money than other people
    b   Being aware you are being exploited
    c   Being unaware of where the true interests of your class lie
    d   Becoming revolutionary

7   In Weber's sociology, your class position is determined by:
    a   A combination of whether you own property and your position in the labour market
    b   Your position in the labour market alone
    c   Whether you own property
    d   Your status

8   Weber calls groups who exercise power or try to influence those with power:
    a   Clubs
    b   Parties
    c   Classes
    d   Status groups

9   Which two of these statements describe changes in the British occupational structure during the twentieth century?
    a   An increasing proportion of paid jobs were held by women

    b   The proportion employed in manufacturing increased
    c   The proportion of people employed in manual work increased
    d   White-collar employment grew

10 Which one of these statements is true?
    a   Income inequality reduced for much of the twentieth century but increased in the last two decades
    b   Wealth inequalities were reduced in the 1990s
    c   Wealth is now fairly evenly spread across the British population
    d   The proportion of people who own shares as individuals has been decreasing in recent decades

11 In 1994 the richest 10% of the British population owned what proportion of marketable wealth?
    a   10%
    b   42%
    c   51%
    d   64%

12 Which one of these writers puts forward a New Right view of the upper class?
    a   John Westergaard
    b   Peter Saunders
    c   John Scott
    d   Leslie Sklair

13 According to Leslie Sklair, the most powerful group in society is:
    a   The ruling class
    b   The upper class
    c   The ruling elite
    d   The transnational capitalist class

14 Which two of these statements describe the Weberian view of the professions?
    a   The professions serve the public interest
    b   The professions predominantly serve the interests of the rich and powerful
    c   Professionalism can be seen as a market strategy
    d   Professions largely serve their own interests

15 Which two of these statements describe the functionalist view of the professions?
    a   Codes of ethics are used as a technique of social closure
    b   Codes of ethics ensure that the professions serve the public interest
    c   The professions deserve their high wages
    d   High professional wages result from monopolistic control of the supply of labour

16 The proletarianization thesis suggests:
    a   The proletariat are becoming middle-class
    b   Some white-collar workers are becoming working-class
    c   Professional workers are adopting working-class culture
    d   Everybody is now proletarian

17 Which two of these writers/co-writers believe that most clerical workers remain middle-class?
    a   Braverman
    b   Lockwood
    c   Stewart, Prandy and Blackburn
    d   Crompton and Jones

18 According to Roberts, Cook, Clark and Semeonoff, the middle class is:
 a Polarized
 b Fragmented
 c United
 d Disappearing

19 According to Savage, Barlow, Dickens and Fielding, a part-time university lecturer without a permanent contract would be a member of the middle class because they possessed:
 a Property assets
 b Organizational assets
 c Cultural assets
 d Personal assets

20 Which two of these attributes are characteristic of proletarian traditionalists, according to David Lockwood?
 a Segregated conjugal roles
 b Joining a union for pragmatic reasons
 c Fatalism
 d Seeing society as a status hierarchy

21 The theory of embourgeoisement suggests that:
 a Affluent workers are joining the bourgeoisie
 b The whole of the working class has become middle-class
 c Affluent workers are becoming middle-class
 d The bourgeoisie are becoming more cultured

22 Which two of these developments did Marx predict would occur in the working class?
 a The working class would become more affluent
 b The working class would adopt middle-class lifestyles
 c The working class would eventually become aware that they were being exploited
 d The working class would get poorer in comparison with higher classes

23 Which one of these groups does Charles Murray not see as part of the underclass?
 a Pensioners
 b Single parents
 c Criminals
 d The work-shy

24 If the daughter of a coal miner becomes a manager this is an example of:
 a Intragenerational upward mobility
 b Horizontal mobility
 c Intergenerational upward mobility
 d Short-range intragenerational mobility

25 The Oxford Mobility Study found:
 a Very little mobility
 b More downward mobility than upward mobility
 c High rates of absolute mobility but big class differences in relative mobility
 d No long-range mobility

26 Marshall, Newby, Rose and Vogler found:
 a Women had more absolute social mobility than men but similar rates of relative mobility
 b Women and men had almost identical patterns of social mobility
 c Women had less absolute social mobility than men and much more chance than men of being upwardly mobile
 d Women were much more likely than men to be downwardly mobile to the bottom of the stratification system

27 Which of these sociologists believes that class position should be based on the individual rather than the family?
 a Parkin
 b Britten and Heath
 c Goldthorpe
 d Stanworth

28 Which of these is not one of the reasons put forward by Pakulski and Waters for the 'death of class'?
 a Globalization
 b A wider distribution of wealth
 c The increased importance of qualifications in determining status
 d All workers enjoying good wages

29 According to John Westergaard, class differences are:
 a Staying much the same
 b Hardening
 c Reducing
 d Disappearing

30 Supporters of which two of these theoretical approaches are most likely to see Britain as meritocratic?
 a Marxism
 b The New Right
 c Functionalism
 d Weberian theories

Develop your analysis and evaluation skills

(see p. 195 for guidance notes)

For each of the following statements, identify which sociologists would argue in favour of and which against the view expressed. Explain the reasons for their view.

1 Stratification is an inevitable and desirable feature of human societies.
2 Britain is now a meritocratic society.
3 The British class system is now dominated by a homogeneous middle class.
4 The working class is an increasingly small and unimportant group.
5 Class is dead.
6 Marxism contributes little to an understanding of class in modern Britain.

Answer all parts of this question
Total: 60 marks
Time allowed: 1 hour 30 minutes

1 mark = 1 minute

ITEM A

In conventional class analysis two approaches dominate: Marxist and Weberian. Weberian theories see class position as partly determined by the job market and they suggest that higher classes in particular will try to exclude others from sharing their advantages by a process of closure of opportunities. This, it could be argued, might explain the position of women and certain ethnic groups.

To check your understanding of this concept see p. 9

Note: exclusivity can apply to groups other than those at the top

In Marxist theory class position is determined by people's relationship to the means of production, either as owners, or as non-owners who can only survive by selling their labour power. Those who neither own the means of production nor sell their labour power (such as children, some women, the elderly/retired, the unemployed, the disabled/ill) have no class position other than by their association with someone in paid labour.

These groups are not easily assigned a class on the basis of work. Interpret and apply this for part [a]

Comments on the question	Question	Advice on preparing your answer
• This is a synoptic question which links theoretical and methodological issues to the topic • What might be different today compared with 100 years ago? See p. 8 on share ownership for one answer	[a] Discuss briefly how Marxist theories of class might create problems in measuring class today. [8 marks]	• See p. 7 for the relevant theory and apply your knowledge of methodology to this problem. E.g. class consciousness and/or the difference between people's occupation and their perception of their class • Interpret the item to show how this occupational-based theory has difficulty dealing with certain groups • Consider ownership – e.g. see p. 8 on measuring assets

Comments on the question	Question	Advice on preparing your answer
• This is a **synoptic** paper so you should show knowledge from different areas of the specification • This could mean **actions** of the in-group to prevent others from joining them, or **attitudes** learned by a group which prevent them from thinking they can join the group concerned • Focus must be on these groups and you could suggest there are differences between ethnic groups and groups of women	[b] Examine how closure of opportunities might explain the social position of women and certain ethnic groups. [12 marks]	• Actions 1 Entry qualifications apply for certain professions, see p. 9 2 Unwritten barriers exist, such as the ability of public schools to dominate certain professions, see Haralambos and Holborn, pp. 604–6 3 Chapter 3, pp. 23–7 and Chapter 4, pp. 32–8 will be of use here 4 Subtle (and sometimes illegal) processes such as sex and race discrimination can be both individual and institutional, and direct and indirect • Attitudes 1 Cultural hegemony and stereotypes (Chapter 13, especially p. 157) 2 Fatalism (p. 11) and hidden curriculum (Chapter 11, pp. 130–1)
• Look at theories and evidence in support of the ideas, and against them • To get the maximum marks you do need to show that you have considered all four aspects • Again remember that this is a synoptic paper and you can bring in evidence from many parts of the specification • 20 marks are for knowledge; 20 marks are for analysis and evaluation	[c] Examine the view that stratification is inevitable and beneficial to both individuals and society. [40 marks]	• Define stratification, see p. 6 • Outline the arguments that see it as inevitable and beneficial, i.e. Parsons, Davis and Moore (pp. 6–7) • Remember to look at both the total society and the possible benefits for all individuals (maybe the security of 'knowing their place') • Now consider the arguments and evidence against inevitability (Marx, Weber and others, see p. 7), against it being beneficial to society (Tumin, p. 6, and Young), and against it being beneficial to individuals (see Tumin, Marxists, feminists, etc.)

Answer all parts of this question
Total: 90 marks   1 mark = 1 minute
Time allowed: 1 hour 30 minutes

ITEM A

Characteristics of the superclass

Adonis and Pollard argue that a new social class has emerged in Britain, a professional and managerial elite which they refer to as the 'Super Class'. This group is made up of both males and females and is based on the old professions who have made their fortunes in the City. The Super Class tend to intermarry and therefore earn combined super-salaries. They can be distinguished from the rest of society by their consumption patterns, which revolve around nannies and servants, second homes, exotic holidays, private health and pension schemes and private education for their children.

ITEM B

Make sure you fully understand how this data is organised

Social class distribution by Registrar General's category, economically active population (%)

Class	Occupation	1971	1981	1991
I	Professional	4	4	5
II	Managerial	18	22	28
IIINM	Skilled non-manual	21	22	23
IIIM	Skilled manual	28	26	21
IV	Semi-skilled	21	19	15
V	Unskilled	8	7	6

Source: extracted from Mark Kirby, *Stratification and Differentiation*, Macmillan, 2000, p. 9

Comments on the question	Question	Advice on preparing your answer
• Everything you need is in Item A. Do not be tempted to go beyond it • No more, no less • Identify only. Don't waste time offering an explanation	[a] Using only the information in Item A, identify two characteristics of the 'Super Class'. [6 marks]	• Don't lift material word for word from the items. Be prepared to put the information into your own words • Focus on salaries and consumption
• No more, no less • Identify only. There is no need to offer an explanation for these patterns	[b] Identify two patterns shown by the data in the table in Item B. [6 marks]	• Always look closely at how data in tables, graphs, etc. are organized • Focus on major patterns and trends

Comments on the question	Question	Advice on preparing your answer
• Don't offer any more • This question is asking you to explain why a problem has come about • Clearly distinguish between the two problems identified	[c] Identify and explain two problems facing sociologists trying to measure the distribution of wealth. [12 marks]	• This a synoptic question. It is demanding some knowledge of methodology
• This a synoptic instruction and means you should dip into a couple of other topics for the evidence as well as taking material from your notes on this unit • Outline means describe. There is no need to offer an explanation	[d] Using your wider sociological knowledge, outline the evidence that suggests that social class is still very important today. [22 marks]	
• Describe the main points and concepts that make up the theory and any evidence that supports it • You can mention other theories but these should be offered as evaluative alternatives to whatever theory you choose to focus on • Assess means weigh up the arguments for and against the theory. Try to be balanced rather than one-sided	[e] Outline and assess one sociological explanation of class inequality. [44 marks]	

Chapter 3

Sex and gender

Specifications

Specification	Relevant module title	Place in module	Level	Assessment	Other relevant modules
AQA	There is no AQA module specifically on this topic (see last column).	n/a	n/a	n/a	This topic is intrinsic to the whole specification and is relevant to every module.
OCR	There is no OCR module specifically on this topic (see last column).	n/a	n/a	n/a	This topic is intrinsic to the whole specification and is relevant to every module.

Sex and gender: essential notes

Introduction

Dr Robert Stoller (1968) defines sex in terms of physical differences between males and females: sex organs, secondary sex characteristics and hormones. These differences mean that women can bear and suckle children whereas men cannot.

Stoller defines gender in terms of the psychological and cultural differences between what is defined as masculine and feminine in particular societies.

This implies that differences between men and women in terms of behaviour and social roles are at least partly social and cultural rather than biological.

Sex and gender differences

Many have argued that differences between males and females are biologically based.

They have claimed that higher amounts of testosterone and other androgens in males make them more aggressive.

However, critics point out that most of the research to support this is based on animal experiments and the results may not be applicable to humans.

The theory of brain lateralization suggests that the left hemisphere of the brain – specializing in verbal and language skills – is dominant in females, while the right hemisphere – specializing in visuo-spatial abilities – is dominant in males. This could explain differences in male and female aptitudes and interests.

However, research findings in this area are contradictory, and both males and females can be very able in areas where the other sex is supposed to have more ability.

Sociobiology

Sociobiologists explain behaviour in terms of reproductive strategies and the desire to pass on your genes to children. The best strategy for women is to seek the most suitable partners since a woman can bear only a limited number of children. The best strategy for men is to get as many women pregnant as possible. This is held to explain differences in male and female behaviour.

Critics point out that this approach cannot explain homosexuality or celibacy. Oakley (1972) argues that it cannot explain societies such as the Trobriand Islands where women take the lead in sexual relationships

Biology and the sexual division of labour

From a study of 224 societies, the functionalist George Peter Murdock (1949) argues that a sexual division of labour develops, in which men do the hunting and heavy work and engage in warfare, while women do the gathering, cooking, repairing clothes and carrying water. This results from practical reasons: men are stronger and are not burdened by pregnancy and nursing children.

Talcott Parsons (1955) argues that women are more suited to expressive roles such as the socialization of children because they give birth and are naturally closer to children.

John Bowlby (1953) argues that children are psychologically damaged by the absence of the natural mother, or mother substitute, during their early years (maternal deprivation).

Ann Oakley (1974) rejects these views, arguing that the division of labour between men and women is based on culture not biology. She points out:

- There are many societies which are exceptions to the general rule, e.g. amongst Mbuti Pygmies there are no specific sex roles.
- In contemporary societies such as China and Cuba a lot of heavy work is done by women.
- The mother-housewife role is a cultural construction. Evidence shows that children do not have to be cared for by their mothers to grow up well-adjusted.

The social construction of gender roles

Many sociologists argue that males and females learn to be masculine and feminine – their roles are socially constructed.

Oakley sees gender role socialization taking place through:
- Manipulation – e.g. dressing girls in 'pretty' clothes.
- Canalization – e.g. directing boys and girls towards different toys.
- Verbal appellations – e.g. telling boys they are strong and girls they are pretty.
- Exposure to different activities – e.g. getting girls to help with domestic tasks.

The mass media reinforce stereotypes of masculinity and femininity.

Kessler and McKenna (1978) point out that in some societies there is a third gender, the *berdache* (found amongst native American tribes). The berdache are 'men' who dress and act in feminine ways and are considered neither male nor female.

Conclusion

Writers such as David Morgan (1986) and Linda Birke (1986) argue that biological and social factors interact to create gender differences.

Gender inequality

Feminist theories try to explain inequalities and differences between men and women and suggest what should be done about them. There are several broad approaches.

Radical feminism

Radical feminists believe that women are exploited by, and subservient to, men. Society is patriarchal, or male-dominated. Men are the ruling class and women the subject class. Radical feminists explain the inequality in various ways, some seeing biology as the cause, others seeing culture or male violence as more important.

Female supremacists see women as superior to men, while female separatists believe that women should stay completely independent of men.

Marxist and socialist feminism

Marxist and socialist feminists see the capitalist system as the main source of women's oppression and stress the importance of the exploitation of women as paid and unpaid workers. Some would like to see a communist society established.

Liberal feminism

This perspective is associated with equal rights campaigners, who want reforms to improve women's position, rather than revolution. They often attribute inequality to sexism, discrimination and sex role stereotyping and socialization.

Black feminism

Black feminists believe that 'race'/ethnic differences between women have been neglected by white feminists, and they stress the particularly deprived position of black women. Brewer argues that class, race and gender combine to give black women multiple sources of deprivation.

The origins of gender inequalities – feminist views

Feminists adopting different approaches have tried to explain how gender inequalities originate.

Shulamith Firestone (1970) argues that the sexual class system is the most fundamental form of stratification. The biological family results from women being burdened by pregnancy, childbirth, breastfeeding and menstruation. They become dependent on men and power psychology develops which maintains female oppression.

Critics point out that in some societies women seem less disadvantaged by biology than in others (see Oakley, pp. 22–3).

Ortner (1974) sees female oppression as cultural. Because women give birth they are defined as closer to nature than men, who are seen as more cultural. Culture is seen as superior to nature.

Coontz and Henderson (1986) criticize Ortner, arguing that not all societies see culture as superior to nature.

The origins of gender inequalities – Marxist and socialist perspectives

Engels argued that gender inequality had a materialist base. The monogamous family only developed once herding of animals replaced hunting and gathering. Men used monogamous marriage to control women's sexuality so that they could identify their own biological children and pass down their herds of cattle to them.

However, Engels's theory is not based on sound empirical evidence.

Coontz and Henderson also provide a materialist explanation. They argue that men became dominant due to the practice of patrilocality, whereby wives went to live with their husband's family. This tended to mean that men gained control of women's labour and the wealth they produced.

Gender and industrialization

This view does not follow a particular feminist perspective, but sees gender inequality as originating from the Industrial Revolution. Oakley (1981) argues that women became disadvantaged because of the creation of the mother-housewife role in the nineteenth century. Children were gradually banned from the workplace in the new mines and factories, leaving women at home to care for them. Unable to earn their own living, women became dependent on men.

However, the importance of the mother-housewife role may have declined in the late twentieth century with more women working.

Gender in contemporary societies – radical feminist perspectives

The radical feminist Kate Millett (1970) argues that modern societies are patriarchal and there are many sources of patriarchy.

- Biology plays some part through superior male strength and the use of violence (though this is now more psychological than real).
- Ideological factors and socialization are important.
- Sociological factors, such as women's role as mothers in family life, also contribute.
- Women have a caste-like status which means that even higher-class women are subordinate to men.
- Educational and economic inequalities hold women back.
- Myth and religion are used to justify male dominance.
- Psychology plays a part since women interiorize patriarchal ideology.
- Rape, sexual violence and the use of force underpin male power.

Critics such as Rowbotham (1979) question the usefulness of a vague term like patriarchy. Rowbotham also denies that all men exploit all women.

Gender in contemporary societies – Marxist and socialist perspectives

- Engels argued that men retained power because of access to work, particularly well-paid work, and he expected inequalities to reduce once women returned to work.
- Marxist feminists such as Benston (1972) argue that women are used as a reserve army of labour, benefiting capitalism by keeping wages low. They are a relatively docile, easily exploited workforce.
- Hartmann (1981) argues that capitalism might create low-paid jobs and a reserve army of labour, but this does not explain why women occupy these positions. She argues that patriarchy provides the key. Men maintain their control over women by exploiting their labour and denying them access to jobs that pay a living wage, so that they stay dependent on their husbands.

Walby – *Theorizing Patriarchy*

Sylvia Walby (1990) provides both a theory of patriarchy, mixing a variety of feminist theories, and an assessment of how much women's lives have improved.

She argues that there has been a move from private patriarchy (the exploitation of women in the home) to public patriarchy (the exploitation of women outside the home).

She identifies six structures of patriarchy:

- Paid employment – here Walby acknowledges some reduction in inequality, with women having more access to paid employment. However, the gap in wages between the sexes has only narrowed slightly. Walby sees lack of well-paid work as the most important factor discouraging women from taking paid employment.
- Household production continues to be based on patriarchal relations of production, with men benefiting from women's unpaid labour. However, women are doing more paid work, and relaxed divorce laws make it easier to escape from exploitative marriages. Some women – e.g. some black women who are exploited at work – may see family life as preferable to paid employment. Marriage brings material benefits for some women, but violence for others.
- Culture continues to differentiate between males and females, but sexual attractiveness has replaced domesticity as the key feature of femininity. This has increased women's freedom in some ways, but it has also subjected them to degrading pornography and sometimes sexual violence.
- Heterosexuality is a patriarchal structure, but it has changed. Women have more freedom to engage in sex outside marriage, but sexual double standards still applaud male promiscuity while promiscuous women are seen as 'slags'.
- It is not clear whether violence against women has increased. While the police take domestic violence against women more seriously than they used to, violent husbands are still rarely convicted.
- The state has become less discriminatory but still remains patriarchal, capitalist and racist. For example, single mothers continue to be treated badly.

Overall, the changes indicate a shift from private patriarchy (women exploited as mothers and housewives) to public patriarchy (women exploited as workers and sex objects). However, the nature of patriarchy varies by social group – e.g. Muslim women are more constrained by private patriarchy than other groups.

In later work Walby detects a generational difference, with younger women experiencing gains in areas such as sexual freedom, educational opportunities and paid employment. However, poorly qualified young women and single parents suffer considerable disadvantages, and most elite positions continue to be male-dominated.

Evaluation

Jackie Stacey (1993) praises Walby for an 'all-encompassing' approach but criticizes her for using the idea of structure rather loosely and ignoring the subjectivity of women.

Anna Pollert (1996) attacks the use of the term patriarchy in general. It usually involves a circular argument: it is used both as a description and as an explanation of inequality between the sexes. Pollert argues that capitalism is a system with an internal dynamic, but that patriarchy is not. She prefers empirical studies of how class, gender and ethnicity relate to one another, rather than theorizing about patriarchy.

Postmodernism, sex and gender

- Postmodern feminism generally rejects the idea that all women share the same interests and their position can be explained in terms of a single theory.

- It emphasizes differences between groups of women – e.g. between lesbian and heterosexual women, women from different classes and ethnic groups, and women of different ages.
- Postmodern feminists celebrate difference.
- They reject the idea of progress, seeing it as a product of male rationality, and therefore they reject the idea of a single path to female liberation.
- They argue that women's position can be improved by deconstructing (taking apart and criticizing) masculine language and thinking.
- They attack the male way of thinking of women as the 'other' (as different from and inferior to men).
- By allowing the voices of different women to be heard, the idea of women as an inferior 'other' can be broken down.

Criticisms
- Sylvia Walby (1992) criticizes postmodern feminism for losing sight of the importance of inequality and the degree to which the experience of oppression and inequality gives women shared interests.
- Postmodern feminists tend to neglect important areas such as male use of violence to maintain power and gender inequalities at work.

Gender and paid employment

In 1970 the Equal Pay Act legislated that women should be paid the same as men for doing the same or broadly similar work. In 1984 an amendment stipulated that women should get equal pay for work of equal value.

The 1975 Sex Discrimination Act made discrimination on the grounds of sex illegal in employment, education and the provision of goods and services.

Despite these Acts and some improvements in the position of women in Britain, women remain disadvantaged at work.
- The proportion of the labour force who are women has risen considerably. In 1961 women made up 32% of the labour force; by 1997 they made up nearly 46%.
- A big majority of part-time workers are women.
- The proportion of married women who work has risen most rapidly.
- Women continue to be less well paid than men. In 1970 women working full-time earned 63% of the average full-time male wage; by 1996 they were still only getting 80% of the average male wage.
- Vertical segregation continues – i.e. women have fewer of the higher-status jobs.
- Horizontal segregation – i.e. where men and women tend to have different types of job – also continues. Women tend to be employed in areas such as personal services, administration, hotels and restaurants. Most routine clerical and secretarial workers are women, as are most primary teachers. Men tend to dominate in areas such as manufacturing, construction and transport. There are more men in higher professions and more women in lower professions, particularly welfare professions.
- Women have made progress in some professions, such as medicine. However, they still hold few elite positions.

There are a number of explanations for gender inequalities at work:
- Human capital theory suggests that women are less valuable to employers than men because they are less committed to work and more likely to take career breaks to raise children. This gives employers less incentive to promote women and invest in their training.

However, a study by Peter Sloane (1994) found that gender continued to influence pay even when qualifications and experience were taken into account.

The dual labour market theory of Barron and Norris (1976) distinguishes:
- The primary labour market of well-paid, fairly secure jobs with prospects.
- The secondary labour market of poorly paid, insecure jobs with few prospects.

Employers try hard to attract and retain primary workers, who are seen as key to the success of their enterprises, but secondary workers are seen as easily replaced. It is difficult to transfer from the secondary to the primary labour market, and women tend to be concentrated in the secondary sector. This is due in part to employer sexism but also to factors such as lack of unionization.

Beechey (1986) criticizes the theory because:
- Some women in crucial, skilled jobs (e.g. working in textiles) still get low pay.
- Women are promoted less than men even when employed in primary sector jobs.
- Marxists such as Braverman (1974) argue that women's work has been deskilled as employers seek to cut costs by taking the skill out of much of the work. Clerical and service sector work, predominantly done by women, has been deskilled.

However, critics of Braverman suggest that the skills required for some jobs have changed or increased rather than decreased, and women often get low pay even when doing skilled jobs.

Another Marxist-influenced theory sees women as a cheap reserve army of labour, brought in during economic booms but thrown out during slumps. This creates flexibility for capitalists and depresses overall wage levels.

According to Beechey, women tend to be in the reserve army because: they are often not in unions; they may be prepared to work for less if their wage is a second income; they are seen as combining work with domestic responsibilities.

However, this theory cannot explain horizontal segregation, and the continued growth of female employment suggests that women are not being used as a temporary, reserve army of workers.
- Linda McDowell (1992) applies post-Fordist theory to female employment. Post-Fordism suggests that there has been a move away from mass production to more flexible production of specialist products. Businesses keep a core of highly skilled workers, but most other workers are temporary or part-time, or work is contracted out to other firms. Women tend to be concentrated in the more flexible jobs, particularly part-time work, although some have benefited from gaining core jobs.

Research by Lovering (1994) found evidence to support this theory in some companies but not in others, suggesting that post-Fordist trends affect only some workers.

- Some feminists stress the role of male trade unionists in restricting women's opportunities. Walby (1986) argues that in some areas (e.g. engineering) trade unions have used exclusion to disadvantage women, while in industries such as textiles women have been disadvantaged by confinement to certain lower-paid areas of work. Low-paid work ensures that women are more likely to take on domestic responsibilities than men.
- Radical feminists see patriarchy rather than capitalism as the main cause of female disadvantage. Stanko (1988) argues that sexual harassment in the workplace is used to keep women in their place. Men use their power in the workplace to protect their position. Women in jobs such as bar and secretarial work are sexualized and are not taken seriously as workers or candidates for promotion.

Lisa Adkins (1995) goes further, arguing that sexual work has become integral to many women's jobs. In service sector jobs where women have contact with men they are expected to engage in sexual servicing: looking attractive, engaging in sexual banter, tolerating sexual innuendo and so on.

- Crompton and Sanderson (1990) argue that there is an interaction between the choices of individuals and the complex structure of the labour market. Qualifications influence the jobs people get, but the value of qualifications changes depending on the demand for different skills. There is a difference between occupational labour markets (in which your job allows you to move between employers easily) and internal labour markets (where your prospects depend on the particular employer you work for). In different areas of employment women are disadvantaged in different ways.
- In pharmacy women have valuable skills in an occupational labour market, but because many women work part-time due to domestic commitments promotion prospects are limited.
- In accountancy women are in a small minority and tend to be the victims of sexist employers in large organizations.
- In building societies women are in a big majority, but in these internal labour markets men are dominant, and women tend to be excluded from training programmes which provide promotion prospects.

Dawn Burton (1994) praises Crompton and Sanderson for producing a sophisticated theory, but questions the reliability of their research which was based on a series of case studies.

Gender and stratification

Some sociologists see women as forming a separate group in the stratification system. However, it is difficult to see them as a class because the wealth and income of individual women vary considerably. Various alternatives have been suggested.

- Kate Millett (1970) sees women as having a 'caste-like status'. Like caste membership, caste is an ascribed status. Social mobility between the sexes is almost impossible and rewards vary between the sexes.

However, Eichler (1980) points out that in castes all members of the highest castes are better off than lower castes. This is not true of men and women, since some women are better off than some men.

- Helen Hacker (1972) sees women as a minority group – a group with physical or cultural characteristics who are singled out and subject to discrimination. She compares women's situation with that of black Americans. Both groups are highly visible, both are given ascribed attributes in terms of the sort of behaviour expected of them, and both suffer from discrimination. The inferior status of blacks and women is rationalized in terms of supposedly innate characteristics, and both groups adopt accommodating behaviour such as being deferential towards more powerful members of society.

Eichler criticizes this approach for being largely descriptive rather than explaining the differences.

- Eichler argues that sex stratification exists alongside class stratification. Women cannot be easily classified in terms of traditional class analysis because much of the exploitation of women takes place in the family rather than in paid work. Wives can be personally dependent on husbands in all classes. Even where both work, the husband often controls the family finances, or the wife does most of the housework.

Eichler sees the family as a quasi-feudal institution in which the wife provides personal services in return for food, shelter, clothing and protection. Her situation is similar to that of a serf.

A problem with Eichler's view is that she is rather unclear about what causes female disadvantage in the first place, and she assumes that men are dominant within all marriages. Also, she analyses the position of married women but neglects the possible exploitation of single women.

Women's liberation – proposals and prospects

Feminism had considerable influence on sociology in the 1970s and 1980s and, arguably, had some influence on social changes.

In the 1990s questions were raised about feminism's future prospects.

- In 1992 Susan Faludi argued that there had been a backlash against feminism. This backlash claimed that feminism had gone far enough – it had achieved equality for women, but it had made their lives unhappy. For example, women pursuing careers and neglecting family life tended to suffer health problems, to become infertile and so on.

Faludi sees these arguments as unfounded. She argues that major inequalities remain. In the USA and Britain men still earn considerably more than women, and Faludi points to research which shows that married women are more likely to be depressed and unhappy than single women with careers.

- Postfeminists argue that the feminism of the 1970s and 1980s is outdated because it sees all women as sharing the same interests and ignores the diverse interests of different groups of women. No one project can liberate all women. Ann Brooks (1997) welcomes this development, arguing that it has highlighted the particular issues surrounding women of colour and lesbians.

However, Whelehan (1995) argues that, while postfeminism has some merit, issues that unite women should not be ignored. She still sees society as essentially patriarchal.

Masculinity

In much early sociology men were simply taken as the norm, while women were different and their behaviour therefore needed explaining. More recently, attention has shifted to focus on the distinctive characteristics of masculinity and how masculinity affects society.

- David Gilmore (1990) argues that masculinity is, in part, socially constructed. What is considered masculine varies from society to society. Biological differences between men and women may be exaggerated or altered by society. In most societies men are seen as impregnators, providers and protectors. They perform important roles for society, taking risks in order to ensure that society survives. Men who succeed in these roles gain high status.

However, in a minority of societies masculinity is very different. In Tahiti, men tend to be timid and passive – there is no warfare and, with a plentiful food supply, no need for men to face danger. Amongst the Semai of Malaysia all violence and aggression are taboo and there is little difference between the behaviours expected of men and women.

Gilmore's work can be criticized for being based on functionalist analysis and for exaggerating the degree to which men protect and provide for women.

- Victor Seidler (1989, 1994) sees masculinity in Western societies as being based on Enlightenment thinking. The Enlightenment (seventeenth- to eighteenth-century science and philosophy in Europe) attacked emotion and superstition and emphasized an objective, detached and scientific approach. Men became associated with these characteristics, while women were seen as more emotional and closer to nature.
- Rutherford (1998) also sees masculinity as traditionally associated with science and reason, but he argues that the idea of masculinity has become more ambiguous. Traditional masculinity

has been challenged by the decline of heavy manual work, divorce, the women's movement, gay and black politics, and an awareness of domestic violence. Consequently there is a split between retributive man (who reasserts traditional masculinity) and new man (who may be more emotional, more concerned about body image and more likely to be involved in childcare). The new man may, in part, be a media myth, but even the existence of the myth creates uncertainty amongst males about how best to be a man.

Rutherford's work is somewhat journalistic and lacks supporting evidence, but it does raise important issues.

- Connell (1995) argues that masculinity develops from both biology and culture, which should be seen as fused together. He argues that masculinity can take a variety of forms. These forms develop and change – some decline, and some become more prominent.

Hegemonic masculinity is the dominant form of masculinity in any society. In contemporary Western societies, white middle-class heterosexual masculinity tends to be dominant. It tries to maintain dominance over subordinate groups, e.g. gay men. However, it is always subject to challenge, and alternative masculinities may exist alongside it without being fully accepted. In his research Connell found four groups of men in which there was evidence of a crisis in the gender order:

- The first group wish to 'live fast die young'. These young working-class men engaged in an exaggerated form of masculinity which involved an acceptance of violence. It involved hostility towards homosexuals, but also an element of contempt towards women. It was largely based on hegemonic masculinity, but Connell sees it as a form of protest masculinity which is a reaction against poverty and educational failure.
- Another group were involved in the environmental movement, which emphasizes equality and cooperation rather than competitiveness. The men were consciously opposed to elements of hegemonic masculinity.
- The 'very straight gays' were homosexual but generally acted in ways that were typical of conventional masculinity. However, they tended towards more egalitarian relationships with partners than is typical of heterosexual hegemonic masculinity.
- Men of reason were part of hegemonic masculinity. They were professionals who saw men as more rational than women.

Connell concludes that the nature of masculinity is contradictory and constantly changing. He is not optimistic about the prospects for transforming masculinity, but he believes there will continue to be challenges to hegemonic masculinity.

1 According to Robert Stoller's distinction between sex and gender, which two of the following would be sex rather than gender characteristics?
   a The difference between male and female sex organs
   b The possession of different levels of hormones by men and women
   c The tendency for men to do more of the heavy work
   d The tendency for women to appear more emotional than men

2 Which two of the following types of hormone tend to be found in higher concentrations in men than in women?
   a Progesterone
   b Oestrogen
   c Testosterone
   d Androgens

3 According to theories of brain lateralization, which one of the following statements is true?
   a The right hemisphere is dominant in females
   b There is no difference between the two hemispheres of the brain
   c The left hemisphere is dominant in females
   d The right hemisphere specializes in verbal and language skills

4 According to sociobiologists, human behaviour is dominated by:
   a A desire to help other people
   b A desire to pass on your genes
   c A desire to make as much money as possible
   d A desire to eat and drink as well as you can

5 Which two of the following types of behaviour does sociobiology have trouble explaining?
   a Promiscuity in men
   b Coyness in women
   c Homosexuality
   d Celibacy

6 Ann Oakley argues that the mother-housewife role is a cultural construction. By this she means:
   a Mothers and housewives are highly regarded in our culture
   b You are considered cultured if you are a mother or a housewife
   c Society's culture creates the expectation that women will do most of the housework and childcare
   d The mother-housewife role is nothing new

7 Gender role socialization refers to:
   a The process by which boys and men and girls and women learn how society expects males and females to behave
   b The way boys and girls socialize with one another
   c The biological differences between males and females
   d The different roles of men and women in society

8 Which one of the following types of feminist places most stress on economic factors in explaining gender inequality?
   a Radical feminists
   b Socialist feminists
   c Liberal feminists
   d Black feminists

9 Which one of the following types of feminist tends to believe that gender inequality can be successfully addressed through equal rights legislation and changing attitudes?
   a Radical feminists
   b Socialist feminists
   c Liberal feminists
   d Black feminists

10 According to Engels, gender inequality originated because:
   a Men used more violence than women
   b Men were more intelligent than women
   c Men wanted to be sure of who their children were
   d Men were physically stronger

11 Marxist feminists such as Benston believe that:
   a Gender inequalities benefit men alone
   b Gender inequalities benefit capitalism alone
   c Gender inequalities benefit both men and capitalism
   d Gender inequalities benefit neither men nor capitalism

12 Which one of the following is not a structure of patriarchy, according to Walby?
   a Paid employment
   b Culture
   c Biology
   d Violence

13 Anna Pollert criticizes the concept of patriarchy for which two of the following reasons?
   a Men are not dominant in society
   b It involves the confusion of description and explanation
   c Gender relations are not a system in the sense that capitalism is
   d The term patriarchy is used in too many different ways

14 Which one of the following is not a statement that postmodern feminists would tend to agree with?
   a The voices of different women need to be heard
   b Deconstructing masculine language is an important feminist project
   c Gender inequality is primarily produced by economic inequality
   d There are many groups of women with different interests

15 Which one of the following is a criticism of postmodern feminism?
   a It neglects language
   b It ignores difference
   c It neglects inequality
   d It emphasizes violence too much

16 By 1996 what percentage of the male wage did women earn?
   a 60%   b 70%
   c 80%   d 90%

17 Horizontal segregation refers to:
   a The tendency for men and women to live in different areas
   b The tendency for men to have higher-status jobs than women
   c The tendency for men and women to do different types of job
   d The tendency for men to occupy elite positions

18 Which one of the following theories suggests that women are particularly likely to be thrown out of work during a recession?
   a Dual labour market theory
   b The reserve army of labour theory
   c The deskilling theory
   d The post-Fordist theory

19 Which one of the following is the main advocate of the theory of deskilling?
   a Oakley
   b Baron and Norris
   c Braverman
   d Beechey

20 Betty Stanko sees a major cause of female disadvantage in the labour market as:
   a Sexual harassment at work
   b Trade unions
   c Biological factors
   d Government legislation

21 Lisa Adkins argues that women's work increasingly involves:
   a Low status
   b Employer discrimination
   c Sexual servicing
   d Restricted opportunities in internal labour markets

22 Kate Millett sees women as:
   a A separate class
   b A minority group
   c Exploited through quasi-feudal institutions
   d Having a caste-like status

23 According to Susan Faludi, feminism is suffering from:
   a A fragmentation of the movement
   b A backlash from men
   c Reduced popularity because of huge progress towards equality
   d The popularity of postmodernism

24 Postfeminism emphasizes:
   a The variety of interests held by different groups of women
   b The importance of the men's movement
   c The end of gender roles
   d The end of gender inequality

25 Post-Fordism claims that:
   a Women are increasingly employed in core jobs
   b Women are increasingly employed in part-time flexible jobs
   c There is a move towards mass production
   d All jobs are being deskilled

26 Eichler argues that women cannot be seen simply as a social class because:
   a Some women are rich
   b Much exploitation takes place in the family
   c Women can move between strata
   d Women should be seen as a minority group

27 Which one of the following is not mentioned by David Gilmore as a traditional role for men?
   a Impregnator
   b Provider
   c Protector
   d Politician

28 Seidler sees masculinity as particularly associated with:
   a Brutality
   b Competitiveness
   c Rationality
   d Emotion

29 According to Bob Connell, the most dominant type of masculinity in any society is called:
   a Ruling-class masculinity
   b Dominance masculinity
   d Elite masculinity
   d Hegemonic masculinity

30 Which one of the following statements would Bob Connell be most likely to disagree with?
   a The nature of masculinity is constantly changing
   b Culture alone shapes masculinity
   c There is something of a crisis in the gender order
   d Some groups of men emphasize cooperation rather than competitiveness

---

Develop your analysis and evaluation skills (see p. 196 for guidance notes)

For each of the following statements, identify which sociologists would argue in favour of and which against the view expressed. Explain the reasons for their view.

1 Gender roles are shaped as much by biology as by culture.
2 Gender inequalities originated with and are maintained by economic inequalities.
3 British society continues to be patriarchal.
4 Patriarchy is no longer a useful concept for feminists.
5 Family responsibilities are largely to blame for women's low wages.
6 Masculinity continues to be characterized by competitiveness, rationality and the use of violence.

AQA style Sex and gender questions

The questions below are examples of where you might be able to use sections of this chapter to answer questions from other areas of the specification.
It is worth remembering that Sex and Gender is part of one of the underlying core themes and thus will come into every part of the specification.

AS Unit 2: Work and Leisure

Comments on the question	Question	Advice on preparing your answer
• Give reasons • Which laws might you consider? • This could mean different things: equality of wages, of promotion and training opportunities, of retirement rights • Other factors outside might explain why they remain unequal in employment	[a] Explain why changes in the law might not bring about equality in employment between men and women. [20 marks]	• See p. 24 for the Acts referred to • Consider cultural differences between men and women (pp. 22–3) • Consider patriarchy (p. 23) and its effects (pp. 25–6) • Notice that not all women and not all men are in the same position (p. 25) • pp. 23–5 might also be very useful here

A2 synoptic Unit 6: Stratification

Notice that although the question is very similar to the one above, different skills and information will be needed to answer it.

Comments on the question	Question	Advice on preparing your answer
• This requires that you bring some evaluation to your reasoning • This question does not have the same tight focus on employment. You should draw on your synoptic understanding from other modules you have studied • What is meant here? Is it equality of opportunity or equality of outcome or both? You should discuss this briefly • This is the focus, but it is worth remembering that differences of age, class and ethnicity may interact as well	[b] Critically examine the reasons why changes in the law may not bring about equality between men and women. [40 marks]	• A quick look at the nature/nurture debate • Gender in contemporary societies (p. 24) • The role of patriarchy (p. 24) • Discrimination (pp. 25–26) • Hegemonic masculinity (p. 27) • In order to fully answer the question you would need to draw on other areas, e.g.: 1 Women in the family (Chapter 8) 2 Women in education (Chapter 11) 3 The role of the mass media and self-identity (Chapters 12 and 13)

Answer all parts of this question

Total: 60 marks   1 mark = 1 minute   Time allowed: 1 hour

ITEM A

This might help in answering part (a)

Jonathan Rutherford believes that the traditional definition of masculinity is under increasing threat because a number of changes have undermined male dominance of the economy and family. Working-class masculinity has been threatened by the decline of manual work which has resulted in high levels of male unemployment. The male roles of breadwinner and head of household have been challenged by working women. Confusion and anxiety about male identity may be responsible for increasing levels of suicide among young men.

Comments on the question	Question	Advice on preparing your answer
• The reasons are in the data. There is no need to go beyond this • Make sure that the examiner can clearly see two reasons • Make sure that you explain the reason you have identified – perhaps with an example • Don't offer more than two points	[a] Using Item A only, identify and explain two reasons why the traditional model of masculinity is under threat. [8 marks]	• Don't lift the material word for word from the item. Try to put it into your own words
• Go beyond simply providing a list. Explain using examples • No more, no less • Don't ignore this crucial instruction	[b] Identify and explain two masculine identities that exist in modern UK society, other than the traditional model of masculinity. [8 marks]	• The section on masculinity (p. 27) will be useful here
• This means 'describe' • This means you should briefly weigh up any arguments/evidence for or against the ways you identify	[c] Outline and briefly evaluate two ways in which males are socialized into masculine norms and values. [18 marks]	• The section on gender role socialization on p. 23 will help you with this task • Focus on agents of socialization
• This means that you need to look at arguments against the view as well as arguments and evidence that support it • They may not be experiencing any such thing, i.e. you might want to conclude that masculinity and femininity are still quite traditional in character	[d] Discuss the view that masculinity and femininity may be experiencing gender transformation. [26 marks]	• Don't forget to discuss both

Chapter 4

'Race', ethnicity and nationality Textbook pp. 198–289

Specifications

Specification	Relevant module title	Place in module	Level	Assessment	Other relevant modules
AQA	There is no AQA module specifically on this topic (see last column).	n/a	n/a	n/a	This topic is intrinsic to the whole specification and is relevant to every module.
OCR	There is no OCR module specifically on this topic (see last column).	n/a	n/a	n/a	This topic is intrinsic to the whole specification and is relevant to every module.

'Race', ethnicity and nationality: essential notes

Introduction

There has been a long history of racism and racial or ethnic conflict. Examples include the enslavement of Africans, anti-Semitism in England, the slaughter of Jews in Nazi Germany, ethnic cleansing in the former Yugoslavia, conflict between Protestant and Catholic ethnic groups and so on.

'Race'

Biological theories of 'race' connect phenotype (physical appearance) with genotype (genetic differences).

- Michael Banton (1987) argues that the term 'race' was not used in English until 1508. Before that everyone was assumed to be descended from Adam and Eve. This was a monogenesist theory – i.e. everybody had the same origin.

  In the eighteenth and nineteenth centuries polygenetic theories developed. These held that there were different 'races' with different origins. They divided people into different groups such as Caucasian, Mongolian, Malay, American (native American) and Ethiopian (black African).

- Drawing on the theory of evolution, Herbert Spencer (1971), argued that different 'races' had evolved to different degrees, with Aborigines amongst the least evolved and white Europeans amongst the most evolved.

- The geneticist Steve Jones (1991, 1994) argues that there are no clear dividing lines between different 'races'. Although there are genetic differences between groups, humans are a very homogeneous species. Genes for skin colour are not linked to other genes, and there are big genetic differences between people of the same supposed 'race'.

To Jones, 'race' is simply a social definition since societies use widely differing definitions and there is no genetic justification for distinguishing 'races'.

- Richardson and Lambert (1985) argue that 'race' has no biological basis but the belief that 'races' exist has important social consequences.

  In particular, doctrines of racial superiority (the belief that particular 'races' are superior to others) influence behaviour.

  Richardson and Lambert criticize the doctrine of racial superiority, pointing out that at different stages of history a wide variety of societies with different 'races' have been the most dominant or technologically advanced.

  Richardson and Lambert conclude that 'race' is a social construct – it is concerned with what people make of physical differences rather than the differences themselves.

Migration and 'race' relations

Some sociologists see the effects of migration as central to understanding race relations.

Migration to Britain

John Richardson (1985) points out that for many centuries Britain has had migration from diverse areas, and it has long had an ethnically diverse population. One example of migration took place with the Norman Conquest, and there was considerable Jewish immigration in the 1870–1914 period, and Polish immigration during the Second World War.

In the 1950s and 1960s there was substantial immigration to Britain from the New Commonwealth, particularly Afro-Caribbean immigration from the West Indies, and Asian immigration from India, Pakistan and, in the 1970s, East Africa.

This migration became politically controversial,

with politicians such as Enoch Powell arguing that it would lead to racial violence.

Immigration laws were progressively tightened, with the 1962 Commonwealth Immigrants Act and the 1971 Immigration Act.

Many commentators, such as Pilkington (1984), argue that such Acts were racially discriminatory since they allowed more white than non-white immigration.

A 1988 Act made it difficult for families of non-white immigrants to come to Britain, and the 1993 Asylum and Immigration Act tightened up rules on people applying for political asylum in Britain.

Commentators such as Cohen argue that such changes have made it difficult for those who are genuinely being persecuted to come to Britain. Skellington and Morris (1992) see immigration laws as discriminatory against black and Asian people. They point out that:

- A great deal of white immigration is allowed – e.g. from European Community countries.
- Britain was a net exporter of people for much of the twentieth century, so arguments that Britain is becoming overcrowded as a result of immigration are spurious.

Britain's non-white ethnic minority population is comparatively small. The 1991 census found 890,000 British people who described themselves as black, and about 1.5 million who described themselves as Indian, Pakistani or Bangladeshi (out of a total population of more than 54 million).

Migration and assimilation

The immigrant-host model examines race relations in terms of the relationship between an immigrant minority and a host majority.

It is often assumed that the immigrant minority will gradually be assimilated into the host majority.

As in functionalist theories of value consensus, the host majority are often assumed to have a shared culture. And as in functionalism, an evolutionary process of adaptation is assumed to take place.

Park – race relations and migration

Robert Park (1950) of the Chicago School first put forward this sort of approach in the 1920s and 1930s. He argued that there was a process of interracial adjustment following migration.

Initial competition and conflict would usually give way to accommodation (in which groups learn to live together) and assimilation (in which the different racial groups merge with minority groups, gradually blending into the majority group).

Park acknowledged that some conflict could remain.

Patterson – *Dark Strangers*

In a study of first-generation immigrants from the West Indies to Brixton, Sheila Patterson (1965) found that some accommodation between the two communities had taken place, and she anticipated that, as with the Irish, assimilation would eventually take place.

Richardson and Lambert – a critique of the immigrant–host model

Richardson and Lambert (1985) criticize the immigrant–host model:

- Concepts such as accommodation and assimilation are too vague and hard to apply to actual situations.
- Assimilation may not be desirable: some prefer the diversity of a multicultural society.
- The model ignores the existence of racism as a barrier to developing harmonious relationships.
- Conflict theorists criticize it for wrongly assuming there is a consensus in host societies.

Castles and Kosack – a Marxist view

The Marxists Castles and Kosack (1973) see migration in terms of the international capitalist system:

- From colonial times, many Third World countries have been used as a source of cheap, easily exploited labour.
- In Europe and elsewhere, migrant workers continue to be exploited as a reserve army of labour.
- 'Race prejudice' against the migrant workers develops among the working class, who see the new workers as a threat to their jobs. This prevents a united working class from developing class consciousness.

Castles and Miller – *The Age of Migration*

In more recent work Castles and Miller (1993) argue that the scale of international migration has led to increasing cultural diversity in most states.

Minority groups have increasingly sought to maintain their culture and identity. In many places this has led to greater acceptance of a plurality of cultures.

However, in some countries which have experienced little migration in recent years there is the danger of exclusionary nationalism (the former Yugoslavia is an example).

Ethnicity

The idea of ethnicity places emphasis on culture rather than the biological differences implied by the term 'race'.

Unlike immigrant-host models there is no assumption that there will be greater integration or assimilation between ethnic groups.

Defining ethnicity

- Milton Yinger (1981) defines an ethnic group in terms of a real, or perceived, difference between one group and others, in some combination of 'language, religion, race ... ancestral homeland ... culture'. It involves participation in 'shared activities built around their (real or mythical) common origin or culture'.
- John Richardson (1990) also sees ethnicity as based upon cultural differences. He criticizes 'racial' categories, arguing that biological differences are not clearcut.

However, there are problems with the term ethnicity:

- Many ethnic groups are subdivided.
- Different aspects of culture, such as language, territorial origin and religion, can produce conflicting categories.

Ethnographic studies of ethnicity examine the culture and lifestyle of ethnic groups.

The Ballards – Sikhs in the Punjab and in Leeds

Roger and Catherine Ballard (1977) studied Punjabi Sikhs in Leeds. They found:

- A strong desire to maintain the distinctive features of Sikh culture in the first generation. This was partly based on the 'myth of return' (the belief that they might one day return to the Punjab).
- A greater interest in materialism and educational achievement in the second generation.
- Children developed multiple presentations of self. They retained an attachment to their parents' culture while acting in more Westernized ways outside the home.
- While racism played some part in shaping behaviour, the preferences of Sikhs themselves were also important.

In later work, Ballard emphasized the differences between groups of British Asians:

- Sikhs tended to come from richer areas than Muslims and had been more economically successful in Britain.
- Cultural factors – such as Muslim wives being less likely to take paid employment than Sikh wives – played some part.

Pryce – West Indians in Bristol

Ken Pryce (1979) studied West Indians in Bristol in the 1970s.

He found a variety of subcultures in the West Indian community, split between two main types of response to life in Britain:

1. The expressive-disreputable orientation involved rejection of a white society that was perceived as hostile and racist.
2. The stable, law-abiding orientation involved acceptance or at least grudging toleration of white society.

Pryce's study shows how ethnic groups can develop different subcultures resulting from different responses to racism and exploitation. The more politically aware young West Indians are continuing a tradition of anti-colonial struggle which started in the Caribbean.

McKay – primordial and mobilizationist explanations of ethnicity

James McKay (1982) looks at explanations for the existence of ethnicity.

Primordial explanations suggest that humans naturally divide the world into people similar to themselves ('us') and people who are different ('them').

McKay criticizes this approach because it cannot explain variations in the strength of ethnic attachments or changes in ethnic identity.

Mobilizationist explanations see ethnicity as actively created rather than an inevitable product of being human. People use ethnic symbols and ethnicity to further their own ends.

McKay sympathizes more with this approach but argues that it fails to explain the emotional strength of ethnic attachments. He believes that the two approaches should be combined.

In some ethnic groups, primordial attachments are strong (e.g. amongst Basque Nationalists); in other groups, ethnicity is more symbolic and based upon mobilization (e.g. Irish people living outside Ireland who take part in a St Patrick's Day parade).

Brown – the causes of ethnic conflict

Michael Brown (1997) examines the causes of ethnic conflict:

1. Systemic explanations explain conflict in terms of the nature of the overall security system. For example, conflict between ethnic groups in the former Yugoslavia could be seen as resulting from the break-up of a powerful, centralized state which kept ethnic conflict in check.
2. Domestic explanations involve the ability of states to deal with the concerns of different ethnic groups. Sometimes states themselves encourage hostility to ethnic groups to distract attention from the failings of the government.
3. Perceptual explanations consider how distortions, myths and false histories can encourage hostility to an ethnic group.

Conflict is most likely where groups who have hostile perceptions of one another live in close proximity without a strong centralized authority to keep them in check. The break-up of the Soviet Union has led to many such conflicts.

More optimistically Brown suggests that ethnic conciliation is possible.

Ethnicity – an evaluation

The idea of ethnicity has certain strengths:

1. The ethnicity approach gets away from the biological determinism of 'race'.
2. It avoids the assumption of eventual assimilation of the host-immigrant model.
3. It recognizes the part ethnic groups play in actively shaping their own lifestyles.
4. It also tends to support multiculturalism.

However, it also has a number of weaknesses:

1. Marxists believe that it ignores social structure.
2. Some commentators believe that it neglects the importance of racism.
3. Some theories of globalization question whether there are still clear distinctions between ethnic groups.

Racism

Approaches which stress the importance of racism tend to be particularly concerned with:

- Constraints placed on 'racial'/ethnic groups by discrimination.
- Inequalities between such groups.

They tend to be less concerned with cultural differences.

Key terms are:

- Prejudice – learned beliefs or values which make people biased against a group.
- Discrimination – actions that disadvantage people because of prejudice.
- Racism – this word has been used in a variety of ways and has a comparatively recent origin. John Rex (1986) sees racism as 'deterministic belief systems about the differences between ethnic

groups'. To John Solomos (1993) racism is not just a question of beliefs but also involves discrimination on the basis of racist beliefs.

- Cultural racism refers to widespread racist beliefs in a particular culture rather than views held by individuals.
- Institutional racism is a controversial term, but it most commonly refers to partly unconscious racism which results from the way institutions are organized or the culture that operates in them. The Stephen Lawrence Inquiry (MacPherson Report, 1999) defined it as 'The collective failure of an organisation to provide an appropriate and professional service to people because of their colour, culture or ethnic origin.' However, it has also been defined in terms of the inequalities between ethnic groups which result from state policy (the structural Marxist view) and in a variety of other ways.

The idea of institutional racism has been criticized:

1 Many see it as poorly defined.
2 Miles criticizes approaches that suggest that institutional racism is simply 'what white people do'.
3 The definition of institutional racism in terms of inequality between groups ignores the possibility that other factors (such as cultural differences) might play a part in creating inequality.

However, it does draw attention to the way in which the policies of some institutions disadvantage ethnic minorities, whether or not there is any conscious discrimination.

The extent of individual racism

Various attempts have been made to measure the extent to which individuals in Britain are racist.

- The British Social Attitudes Surveys found, between 1983 and 1991, a reduction in those who were 'very prejudiced' (from 4% to 2%) and a small reduction in those who were 'a little prejudiced' (from 31% to 29%).
- In a 1995 ICM poll, two-thirds of the sample admitted they were racist, and less than half the black and Asian respondents agreed that 'coloured people felt British'.

A problem with these sorts of studies is that they only measure the racism that people admit to. Furthermore they only measure individual racism, saying nothing about cultural or institutional racism.

Racial harassment

Some studies look at the extent of racism actually experienced by people.

The Policy Studies Institute (PSI) survey published in 1997 estimated that every year 1% of ethnic minority members in Britain were subject to racially motivated attacks; about 2% had property damaged for racial reasons; and about 11–12% experienced racial abuse or insults.

Racism in the press

Racism can also be found in the media. Van Dijk (1991) studied racism in the British press in the 1980s. He found:

- Black people were often associated with inner-city disturbances or violence.
- Ethnic minorities were rarely portrayed as victims of violence.

- There was a great deal of coverage of a story about white children being disadvantaged as a minority in a Bradford school (the Honeyford affair).
- In the late 1980s Islamic fundamentalism was often portrayed as a threat.

Solomos and Back – racism and popular culture

John Solomos and Les Back (1996) have studied racism in popular culture. They argue that there is a long history of racist imagery in British culture.

- British Imperial propaganda in the nineteenth and early twentieth century used images such as John Bull and Britannia which were connected with the notion of white British people civilizing the world.
- In the 1930s there was concern in the popular media about sex between white and non-white people.
- In the 1950s the sheer number of black people entering Britain was portrayed as a problem.
- In the 1960s black people were portrayed as welfare scroungers.
- In the 1970s muggings and riots were associated with Afro-Caribbeans.
- By the late 1980s there was more apparent acceptance in the popular media of black and Asian people in Britain, and there were more multicultural images – e.g. in Benetton's advertising.

Solomos and Back see some progress taking place but argue that racist elements remain in popular culture. For example, black people are sometimes still discussed in the popular media in terms of sexual attractiveness rather than in terms of achievement (e.g. Linford Christie's 'lunchbox').

Inequalities between ethnic groups in Britain

Useful sources of data on ethnic inequality in Britain are the recent Policy Studies Institute (PSI) surveys, and studies carried out by their predecessor, Political and Economic Planning. They are based on questionnaire research and cover periods between 1966 and 1994.

- Employment
1 There are variations in occupational status according to gender and ethnic group.
2 The proportion of the Chinese with professional and managerial jobs is higher than that for whites.
3 African Asians do well in the labour market. Indians do better than Pakistanis and Bangladeshis.
4 Only a small percentage of those of Caribbean origin hold professional and managerial jobs.
5 Most groups of ethnic minority women earn more than white women (though not Pakistani and Bangladeshi women), whereas all groups of ethnic minority men (apart from the Chinese) earn less than white men.
6 There is evidence of some decline in inequality, but overall ethnic minorities still do less well than whites in employment.

- Housing
1 Owner-occupation has grown considerably amongst ethnic minorities, with higher rates than whites for all groups apart from Pakistanis, Afro-Caribbeans and Bangladeshis.

2 Ethnic minorities tend to live in more disadvantaged areas than whites.

Conclusion
Overall, inequalities remain, but they have been reduced and patterns vary considerably between different ethnic groups.

Theories of racism

Psychological theories
Psychological theories tend to see racism as a characteristic of abnormal minorities.

- Adorno (1950) of the Frankfurt School argued that racism stemmed from authoritarian personalities, which were produced by strict disciplining and a lack of love in childhood.
- Dollard (1939, 1957) argued that the frustrations of a repressed childhood resulted in aggression towards ethnic minorities in later life.

Critics of psychological theories argue that racism is widespread in some societies and is not confined to a minority with abnormal personalities.

Cashmore – *The Logic of Racism*
Ellis Cashmore (1987) explored racism in different areas of Birmingham. Racism was present everywhere, but it varied by age group and the area in which people lived. Whites in middle-class areas with small ethnic minority populations tended to be less openly racist than others, but they did discriminate in their positions of authority. There was more open conflict and racism in working-class areas with large ethnic minority populations, but some of the young whites felt a good deal in common with ethnic minority youths.

Cox – a Marxist theory
Oliver Cox (1948) puts forward a Marxist theory. He argues that racism developed with capitalism and served as a justification for the exploitation of slave workforces in colonies.

However, critics have argued that racism exists outside capitalist systems.

The Birmingham Centre for Contemporary Cultural Studies – a neo-Marxist theory
The Birmingham Centre for Contemporary Cultural Studies argues that racism predates colonialism, and that colonialism is only one factor influencing racism. Economic factors are important but specific historical and cultural factors also shape racism, as do the resistance and struggle of ethnic minorities.

Following this approach, Lawrence (1982) argues that the 1970s saw the development of a 'new racism' in Britain. Racism was no longer based on explicitly portraying non-white people as inferior but on portraying their cultures as a threat to the integrity of British culture.

Gilroy – *There Ain't No Black in the Union Jack*
Paul Gilroy (1987) examined both racism and ethnic minority cultures. He discusses the process of race formation in which interaction within and between ethnic minorities and whites shapes the identity of different groups.

Gilroy agrees that there is a new racism based on perceived cultural threats to the supposed British way of life. It emphasizes ethnic absolutism – the idea that ethnic minority cultures are completely alien to white British culture.

However, Gilroy argues that there is increasing overlap. For example, black and white youth culture and music overlap and incorporate elements from different sources. There are therefore some grounds for optimism about a future decline of racism.

Nationalism and identity

Nationalism
Many commentators believe that there has been a recent revival of nationalism despite many predictions that it would decline.

- Benedict Anderson (1983) sees nationalism as different from racism in that you can become a member of a nation whereas you cannot become a member of a different race.
- Robert Miles (1989) and others see close connections between race and nationalism, with racist ideas often used to justify the supposed superiority of people from particular nations.
- Miles sees a central feature of nationalism as a desire for a particular group to have a sovereign nation-state, i.e. an independent state.

McCrone – *The Sociology of Nationalism*
David McCrone (1998) distinguishes between civic nationalism and ethnic nationalism:

- Civic nationalist sentiments are based upon being a member of a particular nation-state, such as the USA, which includes diverse ethnic groups.
- In ethnic nationalism, perceived membership of an ethnic group unites people – e.g. Serbs and Croats in the former Yugoslavia.

McCrone goes on to explain how four different types of nationalism emerged:

1 Nationalism in the modern nation-state – this type of nationalism emerged in countries such as the UK, France and the USA. The nation-state developed with the economic changes of capitalism and the Industrial Revolution, but the building of nationalist identities sometimes exploited existing ethnic and cultural groupings.
2 Nationalism emerged in many countries which were colonies, as they struggled for independence and sought to become post-colonial societies.
3 Neo-nationalism is found in independence movements in Western societies, such as the Basque country and Scotland. It tends to develop in areas with strong economies and a strong civil society.
4 Post-communist nationalism exists in some areas which used to be part of the Soviet Union, and in other areas of Eastern Europe. With the decline of strong centralized authority, groups with particular national and ethnic identities sought to establish national homelands for themselves, and some fought over particular territories.

Cohen – British nationality and identity

Robin Cohen (1994) discusses British nationality and identity. He argues that there is no clear dividing line between being British and not being British. For example, the Scottish and Welsh and people in former colonies may to different extents identify themselves as British or distance themselves from being British.

There is also some overlap between European and American identities and being British, which means that defining who is alien – i.e. non-British – is not clearcut.

Hall – new ethnicities

The complexity of national identity is reflected in the emergence of new ethnicities.

Stuart Hall (1996) sees new ethnicities in terms of the development of new identities in black cultural politics in Britain.

These new identities stress the great variety of differences between people. People see themselves and are seen by others not just in terms of ethnicity but also in terms of age, religion, sexuality, class and gender.

Hall also argues that there is increasing hybridization with the merging and overlapping of different identities. Globalization and migration have led to increasingly diverse populations living in particular areas and therefore different cultures influencing one another.

In some areas the response has been ethnic absolutism, based on trying to maintain ethnic purity and hostility to members of other groups – e.g. ethnic cleansing in the former Yugoslavia.

Hall sees ethnic absolutism and nationalism as major threats in a globalizing world.

Modood – new ethnicities and identities

Some evidence of changing ethnic identities in Britain is provided by survey research carried out by Modood et al (1997).

- This found that by the mid-1990s most British Caribbeans and South Asians thought of themselves both as British and as members of ethnic minorities.
- Older Caribbeans and South Asians born outside the UK identified more with their country of origin than younger generations born in Britain.
- There were considerable variations in people's sense of identity in all ethnic groups.

Back – new ethnicities and urban culture

Research by Les Back (1996) on two London council estates found a mixture of racism and the development of new ethnicities.

- On one estate a number of white youths adopted elements of black youth culture and felt they had as much in common with some black people as with white people.
- Some young black people had a strong sense of British citizenship.

Modernity, postmodernity, racism, ethnicity and identity

- Zygmunt Bauman (1989), a postmodernist, links modernity to racism. He argues that modernity made the Holocaust (the mass extermination of Jews and other groups in Nazi Germany) possible.

1 Bureaucratic planning made mass extermination possible.
2 Modern organizational discipline was used to control the individuals who carried out the exterminations.
3 The existence of modern nation-states allowed Jews to be seen as outsiders.
4 Modern scientific rationalism was used to 'prove' the inferiority of Jews.

- Davis Goldberg (1993) blames modernity for creating racism. He argues that there was no racism in premodern societies.

1 Modernity brought a new liberal conceptual order in which people thought of themselves as rational individuals rather than the subjects of God.
2 Non-Western people whose lands were colonized began to be defined as less than rational by Western liberals and scientists, leading to the development of racism.
3 Non-Westerners were regarded as 'others' and seen in terms of racist and stereotypical images.

Goldberg believes that the development of postmodernism – in which people have more mixed, varied and insecure identities – makes it possible that racism might decline.

- Ali Rattansi (1994) argues that under postmodernism two processes might undermine racism:

1 Decentering the subject rejects the view that people have a strong and unambiguous sense of identity.
2 De-essentialization rejects the view that there are fundamental or unchanging differences between societies or groups of people.

With more fluid identities it becomes hard to maintain rigid, racist views because there are no longer clear distinctions between groups of people.

- Kenan Malik (1996) criticizes postmodern theories.

1 He argues that the Enlightenment philosophy on which modernity was based saw humans as equal and provided the theoretical basis for liberating people.
2 It was not modernity as such which caused racism but the inequality produced by capitalism. The working class was the first group to be seen as 'racially' inferior, and only later did racism become applied to people from different ethnic groups.
3 Malik believes that modern ideas about the equality of humans are a more positive way of tackling racism than the postmodern idea of simply accepting difference. This is because groups who are different may also be or become very unequal.

Ethnic minorities in the labour market and stratification system

A number of attempts have been made to explain the tendency for people from (some) ethnic minorities to get lower pay and to have lower-status jobs.

Discrimination in the labour market

Discrimination is one possible explanation.

Brown and Gay (1985) used bogus job applications to measure the extent of racial discrimination by employers in the 1980s. They found evidence that more than a quarter of employers discriminated against ethnic minority applicants by denying them job interviews.

In the 1990s survey by the Policy Studies Institute, substantial minorities amongst ethnic groups (e.g. 28% of Caribbean people) claimed to have been denied a job because of their race or religion.

Ethnic minorities as an underclass
Some sociologists have seen ethnic minorities as making up an underclass.

- Charles Murray (1984) argued that in the USA there was a growing black underclass made up of single mothers, young men unwilling to work and criminals.
  Their problems stemmed from their culture, which resulted in part from welfare payments that made single parenthood possible and encouraged dependency on benefits rather than earned income.

  However, Lydia Morris (1994) points out that there is no automatic entitlement to benefits for the unemployed in the USA.
- An alternative view of the underclass in the USA is put forward by William Julius Wilson (1987).
1 He sees blacks and Hispanics living in inner cities as making up an underclass, but because of disadvantage rather than because of cultural differences.
2 A combination of racism and lack of skills has held these groups back, and their lack of economic success has reinforced racial stereotypes.
3 Successful blacks and Hispanics have moved out of the inner cities, leaving the least successful behind.
4 Wilson suggests that the term underclass should be abandoned because it has been used by some to unfairly blame the disadvantaged for their problems. He prefers the term ghetto poor which has no such connotations.
- In 1973 Giddens argued that there was an ethnic minority and female underclass in Britain, as a result of structural problems such as low skills and discrimination.
- John Rex and Sally Tomlinson (1979) studied Handsworth, Birmingham, in the late 1970s and found evidence of an ethnic minority underclass.
  They found that blacks and Asians were concentrated in secondary labour market jobs – those with few prospects and little security. For example, a high proportion worked in metal or metal goods manufacturing but only a low proportion in the better-paid vehicle manufacturing sector.

Marxist approaches
- An alternative view is put forward by Marxists such as Castles and Kosack (1973).
1 From a study of immigrant groups in various European countries, they acknowledge that such groups are concentrated in low-paid and low-status work
2 In Britain this is mostly due to discrimination. However, in France, Germany and Switzerland many members of ethnic minorities are migrant workers who lack citizenship rights. Here restrictive laws and regulations prevent them from getting better work.
3 Castles and Kosack see immigrants as a reserve army of labour – easily hired and fired – who are needed to cope with the booms and slumps of capitalist economies. They see them as the most disadvantaged group in the working class rather than as a separate underclass.
- The Marxists Annie Phizaklea and Robert Miles (1980) see ethnic minorities as one faction in the working class. The working class has always contained different factions – e.g. males and females and skilled and unskilled workers.
- Andrew Pilkington (1993) questions all of the above theories which see ethnic minorities as forming a distinct stratum below or at the bottom of the working class.
1 He points out that substantial proportions of all ethnic minorities have non-manual jobs. Indian men are more likely to be in white-collar employment than white men.
2 Although ethnic minorities overall have lower pay and lower-status jobs, there is a great deal of overlap and no evidence of ethnic minorities as a whole forming an underprivileged stratum.

Conclusion
Pilkington's views highlight the need to examine a range of factors (such as age, class background and gender, as well as ethnicity) in trying to understand the labour market, and they show the dangers of over-simplifying the situation.

1   Phenotype refers to:
    a   The physical appearance of different groups
    b   The personality of different groups
    c   The genetic differences between groups
    d   The behaviour of different groups

2   Saying that 'races' are socially defined means:
    a   Races are genetically different
    b   A race is simply what a particular society sees as a race
    c   There is considerable overlap between races
    d   Races do not exist

3   Which one of these statements is not a criticism of the biological theory of 'race'?
    a   Skin colour is only linked to a small number of genes
    b   Humans are a genetically relatively homogeneous species
    c   There are big genetic differences between people of the same supposed 'race'
    d   There are distinct, genetically different racial groups which can be identified through skin colour

4   Which one of these statements about British migration is true?
    a   Britain has always had more immigration than emigration
    b   Immigration to Britain is a comparatively new phenomenon
    c   Britain has had an ethnically diverse population for many centuries as a result of migration
    d   British immigration laws treat all non-British citizens equally

5   Which one of these statements about the immigrant–host model is not true?
    a   The model assumes that the hosts have a shared culture
    b   The model sees assimilation as unlikely to happen
    c   The model sees accommodation as part of the process of adaptation
    d   The model was first developed at the University of Chicago

6   Which one of the following do Castles and Miller not see as being a consequence of recent international migration?
    a   All minority groups have tried to become assimilated into the majority population
    b   Most minority groups have tried to maintain a separate identity
    c   Generally a greater acceptance of cultural diversity has developed
    d   In some countries strong nationalist sentiment has developed against minority groups

7   Which one of these statements is true?
    a   The idea of ethnicity places more emphasis on culture than on genetics
    b   There are always clear dividing lines between ethnic groups
    c   Ethnic groups are based on the locality where the groups live
    d   Ethnic groups are homogeneous

8   Punjabi Sikhs in Leeds were studied by:
    a   John Richardson
    b   Robert Park
    c   Milton Yinger
    d   Roger and Catherine Ballard

9   Ken Pryce conducted an ethnographic study of:
    a   West Indians in Bristol
    b   Bangladeshis in London
    c   Greek Cypriots in London
    d   Pakistanis in Bradford

10 Primordial explanations of ethnicity suggest:
    a   Some ethnic groups are primitive
    b   People define themselves as members of ethnic groups because they believe they have something to gain
    c   Humans have a natural tendency to divide the world into 'us' and 'them'
    d   Ethnic groups develop because of genetic differences

11 Which one of the following does Michael Brown not give as an explanation for ethnic conflict?
    a   A domestic explanation
    b   A global explanation
    c   A perceptual explanation
    d   A systemic explanation

12 Which two of the following are strengths of the ethnicity approach?
    a   It stresses the importance of racism
    b   There are clear distinctions between ethnic groups
    c   It avoids biological determinism
    d   It sees ethnic minorities as active agents

13 Which one of the following is an example of institutional racism?
    a   A widespread belief that an ethnic group is inferior
    b   Policing policies which disadvantage an ethnic group
    c   A member of the public shouting racial insults in the street
    d   An individual harassing somebody because of their 'race'

14 In 1995 what proportion of people admitted they were racist in an ICM poll?
    a   One-tenth
    b   One-half
    c   Two-thirds
    d   Three-quarters

15 Which one of these statements about ethnic minority employment in Britain is true?
    a   All ethnic minorities are disadvantaged in employment
    b   Bangladeshis do particularly well in the labour market
    c   African Asians do particularly well in the labour market
    d   Inequality between ethnic groups in the labour market is increasing rapidly

16 According to Adorno, racism is caused by:
    a   Authoritarian fathers
    b   Weak mothers
    c   Frustration resulting from a repressed childhood
    d   A poor diet in childhood

17 Ellis Cashmore studied racism in:
   a Manchester   b Glasgow
   c Birmingham   d Plymouth

18 Oliver Cox blames racism on:
   a Ignorance   b Capitalism
   c Patriarchy   d Migration

19 New racism is based on the idea of:
   a Biological differences between people
   b Cultural inferiority of ethnic minorities
   c Differences in intelligence
   d Differences in power between racial groups

20 Paul Gilroy believes that:
   a Some ethnic minority cultures are alien to the
     British way of life
   b There are clearcut differences between ethnic
     groups
   c Racism is disappearing in Britain
   d There is increasing overlap between black and
     white youth cultures

21 Which one of these is not a phenomenon caused by
   globalization, according to Stuart Hall?
   a Hybridization
   b Ethnic absolutism
   c A desire for ethnic purity
   d The destruction of ethnic identities

22 Zygmunt Bauman can best be described as:
   a A postmodernist
   b A modernist
   c A Marxist
   d A feminist

23 Which one of these statements best describes the
   views of Kenan Malik?
   a Modernity is responsible for racism
   b Postmodernity will ensure equality between ethnic
     groups
   c Modernity provides the potential basis for
     producing greater equality between ethnic groups
   d Racism is confined to higher social classes

24 Which one of these writers sees the underclass as
   resulting from deficient culture and generous
   welfare systems?
   a Anthony Giddens
   b Charles Murray
   c Lydia Morris
   d William Julius Wilson

25 Goldberg believes that racism was first caused by:
   a Patriarchy
   b Modernity
   c Postmodernity
   d Industrialization

26 Which one of these terms is not associated with
   Rex and Tomlinson's study?
   a Underclass
   b Secondary labour market
   c Dual labour market
   d Class faction

27 Which of the following researchers studied racism
   using bogus job applications?
   a Giddens
   b Rex and Tomlinson
   c Murray
   d Brown and Gay

28 Andy Pilkington believes that ethnic minorities:
   a Have achieved equality with whites in Britain
   b Do not form a distinct underclass
   c Are almost all living in poverty
   d Have an inferior culture to whites

29 Zygmunt Bauman studied:
   a Ethnic cleansing in Yugoslavia
   b Racism in the USA
   c The Holocaust
   d Race riots

30 The Conservative politician who warned of the
   possibility of racial violence in the 1970s was:
   a Enoch Powell
   b Edward Heath
   c Harold Wilson
   d George Brown

31 'Decentering the subject' means:
   a People no longer have strong, unambiguous
     identities
   b People no longer have any identity
   c People are developing stronger identities
   d There is no such thing as identity

32 De-essentialization means:
   a Rejecting sociological explanations
   b Rejecting popular culture as essentially racist
   c Rejecting multiculturalism
   d Rejecting the view that there are unchanging
     differences between human groups

Develop your analysis and evaluation skills

(see p. 198 for guidance notes)

For each of the following statements, identify which sociologists
would argue in favour of and which against the view expressed.
Explain the reasons for their view.

1 There are biologically distinct races some of
  which are superior to others.
2 Racism explains the main inequalities and
  differences between ethnic groups in Britain.
3 Ethnicity is a more useful concept than racism
  in understanding ethnic groups.
4 Both racism and inequalities between ethnic
  groups are dying out in Britain.

5 Nationalism and ethnic conflict are both
  becoming more common, and there are a
  variety of reasons for this change.
6 Ethnic minorities in Britain constitute an
  underclass.
7 Racism is a product of modernity.

AQA style Ethnicity and Race question

The questions below are from different parts of the specification but they are all parts of questions where you will be able to use knowledge from this chapter.

AS Unit 2: Work and Leisure

Comments on the question	Question	Advice on preparing your answer
• This means look at from more than one point of view – does a viewpoint have evidence to back it up? • Plural, so several reasons will be needed here • Are all groups the same? Distinguish between them and consider whether male and female ethnic minority members are in the same position • You might also need to look at the chapter on Work, unemployment and leisure to answer this question fully	[a] Examine the reasons for the continued discrimination of ethnic minority groups in the field of employment. [20 marks]	• Start by explaining this term, see p. 34 • This chapter has several important points: 1 Migration and conflict, pp. 32–3 2 Exclusionary nationalism, pp. 36–7 3 Subcultural values, pp. 33–4 4 Racism, pp. 34–5 5 Inequalities between groups, pp. 35–6 6 Reasons for racism from a variety of perspectives, pp. 34–5 7 Underclass theory, p. 38

A2 synoptic Unit 6: Stratification

Comments on the question	Question	Advice on preparing your answer
• Look at both sides of every argument you consider • You should distinguish between different groups here • This is the focus, not any other feature of life • This means you shouldn't look at education for the answer here • This is a fifth of your total marks, so only spend a fifth of your time, i.e. 18 minutes	[b] Briefly examine the reasons why ethnic minorities are still more likely to be receiving low pay than others with equal skills. [12 marks]	• This question is saying: 'If all else is equal why does discrimination occur?' • The main answer will probably hinge on racism, so pp. 34–5 may be of great use here • Consider the following types of racism: 1 Individual 2 Institutional 3 Cultural • You could bring in ideas from: 1 Communication and the media, Chapter 13 2 Work, unemployment and leisure, Chapter 10 3 Culture and identity, Chapter 12

OCR style 'Race', ethnicity and nationality question, AS Unit 2532: The Individual and Society

Answer all parts of this question
Total: 60 marks   1 mark = 1 minute
Time allowed: 1 hour

ITEM A

Les Back's research in 'Southgate', a council estate in South London, found that a new type of hybrid black-white ethnic culture was developing among young people. For example, Tony, who was a 17-year-old white male, had learnt to talk in the same way as local black people. Debbie, a white female, mainly had black friends. Although racism against black people had not disappeared from the area, both black and white youth shared racist ideas about the Vietnamese living in the area.

This might help in answering part (a)

Comments on the question	Question	Advice on preparing your answer
• The characteristics are in the data. You will not be rewarded for going beyond this • Make sure that the examiner can clearly see the two characteristics you have identified and explained – e.g. number them • Go beyond simply supplying a list – explain using examples • Don't offer more than two points	[a] Using Item A, identify and explain two characteristics of the new type of hybrid black/white ethnicity appearing among young people. [8 marks]	• Don't just copy the material from Item A. Try to put it into your own words
• No more, no less • Make sure that two reasons are clearly seen by the examiner	[b] Identify and explain two reasons why some members of ethnic minority groups living in the UK may be reluctant to identify themselves as British. [8 marks]	• The section on Modood's research on p. 37 will assist you with this task • Try to be very specific when talking about ethnic minority groups – e.g. are you talking about Afro-Caribbeans, Asians, etc.?
• This means describe the way • Don't forget to do this • This can be positive or negative • Evaluation might focus on the fact that other agencies of socialization may be more important in shaping identity	[c] Outline and briefly evaluate two ways in which the workplace may shape the identity of some members of ethnic minority groups. [18 marks]	• Workplace can be interpreted broadly to mean: the type of work people do; the occupational community to which people belong; the home as a workplace for full-time mothers, etc. • You will find pp. 37–8 useful for answering this question • Remember to be specific about ethnic minority groups
• This means that you need to look at arguments and evidence against the view as well as arguments and evidence that support it	[d] Discuss the view that what it means to be British is not clear cut. [26 marks]	• You will need to make clear what British identity is and how it is formed before you can discuss the view that it is not clearcut • You do not have to accept the view – you might want to challenge it • See pp. 36–7 for some arguments that focus on this issue

Chapter 5

Poverty and social exclusion

Specifications

Specification	Relevant module title	Place in module	Level	Assessment	Other relevant modules
AQA	2: Education; Wealth, **Poverty and Welfare**; Work and Leisure	One of three options in this module.	AS	One data-response question.	Material from this chapter may be used in the A2 synoptic module 6.
OCR	Power and Control	**Social Policy and Welfare** is one of six options in this module.	A2	One essay question from a choice of two.	Material from this chapter may be used in the A2 synoptic module.
	Social Inequality and Difference	**Poverty** is included in this synoptic module.	A2	One multi-part data-response question from a choice of two.	This module is synoptic. This means that you will have to link your work here to other topics, key sociological theories and concepts and research methods.

Poverty and social exclusion: essential notes

The definition and measurement of poverty

Since studies of poverty began, researchers have been trying to establish a fixed standard against which to measure poverty. There are three main areas of controversy.

1 Absolute and relative poverty

Some writers argue that a common minimum standard of subsistence can be applied to all societies. Individuals without the resources to maintain a healthy life can be said to be in poverty.

Supporters of the concept of relative poverty dismiss this idea. They believe that definitions of poverty must relate to the standards of a particular society at a particular time. The poverty line will vary according to the wealth of a society.

2 Material and multiple deprivation and social exclusion

Some sociologists assume that poverty consists simply of a lack of material resources – a shortage of the money required to maintain an acceptable standard of living.

Others argue that poverty involves more than material deprivation. They see poverty as a form of multiple deprivation, involving additional factors such as inadequate educational opportunities, unpleasant working conditions and powerlessness. Today many writers prefer to use the term social exclusion to describe a situation where multiple deprivation prevents individuals from participating in social activities such as paid employment.

3 Inequality and poverty

From one point of view any society in which there is inequality is bound to have poverty. Those at the bottom will always be 'poor' and poverty could only be eliminated by abolishing all inequality.

Most sociologists accept that some reduction in inequality is needed in order to abolish poverty but believe that it is possible to establish a poverty line – a minimum standard below which it is not possible to maintain an acceptable standard of living. Thus it would be possible to have a society with some inequality but where poverty no longer exists.

Absolute poverty

There have been many attempts to operationalize (put into a form which can be measured) the concept of absolute poverty.

Drewnowski and Scott (1966) define physical needs in the following way:

- Nutrition: measured by factors such as the intake of calories.
- Shelter: measured by quality of housing and degree of overcrowding.
- Health: measured by infant mortality rates and availability of medical facilities.

Drewnowski and Scott also introduce the idea of basic cultural needs. These broaden the concept of human needs to include education, security, leisure and recreation.

Criticisms of the concept of absolute poverty

The concept of absolute poverty has been widely criticized. It is based on the assumption that there are basic minimum needs for all people in all societies. The problem is that needs vary both within and between societies.

- Within a society

  The nutritional needs of a bank clerk sitting at a desk all day are very different from those of a labourer working on a building site.

- Between societies

  The Bushmen of the Kalahari Desert have very different nutritional needs compared to office workers in London.

  The concept of absolute poverty is even more difficult to defend when it includes cultural needs. These needs vary from time to time and place to place, so that any attempt to establish a fixed standard is bound to fail.

Budget standards and poverty

The budget standards approach to measuring poverty involves calculating the cost of those purchases that are considered necessary to raise an individual or family out of poverty.

Seebohm Rowntree conducted three studies of poverty in York using this approach (1901, 1941, 1951).

Rowntree – trends in poverty

Rowntree drew a poverty line in terms of a minimum weekly sum of money needed to live a healthy life. In the later studies he included extra items which were not strictly necessary for survival, such as newspapers and presents. He found that the percentage of the population in poverty dropped rapidly between 1899 and 1950.

Rowntree believed that increased welfare benefits would eventually eliminate poverty.

Criticisms of Rowntree

- Rowntree's selection of necessities was based on expert views and did not take into account the customs of ordinary people.
- Rowntree's view that poverty was declining was challenged by later writers who adopted a relative definition of poverty.

Bradshaw, Mitchell and Morgan – the usefulness of budget standards

Bradshaw et al. believe that the budget standards approach is still useful because it focuses attention on the amount paid in benefits to those on welfare. Sociologists can assess whether benefits can provide adequately for people's needs. In the 1990s Bradshaw established the Family Budget Unit (FBU) to develop this approach.

Using FBU measures, Oppenheim and Harker (1996) found that in 1995 income support would meet just 34% of a modest but adequate budget for a single man and 40% for a lone mother with two young children.

Townsend – poverty as relative deprivation

Peter Townsend has carried out a number of studies on poverty and has played a major part in highlighting the continuing existence of poverty. He has also been a leading supporter of defining poverty in terms of relative deprivation.

Townsend believes that it is society that determines people's needs. Tea, for example, is not essential but members of British culture are expected to be able to offer visitors a cup of tea.

Townsend argues that relative deprivation needs to be thought of in terms of the resources available to individuals and households, and the way in which these resources affect participation in the community. Poverty involves an inability to participate in social activities that are seen as normal, such as visiting friends or relatives, having birthday parties for children and going on holiday.

Poverty in the United Kingdom

Townsend used his definition of poverty to measure the extent of poverty in Britain. He used a deprivation index which included 12 items that he believed would be relevant for the whole population, and he calculated the percentage of the population deprived of these items. They included:

- Not having had a week's holiday in the last year.
- Children not having had a friend over to play in the last month.
- Not having a refrigerator.
- Having gone through one or more days in the past fortnight without a cooked meal.
- Not usually having a Sunday joint.

On the basis of these calculations Townsend found that 22.9% of the population (12.46 million people) were living in poverty in 1968–9.

Criticisms of Townsend's research

- Piachaud (1981, 1987) claims that the index on which Townsend's statistics are based is inadequate. Going without a Sunday joint or eating salads may reflect cultural preferences rather than deprivation.
- Townsend claims that he has identified a 'poverty line' – deprivation increases rapidly when income drops below a particular level. Piachaud rejects this view.
- Piachaud argues that the implications of Townsend's definition of poverty are that poverty will remain as long as people behave in different ways – choosing to be vegetarian or not going on holiday, for example.

The London study

In 1985–6 Townsend used a new approach to defining poverty in a study based in London. He distinguished between:

- Material deprivation, which included deprivation in terms of diet, housing, clothes, work and environment.
- Social deprivation, which covered lack of employment rights, family and leisure activities, community participation and educational opportunities.

Townsend allowed for greater variations in taste in this study and also distinguished between objective deprivation (measured by a deprivation index) and subjective deprivation (measured by asking people the level of income their household needed to escape poverty).

Townsend found that both methods of determining the poverty threshold showed that government benefit levels were inadequate.

Mack and Lansley – *Poor Britain*

Joanna Mack and Stewart Lansley (1985) took note of many of the criticisms of Townsend's work in their study of poverty in Britain.

- Their deprivation index included a question asking respondents whether they lacked a particular item through choice or necessity.
- They selected the items in their deprivation index on the basis of asking respondents what they considered to be necessities in modern Britain.

They found poverty to be widespread, although on a lesser scale than Townsend. However, in a follow-up study (1990) they found that the numbers in poverty had risen significantly. Mack and Lansley believed that this increase was due to changes in the benefits system.

Criticisms of Mack and Lansley

- The inclusion of extra items in the 1990 index raises questions about the comparability of the two studies.
- The deprivation index was constructed by the public but the list they chose from reflected the researchers' values rather than a general consensus.
- The researchers defined poverty as lacking three or more items from their list. A different definition would have produced very different results.
- Walker (1987) points out that Mack and Lansley's method does not take into account the quality of items, only whether or not they exist.

Social exclusion

In recent years some commentators have tried to broaden the issues surrounding deprivation by using the term social exclusion rather than poverty. The use of the term has several implications:

- It looks beyond a simple lack of material resources and includes those excluded from key parts of society, such as the unemployed, those who do not register to vote, and isolated elderly individuals who live alone and lack a role in the social system.
- It forces us to consider those who do the excluding (the comfortably-off majority) as well as those who are excluded.
- Policies aimed at reducing social exclusion need to try to change wider social and economic structures; social exclusion cannot be tackled by simply increasing welfare payments.

The government set up a Social Exclusion Unit in 1997. This aimed to encourage social inclusion by tackling social problems such as truancy and unemployment.

Some problems with social exclusion

- It is difficult to define and measure with any accuracy.
- There is a risk that using the term may distract policy-makers from dealing with the material disadvantages that often give rise to social exclusion.
- There is a risk that the concept may be used to justify cutting welfare payments on the grounds that this will encourage the excluded to earn a living, which will in turn lead to their greater involvement in society.

Some countries, such as the USA, have an official poverty line, but Britain does not. Britain does, however, produce figures on low incomes.

- Nearly all the official figures suggest that there has been a rise in poverty over recent decades, particularly since 1979. The poorest 10% of the population have become worse off in real terms.
- The amount of homelessness has increased, suggesting that absolute poverty has returned as a serious problem in Britain.

The social distribution of poverty

The chances of experiencing poverty are not equally distributed. Some groups are much more prone to poverty than others.

Economic and family status

- Being in paid employment on a full-time basis greatly reduces the risk of poverty. Retirement and unemployment are both strongly associated with poverty.
- Lone parenthood leads to a high risk of poverty.
- Over a quarter of pensioner couples are poor, although some evidence suggests that the elderly are becoming less prone to poverty.

Gender and poverty

The Child Poverty Action Group (Oppenheim and Harker, 1996) estimates that in 1992 there were about 5.2 million women but only 4.2 million men in poverty.

- Women are less likely than men to have occupational pensions and income from investments.
- Married women are less likely than married men to be working.
- Women who are working are more likely than men to be low-paid.
- More women than men work part-time.
- More women than men rely on benefits as their main source of income.
- Lone parents are vulnerable to poverty, and about 90% are women.
- The majority of pensioners are women.

Ethnicity and poverty

Berthoud's study (1997) concludes that:

- Poverty is common among most ethnic minority groups. Their poverty usually stems from unemployment and low pay.
- Pakistani and Bangladeshi households tend to be at high risk of poverty because of unemployment and the fact that relatively few women have paid employment.

Alcock (1997) argues that social exclusion resulting from racism is often as much a problem for ethnic minority groups as material deprivation.

Poverty and disability

It has been estimated that nearly half of all disabled people live in poverty. The figure is high because:

- Most households containing a disabled person receive no income from employment.
- Disabled people tend to have high spending costs.

Individualistic and cultural theories of poverty

The earliest theories of poverty placed the blame for poverty on the poor themselves. Those who suffered from very low incomes were unable or unwilling to provide for their own well-being. Although most sociologists reject these views, they are still popular with a minority of the general public.

The New Right – the culture of dependency

The politics of the Conservative governments (1979–97) were influenced by the ideas of the New Right. A central plank of their policies was the claim that the welfare state was leading to a culture of dependency. Writers such as David Marsland have used this concept to help explain poverty.

Marsland – poverty and the generosity of the welfare state

David Marsland (1996) claims that much research on poverty has exaggerated the extent of poverty in Britain, because relative definitions of poverty have confused poverty with inequality. In fact, steadily rising living standards have largely eradicated poverty.

For most people, low income results from the generosity of the welfare state. Marsland believes that universal welfare provision (the provision of benefits such as education and health services to all members of society regardless of whether they are on low or high incomes) has created an expectation that the state will look after people's problems – a culture of dependency.

Criticisms of Marsland

- Marsland ignores some important evidence such as the fact that the real incomes of the poorest have been falling.
- Jordan (1989) claims that societies that rely on means-tested benefits (welfare benefits that only go to the most needy) tend to develop a large underclass. If members of the underclass take low-paid jobs they lose benefits and end up worse off.
- Dean and Taylor-Gooby (1992) interviewed social security claimants and found that their attitudes and ambitions were little different from those of other members of society. They wanted to earn their own living and would prefer not to have to rely on benefits. The study found little evidence of a dependency culture.

The culture of poverty

Many researchers have noted that the lifestyle of the poor differs from that of other members of society. This observation has led to the concept of a culture of poverty (or, more correctly, a subculture of poverty), with its own norms and values.

The idea of a culture of poverty was first introduced by Oscar Lewis (1959, 1961, 1966) in the late 1950s. His fieldwork in Mexico led him to identify a particular design for living which had the following elements:
- Individuals feel marginalized and helpless.
- There is a high rate of family breakdown.
- There is lack of participation in social institutions.

These attitudes and behaviours are passed on to the next generation, making it very difficult to break out of poverty as members of the subculture are not able to take advantage of opportunities that may be offered.

Criticisms of the culture of poverty idea

A great deal of research in both the developed and developing worlds has failed to identify a clear culture of poverty.

Recent qualitative research conducted by the Joseph Rowntree Foundation and summarized by Elaine Kempson (1996) provides support for the argument that no more than a small proportion of those on low income are part of a culture of poverty.

The studies found that many people looked very hard for work but encountered considerable barriers in their search for a job. Age, lack of skills, poor health and disability, for example, were all problems.

These kinds of barriers (known as situational constraints) may well be a more significant factor in keeping individuals on low incomes than a 'culture of poverty'.

The underclass and poverty

In recent years the concept of an underclass has become widely used and increasingly controversial.

Murray – the underclass in Britain

Charles Murray (1989, 1993) is an American sociologist who visited Britain in 1989 and 1993. He claimed that, like the USA, Britain was developing an underclass.

This underclass did not just consist of the poorest members of society. It consisted of those whose lifestyles involve a 'type of poverty' characterized by what Murray calls 'deplorable behaviour', such as refusal to accept jobs, delinquency and having illegitimate children.

Murray puts forward evidence in three areas to support his claim:
- Illegitimacy

Murray argues that illegitimacy is rapidly increasing, particularly among women from the lower social classes. The absence of a father means that illegitimate children will tend to 'run wild'. According to Murray, cohabitation does not provide the same stability as marriage.
- Crime

Murray associates the development of an underclass with rising crime. He argues that crime is damaging because it fragments communities. People become suspicious of each other and, as crime becomes more common, young boys start to imitate older males and take up criminal activities themselves.
- Unemployment

Murray does not see unemployment itself as a problem; instead it is the unwillingness of young men to take jobs that creates difficulties. Young men without jobs cannot support a family, so they are unlikely to get married when they father children, and the illegitimacy rate rises. In the absence of family responsibilities they find other, more damaging, ways to prove themselves – for example, through violent crime.

Causes and solutions

Murray argues that the benefits system needs to be changed to get rid of disincentives to marriage and to discourage single parenthood. Single mothers can now afford to live on benefits and so males who father children are often isolated from the responsibilities of family life. To force pregnant women to marry, Murray advocates cutting benefits for unmarried women entirely.

Critics of Murray

Unsurprisingly Murray's views have come under serious attack.

Walker – blaming the victims

Walker (1990) argues that:
- Lone parenthood is often short-lived – most lone parents find a new partner in a relatively short time.
- Most of the so-called underclass have conventional attitudes. They want stable relationships and paid employment. It is not their values that prevent them from achieving their aims, but lack of opportunities.

Brown – single motherhood

Joan C. Brown (1990) points out that:
- Where there is a concentration of single mothers in a particular neighbourhood, this is the result of council housing policy not values that undermine family life.
- Divorce is common in all strata of society and is not confined to the lower classes.

Heath – underclass attitudes

Anthony Heath (1990) collected data to test the claim that the attitudes of the underclass are different. Most of the evidence suggests that the majority of the underclass have conventional aspirations. They want jobs and happy marriages, but they are slightly less likely than other members of society to believe that people should get married before having children.

Field – *Losing Out*

Frank Field is a Labour MP who has campaigned against poverty. He believes that there is an underclass but he sees it in a very different way from Murray.

The composition of the underclass

According to Field the underclass consists of three main groups:
- The long-term unemployed, particularly school-leavers who have never had a job and older workers who have been unemployed for long periods.
- Single-parent families. This group is increasing but for many it is only a temporary stage. It is those who are dependent on benefits for long periods who are members of the underclass.
- Elderly pensioners who depend on state benefits because they do not have an occupational pension. Unlike the first two groups the elderly make up a declining proportion of the very poor.

All the members of Field's underclass rely on state benefits which are too low to give them an acceptable standard of living, and they have little chance of escaping this dependence.

The causes of the underclass

Field identifies four main causes for the development of the underclass:
- Rising levels of unemployment.
- Social changes and government policy have widened the gap between higher and lower classes.
- Living standards as a whole have risen but the poorest members of society have been excluded from the benefits enjoyed by the increasingly affluent.
- Successful members of the working class have cut themselves off from those who have had less success. They are now more likely to blame the poor for their plight.

Blackman – the homeless and the underclass

Shane Blackman (1997) conducted an ethnographic study of the young homeless in Brighton. He argues against Murray's view that the underclass reject society's values. What the young homeless needed was jobs and homes, not a different culture. Blackman sees members of the so-called 'underclass' as victims of society whose behaviour changes when they are given genuine opportunities to improve their situation.

Conflict theories of poverty

The sociology of poverty has increasingly come to be studied within a conflict perspective. Conflict theorists argue that poverty continues to exist because society fails to allocate its resources fairly. To some extent conflict theorists disagree about the reasons why society has failed to eradicate poverty.
- Some regard poverty as the result of the failings of the welfare state.
- Others place more emphasis on the disadvantages faced by the poor in the labour market.
- Marxists believe that poverty is an inevitable consequence of capitalism.

Poverty and the welfare state

Recent studies of relative poverty have found that those who rely on state benefits for their income are among the largest groups of the poor. However, it is widely assumed that the welfare state makes a major contribution to reducing poverty, and that it redistributes resources from the rich to the poor.

Many sociologists have challenged this view.

Tax
- Giles and Johnson (1994) show that tax changes between 1985 and 1995 made the richest better off and the poorest worse off.

Education
- Smith, Smith and Wright (1997) identify a range of ways in which the poor are disadvantaged by educational policy, for example by cuts in the provision of free school meals.

Housing
- Ginsburg (1997) notes that recent housing policy has been aimed at encouraging home ownership, while

spending on new council houses has been restricted.

Health

- Benzeval (1997) has found a growing health gap between the rich and poor in Britain.
  Overall there is little evidence that government policies redistribute resources to the poor.

Poverty, the labour market and power

Not all of those who experience poverty rely on state benefits for their income. A considerable proportion of the poor are employed but receive wages that are too low to meet their needs. Sociologists have put forward explanations to explain low pay.

The dual labour market

Some sociologists suggest that there are two labour markets:

- The primary labour market includes jobs that offer job security, promotion prospects, training opportunities and relatively high wages.
- The secondary labour market offers the opposite. Women and ethnic minorities are particularly concentrated here.

Changes in the labour market

Dean and Taylor-Gooby (1992) argue that changes in the labour market have made people in Britain vulnerable to poverty.

- Manufacturing industry has declined, and there has been an increase in service sector jobs.
- A considerable number of service sector jobs do not provide security and are part-time – they form part of the secondary labour market.
- Economic change has affected different parts of the country at different times, leading to regional unemployment and poverty.
- The decline of trade unionism has reduced the ability of workers to defend their rights.

Post-Fordism, globalization and poverty

Enzo Mingione (1996) argues that increases in international poverty are linked to a shift from Fordist to post-Fordist production in the world economy.

This involves a decline in heavy industry and mass production and an increase in the service sector and more flexible production. This results in an increase in casual, insecure and temporary employment.

Globalization means that companies can move investment from country to country in search of cheap labour and freer trade. This makes more people vulnerable to poverty as jobs are less secure, and the increasing numbers of women in work mean that more families rely on two earners.

Poverty and the capitalist system

Marxists believe that the poor are not a separate group in society but simply the most disadvantaged section of the working class. Westergaard and Resler (1974) argue that concentrating on the poor diverts attention away from wider structures of inequality.

Marxists believe that poverty exists because it benefits the ruling class in the following ways:

- Low wages help to reduce wage demands as workers tend to assess their incomes in terms of the baseline provided by the low-paid.
- Since the state reflects the interests of the ruling class it can be expected to do little except reduce the harsher effects of poverty. Westergaard and Resler argue that the welfare state was created to 'contain' the demands of the labour movement. With the increased emphasis on market forces, Westergaard (1994) argues that Marxist views are more relevant than ever. However, they are less successful than other conflict approaches in explaining why particular groups and individuals become poor.

Poverty and social exclusion – solutions and values

New Right solutions

After 1979 the Conservative governments of Margaret Thatcher and John Major were inspired by New Right ideas. They decided to:

- Reduce welfare expenditure so that a more dynamic economy could be created. As the economy grew and living standards rose, wealth would 'trickle down' to those on low incomes.
- Move away from universal benefits in order to reduce the dependency culture which made people rely on state benefits.
- Target resources to the poor so that benefits would only go to those in genuine need.

Criticisms of New Right policies

Most of the evidence included earlier in this chapter suggests that poverty actually worsened during this period. Carey Oppenheim (1997) found no evidence of a 'trickle-down' effect, although the government claimed that its policies had increased the income of the poorest 20% of the population.

Welfare and redistribution as solutions to poverty

Some believe that the answer to poverty is to be found in improving welfare provision.

- Mack and Lansley (1985) claim that raising benefit levels could have a significant impact on poverty. Their research showed considerable public support for this.
- Peter Townsend (1997) argues for a national plan to eliminate poverty. The plan might ultimately require the development of a kind of international welfare state.
- Walker and Walker (1994) argue for increased emphasis on universal benefits and for governments to do more to provide work for the unemployed, the disabled and lone parents.

Marxist solutions

Because Marxists see poverty as simply one aspect of inequality, eliminating it involves a radical change in the structure of society.

Westergaard and Resler (1976) maintain that no substantial redistribution of wealth can occur until capitalism is replaced by socialism.

However, there seems little prospect of a revolution occurring at the moment, and there is no evidence that the few remaining communist countries have eliminated poverty.

'New Labour' – 'A hand up, not a hand-out'

The 'New Labour' government which took office in Britain in 1997 claimed it had policies that would reduce poverty and social exclusion – what the poor needed was a 'hand up, not a hand-out'. In other words, they needed to be given the support they needed to help themselves rather than simply depending on state benefits.

Some changes made by the Labour government, such as the creation of the Social Exclusion Unit, offered new opportunities, though some contained an element of compulsion because of the threat of lost benefits. The government also showed little willingness to increase benefits. Its policies contained a novel mix of contradictory ideologies, influenced by both left-wing sociologists such as Peter Townsend and New Right thinkers such as Charles Murray.

Test your knowledge and understanding

(answers on p. 214)

1 The view that individuals without the resources to maintain a healthy life can be said to be in poverty is based on which definition of poverty?
   a Absolute definition
   b Relative definition
   c Multiple deprivation
   d Social exclusion

2 Which of the following is not a physical need according to Drenowski and Scott?
   a Shelter
   b Cultural needs
   c Nutrition
   d Health

3 In which year did Rowntree's first study of poverty take place?
   a 1891
   b 1901
   c 1911
   d 1921

4 What is meant by the budget standards approach to measuring poverty?
   a Constructing a poverty line which is applicable to all societies
   b Measuring how effectively households manage their budgets
   c Using an absolute definition of poverty to measure it
   d Measuring poverty by calculating the cost of purchases necessary to maintain a satisfactory minimum standard of living

5 Which one of the following items was part of Townsend's deprivation index in his study of poverty in the United Kingdom?
   a Not having a Christmas party
   b Not going to the pub once a week
   c Not usually having a Sunday joint
   d Not being able to afford cigarettes

6 Which one of the following did Townsend not attempt to measure in his 1985–6 study of poverty in London?
   a Material deprivation
   b Subjective deprivation
   c Social exclusion
   d Social deprivation

7 Three of the following are criticisms of Mack and Lansley's research. Which is the odd one out?
   a Their research only measures absolute poverty
   b Their research does not take into account the quality of items in their deprivation index
   c Their deprivation index is different in their two studies so their results cannot be compared
   d The public chose the items to be included in the deprivation index but the list from which they chose reflected the researchers' values

8 Which one of the following can be considered to be a criticism of the idea of 'social exclusion'?
   a It does not look beyond poverty as a simple lack of material resources
   b It is difficult to define and measure with any accuracy
   c It does not make us consider both the excluded and those who do the excluding
   d It does not make policy-makers aware of the need to change social and economic structures

9 Three of the following are associated with a high risk of poverty. Which is the odd one out?
   a Unemployment
   b Retirement
   c Lone parenthood
   d Employment

10 Three of the following are reasons why women are more likely to be in poverty than men. Which is the odd one out?
   a They are more likely to be lone parents
   b They are more likely to work part-time
   c They are more likely to have low educational qualifications
   d They are less likely to have occupational pensions

11 Which one of the following views influenced the Conservative government 1979–97?
   a Marxism
   b The New Right
   c Functionalism
   d Feminism

12 The provision of welfare benefits to all regardless of their income is known as:
   a A welfare state
   b Means-tested benefits
   c Universal welfare provision
   d Redistribution of wealth

13 Which one of the following has been responsible for eradicating most poverty in Britain, according to the New Right?
   a The welfare state
   b Rising living standards
   c Means-tested benefits
   d The culture of poverty

14 Which one of the following is not associated with the culture of poverty?
   a Feeling of marginalization
   b High rate of family breakdown
   c Lack of participation in social institutions
   d Situational constraints

15 Which two of the following does Murray put forward as evidence of the existence of an underclass in Britain?
   a Rising illegitimacy rate
   b Rising standard of living
   c Rising crime rate
   d Rising level of welfare payments

16 Which one of the following is a Labour MP who has campaigned against poverty and used the idea of an 'underclass'?
   a Tony Blair
   b Ann Widdecombe
   c Frank Field
   d Claire Short

17 Which one of the following statements are conflict theorists likely to agree with?
   a Poverty is the result of individual inadequacy
   b The welfare state has done much to eliminate poverty
   c The welfare state has done very little to redistribute resources from the wealthy to the poor
   d Poverty is the result of a culture of poverty

18 Three of the following are reasons why changes in the labour market have made people in Britain more vulnerable to poverty. Which is the odd one out?
   a The decline in manufacturing industry
   b Growth in high technology industries
   c Increases in regional unemployment
   d The decline of trade unionism

19 Marxists might well agree with three of the following statements. Which is the odd one out?
   a The poor are merely the most disadvantaged section of the working class
   b Low wages help to reduce wage demands in capitalist societies
   c The welfare state 'contains' the demands of the working class
   d It is possible for the welfare state to eliminate poverty

20 Which two of the following statements would the New Right be likely to agree with?
   a Universal welfare benefits help create a dependency culture
   b Means-tested benefits are socially divisive
   c Reducing welfare expenditure makes the economy more dynamic and benefits the poor, as wealth will 'trickle down'
   d The welfare state should redistribute wealth from the rich to the poor

Develop your analysis and evaluation skills

(see p. 199 for guidance notes)

For each of the following statements, identify which sociologists would argue in favour of and which against the view expressed. Explain the reasons for their view.

1 Poverty is best understood in terms of relative deprivation.
2 Constructing a 'poverty line' is an impossible task.
3 The welfare state produces a culture of dependency.
4 The existence of an underclass is crucial in understanding poverty in Britain today.
5 Poverty cannot be abolished without major changes to social and economic structures.

Answer all parts of this question
Total: 60 marks
Time allowed: 1 hour 15 minutes

1 mark = 1.25 minute

ITEM A

In Britain there is no official measure of poverty. However, those living on or below 50% of average income are often taken to be the poor. The real incomes of this poor group have fallen in the last 20 years whilst those of the top wage earners have increased. These changes not only produce greater inequality but can also give rise to problems of social exclusion.

This is one of the measures of poverty for part [d]

Before answering part [e], check your understanding of this term (see p. 45)

The background to changes in income distribution can be found in Chapter 2, p. 8 Although actual incomes of the poor have not fallen, their purchasing power has. This will help you to answer part [a]

ITEM B

A major new piece of research on *Poverty and Social Exclusion*, published by the Joseph Rowntree Foundation (2000), produced some headline press coverage recently with the news that 2 million children in Britain went without some of the 'necessities of life'. Not only are these children members of low income families, but they go without two or more items that parents regard as necessary for living in a society such as Britain.

Source: Sue Middleton, 'Measuring poverty in Britain', *Sociology Review*, vol. 10, no. 3, February 2001

This is another way of measuring poverty for your answer to part [d]

You cannot use this group in your answer to part [c]

You can apply this material to help you answer part [b], but this group cannot be used in your answer to part [c]

Comments on the question	Question	Advice on preparing your answer
• The item gives you the context for this question	[a] Explain what is meant by 'real income'. [Item A, line 3] [2 marks]	• The important word here is 'real', which has a very particular meaning in this context, so be sure to read carefully
• The item gives you the context and some help in answering this question • No more – a waste of time; no less – you will fail to gain all marks	[b] Suggest **two** reasons why children are particularly vulnerable to poverty. [Item B] [4 marks]	

Comments on the question	Question	Advice on preparing your answer
• Write your answer as a list – you do not need to explain or develop your answer • If you give more than this only the first three may be taken into consideration in the marking	[c] Identify **three** other groups of people who are prone to poverty apart from those mentioned in the items. [6 marks]	• Select from a number of groups (see pp. 45–6) • Do not include 'children', 'low income families' and those living on or below 50% of average income
• Do not forget the second part of this question • This could be: 1 A practical problem of using the measure 2 The inappropriateness of the definition that gives rise to the measure	[d] Identify and **explain** one **criticism** for each of the **two** ways of measuring poverty mentioned in the items. [8 marks]	• Both these issues are discussed on pp. 43–5 • Select an appropriate point and apply to the measures in the item
• The question does not say that these have to be in current operation • Make sure that you know what the term means (see p. 45)	[e] Examine **social policies** designed to prevent **social exclusion.** [20 marks]	• Different approaches to the problem are discussed on pp. 48–9 • You must show how the policy will try to prevent the problem and how far it might be successful
• Use additional material to that contained in the items • The plural tells you that you should examine more than one theory • Any reference to this should recognize alternative definitions in the answer	[f] Using material from the items and elsewhere, assess sociological theories that argue that **poverty** is produced by structural inequality. [20 marks]	• The link between inequality and poverty is explained on p. 43 • Structural theories adopt a relative view of poverty • Examples of these theories: Field, p. 47; conflict theories, pp. 47–8 • You can use individualistic and cultural theories (p. 46) to show that structural theories do not explain every issue

OCR style Poverty and Social Exclusion question, A2 Synoptic Unit 2539: Social Inequality and Difference

Answer all parts of this question

Total: 90 marks   1 mark = 1 minute   Time allowed: 1 hour 30 minutes

Make sure you clearly understand the data. Double-check any statistics that you use in your response.

ITEM A

Percentages in poverty, by family type

	% of group in poverty		
	1979	1995	1999
Pensioner couples	21%	23%	25%
Single pensioners	12%	32%	37%
Couples with children	8%	23%	24%
Single with children	10%	55%	62%
Single without children	7%	23%	22%

ITEM B

These might be useful for answering part (b)

When Murray uses the term 'underclass' he is focusing on a certain type of poor person, defined not by his condition, e.g. long-term unemployed, but by his deplorable behaviour in response to that condition, e.g. unwilling to take the jobs that are available to him. Murray concludes that Britain has a growing population of working-aged healthy people who subscribe to a culture of welfare dependency, laziness and crime which is contaminating the life of entire neighbourhoods. Murray claims that these people are raising their children to see this way of life as normal.

Comments on the question	Question	Advice on preparing your answer
• Do not go beyond the data in Item A • There is no need to offer any explanations for these changes • Make sure that you get the dates right • Double-check any figures that you have used	[a] Using only the information in Item A, identify two main changes in the type of family in poverty in 1999 compared with 1979. [6 marks]	• To identify the 'main' changes, you should work out which two family groups were likely to experience poverty in 1979 and which two were likely to experience it in 1999 • Don't over-complicate the task
• There is no need to go beyond Item B for your answer • No more, no less • There is no need to offer an explanation for these characteristics	[b] Identify two characteristics of the underclass according to Item B. [6 marks]	• See the margin notes and arrows linked to Item B above
• Don't just compile a list. You must explain why what you have identified is a problem • Scale means amount of poverty • You must be clear in your understanding of this concept	[c] Identify and explain two problems in measuring the scale of poverty using relative definitions. [12 marks]	• This is a synoptic question and you should use your knowledge and methodology to answer it • You need to focus on the practical problem of using such definitions (e.g. how do you make sure that a survey population shares your definition of poverty) rather than theoretical problems • pp. 44–5 may be useful in helping you to answer this question
• A synoptic instruction. As well as using material from this unit for this evidence, you should dip into two or three other areas that you have studied • Describe the evidence only. There is no need to explain it	[d] Using your wider sociological knowledge, outline the evidence for the view that poverty has a significantly negative effect on the life-chances of individuals. [22 marks]	• Focus on data in the form of statistics or trends, and sociological studies of poverty and its effects • You will find evidence in this resource, e.g.: 1 Family poverty, p. 93 2 The feminization of poverty, pp. 25–6 3 Poverty and health, pp.46–8 4 Education and poverty, p. 47 • See p. 6 for a definition of this concept

Comments on the question	Question	Advice on preparing your answer
• Do not go beyond the data in Item A • There is no need to offer any explanations for these changes • Make sure that you get the dates right • Double-check any figures that you have used	[a] Using only the information in Item A, identify two main changes in the type of family in poverty in 1999 compared with 1979. [6 marks]	• To identify the 'main' changes, you should work out which two family groups were likely to experience poverty in 1979 and which two were likely to experience it in 1999 • Don't over-complicate the task
• There is no need to go beyond Item B for your answer • No more, no less • There is no need to offer an explanation for these characteristics	[b] Identify two characteristics of the underclass according to Item B. [6 marks]	• See the margin notes and arrows linked to Item B above
• Don't just compile a list. You must explain why what you have identified is a problem • Scale means amount of poverty • You must be clear in your understanding of this concept	[c] Identify and explain two problems in measuring the scale of poverty using relative definitions. [12 marks]	• This is a synoptic question and you should use your knowledge and methodology to answer it • You need to focus on the practical problem of using such definitions (e.g. how do you make sure that a survey population shares your definition of poverty) rather than theoretical problems • pp. 43–44 may be useful in helping you to answer this question
• A synoptic instruction. As well as using material from this unit for this evidence, you should dip into two or three other areas that you have studied • Describe the evidence only. There is no need to explain it	[d] Using your wider sociological knowledge, outline the evidence for the view that poverty has a significantly negative effect on the life-chances of individuals. [22 marks]	• Focus on data in the form of statistics or trends, and sociological studies of poverty and its effects • You will find evidence in this resource, e.g.: 1 Family poverty, p. 93 2 The feminization of poverty, pp. 25–6 3 Poverty and health, pp.46–8 4 Education and poverty, p. 47 • See p. 6 for a definition of this concept
• Describe the main features of the argument and its supporting evidence • Examine specific evidence against the view, and describe alternative views if they are appropriate	[e] Outline and assess the view that the behaviour of an underclass is the main cause of poverty in the UK today. [44 marks]	• Item A may prove useful as an introduction • Remember that you don't have to agree with the view • See pp. 46–7 for an account of this view

Comments on the question	Question	Advice on preparing your answer
• Describe the main features of the argument and its supporting evidence • Examine specific evidence against the view, and describe alternative views if they are appropriate	[e] Outline and assess the view that the behaviour of an underclass is the main cause of poverty in the UK today. [44 marks]	• Item A may prove useful as an introduction • Remember that you don't have to agree with the view • See pp. 46–7 for an account of this view

Chapter 6

Crime and deviance

Specifications

Specification	Relevant module title	Place in module	Level	Assessment	Other relevant modules
AQA	6: **Crime and Deviance**; Stratification and Differentiation	One of two options in this module	A2	One three-part synoptic question.	This module is synoptic. This means that you will have to link your work here to other topics, key sociological theories and concepts and research methods.
OCR	Power and Control	**Crime and Deviance** is one of six options in this module.	A2	One essay question from a choice of two.	Material from this chapter may be used in the A2 synoptic module.

Crime and deviance: essential notes

Introduction: the definition of deviance

At its simplest, deviance is behaviour that does not follow the norms and expectations of a particular social group. Deviance is relative: what is regarded as deviant varies from time to time and place to place. In other words, deviance is culturally determined.

For instance, at certain times in Western society it has been considered deviant for women to smoke, wear make-up and consume alcoholic drinks in public. Homosexuality used to be a criminal offence in Britain, but in 1969 homosexual acts between consenting males were made legal, and in 1994 the age of consent was reduced to 18.

Physiological and psychological theories of deviance

Physiological theories

Physiological or biological theories of deviance argue that some individuals are prone to deviance because of their genetic make-up.

Moir and Jessel (1997), for example, argue that:
- Low intelligence is inherited and leads to impulsive behaviour.
- Crime and delinquency can be caused by low levels of serotonin, a chemical which inhibits impulsive and anti-social behaviour.
- Lack of serotonin can lead to Attention Deficit Disorder (ADD) in children which makes them prone to delinquency.
- Biological differences make men more likely to commit crimes than females.
- Some female crime is the result of Premenstrual Syndrome (PMS).

- Environmental factors interact with genes.

Criticisms of physiological theories

1 Behaviour that results from biological causes may not necessarily lead to criminal acts. Aggressive behaviour, for example, can be channelled into socially acceptable activities, such as boxing or competitive business. Behaviour only becomes criminal when a law has been passed outlawing that behaviour.
2 Biological factors alone cannot explain crime.
The geneticist Jones (1994) argues that the link between genetics and crime is 'distant'.

Psychological theories

Psychological theories see the deviant's abnormality as lying in mental processes rather than physical differences.

Bowlby (1946) explained deviance in terms of a child's early socialization. He argued that children need the emotional security provided by a loving relationship with their mother. If they were deprived of this, a psychopathic personality could develop. Psychopaths act impulsively, rarely feel guilt and show little response to punishment or treatment. Bowlby argued that persistent delinquents had suffered from maternal deprivation during the early years of their lives.

Criticisms of psychological theories

1 These theories neglect social factors in the explanation of deviance.
2 The methodology of many of these studies is suspect.
3 Many sociologists reject the priority given to early childhood experience. Bowlby's work has been attacked for attempting to justify the view that women with children should not go out to work.
4 Psychoanalytic theories based on the work of Freud are difficult to test because they rely on inner

processes of the mind which are not accessible to researchers.

Deviance: a functionalist perspective

The functions of deviance
A functionalist analysis of deviance looks for the source of deviance in the nature of society rather than in the biological or psychological nature of the individual. Although functionalists agree that social control mechanisms such as the police and the courts are necessary to keep deviance in check, many argue that a certain amount of deviance can contribute to the well-being of society.

Durkheim (1895) believed that:
- Crime is an 'integral part of all healthy societies'. This is because individuals are exposed to different influences and will not all be committed to the shared values and beliefs of society.
- Crime can be functional. All societies need to progress and all social change begins with some form of deviance. In order for change to occur, yesterday's deviance must become tomorrow's normality. Nelson Mandela, once imprisoned as a 'terrorist', eventually became president of South Africa.
- Societies need both crime and punishment. Without punishment the crime rate would reach a point where it became dysfunctional.

Durkheim's views have been developed by A. Cohen (1966) who discussed two possible functions of deviance:
1 Deviance can be a 'safety valve', providing a relatively harmless expression of discontent. For example, prostitution enables men to escape from family life without undermining family stability.
2 Deviant acts can warn society that an aspect is not working properly – for example, widespread truanting from school.

Merton – social structure and anomie
Robert K. Merton (1938) explains how deviance can result from the culture and structure of society. He begins from the functionalist position of value consensus – that is, all members of society share the same values. In the USA, members of society strive for the goal of success, largely measured in terms of wealth and material possessions. The means of reaching this goal are through talent, ambition and effort. Unfortunately, Merton argues, little importance is given to the means of achieving success. The result is an unbalanced society where winning is all and the 'rules' are not very important. This situation of 'normlessness' is known as anomie. Individuals may respond in different ways:
- Conformity
The most common response is conformity. Conformists strive for success through the accepted channels.
- Innovation
People from lower classes may have few qualifications and turn to crime to achieve material success.
- Ritualism
Some people, particularly from the lower middle classes, may abandon the ultimate goal of wealth but continue to conform to the standards of middle-class respectability.
- Retreatism
Retreatists are 'drop-outs' who have rejected both the shared value of success and the means provided to achieve it.
- Rebellion
Rebels reject both goals and means but replace them with different ones. They wish to create an entirely new kind of society.

Evaluation of Merton
1 Taylor criticizes Merton for failing to consider wider power relations in society – that is, who actually makes the laws and who benefits from them.
2 Merton assumes that there is a value consensus in American society and that people only deviate because of structural strain in society.
3 Merton's theory exaggerates working-class crime.
4 Taylor, Walton and Young (1973) argue that the theory cannot account for politically motivated crime where people break the law because of commitment to a cause.
5 Merton has been defended by Reiner (1984) who believes that Merton's theory can be adapted to take into account most of these criticisms.
6 Merton's theory can be applied to some contemporary trends in crime. For example, it can be argued that Thatcherism in the 1970s and 1980s created a greater emphasis on individual success and contributed to a rise in property crime.

Structural and subcultural theories of deviance

Structural theories of deviance explain the origins of deviance in terms of the position of the individual in society.

Subcultural theories of deviance explain deviance in terms of the subculture of a particular social group. Certain groups develop norms and values which are different from those held by other members of society.

Cohen: the delinquent subculture
Albert Cohen's work (1955) modified Merton's position and combined both structural and subcultural theories of deviance. Cohen criticizes two aspects of Merton's theory of working-class deviance:
1 Cohen argues that deviance is a collective rather than an individual response.
2 He also believes that Merton ignored non-utilitarian crimes. These are crimes that have no financial reward, such as vandalism and joy-riding.

Lower-working-class boys want success but cannot achieve their goals because cultural deprivation leads to educational failure and dead-end jobs. They suffer from status frustration and turn to criminal paths to achieve success. An alternative set of norms and values is adopted – a delinquent subculture – which reverses mainstream culture by valuing activities such as stealing, vandalism and truancy.

Evaluation of Cohen
Box (1981) argues that Cohen's theory only applies to a minority of delinquents. The rest accept mainstream

standards of success but resent being seen as failures and turn against those who they feel look down on them.

Cloward and Ohlin – *Delinquency and Opportunity*

Richard A. Cloward and Lloyd E. Ohlin (1962) accept Merton's explanation of deviance in terms of the legitimate opportunity structure, but they argue that he failed to consider the illegitimate opportunity structure. Just as the opportunity to succeed by legitimate means varies, so does the opportunity to succeed by illegitimate means. For example, in one area there may be a thriving criminal subculture, while in another area this subculture may not exist. Thus, in the first area, the adolescent has more opportunity to become a successful criminal.

Like Merton, Cloward and Ohlin believe that there is greater pressure on the working classes to deviate because they have less opportunity to succeed by legitimate means. They identified three possible responses to this situation:

1 Criminal subcultures emerge in areas of established organized crime where young people are exposed to deviant values and role models. In this situation young people have the opportunity to rise within the established criminal hierarchy.
2 Conflict subcultures develop in areas where there is little access to either legitimate or illegitimate opportunity structures. The response to this situation is often gang violence, which serves as a release from anger and frustration and as a means of achieving prestige in terms of the values of the subculture.
3 Retreatist subcultures are organized mainly around illegal drug use and occur because members have failed to succeed in both legitimate and illegitimate opportunity structures.

Evaluation of Cloward and Ohlin

1 Taylor, Walton and Young (1973) criticize Merton, Cohen, and Cloward and Ohlin for assuming that everybody is committed to the success goal of achieving wealth. They point out that there are other possible goals and that some groups, such as 'hippies', make a conscious choice to reject conventional goals.
2 The marketization of capitalist societies has made these theories increasingly relevant. Nigel South (1997) believes that the British drug trade is largely based around 'disorganized' crime, which can be compared to Cloward and Ohlin's conflict subcultures, although some of it is based around professional criminal organizations and more closely resembles a criminal subculture. Many of the drug users themselves are part of a retreatist subculture.

Miller – lower-class subculture

Walter B. Miller (1962) believed that the lower classes had their own distinctive values which were passed on from generation to generation and which actively encouraged lower-class men to break the law. He identified various 'focal concerns' of the 'lower class' which included:

● Toughness: a respect for courage
● Smartness: the capacity to 'outsmart' others

● Excitement: the search for thrills
  Miller believed that delinquency was the result of an exaggerated conformity to these 'focal concerns'.

Evaluation of Miller

1 Many sociologists would reject Miller's picture of an isolated lower class whose values bear no relation to the mainstream culture.
2 Gill's study of a working-class area (1977) supported Miller by finding that residents did not believe it was wrong to commit some crimes, such as stealing from an unoccupied house.
3 Other sociologists, such as Braithwaite (1989), argue that crimes that involve direct harm to the victim are seen as wrong in all classes in Western societies.

The underclass and crime

Murray – welfare, culture and criminality

Some sociologists have suggested that an underclass now exists which does not share the same values as other members of society. Charles Murray (1989) believes that the underclass is responsible for a large proportion of crime, and he blames welfare benefits which have made it possible for young women to become single parents and for young men to reject the idea that it is important to hold down a job.

Inequality, the underclass and crime

Other sociologists reject Murray's 'New Right' views but still believe that an underclass exists. Taylor (1997) argues that young, unskilled working-class males have been affected by increasing inequality and declining job prospects. Underclass criminal activity is the result of material deprivation rather than an unacceptable culture.

Evaluation of underclass theories of crime

Many sociologists have questioned the idea that there is a distinctive underclass culture.
  Most criticisms refer to the views of Charles Murray:

1 Tham (1998) compared welfare policies and crime rates in Britain and Sweden. During the 1980s and 1990s he found that crime increased more rapidly in Britain than in Sweden which had a more generous welfare state. He claims that crime rates are closely linked to levels of inequality.
2 Mooney (1998) argues that there is no link between single parenthood and criminality. Her research indicates that single parents are more likely to become the victims of crime than to become criminals themselves.

Matza – delinquency and drift

In contrast to many structural and subcultural theories, David Matza (1964) argues that delinquents are, to a considerable extent, committed to the same values as other members of society. Deviance becomes possible when 'techniques of neutralization' are used which temporarily release them from the hold society has over them.
  Techniques of neutralization include:

● Denial of responsibility for a deviant act – blaming parents or the area they live in, for example.

- Denial of injury resulting from the act – they claim that no harm was done, that it was just a bit of 'mischief'.
- Denial that the act was basically wrong – an assault on a homosexual or a robbery from an expensive shop, for instance, may be seen as 'rough justice'.
- Condemnation of those who enforce the rules – the police may be seen as corrupt or teachers as unjust.
- Appeal to higher loyalties – the law may be broken to help family or friends.

Matza argues that the use of techniques of neutralization throws serious doubt on the idea of deviant subcultures.

- Their existence is evidence of guilt and shame, which suggests at least a partial acceptance of mainstream values.
- One set of mainstream values is sometimes used to justify breaking another. Thus, assaulting homosexuals is justified since it supports mainstream sexual behaviour.

Subterranean values

Once potential delinquents have freed themselves from social constraints, they are in a state of drift and may go on to commit deviant acts. Matza explains the attraction of deviance in terms of subterranean values. These values encourage enjoying yourself, acting on the spur of the moment, being aggressive and seeking excitement. Respectable members of society only express these values at carefully controlled moments, but delinquents express them at inappropriate times – for example, seeking excitement in school or being aggressive while at work.

Evaluation of Matza

1 Matza's work challenges earlier theories of delinquency which suggest that delinquents are 'sick' or different from other members of society. He stresses the choices that all members of society have.
2 Box (1981) questioned the evidence that Matza used. Delinquents may not be sincere when they express regret for their actions.
3 Jones (1998) believes that Matza's theory cannot adequately explain persistent delinquency and violent acts.

Deviance and official statistics

Many theories of deviance are based on the official statistics provided by government organizations such as the police and the courts. These statistics tend to show two main trends:

1 Some social groups appear to be more involved in crime than others. They are:
- The working class
- The young
- Males
- Some ethnic minorities

These groups appear to be more likely to commit crimes than the middle class, the elderly, females and whites. Sociologists such as Merton and Miller have taken these statistics at face value and gone on to explain why these groups appear to commit a disproportionate amount of crime.

2 Crime rates in Britain remained low until the 1950s but have increased rapidly since then, although there was some decline in the mid-1990s. Often the release of crime figures receives widespread publicity and leads to concern that the country is experiencing a 'crime wave'.

Unrecorded crime

Not all the crimes that take place are recorded by the police. For a crime to be recorded at least three things must happen:

1 Somebody must be aware that a crime has taken place.
2 That crime must be reported.
3 The police or other agency must accept that a law has been broken.

Some crimes, such as tax evasion, do not have an obvious victim, and it is these that are least likely to be reported. However, attempts have been made to estimate the amount of crime which victims are aware of but which is not reported to the police or not recorded as a crime by them.

Victimization studies

In 1983 the Home Office published the first British Crime Survey. This survey takes place every two years and represents an attempt to overcome the limitations of official crime statistics. Instead of relying on police records, it uses victimization studies. These involve asking individuals if they have been the victim of crime in the previous year, whether they reported the crimes and whether the police recorded them.

Some of their key findings are outlined below:

- Less than half of all crimes are reported to the police. Reporting varies enormously according to the crime – in 1997, 97% of vehicle thefts were reported, compared to just 26% of acts of vandalism.
- The usual reasons for non-reporting were that the crime was thought to be too trivial or that the victim believed that the police could not do anything or would not be interested. Only a tiny minority were frightened of reprisals or of the police themselves.
- Around half of all incidents reported to the police were not recorded as crimes. This was because the police judged the incident as too trivial, did not believe that it had taken place or felt that there was insufficient evidence to proceed.
- In terms of trends in the overall crime rate, figures from the *British Crime Surveys* are generally in line with the official police figures.

Data from the *British Crime Surveys* are still not entirely reliable. Young (1988) identifies three main problems:

1 A substantial minority refuse to cooperate with the survey. These people are not likely to be representative of the population, thus distorting the figures.
2 Victims of crimes such as domestic violence and sexual crimes may not be willing to reveal them.
3 Changes in attitudes may affect the public's willingness to regard acts as criminal. For example,

people may have become less tolerant of crimes of violence or vandalism and so may be more willing to report them.

The characteristics of offenders – self-report studies

Self-report studies attempt to discover the characteristics of criminals. They use questionnaires or interviews and ask individuals to admit to the number and types of crime they have committed. The data can then be compared with official conviction rates to discover which types of offenders are most likely to be convicted.

- Using data from 40 self-report studies from different countries, Box (1981) rejected the impression created by official statistics that working-class youths are more likely to engage in delinquency than middle-class youths.
- A more recent study by Graham and Bowling (1995) found that social class had no influence on whether young British males and females would admit to having committed offences, although the lower classes were more likely to admit to more serious offences.

Evaluation of self-report studies

1 Individuals may wish to conceal their criminal acts. However, it is estimated that around 80% of those who reply do tell the truth.
2 It is likely that self-report studies identify more offenders than the official statistics.

Bias in official statistics

Self-report studies indicate that there may be police bias against working-class delinquents. Support for this view is provided by Chambliss's study (1973) of two American delinquent gangs:

1 The working-class 'roughnecks' were viewed with suspicion and each of them was arrested at least once.
2 The middle-class 'saints' were never arrested, although they carried out more serious delinquent acts than the 'roughnecks'.

Chambliss claims that the police do not take middle-class delinquency seriously – such activities are often dismissed as 'harmless pranks'.

White-collar crime

Edwin Sutherland (1960) was the first sociologist to study 'white-collar crime'. He defines it as 'crimes committed by persons of high social status and respectability in the course of their occupations'.

White-collar crimes may include a variety of offences, such as:

- Bribery and corruption in business and politics
- Misconduct by professionals such as lawyers or doctors
- The breaking of trade regulations, food and drug laws and safety regulations
- Misrepresentation in advertising

There is much evidence to suggest that these sorts of offences are widespread. Here are just a few recent examples.

- Bribery and corruption

A member of the last Conservative government, Jonathan Aitken, was found to have accepted

hospitality at the Paris Ritz from Mohammed Al Fayed in return for asking questions in Parliament. He was later imprisoned for trying to cover this up.

- Fraud

Robert Maxwell was the owner of Mirror Group newspapers before his mysterious drowning in 1991. Maxwell had used money from the pension fund of Mirror Group employees to stave off the collapse of his business empire.

- Health and safety

According to Streeter (1997), in the late 1990s the effects of asbestos were killing 3,500 people per year. The actions which resulted in these deaths may not have been illegal but their consequences in terms of loss of life were extremely serious.

- Illegal actions by government organizations

In his book *Spycatcher*, Peter Wright (1987) claimed that, during the 1960s, the security services were involved in numerous unauthorized buggings and burglaries.

A number of factors combine to reduce the apparent extent and seriousness of white-collar crime:

- White-collar crimes are difficult to detect as many do not have obvious 'victims'.
- In cases of bribery and corruption all those involved will benefit, so nobody is likely to report the offence.
- In cases where the victim is the public at large (such as misrepresentation in advertising) few members of the public have the expertise to realize that they are being misled, and government agencies do not have the resources to follow up more than a few cases.

Even if they are detected, few white-collar crimes lead to prosecutions. The power and influence of many of those involved mean that a 'blind eye' is often turned or an 'official warning' given. Cases of professional misconduct are usually dealt with by the relevant professional association which may simply hand down a reprimand.

Official statistics probably significantly underestimate the extent of white-collar and corporate crime. As a result, crime is viewed as predominantly working-class behaviour.

Deviance – an interactionist perspective

Most of the theories considered up to now have looked at the factors that supposedly direct the behaviour of deviants. This emphasis on the idea that deviants simply react to external forces is similar to a positivist position. Interactionists take a different approach. They examine:

- How and why particular individuals and groups are defined as deviant.
- The effects of such a definition on their future actions.

Becker – labelling theory

The definition of deviance

Howard S. Becker (1963) suggests that there is really no such thing as a deviant act. An act only becomes deviant when others perceive it as such. He gives the example of a brawl involving young people:

- In a low-income neighbourhood this may be

defined by the police as delinquency.

- In a wealthy neighbourhood it may be defined as youthful high spirits.

The acts are the same but the meaning given to them by observers is different. If youngsters are defined as delinquent and convicted then they have become deviant. In other words they have been labelled as deviants.

Possible effects of labelling

Once an individual or group is labelled as criminal, mentally ill or homosexual, others see them only in terms of that label. It becomes what Becker calls a master status. Labelling also causes the labelled group or individual to see themselves in terms of the label. This may produce a self-fulfilling prophecy in which the label actually makes itself become true.

Becker identifies a number of stages in this process:
1 The individual is labelled as deviant and may be rejected from many social groups.
2 This may encourage further deviance. A drug addict may turn to crime because employers refuse to give him/her a job.
3 Ex-convicts find it difficult to get jobs and may be forced to return to crime.
4 The deviant career is completed when individuals join an organized deviant group, thus confirming and accepting their deviant identity.
5 Now a deviant subculture may develop which includes norms and values which support their deviant behaviour.

Young – labelling and marijuana users

Becker's approach is used by Jock Young (1971) in his study of 'hippie' marijuana users in London.
1 The police see hippies as dirty, lazy drug addicts.
2 Police action against marijuana users unites them and makes them feel different.
3 As a result they retreat into small groups.
4 Deviant norms and values develop in these closed groups. Hair is grown longer, clothes become more unconventional and drug use becomes a central activity.

Thus a self-fulfilling prophecy is created.

Lemert – societal reaction – the 'cause' of deviance

Edwin M. Lemert (1972) distinguishes between 'primary' and 'secondary' deviance.

Primary deviance consists of deviant acts before they are publicly labelled. Trying to find the causes of primary deviance is not very helpful because:

- Samples of deviants are inevitably based only on those who have been labelled, and they are therefore unrepresentative.
- Most deviant acts are so common that they may be, in statistical terms, normal. Most males may at some time commit a homosexual act, engage in delinquency and so on.

The important factor in creating 'deviance' is the reaction of society – the public identification of the deviant. Secondary deviance is the response of the individual to that societal reaction.

Goffman – deviance and the institution

Erving Goffman's examination of the treatment of mental patients in institutions illustrates the idea of secondary deviance. He shows how deviance can actually be created by the societal reaction to it.

When inmates arrive in the mental hospital, pressure is placed on them to accept the institution's definition of them as 'mentally ill'. The inmates' individuality is removed through what Goffman calls a mortification process:

- Their clothes are removed and their possessions are taken away and stored.
- The patient may be washed and disinfected and their hair may be cut.
- They may then be issued with a new 'identity' in the form of regulation clothes and toilet articles.
- Every day is strictly controlled with a set of compulsory activities.
- Inmates are allowed little freedom of movement and few opportunities for initiative.
- Their actions are continually watched and assessed by staff.

The effect of all this is to leave inmates unprepared for life on the outside. This is because:

- Some have accepted the institution's definition of them as helpless deviants.
- Others believe they are unable to function at all in the outside world.
- The label 'ex-mental patient' makes re-entry into society very difficult.

Goffman's research took place several decades ago and may not be so applicable today. However, his work was influential in producing improvements in the treatment of the mentally ill.

Labelling theory and social policy

Stephen Jones (1998) identifies two main policy implications of labelling theory:
1 As many types of behaviour as possible should be decriminalized. For example, in some countries, such as the Netherlands, cannabis has been effectively legalized.
2 When the law has to intervene, it should avoid giving people a self-concept in which they view themselves as criminals. For example, warnings and cautions could be used to deal with delinquents rather than placing them in institutions.

However, these policies became less popular during the 1990s. Recently the emphasis has been on the 'naming and shaming' of offenders such as paedophiles and kerb-crawlers.

Evaluation of the interactionist approach

Labelling theory enjoyed great popularity in the 1960s but provoked strong criticism in the 1970s. The key criticisms are as follows:
1 Taylor, Walton and Young (1973) argue that labelling theory is wrong in suggesting that deviance is created by the social groups who define acts as deviant. Some acts – such as premeditated killing for personal gain – will always be regarded as deviant in our society.
2 Many sociologists claim that the interactionist approach fails to explain why individuals commit deviant acts in the first place (primary deviance).
3 It is claimed that labelling theory is too

deterministic. It assumes that, once a person has been labelled, their deviance will automatically increase. Ackers (1975) suggests that individuals might simply choose to be deviant, regardless of whether they have been labelled.

4 Interactionists fail to explain why some people are labelled rather than others and why some activities are against the law and others are not. In other words it ignores the wider issue of the distribution of power in society.

Interactionists such as Plummer (1979) have strongly defended labelling theory against these criticisms. It is certainly true that the interactionist approach has had a significant influence on the sociology of deviance, particularly more recent approaches such as new left realism.

Traditional Marxist perspectives on deviance

Who makes the law? Who benefits?

● From a Marxist perspective, laws are made by the state which represents the interests of the ruling class.
● Snider (1993) notes that the capitalist state is often reluctant to pass laws that threaten the profitability of large businesses. Often the state has worked hard to attract large corporations and does not want to risk alienating them.
● Pearce (1976) argues that many laws which appear to benefit only the working class, in reality benefit the ruling class as well. Factory legislation protecting the health and safety of workers benefits capitalists by keeping workers fit for work and loyal to their employers.
● Chambliss (1976) suggests that much of what takes place in the creation of rules is 'non-decision making'. Many issues – such as the way wealth is distributed – never reach the point of decision.

Who breaks the law? Who gets caught?

● Marxists argue that crime is widespread in all parts of society. There are many examples of illegal behaviour by white-collar criminals and corporations.
● Snider (1993) argues that many of the most serious deviant acts in modern societies are corporate crimes. She claims that corporate crime costs more in terms of loss of money and life than crimes such as burglary and robbery.
● In a study of crime in the USA Chambliss (1978) concludes that:
1 Those who operate organized crime in America belong to the economic and political elite.
2 The ruling class as a whole benefits from organized crime as money used from crime is used to finance legal business operations.
3 Corruption of local politicians and law enforcement agencies is essential for organized crime to flourish.
4 Criminal acts that favour ruling-class interests will not be penalized.

Why break the law? Why enforce the law?

Many Marxists see crime as a natural 'outgrowth' of capitalist society.

● Chambliss (1976) argues that the greed, self-interest and hostility generated by capitalist society motivate crimes at all levels within society. Members of all classes use whatever opportunities they have to commit crime.
● Given the nature of capitalist societies, crime is rational. Gordon (1976) argues that in a society where competition is the order of the day, individuals must fend for themselves in order to survive.

Gordon goes on to suggest that law enforcement in the USA supports the capitalist system in three main ways:
1 Individuals who commit crimes are defined as 'social failures' and seen as responsible for their actions. In this way blame and condemnation are directed at the individual rather than the capitalist system.
2 The imprisonment of selected members of the working class neutralizes opposition to the system. For example, American blacks are heavily over-represented amongst those arrested for street crimes such as robbery and aggravated assault.
3 Defining criminals as 'animals and misfits' provides a justification for their imprisonment. This keeps them hidden from public view and so the embarrassing extremes produced by the capitalist system are swept under the carpet.

Evaluation of conventional Marxism

Marxist theories have come in for some heavy criticism:
1 Feminists have argued that Marxist theories ignore the importance of patriarchy in influencing the criminal justice system. Marxists have also been accused of neglecting the importance of racism in the enforcement of law.
2 Crime has not been eradicated in communist societies based on Marxist principles.
3 Stephen Jones (1998) points out that capitalism does not always produce high crime rates. For example, in Switzerland the crime rate is very low.
4 Perhaps the distribution of power is not as simple as some Marxists suggest. Jones gives the example of insider trading (taking advantage of 'insider' knowledge to make huge profits on the stock exchange). This is illegal, which suggests that capitalists do not always get the laws they want.
5 'Left realists' (see pp. 63–5) believe that Marxists put too much emphasis on corporate crime. Other crimes such as burglary cause greater harm than Marxists imply. Their victims are usually working-class and the consequences can be devastating for them.
6 Postmodern criminology rejects Marxist criminology as being neither believable nor defensible (see pp. 67–8).

Despite these criticisms, Marxism has been an influence on a number of critical perspectives on deviance. Some have drawn their inspiration from Marxism and can be referred to as neo-Marxist approaches. Others owe less to Marxism and are better defined as radical approaches.

Deviance – neo-Marxist and radical perspectives

Neo-Marxist approaches to deviance are strongly influenced by Marxism but do not accept that there is a straightforward link between the structure of capitalist society and deviance.

Taylor, Walton and Young – The New Criminology

In 1973, Taylor, Walton and Young published The New Criminology. This influential book criticized many existing theories of crime. The authors accept some key assumptions of Marxism but adopt a more liberal and tolerant view, influenced by labelling theory.

They outline what they call a 'fully social theory of deviance'. The criminologist must consider the following aspects of deviance:

1 The way in which wealth and power are distributed.
2 The circumstances surrounding the decision of an individual to commit an act of deviance.
3 The meaning of the deviant act for the person involved. Was the individual 'kicking back' at society through an act of vandalism, for example?
4 The ways in which other members of society, such as the police, respond to the deviant act.
5 This reaction needs to be examined in terms of the way society is organized. Who has the power to make rules and decide how deviant acts should be dealt with?
6 The impact of the deviant label. This may have a variety of effects – the deviant may accept the label as justified, or they may ignore the label, or it may lead to greater deviance (see pp. 60–1).
7 Finally, criminologists need to look at the relationship between all these different aspects so that they can be fused into one complete theory of deviance.

Evaluation of The New Criminology

The New Criminology has been criticized in a number of ways:

1 Feminists have criticized its concentration on male crimes.
2 Some 'new left realist' criminologists have accused it of neglecting the impact of crime on victims and romanticizing working-class criminals (see pp. 63–5).

In 1998 Paul Walton and Jock Young re-evaluated their earlier work. They accept some of the criticisms but argue that recent approaches such as 'realist criminology, feminist criminology and postmodern criminology are all committed to creating a more equitable and just society'. In that respect they are a continuation of the traditions of *The New Criminology*.

Walton and Young only outlined the main features of their approach to studying crime and deviance. It was left to others to put their theory into practice.

Policing the Crisis – mugging, the state and law and order

Stuart Hall *et al.* (1979) attempt to provide a 'fully social theory of deviance' in their explanation of the crime of 'mugging' in Britain in the 1970s.

The authors argue that there was a 'moral panic'

about crime and mugging in particular – a crime associated with black youth. (A moral panic is an exaggerated outburst of public concern over the morality and behaviour of a group in society.) Hall *et al.* found no evidence to indicate that the crime of mugging was new or increasing.

The moral panic over mugging could only be explained in the context of the problems facing British capitalism at the start of the 1970s. Economic problems and industrial and social unrest meant that the hegemony (ideological domination) of the ruling class was under threat and it had to turn to force to control the crisis. Mugging was presented as a key element in the breakdown of law and order.

The moral panic over mugging helped capitalism in two ways:

1 The public were persuaded that society's problems were caused by 'immigrants' rather than the faults of the capitalist system.
2 The government was able to justify the use of force to suppress the groups that were challenging them.

The societal reaction to the threat of violence led to the labelling of large numbers of young blacks as deviants. Labelling helped to produce the figures that appeared to show rising levels of black crime, which in turn justified stronger police measures.

Policing the Crisis – an evaluation

Given the range of issues the study deals with, it is not surprising that other sociologists have raised criticisms.

● Downes and Rock identify two weaknesses:
1 The study claims that black street crime was not rising while at the same time arguing that it was bound to rise as a result of unemployment.
2 The study fails to show how the moral panic over mugging was caused by a crisis of British capitalism.
● Young argues that the study provides no evidence that the public were panicking about mugging, nor does it show that the public identified the crime with blacks. However, he also argues that it would have been quite rational if the public had been concerned about street crime.

Left realism

Left realism has developed since the 1980s and is particularly associated with Jock Young. Left realists take the view that crime is a real problem which must be taken seriously, and they present a number of criticisms of previous criminology:

● Some sociologists have tried to explain the huge rise in street crime since the Second World War by pointing to the unreliable nature of criminal statistics. Young (1993) argues that the rises have been so great that they cannot simply be explained by changes in reporting and recording.
● Some sociologists have advanced the view that the chances of being a victim of street crime are minimal. However, Lea and Young (1984) point out that, while this is true, particular groups face high risks. These groups are the poor and deprived, ethnic minorities and inner-city residents. Those with low incomes also suffer more if they are

robbed or burgled.

- Left realists have carried out a number of victimization studies and found widespread fear of crime. Many people, particularly women, altered their behaviour to avoid becoming victims of crime.
- Lea and Young attack the idea that offenders can sometimes be seen as promoting justice. They attack the image of the criminal presented in parts of *The New Criminology* as a type of modern-day Robin Hood.
- While accepting that white-collar and corporate crime are commonplace and serious, left realists argue that recent criminology has concentrated too much on such crimes.
- Left realists have acknowledged the importance of under-reported and under-recorded crimes such as sexual assaults and harassment, racially motivated attacks and domestic violence. They claim to take all crimes equally seriously.

Ethnicity and crime

Lea and Young accept that policing policies and police racism exaggerate the black crime rate. However, they do believe that there has been an increase in the number of crimes committed by blacks and that this is the result of unemployment and racial discrimination. They find it hard to understand how 'left idealists' such as Gilroy (1983) can argue that the disproportionate number of black males convicted of crimes in Britain is caused by police racism. They are even more critical of Gilroy's claim that such black crime as there is results from a continuation of an 'anti-colonial struggle'.

This is not plausible because:

- Most first-generation immigrants appear to have been law-abiding.
- Most of the victims of black crime are themselves black.

The explanation of crime

Lea and Young base their attempt to explain crime around three key concepts: relative deprivation, subculture and marginalization.

1 Relative deprivation

Deprivation will only lead to crime where it is experienced as relative deprivation. A group experiences relative deprivation when it feels deprived relative to similar groups or when its expectations are not met. In modern societies advertisers stress the importance of economic success and promote middle-class lifestyles and patterns of consumption.

Rather like Merton (see p. 57), Lea and Young argue that rising crime is partly the result of rising expectations of high standards of living, combined with restricted opportunities to achieve this.

2 Subculture

Groups develop lifestyles to cope with the problem of relative deprivation, and subcultures can form as a result. However, these vary. Second-generation West Indian immigrants' subcultural solutions include the Rastafarian and Pentecostal religions as well as 'hustling' for money and street crime.

3 Marginalization

Marginal groups are those that lack organizations to represent their interests in political life. These groups are particularly prone to the use of violence and rioting as forms of political action. The key to avoiding marginality is employment, as workers have clearly defined objectives, such as higher wages. Young unemployed West Indians do not have clearly defined aims or pressure groups to represent them. They feel a general sense of resentment which can lead to them taking to the streets and rioting.

Social change and the problem of crime

Recently Young (1997) has argued that we are entering a period of late modernity which is making the problem of crime worse in a number of ways:

1 Late modernity is characterized by great uncertainty and instability in areas such as family life and work, which make people feel less secure and stable.
2 There is less consensus about moral values. Instead an increasing variety of subcultures claim that their values are legitimate.
3 In the world of leisure there is an emphasis on immediacy and personal pleasure. People expect to be able to buy the consumer goods of their choice and to have lots of fun. At the same time there are fewer secure jobs and there is rising inequality.
   In these circumstances increasing numbers of people are likely to experience marginalization and relative deprivation.
4 Informal social controls are becoming less effective as families and communities disintegrate.

Policing problems

Kinsey, Lea and Young (1984) argue that there are a number of flaws in current policing:

1 The clear-up rate is very low so the police are unable to deter criminals.
2 The police spend very little time actually investigating crime.
3 The police rely on a flow of information from the public, but public confidence in the police is declining, particularly in inner-city areas and among members of ethnic minorities.
4 Without the support of the public, the police have to resort to what the authors call military policing – stopping and searching large numbers of people or using surveillance technology. As a result, those who are not directly involved with the police come to see them as an alien force intent on criminalizing local residents – a process known as the mobilization of bystanders.

Improving policing

Kinsey, Lea and Young argue that the key to police success lies in improving relationships with the community. To achieve this they recommend that:

- The public should have much more say in shaping police policy.
- The police should spend as much time as possible actually investigating crime.

Tackling the social causes of crime

Young (1992, 1997) does not believe that crime can be dealt with simply by improving the efficiency of the

police. Left realists see the problem of crime as rooted in social inequalities. Young suggests:
- Improving leisure facilities for the young
- Reducing income inequalities
- Raising the living standards of poorer families
- Reducing unemployment and creating jobs with prospects
- Providing community facilities which enhance a sense of belonging

The square of crime
Left realists believe that crime can only be understood in terms of the relationship between the four elements in the diagram below.

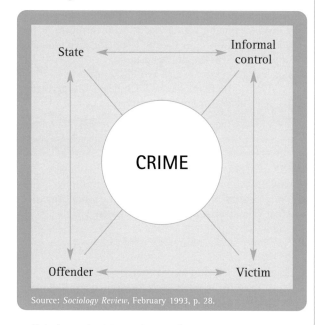

Source: *Sociology Review*, February 1993, p. 28.

It is important to understand:
1 Why people offend
2 What makes the victims vulnerable
3 The factors that affect public attitudes and responses to crime
4 The social forces that influence the police

Evaluation of left realism
Left realism has been criticized in a number of ways:
- Hughes (1991) argues that it fails to explain the causes of street crime. Left realists have not gathered empirical data about offenders' motives.
- Hughes also attacks left realism for its reliance on subcultural theory which has been heavily criticized (see pp. 57–9).
- Jones (1998) argues that left realism fails to explain why some people who experience relative deprivation turn to crime while others do not.
- Jones also identifies flaws in the emphasis on victims. Left realists take victims' accounts of fear of crime at face value and never ask victims for their views about the causes of crime. They also only take into account the views of victims in urban areas where crime rates are high, thus giving a misleading impression of how harmful crime is.
- Ruggiero (1992) argues that left realists have neglected corporate and organized crime and that

this type of crime cannot really be understood within the framework of their theory.

However, Hughes also points out some strengths of left realism:
- It has revived useful concepts such as relative deprivation.
- It has promoted debate and theoretical development within sociology.
- It has highlighted the problem that street crime poses for weaker members of society.
- It has explored the position of victims much more than previous theories.
- It avoids the worst excesses of both right- and left-wing approaches by neither glorifying nor attacking the police.

Left realism and social policy
Left realism has had more influence on crime policies than other theories. The police in Britain now employ civilians to do routine tasks, thus freeing police officers to investigate crime. The police are also beginning to take crimes such as domestic violence seriously.

However, the reduction of inequality – a key factor underlying crime rates for left realists – has not been addressed.

Right realist criminology

Wilson – Thinking About Crime
- James Q. Wilson (1975) denies that trying to get rid of poverty will lead to reductions in crime. This policy failed in the USA in the 1960s, and many poor people (for example, those who are elderly or sick) do not commit crimes.
- Wilson concentrates on street crime, which he believes the general public are most concerned about.
- He sees crime as the result of rational calculation. People will commit crime if the likely benefits exceed the likely costs. In reality the chances of getting caught for a particular crime are quite small. If offenders do not believe they are going to get caught or if punishments take place long after offences, then even severe punishments will not deter people.
- Strong communities are an effective way of dealing with crime. People who are disgraced by their involvement in crime will lose their standing in the community. The problem is that crime itself undermines communities.
- Wilson and Kelling (1982) believe that it is crucial to try to maintain the character of neighbourhoods and prevent them from deteriorating. The role of the police is to clamp down on the first signs of undesirable behaviour. They should try to keep drunks, prostitutes, drug addicts and vandals off the street so that law-abiding citizens feel safe.

Wilson and Herstein – Crime and Human Nature
Wilson and Herstein (1985) argue that some people are born with a predisposition towards crime. Their potential for crime is likely to be realized if they are not properly socialized. Where close-knit nuclear families are absent, effective socialization is unlikely.

Wilson and Herstein still believe that people have free will. Ultimately they choose whether to commit crime by weighing up the costs and benefits. Unfortunately it is too easy to live off welfare benefits, and the potential gains from crime are increasing as society becomes more affluent.

For many people the benefits of crime come to outweigh the costs, and the crime rate increases.

Evaluation of right realism
Some aspects of right realist thinking have been influential. 'Zero tolerance' policing is based on the idea that it is effective to clamp down at the first sign that an area is deteriorating.

However, the views of Wilson and others have come under serious attack.

1 Matthews (1992) finds little evidence that tolerating broken windows and minor incidents has led to an increase in crime.

2 Jones (1998) argues that:
- Factors such as lack of investment are far more important in determining whether a neighbourhood declines.
- Concentrating attention on minor offenders would mean that more serious offenders would be more likely to get away with their crimes.
- If some neighbourhoods were made more orderly then the disorderly and criminals would simply move their activities.
- The biological approach ignores the role of inequality and unemployment in causing crime and neglects white-collar and corporate crimes.
- Finally, despite the influence of right realist policies, the crime rate in the USA continues to rise.

Marketization, globalization, inequality and crime

Some sociologists are particularly critical of the increasing importance of market forces in Western capitalist societies and have analysed the impact this has had on crime.

Taylor – The Political Economy of Crime
Ian Taylor (1997) is interested in how changes in the global economy and the ways in which some politicians have responded to these changes have affected crime.

Marketization and opportunities for criminality
- The deregulation of financial markets has provided increased opportunities for crimes such as insider trading, where financiers use privileged knowledge to make a financial killing.
- Marketization has increased opportunities for crimes such as insurance fraud and false claims for subsidies from the European Commission.

Changes in employment and unemployment
- Unemployment has become a more or less permanent feature of some areas. Lack of opportunity and hope leads some to turn to crime.
- Changing patterns of work have created more opportunities and incentives for criminal activity.

Ruggiero, South and Taylor (1998) believe that subcontracting encourages the employment of people who are working illegally or in conditions or at wage levels that fail to conform to national laws.

Materialism and inequality
Success is increasingly portrayed in terms of a lifestyle associated with expensive consumer goods. At the same time, inequalities have increased rapidly. Taylor sees crimes such as car theft as related to these changes.

Drugs and globalization
- Taylor argues that there are few opportunities for young working-class men in cities such as Los Angeles which are suffering from deindustrialization. At the same time, the culture of entrepreneurship encourages many young blacks, who confront the additional problem of racism, to pursue illegitimate opportunities in the drugs business.
- For less successful, Third World countries, producing the crops from which drugs are derived requires little technology or investment and offers high profits.

Gender and crime

In 1977 Carol Smart put forward the following reasons to explain the neglect of women in criminology:
- Women tend to commit fewer crimes than men.
- Most crimes committed by women appear to be of a comparatively trivial nature.
- Sociology and criminology tend to be dominated by men.
- Traditional criminology is motivated by a desire to control problem behaviour. As women's behaviour is less of a problem than men's it has received less attention.

Official statistics indicate that women in all age groups appear to commit far less crime than men. This pattern has raised three main questions:
1 Do women really commit fewer crimes than men, or are the figures misleading?
2 Is the proportion of crimes committed by women increasing, and is this linked to 'women's liberation'?
3 Why do some women break the law?

Leniency towards female offenders: the 'chivalry' thesis
- Campbell (1981) conducted a self-report study (see p. 60) and found that:
1 Female suspects were more likely than male suspects to be cautioned rather than prosecuted.
2 The rate of male:female juvenile offending was 1.33:1.0 rather than the official figure of 8.95:1.0.
- Hood (1989) compared the sentencing of men and women and found that men were more likely to be given custodial sentences than women.

Evidence against the 'chivalry' thesis
- Box (1981) reviewed the data from self-report studies in Britain and the USA and concluded that the official statistics on gender and crime were fairly accurate.
- Farrington and Morris (1983) conducted a study of sentencing in magistrates' courts. Although men

received more severe sentences than women, the differences disappeared when the severity of offences was taken into account.

- Walklate (1995) believes that it is the female victim rather than the male suspect who ends up on trial in rape cases. Women have to establish their respectability if their evidence is to be believed.
- In a study of domestic violence Dobash and Dobash (1979) found that police officers were very unlikely to make an arrest in cases of domestic violence.

Double standards in criminal justice

Heidensohn (1985) argues that the justice system is influenced by attitudes to gender in society as a whole. Women are treated more harshly when they deviate from norms of female sexuality. Sexually promiscuous girls are more likely to be taken into care than similar boys. On the other hand, courts may be reluctant to imprison mothers with young children.

Carlen (1997) argues that women are more likely to be sentenced according to the court's assessment of them as wives, mothers and daughters rather than the seriousness of their crimes.

The causes of female crime and deviance

Physiological causes

Some of the earliest attempts to explain female criminality were based on biological theories. Lombroso (1895) compared the anatomical features of female criminals and non-criminals. He believed that male criminals could be identified by physical abnormalities such as having an extra toe or nipple. Few women had these features; therefore they were not 'born criminals'.

Lombroso's work has long been discredited. However, biological theories have recently reappeared. Moir and Jessel (1997) explain some violent crime as being linked to Premenstrual Syndrome (PMS). Most sociologists, however, focus on social causes of female crime.

Female crime and women's liberation

Fran Adler (1975) claimed that women's liberation had led to a new type of female criminal and an increase in women's contribution to crime. Women were taking on male social roles in both legitimate and illegitimate areas of activity. Instead of confining themselves to 'feminine' crimes such as shoplifting, women were getting involved in robbing banks, mugging and even murder.

Adler's views have proved to be very controversial. Box and Hale's (1983) review of the debate concludes that if female crime has increased this is more likely to be due to unemployment and inadequate welfare benefits. Most female criminals are from lower-class backgrounds and are the least likely to have been touched by women's liberation.

Carlen – women, crime and poverty

Pat Carlen (1985) conducted unstructured interviews with 39 convicted female offenders. She argues that working-class women have been controlled through the promise of rewards stemming from the workplace and family. When these rewards are not available, or

are not seen as worth the sacrifice, then criminality becomes a possibility.

Female conformity

Heidensohn – women and social control

Frances Heidensohn (1985) attempts to explain why women commit fewer crimes than men. She argues that patriarchal societies control women more effectively than men, making it more difficult for them to break the law.

- Control of women at home
  The time spent on housework and in caring for children means that women have little time for crime. Daughters are given less freedom than sons to come and go as they please.
- Control of women in public
  Women often choose not to go out into public places because of fear of becoming a victim of crime or harassment. They also limit their behaviour in public for fear of being labelled a 'slag, slut or bitch'.
- Control of women at work
  Women are usually controlled by male superiors at work and may be intimidated by various forms of harassment.

Masculinities and crime

Messerschmidt – Masculinities and crime

James W. Messerschmidt analyses why different groups of males turn to different types of crime in their attempts to be masculine.

Masculinities and crime in youth groups

- In order to achieve success white middle-class boys have to be subservient to schoolteachers. Outside the school they try to demonstrate some of the characteristics they repress within the school. This may involve pranks, vandalism, minor thefts and excessive drinking. Such young men adopt an accommodating masculinity.
- White working-class boys have less chance of academic success and tend to construct masculinity around the importance of physical aggression. They try to be tough and oppose the authority of teachers. Theirs is an oppositional masculinity.
- Lower-working-class ethnic minority boys do not expect to be able to hold down a steady job and support a family. They use violence to express their masculinity and may become involved in more serious property crime than white working-class youths. This offers them some prospect of material success.

Postmodernism and criminology

Smart (1995) argues that traditional approaches to crime all adopt a version of positivism in the following ways:

- They try to find the causes of criminality.
- They try to find ways of eradicating crime.
- They assume that scientific methods are the best way of discovering the truth about crime.
- They believe that it is possible to find an overall theory to explain crime.

Postmodernists reject these traditional approaches to crime.

- They do not believe that crimes can be linked together and that common factors which cause them can be identified. They regard each criminal act as unique.
- They do not believe that it is possible to engineer reforms to improve society. Effective ways of dealing with crime must be local and individual.

Evaluation of postmodern approaches

Lea (1998) believes that postmodernism has made a useful contribution to the study of the control of crime. In the postmodern world informal control mechanisms come to dominate at the expense of the central state. Private security firms watch over shopping malls, and closed-circuit television (CCTV) follows our movements around city and town centres. Security firms prevent undesirables from entering some estates. People are treated differently in different areas and seen increasingly as customers and consumers.

However, Lea also believes that postmodernism is regressive since it denies the possibility of being able to do anything to change unequal and unjust societies.

Sociology, values and deviance: whose side are we on?

- Becker (1970) is an interactionist sociologist. He believes that a value-free sociology is not possible. His sympathies lie with the 'underdog' who is labelled by the agencies of social control.
- Gouldner (1971) takes a different, more radical view. He accuses interactionists of taking a liberal position which advocates cosmetic reform rather than radical change. In criticizing the agents of social control, labelling theorists like Becker fail to attack the real causes of deviance which lie in society itself.

Since the issues of crime, deviance and conformity are about basic ideas of right and wrong, it is hardly surprising that values influence this area of sociology to a great extent. Many of the theories examined in this chapter reflect how their authors think society ought to be arranged, as much as how they think it actually is.

1 Which one of the following statements is true?
   a Sociologists believe that deviance is a social construction
   b Sociologists believe that deviance is usually dysfunctional for societies
   c Sociologists believe that deviance is the breaking of laws
   d Sociologists believe that deviance has a positive effect on society

2 Which one of the following statements is true?
   a Physiological theories of deviance believe that deviance is caused by society
   b Physiological theories of deviance believe that deviance is the result of cultural deprivation
   c Physiological theories of deviance believe that deviance has biological causes
   d Physiological theories of deviance believe that deviance is the result of environmental factors

3 Which one of the following did Durkheim believe?
   a Deviance acts as a safety valve for society
   b Deviance is dysfunctional for society
   c Deviance is inevitable in societies
   d All individuals are committed to shared values and beliefs

4 According to Merton, which one of the following is not a response to anomie?
   a Conformity   b Innovation
   c Alienation   d Ritualism

5 According to A. Cohen, which one of the following is not true of the delinquent subculture?
   a Lower-class boys suffer from status frustration
   b Lower-class boys turn to criminal activities to achieve success
   c Lower-class boys want success but cannot achieve it legally
   d For lower-class boys, delinquency is an individual response to their situation

6 According to Cloward and Ohlin, which one of the following is the most accurate definition of the illegitimate opportunity structure?
   a The chances of an average youth becoming a delinquent
   b The chances the adolescent has of engaging in various kinds of illegal activities
   c The chances of getting a job for those with a criminal record
   d An area of established organized crime
   e The chances of those born to unmarried parents becoming delinquents

7 Three of the following are criticisms of Murray's view of the underclass and crime. Which is the odd one out?
   a The underclass do not share the same values as other members of society
   b Crime rates are not linked to generous welfare states
   c There is no link between single parents and criminality
   d There is no distinctive underclass culture

8 Which of the following best defines 'techniques of neutralization'?
   a Ways of justifying and excusing deviant acts
   b Ways of disguising deviant acts
   c Ways of making up for deviant acts
   d Ways in which the police ensure that they are unbiased

9 Which one of the following groups does not appear to be disproportionately involved in crime?
   a Men   b Afro-Caribbean men
   c Asian men   d The working class

10 Which one of the following crimes is likely to have high rates of reporting and recording?
   a Tax evasion   b Burglary
   c Use of illegal drugs d Rape

11 Three of the following are sources of statistical information about crime. Which is the odd one out?
   a Self-report studies
   b The New Criminology
   c The British Crime Survey
   d Victimization studies

12 Which one of the following is an example of white-collar crime?
   a Fraud   b Burglary
   c Domestic assault   d Murder

13 Three of the following are reasons why white-collar crime is under-represented in criminal statistics. Which is the odd one out?
   a It is not serious
   b It is often difficult to detect
   c There is often no direct victim
   d It is often dealt with informally

14 Which one of the following adapted well-known sayings is an accurate description of labelling theory?
   a All the world's a deviant
   b Deviance is in the eye of the beholder
   c To be or not to be a deviant
   d Deviants should be seen and not heard

15 The term 'master status' can be applied in which one of the following situations?
   a When an individual or group is labelled as superior to others
   b When an individual or group occupies a high position in society
   c When an individual or group is judged only on the basis of a label that has been applied to them
   d When an individual or group is able to control and dominate others

16 Secondary deviance can be defined as which one of the following?
   a Less significant acts of deviance
   b The labelling of an individual as deviant
   c An act of deviance before it is publicly labelled
   d Deviance caused as a result of an individual or group being labelled

17 In which decade was labelling theory most popular?
   a 1920s   b 1940s
   c 1960s   d 1980s

18 Which two of the following statements most closely reflect a Marxist view of deviance?
   a Laws reflect the interests of the powerful in society
   b Most crime is the responsibility of an underclass
   c Laws protect all members of society
   d Corporate crime is a serious problem which is ignored in most cases

19 Three of the following authors are associated with *The New Criminology.* Which is the odd one out?
   a Paul Walton
   b Ian Taylor
   c Howard Becker
   d Jock Young

20 According to the authors of *Policing the Crisis*, the mugging moral panic helped capitalism in two ways. Identify the two ways from the following list:
   a Inequality was made to appear legitimate
   b Black muggers were used as a scapegoat for social problems
   c The use of force to suppress opposition was justified
   d Capitalists made more profits

21 Three of the following views are associated with left realism. Which is the odd one out?
   a The crime rate has been rising
   b There is widespread fear of crime
   c Laws benefit the ruling class
   d All crimes should be taken equally seriously

22 Which of the following is a definition of relative deprivation?
   a The feeling of being worse off than other people
   b The feeling of being worse off than others in your family
   c The feeling of being poor
   d The feeling of being socially isolated

23 Which one of the following is not part of the 'square of crime'?
   a The victim
   b The offender
   c The public
   d The state

24 Which one of the following measures to combat crime is most likely to be supported by right realists?
   a Reducing poverty
   b Zero tolerance policing
   c Increased leisure facilities for young people
   d Reducing inequality

25 Which one of the following, according to Ian Taylor, is not a way in which marketization has increased opportunities or incentives for crime?
   a Success is increasingly portrayed in terms of ownership of expensive consumer goods, thus encouraging theft
   b More flexible working practices encourage subcontracting. This provides an incentive to employ workers illegally or pay them below minimum wages
   c Deregulation of financial markets has created more opportunities for fraud and insider trading
   d Increasing family breakdown has created more single-parent families which are a breeding ground for deviant norms and values

26 Which one of the following is a reason put forward to explain why women have been neglected in criminology until recently?
   a They are often the victims of crime
   b They commit less crime than men
   c The proportion of offences committed by women is increasing
   d They are subject to more social control than men

27 The 'chivalry thesis' is:
   a The idea that crimes committed by women tend to be trivial
   b The idea that women will be treated more leniently by the police and courts
   c The idea that women will be treated less severely by criminals
   d The idea that it is easier for women to become police officers and judges

28 According to Messerschmidt, what type of masculinity is usually adopted by white middle-class boys?
   a Accommodating masculinity
   b Oppositional masculinity
   c Hegemonic masculinity
   d Traditional masculinity

29 Which one of the following statements would postmodernist criminologists support?
   a Sociology should try to identify the underlying causes of crime
   b Scientific methods are the best way of finding out about crime
   c Each criminal act is unique and cannot be fitted into general theories
   d It is possible to reform society to reduce crime rates

30 Which one of the following statements is closest to Becker's view?
   a Sociologists should be completely neutral
   b Sociologists should be on the side of law and order
   c Sociologists should deliberately take the side of the 'underdog'
   d Sociologists should take a radical view

Develop your analysis and evaluation skills

(see p. 200 for guidance notes)

For each of the following statements, identify which sociologists would argue in favour of and which against the view expressed. Explain the reasons for their view.

1 The origins of deviance lie in the individual's position in society.

2 Official statistics of crime are completely unreliable.

3 Deviance is simply a label attached to some people's behaviour.

4 Deviance can best be understood by looking at the workings of capitalism.

5 'Zero tolerance' policing is an effective approach to reducing crime.

6 The police and courts treat women more leniently than men.

Answer all parts of this question
Total: 60 marks   1 mark = 1.5 minutes
Time allowed: 1 hour 30 minutes

ITEM A

Use this to help you answer part [a]

The key to doing good quality research on a difficult topic such as armed robbery is trust. There are normally problems of access and of generating a suitable sample of offenders like these, but establishing trust in the research process is of paramount importance because it directly affects the quality and quantity of the information gathered from stigmatized, marginalized and excluded groups such as armed robbers.

Source: adapted from Roger Matthews, 'Doing research on armed robbery', *Sociology Review*, vol. 10, no. 3, February 2001

Comments on the question	Question	Advice on preparing your answer
• Use the three descriptors of the group as the organizing principle and apply to show how trust may affect these • This question is testing your synoptic understanding of methods	[a] Examine how trust [Item A, line 2] can affect the quantity and quality of the information when studying any stigmatized, marginalized and excluded group. [8 marks]	• Concerns about confidentiality may stop people giving any information • See p. 45 for an explanation. Box (p. 174) recognizes that these groups may tell you what you want to hear • Problems of access and ethics are discussed by Polsky (Chapter 14,)
• This question is testing your synoptic understanding of theory and methods. The best answers might distinguish between the two terms • Note the negative phrasing of the question	[b] 'The personal and political sympathies of sociologists make it impossible to have a value-free sociology of deviance.' Discuss this view. [12 marks]	• A general debate can be found in Chapter 14, p. 177 • The application to this specific issue, with particular reference to Becker's commitment to the underdog and Gouldner's response, is set out on p. 68

Comments on the question	Question	Advice on preparing your answer
• This question is testing your synoptic understanding of theory and the links between substantive areas of sociology • Deviance occurs in all modules, including Families, Education, Work, Religion, Politics • Criticisms and alternative views should be recognized • Identify the quote as a functionalist perspective	[c] With reference to material from any part of the course, assess the view that deviance 'is a beneficial part of all healthy societies'. [40 marks]	• The functions of deviance are outlined on p. 57 • Merton's theory (p. 57) recognizes that deviance can highlight where there are dysfunctions in society • Political or religious deviance can bring about change • Deviance of children in families and education can reinforce the norms and values of society • It has been claimed that prostitution is a safety valve to protect the family • Deviance provides work for social control and welfare agencies • Functionalist ideas are criticized on p. 57 • Alternative theoretical approaches are discussed in Chapter 15 and would need to be used selectively to focus on the question

Answer all parts of this question

Total: 60 marks   1 mark = 1 minute

Time allowed: 1 hour

Comments on the question	Question	Advice on preparing your answer
• Make sure that you describe both views in a detailed way with supporting evidence in the form of sociological theories and studies • Look at the range of arguments within both positions • Make sure that your response is balanced – especially in terms of criticism – between both views	Outline and assess the view that criminal behaviour is a product of deviant culture rather than a rational response to social and economic inequality. [60 marks]	• This is an essay question. Spend at least 10 minutes putting together an essay plan • An introduction is necessary to 'set the scene', i.e. to make clear what theoretical positions and sociological names produced the two views in the question • Begin by outlining the 'deviant culture' argument. The section on pp. 57–9 should be useful in helping you to summarize these arguments • The 'social and economic inequality' argument should be outlined as a critique of the previous theory, with supporting evidence. The section on pp. 62–5 will assist you in this • Try to finish with an evaluative conclusion – i.e. on the basis of the evidence, take a side

Chapter 7

Religion

Specifications

Specification	Relevant module title	Place in module	Level	Assessment	Other relevant modules
AQA	4: Power and Politics; **Religion**; World Sociology	One of three options in this module.	A2	One compulsory short data-response question and one essay question from a choice of two.	Material from this chapter may be used in the A2 synoptic module 6.
OCR	Culture and Socialization	**Religion** is one of four options in this module.	AS	One or two two-part structured questions from a choice of two.	Material from this chapter may be used in the A2 synoptic module.

Religion: essential notes

Introduction – definitions of religion

Religious beliefs of some sort are present in every known society but their variety seems endless. Any definition of religion must encompass this variety.

Two main approaches have been taken to defining religion.

1 Functional definitions – these define religion in terms of the functions it performs for society and individuals.
   Example
   Yinger: 'a system of beliefs and practices by means of which a group of people struggles with the ultimate problems of human life' (quoted in Hamilton, 1995).
2 Substantive definitions – these are concerned with the content of religion.
   Example
   Durkheim (1961) defined religion in terms of a distinction between the sacred and the profane. Sacred objects produce a sense of awe and respect, whereas profane objects do not.

Evaluation

All definitions emphasize certain aspects of religion and ignore others. Functional definitions tend to be too inclusive (it is too easy to qualify as a religion); while substantive ones tend to be too exclusive (it is difficult to qualify as a religion).

Religion – a functionalist perspective

Functionalist analysis is concerned with the contribution religion makes to meeting society's needs, such as social solidarity, value consensus, and harmony and integration between its parts.

Emile Durkheim

- Durkheim (1912) argued that, in worshipping God, people are in fact worshipping society. Society is more important and more powerful than the individual, just as God is.
- Religion reinforces the shared values and moral beliefs – what Durkheim called the conscience collective – that hold society together. By defining these shared values as sacred, religion provides them with greater power.
- In worshipping society, people are, in effect, recognizing the importance of the social group and their dependence on it. In this way religion strengthens the unity of the group: it promotes social solidarity.
- Through acts of collective worship, members of society express, communicate and understand the moral bonds which unite them.

Criticisms

1 Durkheim only studied a small number of Aboriginal tribes. It may be misleading to generalize from this small sample.
2 Most sociologists would not go as far as Durkheim in arguing that religion is, in fact, the worship of society.
3 Hamilton (1995) points out that Durkheim's theory may only be applicable to small non-literate societies. Modern societies are characterized by diversity.
4 Hamilton also argues that Durkheim overstates the degree to which common values influence individual behaviour. Often religious beliefs will conflict with dominant values.

Bronislaw Malinowski

Like Durkheim, Malinowski (1954) uses data from small-scale, non-literate societies to support his ideas. He focuses on the role of religion in dealing with situations of emotional stress that threaten social solidarity. He identifies two sorts of events that may create this kind of stress:

1 Anxiety and tension tend to disrupt social life. Situations that produce these emotions include crises of life such as birth, puberty, marriage and death. Malinowski notes that in all societies these life crises are surrounded by religious ritual. At a funeral ceremony, for example, the social group unites to support the bereaved. The expression of social solidarity reintegrates society.

2 Actions that cannot be fully controlled or predicted also produce tension and anxiety. From his observations in the Trobriand Islands, Malinowski noted that such events were surrounded by ritual. Rituals reduce anxiety by providing confidence and a feeling of control.

Criticisms

Malinowski has been criticized for exaggerating the importance of religious ritual in helping people to cope with situations of stress and uncertainty.

Talcott Parsons

- Parsons argued that religious beliefs provide guidelines for human action and standards against which people's conduct can be evaluated. The Ten Commandments, for example, provide the basis for many social norms.
- Like Malinowski, Parsons sees religion as dealing with problems that disrupt social life – problems such as unforeseen, unpredictable events and situations of uncertainty.
- Another main function of religion for Parsons is to make sense of all experiences, no matter how meaningless or contradictory they appear. Religion provides a range of answers to questions about suffering, evil and so on.

Criticisms of the functionalist approach

The functionalist perspective emphasizes the positive contributions of religion to society and ignores its dysfunctional aspects. Functionalism neglects the instances where religion can be seen as a divisive and disruptive force, as with Catholics and Protestants in Northern Ireland and Hindus and Muslims in India.

Religion – a Marxist perspective

To Marx (1963), religion is an illusion which eases the pain produced by exploitation and oppression. It is a series of myths that justify and legitimate the domination of the ruling class. As such it forms the basis of much ruling-class ideology.

Marx famously described religion as the 'opium of the people'. Like a drug, it dulls pain and creates a dream world rather than bringing true happiness. It dulls the pain of oppression in the following ways:

- It promises a paradise of eternal bliss in life after death, making life bearable by giving people something to look forward to.

- Some religions make a virtue of the suffering produced by oppression. In particular, those who suffer poverty with dignity and humility will be rewarded in the afterlife. Religion thus makes poverty more tolerable.
- Religion can offer the hope of supernatural solutions to problems on earth. Anticipation of this future can make the present more acceptable.
- Religion often justifies the social order and a person's position within it. In this way social arrangements appear inevitable, and those at the bottom can accept and come to terms with their situation. In the same way, poverty and misfortune can be seen as a punishment for sin.

Religion and social control

For Marxists, religion does not simply cushion the effects of oppression. It also acts as a mechanism of social control, keeping people in their place.

- By making unsatisfactory lives bearable, it discourages people from attempting to change their situation.
- By offering an illusion of hope in a hopeless situation, it prevents thoughts of overthrowing the system.
- By providing justifications for society, religion distorts reality and helps to produce false class consciousness. This blinds members of the oppressed class to their true situation.
- Ruling classes also adopt religious beliefs to justify their dominance to themselves and others.

Evidence to support Marxism

There is considerable evidence to support the Marxist view of religion. Here are two examples.

1 There are many examples from history where ruling groups have used religion to justify their dominance. The caste system in traditional India was justified by Hindu religious beliefs; whilst in medieval Europe, kings and queens ruled by 'divine right'.

2 Bruce (1988) points out that, in the USA, conservative Protestants – the 'New Christian Right' – consistently support right-wing political candidates. Although they have had a limited influence on American politics, they have tended to defend the interests of the rich and powerful at the expense of other groups in the population.

The limitations of Marxism

- Some evidence suggests that religion does not always legitimate power and that it can sometimes provide an impetus for change.
- The fact that religion sometimes acts as an ideological force in the way suggested by Marx does not explain its existence.

Maduro – the relative autonomy of religion

Some neo-Marxists deny that religion is always a conservative force. Maduro (1982) claims that religion can be revolutionary. Members of the clergy can develop revolutionary potential where oppressed members of the population have no outlet for their grievances. This has occurred in Latin America where some Catholic priests have criticized ruling groups and helped organize resistance. This is known as liberation theology (see p. 77).

Gender, feminism and religion

Feminist theories follow Marxist theories in arguing that religion can be an instrument of domination and oppression. However, unlike Marxism, they see religion as a product of patriarchy (see p. 23) rather than capitalism.

- Armstrong (1993) points out that women occupy a marginal position in most major religions. Although they have made gains in many areas of life, their gains in most religions have been very limited.
- Women continue to be excluded from key roles in many religions (although the Church of England finally allowed the ordination of women priests in 1992). This is despite the fact that women often participate in organized religion more than men.

Women and resistance to religious oppression

Sociologists have come to acknowledge that women can no longer be seen as passive victims of religious oppression.

- Badawi (1994) notes that aspects of Islam are positive for women. For example, Islamic women keep their own family name when they get married.
- Watson (1994) examines the veiling of Islamic women. This practice is seen by many non-Muslim writers as a form of social control. However, Watson argues that veiling can have advantages for women in that it can reduce, or allow them to cope with, male oppression. For example, it reduces the possibility of sexual harassment and allows Muslim women to be judged for what they are rather than what they look like.

Stark and Bainbridge – religion and compensators

Unlike functionalist sociologists, Stark and Bainbridge see religion as meeting the needs of individuals rather than those of society as a whole.

Religion might not actually provide people with eternal life, but what it does offer is a 'compensator'. Compensators are a type of IOU – if individuals act in a particular way, they will eventually be rewarded. In the absence of immediate rewards, people are likely to turn to compensators.

Since religion answers universal questions and offers compensators that meet universal human needs, religion can neither disappear nor seriously decline.

Evaluation

1 Wallis and Bruce (1986) argue that the available evidence contradicts Stark and Bainbridge's theory, as established religions are declining (see pp. 79–82 on the secularization debate).
2 They also criticize Stark and Bainbridge for ignoring social and cultural influences on the questions individuals ask and the rewards they seek.

Religion and social change

Religion as a conservative force

Functionalists and Marxists have generally dismissed the possibility that religion can cause changes in society. They believe that religion acts as a conservative force and that it is changes in society that shape religion and not vice versa.

Religion can be seen as a conservative force in two senses.

1 Functionalists have claimed that it acts in this way because it promotes integration and social solidarity. In this way it facilitates the continued existence of society in its present form. Marx had similar views, although he saw religion as maintaining the status quo in the interests of the ruling class rather than those of society as a whole.
2 'Conservative' can also refer to traditional beliefs and customs. In some circumstances religion can support social change while at the same time promoting traditional values. This often occurs when there is a revival in fundamentalist religious beliefs.

Conservatism, fundamentalism and social change

Recent years have seen the rise of fundamentalist religious beliefs in different parts of the world. Taylor (1987) defines fundamentalism as involving the following:

1 A group perceives a challenge to an ultimate authority, usually a god, in which they believe.
2 The group decides that the challenge cannot be tolerated.
3 They reaffirm their belief in the authority that is being challenged.
4 They oppose those who have challenged the established beliefs and often use political means to further their cause.

If fundamentalists are successful, they succeed in defending traditional values, but at the same time they change society by reversing innovations that have taken place.

The most dramatic example of this process has been in Iran. During the 1960s and 1970s, Iran underwent a process of liberalization. Attitudes to women changed and there were good relations with the West. In 1979 the Iranian revolution took place, partly inspired by Islamic fundamentalism, and these changes were reversed.

In this case, religious beliefs contributed to producing revolutionary change. Religion did not act as a conservative force in one sense of the word. Nevertheless, in terms of supporting traditional values, it did act as a conservative force.

Weber – *The Protestant Ethic and the Spirit of Capitalism*

Both functionalists and Marxists emphasize the role of religion in promoting social integration and impeding social change. However, Weber (1930) argued that in some circumstances religion can lead to social change.

In his most famous book, *The Protestant Ethic and the Spirit of Capitalism*, Weber examines the relationship between the rise of a certain form of Protestantism known as Calvinism and the development of Western industrial capitalism.

Calvinist Protestantism originated in the seventeenth century. Calvin thought that there was a distinct group of the elect – those chosen to go to heaven – and that they had been chosen by God even before they were born. Those who were not among the elect could never gain a place in heaven.

This produced a psychological problem for Calvinists. They did not know whether they were among the elect. They suffered from an uncertainty about their status, and their behaviour was an attempt to convince themselves that they had been chosen to go to heaven.

The Protestant ethic

The Protestant ethic enabled Calvinists to convince themselves that they were among the elect. The ethic was ascetic, encouraging abstinence from life's pleasures, a simple lifestyle and rigorous self-discipline. It produced individuals who worked hard in their careers or callings. Making money was a concrete indication of success in one's calling, and success meant that the individual had not lost grace in God's sight.

The spirit of capitalism

Weber argued that underlying capitalism is the spirit of capitalism – a set of ideas, ethics and values. He claimed that ascetic Protestantism was a vital influence in the creation and development of the spirit and practice of capitalism, because the methodical and single-minded pursuit of a calling encourages the creation of wealth and restrictions on spending. This accumulation of capital produced the early businesses that expanded to create capitalist society.

Evaluation

Weber's book has received both criticism and support.

1 It has been argued that Calvinism was strong in some parts of the world where capitalism did not develop until much later, such as Switzerland and Scotland. However, Marshall (1982) counters this by pointing out that Weber did not claim that Calvinism was the only factor necessary for the development of capitalism.
2 Kautsky (1953) argues from a Marxist perspective that early capitalism preceded and largely determined Protestantism. In his view, Protestantism became the ideology capitalists used to legitimate their position.
3 Another criticism questions the view that it was the religious beliefs of Calvinists that led to them becoming business people. Instead they devoted themselves to business because they were excluded from holding public office and joining certain professions by law.

Religion and social change – conclusion

Many sociologists now accept that religion can be a force for change. Nelson (1986) points to a number of instances where religion has undermined stability or promoted change:

- In Northern Ireland, Roman Catholicism has long been associated with Irish Republicanism.
- In the USA in the 1960s the Reverend Martin Luther King played a leading role in establishing civil rights.
- Also in the 1960s a number of radical groups emerged within the Roman Catholic church in Latin America. They preached liberation theology, arguing that it was

the duty of church members to fight against unjust and oppressive right-wing dictatorships.
- In Iran, Islamic fundamentalism played a part in the 1979 revolution.
- The Roman Catholic church in Poland opposed the communist state and supported the free trade union Solidarity.
- In South Africa, Archbishop Desmond Tutu was a prominent opponent of apartheid.

Conservative or radical religion?

McGuire (1981) examines the factors that influence the type of role that religion plays in society. She identifies four main factors that determine the potential of religion to change society.

1 Beliefs – the beliefs of a particular religion will influence its role in society. For example, religions that emphasize adherence to strong moral codes are more likely to produce members who are critical of society and seek to change it.
2 Culture – in societies where religious beliefs are central to the culture, anyone wishing to produce change tends to use a religious legitimation for their actions. In Britain, however, religion plays a less central role, so it is less significant in justifying social change.
3 Social location – where an established church or other religious organization plays a major role in political and economic life, there is considerable scope for religion to have an impact on processes of change.
4 Internal organization – religions with a strong, centralized source of authority have more chance of affecting events.

Religious organizations

Table 7.1 (on the following page) illustrates some of the key differences between the main kinds of religious organizations. However, some sociologists have suggested that these categorizations may be over-simplified when applied to contemporary societies.

The church

- Bruce (1996) argues that the concept of a church is primarily useful in describing pre-modern Christian societies. The development of religious pluralism (many different religious groups) in modern societies makes it difficult for the state to lend exclusive support to one religion because a single set of religious beliefs is no longer taken for granted and reinforced by all groups in society.
- Robertson (1987) argues that there has been an increase in church–state tensions throughout the world. There is little room for religious concerns in the world of international trade and diplomacy, so governments may come into conflict with the moral concerns of domestic churches.

Denominations

- Stark and Bainbridge (1985) are critical of the concept of a denomination. They claim that the division of religious organizations into separate types obscures rather than clarifies the differences between them.

	Church	Denomination	Sect
Sociologist identifying these factors	Troeltsch (1931)	Niebuhr (1929)	Troeltsch (1931)
Example	Roman Catholic Church	Methodism	Jehovah's Witnesses
Social background of members	Members are drawn from all classes in society, although the upper class are particularly likely to join	Does not have universal appeal; not connected with the upper class	Connected with the lower classes
Relationship to state	Sometimes closely related to the state	Does not identify with the state and approves the separation of church and state	
Relationship to society	Churches accept and affirm life in this world	Members generally accept the norms and values of society	Members reject the values of the world that surrounds them
Demands on members	Members do not have to demonstrate their faith to become members of a church	Some minor restrictions may be placed on members – e.g. Methodists are discouraged from drinking and gambling	Members may be expected to withdraw from life outside the sect. Deep commitment demanded from members
Tolerance	Often churches will jealously guard their monopoly of religious faith	Denominations do not claim a monopoly of religious truth and are tolerant of other religions	Sects tend to believe that they possess a monopoly of religious truth
Type of organization	A formal organization with a hierarchy of paid officials	Usually smaller than a church but still a formal organization with a hierarchy of paid officials	Central authority often rests with a charismatic leader whose special qualities persuade others to follow him

Table 7.1 Comparing religious organizations: churches, denominations and sects

Sects

- Bruce acknowledges that sects can prosper in modern societies where people have more opportunity to form subcultures. Even with the greater toleration of contemporary societies, however, some sects may come into serious conflict with the wider society. In the 1990s there were a number of instances involving the deaths of sect followers – for example, the deaths of more than 80 Branch Davidians in the siege at Waco in Texas.
- Wilson (1982) argues that Troeltsch's description of sects does not account for the increase in the number of sects in Europe and the USA in recent decades. Some of these new religious movements are examined in the next sections.

Cults

Cults tend to be more individualistic than other organized forms of religion because they often lack a fixed set of beliefs. They tolerate other beliefs, and their own beliefs are often vague. They often have customers rather than members, and customers may have relatively little involvement with the organization once they have learned the basics. Many aspects of the New Age movement (see p. 81) are based around cults.

Wallis – The Elementary Forms of the New Religious Life

The development of a range of new religions in the 1970s led Wallis (1984) to categorize these as new religious movements. He divides new religious movements into three main groups based on their relationship to the outside world. He distinguishes between them according to whether the movement and its members reject, accommodate or affirm the world.

World-rejecting new religious movements

- World-rejecting new religious movements have most of the characteristics of a sect described by Troeltsch.
- Their ideology is highly critical of the outside world, and the movement expects or seeks change.
- In order to achieve salvation, members are expected to have a sharp break from conventional life when they join the movement. Organizations of this type act as total institutions, controlling all aspects of their members' lives. As a result, they often develop a reputation for 'brainwashing' their members, since families and friends find it hard to understand the change that has taken place in a member.
- Most are based around a communal lifestyle, and as such develop unconventional ways of living. The ill-fated Branch Davidians in Waco, Texas, are a case in point.

World-accommodating new religious movements

- World-accommodating new religious movements are usually offshoots of an existing major church or denomination. For example, Pentecostalist groups are variants of Protestant religions.
- Typically these groups neither accept nor reject the world as it is, they simply live with it. They are concerned with religious rather than worldly questions.
- World-accommodating sects seek to restore the spiritual purity to a religion, which they believe has been lost in more conventional churches and denominations. Pentecostalists, for example, hold that the belief in the Holy Spirit has been lost in other Christian religions.

World-affirming new religious movements

- World-affirming new religious movements are very different from all other religious groups and may lack some of the features normally associated with a religion. However, these groups do claim to be able to provide access to supernatural or spiritual powers, and in that sense can be regarded as religions.
- Rather than rejecting existing society or existing religions, world-affirming groups accept the world as it is. They offer the follower the potential to be successful in terms of the dominant values of society by unlocking spiritual powers within the individual.
- Followers of world-affirming movements carry on normal lives and there is little social control over the members or customers.
- An example of a world-affirming new religious movement is Transcendental Meditation or TM. TM is based on the Hindu religion and was first introduced to the West in the late 1950s, achieving prominence when adopted by the Beatles in 1968. It is claimed that the meditation technique can

provide 'unbounded awareness' which can have beneficial effects for individuals and society.

- To Wallis, most world-affirming movements are cults, since, unlike sects, they tolerate the existence of other religions, have a rapid turnover of membership and are relatively undemanding on their followers.

Evaluation

Wallis realizes that no religious group will conform exactly to his categories. He recognizes that some groups occupy the middle ground, incorporating elements of all three categories.

Beckford (1985) offers some criticisms of Wallis:

1 He argues that Wallis's categories are difficult to apply. It is not clear whether it is the teachings of the movement or the beliefs and outlooks of individual members that distinguish the different attitudes to the world.
2 Wallis pays insufficient attention to the diversity of views that exists within a sect or cult.
3 Beckford also questions the value of defining some groups as 'world-rejecting'. In his view, no group is able to reject the world altogether.

Reasons for the growth of sects, cults and new religious movements

Religious sects and cults have existed for centuries, but the 1960s saw the growth of many new examples of these religious groups. This growth can be explained in terms of why individuals choose to join or in terms of wider social changes. In fact the two explanations are linked, because social changes affect the number of people available as potential recruits.

Marginality

Weber provided one of the earliest explanations for the growth of sects. He argued that they were likely to arise within groups that were marginal in society. Members of groups outside the mainstream of social life often feel that they are not receiving the rewards they deserve. Some sects offer explanations for the disprivilege of members and promise them a better future either on earth or in the afterlife.

In part, the growth of sects such as the Black Muslims in the USA in the 1960s was accomplished through recruitment from disadvantaged groups.

However, most of the members of world-rejecting sects in the 1960s and 1970s came from young, white, middle-class backgrounds. Wallis (1984) does not believe that this contradicts the marginality theory. Many of the recruits had become marginal in society because they were 'hippies, drop-outs, surfers, LSD and marijuana users'.

Relative deprivation

Relative deprivation refers to subjectively perceived deprivation. In objective terms the poor are more deprived than the middle class, but in subjective terms certain members of the middle class may feel more deprived than the poor. They do not lack material wealth, but they feel spiritually deprived in a world they see as too materialistic, lonely and impersonal. They seek salvation in the sense of community offered by the sect.

Social change

Wilson (1970) argues that sects arise during periods of rapid social change when traditional norms are disrupted. He uses the example of the early Methodist movement, which had the characteristics of a sect. This grew up as the response of the urban working class to industrialization. In a situation of change and uncertainty, it offered the support of a close-knit community, clear norms and values, and a promise of salvation.

Bruce (1995, 1996) believes that the weakness of conventional religions has encouraged some people to consider less traditional alternatives. As modern societies developed, faith in traditional forms of authority declined and denominations became popular. In contemporary secular societies, cults have become more popular because they require fewer sacrifices and less commitment than churches and sects.

The appeal of world-rejecting new religious movements

- Wallis (1984) argues that world-rejecting new religious movements were attractive to young people in the 1960s because they offered a more spiritual and caring way of life.
- Bruce (1995) sees their appeal as deriving from the failure of the youth 'counter-culture' to radically change the world. Disillusioned young people sought their path to salvation through religion instead of peace and love.

The appeal of world-affirming new religious movements

- Bruce believes that world-affirming movements have grown because people find it difficult to gain satisfaction and a sense of identity from their work in contemporary societies. They no longer have a sense of calling to their work and may not identify strongly with their workmates. World-affirming movements offer a solution – they offer people both success and a spiritual element to their lives.

Secularization

Support for the secularization thesis

Many classical sociologists believed that industrialization and the growth of scientific knowledge would lead to secularization, which can broadly be defined as the process of religious decline. Many contemporary sociologists have followed in their footsteps, arguing that modern societies are not compatible with the retention of a central role for religion. For example, Wilson (1966) defines secularization as 'the process whereby religious thinking, practice and institutions lose social significance'.

Problems with the secularization thesis

1 Some sociologists have questioned the idea that religion was as important in the past as has been widely assumed.
2 The role of religion in different modern societies varies considerably. It is possible that secularization is a feature of some societies but not others.
3 The concepts of religiosity and secularization are not given the same meaning by different

sociologists. Problems arise because of the absence of a generally agreed definition.

4 Some postmodernists argue that faith and religion may be rediscovered in a postmodern world in which science and rationality have limited appeal.

The question of secularization will now be discussed in terms of some of the varying definitions that have been used.

Institutional religion – participation

Some researchers have measured the importance of religion in society in terms of institutional factors such as church attendance, membership and participation in religious ceremonies.

Some of this evidence does point towards secularization but:

- The patterns vary between countries.
- The reliability and validity of the statistics are open to question.

Church attendance in Britain

- Church attendance figures show a continuing drop in attendance throughout the twentieth century, particularly in Anglican, Baptist, Catholic and United Reformed churches.
- Attendance at special Christian ceremonies such as baptisms and marriages has also declined. In 1900, 65% of children were baptized; by 1993 it had dropped to 27%.

Church membership in Britain

- Overall, there has been a decline in membership of religious organizations in the UK.
- Institutional Christian religions have declined most, while many non-Christian and smaller religions have gained members.

Religious participation in the USA

- Rates of religious participation in the USA are much higher than those in Britain.

Interpreting the evidence on participation and membership

Most of the long-term evidence on membership and attendance in Britain seems to support the secularization theory. Although recent years have seen a growth in smaller religious organizations, there is little doubt that fewer people attend a place of worship or belong to a religious organization.

In the USA, however, the evidence seems to support those who question the secularization theory.

In both cases, the reliability and validity of the statistics are open to question:

- Nineteenth-century statistics pose problems because the methods of data collection do not meet today's standards of reliability.
- Different criteria are used to record membership in different religions.
- US statistics are based on survey evidence, and it has been suggested that more people claim to attend a place of worship than actually do.

The decline in church attendance in Britain can be interpreted in a number of different ways:

- Martin (1969) claims that in the nineteenth century church-going was a sign of middle-class respectability to a greater extent than it is today.
- Religion today may be expressed in other ways. Religion may have become privatized; people develop their own beliefs and see religious institutions as less important.

Belief, church-going and atheism

Opinion poll data generally find that many more people retain religious beliefs than are members of religious organizations or regular attenders at places of worship. Only 10% of people in Britain and 1% of people in Northern Ireland denied the existence of God outright in the 1991 *British Social Attitudes Survey*.

However, Bruce (1995) points out that the results of a number of surveys show a decline in the belief in sin, the soul, heaven, life after death, and the devil.

Religious belief and participation may be the obvious place to look for evidence of secularization. However, some theorists, such as Casanova (1994), argue that that the role of religion in society is more significant in assessing whether secularization is occurring.

Institutional religion – disengagement, differentiation and societalization

Disengagement

Some sociologists have seen the truly religious society as one in which the church as an institution is very powerful in every aspect of society. A disengagement or withdrawing of the church from wider society is seen as secularization. Martin (1969) sees this view as concerned with decline in the power, wealth, prestige and influence of the church. In medieval Europe, the church and state were very close; today the church is hardly represented in government.

However, Martin points out that the church's contemporary concern with purely spiritual matters represents a purer form of religion, unblemished by secular concerns such as politics.

Casanova (1994) believes that religion is still important in public life. During the 1980s, religion was linked to political conflicts such as the conflict between Jews and Muslim Arabs in the Middle East and between Protestants and Catholics in Northern Ireland. Casanova does not reject the secularization theory, but he does argue that there has been a deprivatization of religion.

Structural and social differentiation

An alternative to the view that disengagement equals secularization is provided by Parsons (1951, 1960, 1965). Parsons agrees that the church has lost many of its former functions. He argues that the evolution of society involves a process of structural differentiation: parts of the social system become more specialized and so perform fewer functions.

However, this process does not necessarily lessen the importance of social institutions. As we saw in a previous section (p. 75), Parsons argues that religious beliefs still give meaning and significance to life.

Bruce (1995) discusses what is essentially the same process but he refers to it as social differentiation. He argues that social life in modern societies is dominated by the logic of capitalist production with its emphasis on efficiency and profit. Religious faith is not significant.

Societalization

Bruce uses the term societalization to refer to a process in which social life becomes fragmented and ceases to be locally based. The decline of communities in modern societies undermines religion in three ways:

1 Churches can no longer serve as the focal point for communities.
2 People's greater involvement with the broader society leads them to look more widely for services. They are less likely to turn to the local vicar or priest for support.
3 The cultural diversity of the society in which people live leads them to hold beliefs with less certainty.

Institutional religion – religious pluralism

Some researchers imply that the truly religious society has one faith and one church. This picture is influenced by the situation in some small-scale societies, such as the Australian Aboriginals, described by Durkheim (see p. 74).

Modernization and industrialization tend to create a plurality of cultural and religious groups. This reminds individuals that their beliefs are a matter of personal choice and no longer part and parcel of their membership of society.

Some argue that religious pluralism is not incompatible with a society in which religion thrives. It is not necessary for everyone to share the same beliefs for religion to be important. Northern Ireland is a case in point.

Pluralism in modern societies stems from two main sources which we will now examine:

1 The existence of different ethnic groups.
2 The growth of sects and cults.

Ethnicity and religious diversity

Bruce (1996) acknowledges that certain ethnic groups retain strong religious beliefs. However, he does not see this as an argument against the secularization theory. He believes that religion remains strong because of its social importance rather than because of any deep religious convictions among members of the groups.

Bruce argues that religion tends to serve one of two main purposes for ethnic groups:

1 Cultural defence – where two communities are in conflict and they are of different religions, their religious identity becomes a way of asserting their ethnic pride. Bruce gives the example of Ian Paisley's Democratic Unionist Party in Northern Ireland. Only a tiny percentage of the population of Northern Ireland are members of the religious group associated with the party, but many more support the party. This is because, according to Bruce, ethnic Protestants identify with the party's opposition to a united Ireland, not because of the religious convictions of the party's leaders.

2 Cultural transition – in this case religion is used as a resource for dealing with situations where people have to adjust their identity. For example, Asian and Afro-Caribbean migrants to Britain can use mosques, temples and churches as centres for their communities, and they can use their religion as a way of coping with the difficulties of being Asian or black and British.

Bruce believes that these processes keep religion relevant but do not create a religious society. Brown (1992) disagrees and sees 'ethnic defence' as a key function of religion in the modern world.

There is certainly plenty of evidence that religion remains strong among many ethnic minorities. Chryssides (1994) argues that in Britain the religions of immigrant groups and their descendants have had three paths open to them:

1 Apostasy – religious beliefs are abandoned in a hostile environment.
2 Accommodation – religious beliefs are adapted to take account of the changed situation.
3 Renewed vigour – religion is asserted more strongly as a reaction to the hostility against it.

Examples of all three responses can be found, but the general pattern is one of accommodation and renewed vigour, with buildings being converted into mosques and religious practices being maintained or adapted.

Sects, cults and secularization

The apparent vitality of sects (see pp. 78–9) seems to provide evidence against the theory of secularization.

● Greeley (1972) believes that the growth of new religious movements represents a process of resacrilization: interest and belief in the sacred are being revived.
● Since the 1980s, interest has grown in a range of beliefs such as tarot cards, astrology and traditional medicines. These sorts of ideas have been referred to as 'New Age'. Heelas (1996) regards the 'New Age' movement as significant. He points out that opinion poll evidence suggests substantial belief in reincarnation, horoscopes and flying saucers.

Other sociologists see the growth of sects and new religious movements as evidence of secularization.

● Wilson (1982) believes that sects are the last outpost of religion in societies where religious beliefs and values are of little significance.
● Bruce (1995, 1996) argues that new religious movements recruit very small numbers compared to the decline in mainstream Christian religions. World-rejecting sects have affected the smallest number of people, while world-accommodating groups – who have least influence on people's lives – have recruited the most.

Institutional religion – the secularization of religious institutions in the USA

Herberg – denominations and internal secularization

According to Herberg (1960), the main evidence for secularization in the USA is to be found in the decline of the religiosity of churches and denominations themselves. These organizations have compromised their religious beliefs to fit in with the wider society.

Herberg claims that the major denominations in America have undergone a process of secularization. They increasingly reflect the American 'way of life' rather than the word of God.

Herberg's argument has been challenged using the example of the New Christian Right in the USA.

The New Christian Right

Roof and McKinney (1987) note the growth of conservative Protestant religions (sometimes called the New Christian Right) which seem to combine a serious commitment to religious teachings with a refusal to compromise religious beliefs. As such, they appear to contradict Herberg's claims.

Criticism

Bruce (1988) argues that the New Christian Right has had very little impact. Very few of its members who have stood for national office have won their elections, for example. The only reason it gets so much attention, Bruce argues, is because its members are unusual for holding strong religious convictions in a secular world.

Religion and society – desacrilization

A number of sociologists have argued that society has been undergoing a process of desacrilization. This means that supernatural forces are no longer seen as controlling the world, and action is no longer directed by religious belief.

Disenchantment

Weber provided one of the earliest statements of the desacrilization theory. He believed that modern societies are characterized by disenchantment: they are no longer charged with mystery and magic; the supernatural has been banished from society. Instead they are based on rational action: actions are based on deliberate and precise calculation and logic.

Science and reason

Bruce (1988) stresses the specific role of scientific beliefs in undermining religion. He argues that technological advances reduce the number of things that need to be explained in religious terms. Science has given individuals a greater sense of control over the natural world and less need to resort to supernatural explanations and remedies.

Bruce acknowledges that such events as the death of a loved one may lead people to turn to God. However, they usually do this as individuals and as a last resort after rational explanations have been exhausted.

The theory of postmodernism suggests that societies have begun to move beyond the scientific rationality of modernity, partly because of growing distrust of science. People are increasingly aware of the failures of science (such as the failure to find a cure for AIDS) and the damaging side-effects of science and technology (such as environmental damage).

Secularization – international comparisons

By concentrating on Britain and the USA, sociologists have taken a rather narrow view of social change and religion. Martin (1978) has looked at the changing role of religion in a range of societies. He finds different patterns of belief and participation in different societies.

Martin argues that the role and strength of religion in modern societies are determined by a number of factors:
1 The degree of religious pluralism and the dominant religion.
2 The political system and the relationship between church and state.
3 The extent to which religion helps to provide a sense of national, regional or ethnic identity.

Far from predicting the downfall of religion, Martin argues that it is likely to increase in importance because:
- Religion is no longer closely associated with rich and powerful elites. It has therefore become more acceptable to people from lower social classes.
- Rationalism has lost some of its appeal. There is growing interest in the supernatural and the religious.

Contemporary religious revivals

Kepel (1994) claims that any trend towards secularization was reversed in around 1975. Since then religious revivals have taken place around the world, often aimed at changing whole societies. Examples include Christianity in the USA and Europe, Judaism in Israel, and Islam throughout the world.

Secularization – conclusion

As the views of sociologists such as Martin and Kepel illustrate, the theory of secularization has not been definitely proved or disproved. This is partly because different writers have used the term 'secularization' in different ways. This has led to confusion since writers discussing the process of secularization are often arguing about different things.

Martin (1969) has actually suggested the removal of the term 'secularization' from the sociological vocabulary. Instead, he supports a careful and detailed study of the ways in which the role of religion has changed at different times and in different places.

(answers on p. 215)

1 Which one of the following statements would a functionalist be most likely to agree with?
   a Religion often causes social change
   b Religion often causes conflict in society
   c Religion reinforces shared values
   d Religion is an ideological tool

2 Three of the following statements are criticisms of Durkheim's views on religion. Which is the odd one out?
   a His sample of societies was so small it was not possible to generalize from it
   b He ignored the fact that religious beliefs often conflict with dominant values
   c His theories are only applicable to small traditional societies
   d He ignored the role of religion in meeting the needs of societies

3 Parsons would probably agree with three of the following statements. Which is the odd one out?
   a Religion helps people to make sense of their experiences
   b Religion helps deal with the problems that disrupt social life
   c Religion has some dysfunctional aspects
   d Religion provides guidelines for human action

4 Marx would probably agree with three of the following statements. Which is the odd one out?
   a Religion acts as a mechanism of social control
   b Religion is the opium of the people
   c Religion is functional for society
   d Religion creates false class consciousness

5 Which major religion is associated with the Indian caste system in which social position is fixed at birth?
   a Hinduism   b Buddhism
   c Islam   d Sikhism

6 Three of the following statements would be supported by most feminists. Which is the odd one out?
   a Women are excluded from key roles in most religions
   b Religion is an instrument of domination and oppression
   c Religious beliefs help women to deal with their problems
   d Most religious beliefs support patriarchy

7 Stark and Bainbridge believe that religion is never likely to disappear. What is their main reason for believing this?
   a Religion functions to hold societies together
   b Religion meets the needs of individuals in society
   c There is no evidence of significant religious decline in Britain
   d Religions have adapted well to social change

8 Which one of the following sociologists is most likely to believe that religion can play a role in changing societies?
   a Weber   b Marx
   c Parsons   d Durkheim

9 Many sociologists believe that religion is a conservative force in society. Which one of the following statements reflects this view?
   a Religion is unlikely to be a key factor in causing social change
   b Most religious believers are right-wing
   c Religion is very powerful
   d Religious fundamentalism is becoming increasingly popular

10 Which one of the following Christian sects did Weber use as an example in his book *The Protestant Ethic and the Spirit of Capitalism?*
   a Protestantism   b Pentecostalism
   c Calvinism   d Lutheranism

11 Which one of the following definitions best describes Weber's concept of the 'spirit of capitalism'?
   a A set of values which encourage the accumulation of wealth
   b A set of values which encourage a simple life and the avoidance of alcohol and other pleasures
   c The view that capitalism is the best economic system
   d A set of values based on Protestant beliefs

12 What name is given to the radical approach of Catholic priests in South America during the 1960s and 1970s?
   a The Protestant ethic
   b Liberation theology
   c The New Christian Right
   d Islamic fundamentalism

13 Three of the following are factors identified by McGuire as affecting the type of role religion plays in society. Which is the odd one out?
   a Internal organization   b Social location
   c Beliefs   d Secularization

14 Three of these characteristics are associated with churches. Which is the odd one out?
   a They are not usually linked to the state
   b Members are drawn from all sections of society
   c They accept and affirm life in this world
   d Believers do not have to demonstrate their faith to become a member

15 Three of these characteristics are associated with sects. Which is the odd one out?
   a They tend to reject the values of society
   b Central authority often rests with a charismatic leader
   c They are formal organizations with a hierarchy of paid officials
   d Members are often expected to withdraw from conventional life

16 Which one of the following organizations could be classed as a denomination?
   a Jehovah's Witnesses
   b The Church of England
   c Methodism
   d Scientology

17 Members of which sect died in the siege at Waco in Texas?
   a Moonies   b The People's Temple
   c Branch Davidians   d Roman Catholicism

18 Three of the following are characteristics of world-affirming new religious movements, according to Wallis. Which is the odd one out?
   a They claim to provide access to spiritual or supernatural powers
   b They are usually offshoots of a major church or denomination
   c They offer followers the potential to be successful
   d They tolerate the existence of other religions

19 Which one of the following explanations for the growth of sects was suggested by Weber?
   a They appeal to those in society who feel marginalized
   b They appeal to those who feel spiritually deprived
   c They arise during periods of rapid social change when traditional norms are disrupted
   d They arise as a result of the weakness of more conventional religions

20 Which one of the following is the most widely accepted definition of secularization?
   a The process whereby there is a decline in church membership and attendance
   b The process whereby people's belief in god or gods declines
   c The process whereby religious thinking, practice and institutions lose social significance
   d The process whereby people look more to science than to religion for explanations of the world

21 One of the following statements about religious participation is false. Can you identify it?
   a Church attendance is declining in Britain
   b Church attendance is declining in the USA
   c Non-Christian religions in Britain have gained members
   d Christian religions in Britain have lost members

22 According to opinion polls, approximately what percentage of people in Britain deny the existence of God completely?
   a 10%   b 20%   c 40%   d 60%

23 What is the name given to the process whereby the church withdraws from wider society?
   a Structural differentiation
   b Social differentiation
   c Societalization
   d Disengagement

24 What term is used to describe a society containing a wide variety of religious groups?
   a Cultural diversity
   b Religious pluralism
   c Ethnic diversity
   d Privatization of religion

25 Bruce argues that when two communities are in conflict their religious identity can become a way of asserting their ethnic pride. What term does he use to refer to this?
   a Cultural transition
   b Cultural defence
   c Cultural diversity
   d Cultural pluralism

26 Chryssides argues that in Britain the religious beliefs of immigrant groups have three paths open to them. Which of the following is not one of those paths?
   a Denial   b Apostasy
   c Accommodation   d Renewed vigour

27 Which one of the following statements is a definition of desacrilization?
   a Supernatural forces are no longer seen as controlling the world
   b There is a decline in sacred objects and symbols
   c Secularization is occurring
   d Conventional religions are losing support

28 What does Bruce identify as being particularly important in undermining religious belief?
   a The development of Communism
   b The development of science
   c The development of the nation-state
   d The development of industrial production

29 Kepel argues that a religious revival is taking place around the world. Which one of the following is not a possible example of this 'religious revival'?
   a Christianity in the USA
   b The Church of England in the UK
   c Judaism in Israel
   d Islam throughout the world

30 What view does Martin hold about the debate on secularization?
   a The case for secularization has been proved
   b The case against secularization has been proved
   c Secularization is occurring in certain societies but not in others
   d Secularization is not a useful term for understanding the changing role of religion in society

Develop your analysis and evaluation skills

see p. 201 for guidance notes

For each of the following statements, identify which sociologists would argue in favour of and which against the view expressed. Explain the reasons for their view.

1 The functionalist perspective on religion ignores the role of religion in causing conflict in society.
2 Religion is a conservative force in society.
3 The growth of new religious movements since the 1960s is due to rapid social change.
4 Church membership and attendance statistics indicate a clear decline in religiosity.
5 Secularization is occurring in modern societies.

Answer the question in Part One and one question from Part Two

Total: 60 marks   1 mark = 1.5 minutes

Time allowed: 1 hour 30 minutes

Part One

ITEM A

Church of England Sunday attendance has sunk to the lowest ever, according to Church statistics published in 1994. Even Christmas services were affected, with numbers falling by 7%, although church officials blamed poor weather and took some comfort from the fact that Easter services had become more popular.

Churchgoers' direct donations had increased by more than inflation and this was interpreted as a sign of a more committed membership.

Criticisms
- Only one religious institution
- Out of date
- Cannot generalize from one year's figures
- Ideological bias in interpreting the data

Measures of religious practice

Comments on the question	Question	Advice on preparing your answer
• There are many points you can pick up on from the item with careful and critical reading • You must go beyond the information in the item to gain full marks	[a] Using material from Item A and elsewhere, examine some of the problems in measuring religious practice. [8 marks]	• See p. 80 and answer 4 in the Guidance notes for Chapter 7 (p. 201)
• This requires that you demonstrate evaluation skills • This means that you can use these and others • Make sure that you understand and use this term correctly (see Chapter 14, p. 171–4)	[b] Discuss how far religious practices such as those in Item A are a valid indicator of religiosity. [12 marks]	• p. 80 looks at participation as a form of religious practice • Other aspects of religiosity can be found on pp. 79–82

Part Two

Answer **one** question from this part

Comments on the question	Question	Advice on preparing your answer
• Identify the source of this view as a Weberian one • Make specific criticisms of this material • Suggest alternative evidence and arguments that would oppose this view • The best answers will consider both these parts of the question • Better answers will see social change as a problematic concept	Either: Assess the evidence and arguments that religious beliefs can encourage social change. [40 marks]	• Weberian views, pp. 76–7 • Evidence for this, pp. 76–7 • Critique, p. 77 • Alternative views: Marxist, p. 73; functionalist, pp. 74–5 • See also answer 2 in Guidance notes, p. 201 • You should also look at the evidence that religion stifles social change
• You cannot successfully do this by writing two consecutive descriptive accounts. You need to identify similarities and differences in the two approaches • Consider the following questions: 1 What perspective do they adopt? 2 What is the origin of religion? 3 How does religion perform social control functions? 4 What purpose does religion serve for individuals and society? 5 What evidence can be used in support of or against each? • A question that looks deceptively simple, but you need to be prepared!	Or: Compare and contrast functionalist and Marxist explanations of the role of religion in society. [40 marks]	• You will need to analyse functionalist accounts (pp. 74–5) and Marxist accounts (p. 78), then use the answers to the questions opposite to write a short paragraph for each theory • You can use other theories, e.g. Weber (pp. 76–7), to show that they both fail to address change; and/or postmodernism on the death of the metanarrative (p. 149)

Answer both parts of this question

Total: 45 marks   1 mark = 1 minute

Time allowed: 45 minutes

Comments on the question	Question	Advice on preparing your answer
• Make sure that the examiner can see that you have clearly identified two characteristics • No more, no less • Make sure that you develop an explanation of why or how what you have identified qualifies as a characteristic of secularization	[a] Identify and explain two characteristics of secularization. [15 marks]	• You will find a definition of this term on p. 79 • The section on pp. 79–82 includes material that will help you with this task
• Describe the view as fully as possible using supporting evidence in the shape of statistical data and sociological studies • Consider arguments/evidence against the view and/or alternative view(s)	[b] Outline and assess the view that people join religious sects and cults as a way of coping with rapid social change. [30 marks]	• Remember that this is only one view. It is perfectly legitimate for you to challenge it • You should construct an introduction which defines sects and cults and which identifies where the view originates • You will find information on the social change argument on pp. 76–7

Chapter 8

Families and households

Specifications

Specification	Relevant module title	Place in module	Level	Assessment	Other relevant modules
AQA	1: **Families and Households**; Health; Mass Media	One of three options in this module.	AS	One data-response question	Material from this chapter may be used in the A2 synoptic module 6.
OCR	Culture and Socialization	**Family** is one of four options in this module.	AS	One or two two-part structured questions from a choice of two.	Material from this chapter may be used in the A2 synoptic module.

Families and households: essential notes

Is the family universal?

Variations in family structure
- The nuclear family
  This is the smallest family unit and consists of a husband, wife and their dependent offspring.
- The extended family
  This is a larger family grouping consisting of other members related by birth, marriage or adoption.

Murdock: the family – a universal social institution
In 1949 Murdock looked at 250 societies and claimed that some form of family existed in each.

He defined the family as a social group characterized by:
- Common residence
- Economic cooperation
- Reproduction
- Adults of both sexes, two of whom maintain a socially approved sexual relationship
- One or more children (own or adopted) of these adults

He concluded that the nuclear family is universal, either on its own or as the base unit within an extended family.

Evaluation of Murdock
Murdock's definition of the family includes at least one adult of each sex. However, many children, both today and in the past, have been raised in households that do not contain adults of both sexes.
- Gough's analysis (1959) of the Nayar society in India, before British rule was established in 1792, shows that women had several 'husbands' who took no responsibility for the care of their offspring.
- A significant proportion of black families in the West Indies, Central America and the USA are

matrifocal (female-headed) families and do not include adult males.
- Sheeran (1993) argues that the 'female-carer core' is the most basic family unit. In Britain, for example, children usually have one woman who is primarily responsible for their care. This primary carer is not always the biological mother. It could be a grandmother, elder sister, aunt, adoptive mother or other female.
- Gay and lesbian households may well contain children, either from a previous heterosexual relationship or as the result of new reproductive technologies. Callahan (1997) argues that gay and lesbian households should be seen as families. If marriage were available, many gay and lesbian couples would marry, and their relationships are not significantly different from those in heterosexual households.

Whether the family is regarded as universal ultimately depends on how the family is defined. It may be a somewhat pointless exercise to try to find a single definition that embraces all the types of household and relationship that can reasonably be called families.

The family – a functionalist perspective

The analysis of the family from a functionalist perspective involves three main questions:
- What are the functions of the family for society?
- What are the functional relationships between the family and the wider social system?
- What are the functions of the family for individuals?

Murdock – the universal functions of the family
Murdock (1949) argues that the family performs four basic functions for individuals and society and that these are applicable to all societies:

1 Sexual – essential for the continuation of the society
2 Reproductive – as for sexual
3 Economic – essential for survival (for example, the production and preparation of food)
4 Educational – essential for passing on the society's culture to the next generation

Criticisms of Murdock

1 Murdock does not consider whether the above functions could be performed by other social institutions.
2 Morgan (1975) points out that Murdock presents the nuclear family as a totally harmonious institution. Later sections will question this view.

Parsons – the 'basic and irreducible' functions of the family

Parsons (1955, 1965) argued that the family retains two 'basic and irreducible' functions which are common to the family in all societies. These are the 'primary socialization of children' and the 'stabilization of adult personalities'.

Primary socialization

Primary socialization refers to socialization during the early years of childhood. The child's personality is moulded to the point where the central values of the society's culture become a part of him or her. Parsons could think of no other social institution that could provide the warmth, security and mutual support necessary for the successful socialization of individuals.

Stabilization of adult personalities

The emphasis here is on the marital relationship and the emotional security the couple provide for each other. This acts to balance out the stresses and strains of everyday life. The family also allows adults to 'act out' the childish parts of their personalities.

Criticisms of Parsons

1 Parsons presents an idealized view of the family.
2 His picture is based largely on the American middle-class family. He ignores variations in families – for example, among different classes and ethnic groups.
3 Like Murdock, Parsons fails to explore alternatives to the family.
4 Parsons sees socialization as a one-way process and ignores the active role that children play in creating their own personalities.
5 Some contemporary perspectives argue that the family cannot be seen as performing functions on its own. It has to be seen in relation to other social institutions.

Critical views of the family

The functionalist view that the family benefits both society and its members has come under strong attack.

Leach – *A Runaway World?*

Leach (1967) was an anthropologist who studied small-scale pre-industrial societies where families were often part of a wider kinship unit and a close community. By comparison, in modern societies the nuclear family is largely isolated from kin and the wider community.

The result is that the demands made on the nuclear family are too great. Family members demand too much from each other and create barriers between themselves and the wider society. The result is conflict.

Laing – *The Politics of the Family*

R.D. Laing's work was based on the study of families where one member was diagnosed as schizophrenic. He shows how the family can be a destructive and exploitative institution in which there is constant demand for mutual concern and attention and considerable potential for harm as a result.

Criticisms of Leach and Laing

1 Neither has conducted detailed fieldwork on the family in contemporary industrial society.
2 Both talk about 'the family' without reference to variations in families – for example, according to social class.
3 To some degree each starts with a picture of a society out of control. Such a view will inevitably result in an unbalanced and extreme picture of the family. However, functionalists can equally be accused of the opposite bias.

Marxist perspectives on the family

Engels – the origin of the family

Engels (1972, originally published 1884) attempted to trace the evolution of the family through time. The monogamous nuclear family developed to solve the problem of the inheritance of private property. Property was owned by males, who needed to be sure of their heirs in order to pass it on. They needed greater control over women so that there would be no doubt over the paternity of their offspring. The monogamous family provided the most efficient device for this purpose.

Zaretsky – personal life and capitalism

Zaretsky (1976) sees the family as a major prop to the capitalist system.

- The capitalist system is based on the domestic labour of housewives who reproduce future generations of workers.
- The family consumes the products of capitalism and this enables the bourgeoisie to keep profits up.

Feminist perspectives on the family

The influence of feminism

In recent years feminism has had more influence on the study of the family than any other approach.

Feminists have been highly critical of the effects of family life upon women.

Feminist approaches have:

- Introduced the study of areas of family life such as housework and domestic violence.
- Challenged established views about male dominance in families.

- Highlighted the economic contribution to society of women's domestic labour.
- Focused on power relationships within the family, in particular the ways in which men benefit from families at the expense of women.

Some recent feminist approaches have questioned the tendency of some feminists to make blanket condemnations of family life and have emphasized the different experiences of women in families.

Marxist feminist perspectives on the family
Marxist feminists argue that the family and its exploitation of women serve the needs of capitalism.
- Benston (1972) points out that the fact that the husband must pay for the production and upkeep of the next generation weakens his bargaining power at work – he cannot go on strike because he has a family to support.
- Ansley (1972) argues that the emotional support provided by wives acts as a safety valve for the husbands' frustration at working within the capitalist system.
- Feeley (1972) sees the family as an authoritarian unit dominated by the husband. It teaches children to submit to parental authority and accept their place in the hierarchy of capitalist society.

Criticisms
1 Variations in family life – according to class and ethnic group, for example – are ignored.
2 Morgan (1975) points out that Marxist approaches often assume the existence of very traditional families – a type of family that is becoming less common.
3 Marxist feminists may exaggerate the harm done to women in the family. They are reluctant to concede that there may be positive elements to family life.
4 They also tend to portray women as the passive victims of exploitation.

Radical feminist perspectives on the family
There are many different types of radical feminism. Bryson identifies two characteristics they have in common:
1 Radical feminism is new and not adapted from existing theories.
2 It sees the oppression of women as the most significant aspect of society. Society is seen as patriarchal or male-dominated.
- Delphy and Leonard (1992) argue that the family is a patriarchal and hierarchical institution through which men dominate and exploit women. Wives may resist male domination but they find it difficult to escape from the patriarchal family.
- Purdy (1997) argues that women's disadvantages largely result from childcare responsibilities. She believes that there are many disadvantages of motherhood. It is expensive and a long-term commitment in terms of time and energy. She advocates a 'baby-strike'. Only then would men take women's demands for equality seriously.

Criticisms
Many of the criticisms of Marxist feminism also apply to radical feminism.

Difference feminism
Neither Marxist nor radical feminism is very sensitive to differences between families. Both can be criticized for failing to acknowledge the variety of domestic arrangements and the range of effects family life can have.

Increasingly feminists have begun to highlight these differences. These feminists have been referred to as difference feminists. Their work often has links with postmodern theories of the family.
- Nicholson (1997) believes that there is a powerful ideology supporting traditional families while devaluing other types. She believes that alternative families are often better than traditional ones for the women who live in them. Nicholson concludes that all types of family and household should be accepted because they could suit different women in different circumstances.
- Calhoun (1997) focuses on lesbian families. She argues that modern family life is characterized by choice, and lesbian and gay families are 'chosen families'. Calhoun believes that gay and lesbian relationships are just as much family relationships as those of heterosexual couples.

Criticisms
1 Some difference feminists lose sight of the inequalities between men and women in stressing the range of choices open to people.
2 They also tend to neglect the common experiences shared by most women in families.

The family, industrialization and modernization

A major theme in the sociology of the family has been the relationship between the structure of the family and the process of industrialization (the move from an agricultural system to the mass production of goods in a factory system).

The pre-industrial family
One form of pre-industrial family found in some traditional peasant societies is known as the classic extended family.

Arensberg and Kimball's study of Irish farmers (1968) found the basic family unit to be the extended family, consisting of a male head, his wife and children, his ageing parents who have passed the farm on to him, and any unmarried brothers and sisters. Together they work as a unit of production, producing the goods necessary for the family's survival.

Some people have argued that, as industrialization proceeds, the classic extended family breaks up and the nuclear family emerges as the predominant family form.

Parsons – the 'isolated nuclear family'
Parsons (1959, 1965; Parsons and Bale 1955) argued that the isolated nuclear family is the typical family form in modern industrial society. It is isolated in the sense that relationships between the nuclear family and wider kin are a matter of choice rather than obligation. There are three key reasons for its suitability in industrial societies:

1 The evolution of society involves a process of structural differentiation. This means that institutions evolve which specialize in fewer functions. Specialist institutions such as businesses, schools and hospitals take over many of the functions of the family.

2 Parsons argued that there is a functional relationship between the isolated nuclear family and the economic system. In modern societies individuals are required to move to places where their particular skills are in demand. The isolated nuclear family is more suited to geographical mobility as it is not tied down with binding obligations to wider kin.

3 The isolated nuclear family is the best family form for societies where status is achieved rather than ascribed (fixed at birth). If adult children remained as part of an extended family unit, conflicts could arise if the son achieved a higher social position than his father, because within the family the father has more status.

Criticisms of Parsons

Cheal (1991) is sceptical about what he calls the modernist view of the family advocated by Parsons. Parsons argues that the nuclear family is well-adapted to modern societies and sees it in a positive light. Cheal argues that:

- There is nothing inevitable about modern institutions developing in such a way that they function well together.
- Parsons makes over-generalized statements about the family which have not stood up well to the passage of time.

Detailed historical accounts of the development of the family have also cast doubt on Parsons's views.

Laslett – the family in pre-industrial societies

Peter Laslett (1972, 1977) has studied family life and composition in pre-industrial England. For the period 1564 to 1821 he found that only about 10% of households contained kin beyond the nuclear family. His low figure may be due to:

- Short life expectancy
- Late marriage

Laslett found no evidence to support the view that the classic extended family was widespread in pre-industrial England.

Anderson – household structure and the Industrial Revolution

Using data from the 1851 census, Anderson found that in Preston almost a quarter of households contained kin other than the nuclear family. The bulk of these extended families occurred among the poor.

Anderson suggests the following reasons for this pattern:

1 In the absence of a welfare state, individuals were dependent on their kin in times of hardship.

2 The high death rate led to a large number of orphans who found a home with their relatives.

3 Additional members of a household lowered the share of the rent paid by each individual.

4 It was normal in factory towns for employers to recruit through kin.

Young and Willmott – four stages of family life

In their book, *The Symmetrical Family* (1973), Young and Willmott suggest that the family has gone through four main stages. We will concentrate on their analysis of the working-class family and the first three stages.

Stage 1 – the pre-industrial family

The pre-industrial family is a unit of production. It was gradually supplanted as a result of the Industrial Revolution. It did, however, continue into the nineteenth century and there are still some examples in farming families today.

Stage 2 – the early industrial family

This type developed in the nineteenth century and reached its peak in the early twentieth century. The family ceased to be a unit of production and responded to the new industrial society by extending its network to include relatives beyond the nuclear family.

This type of family is still found in some well-established working-class communities and is documented in Young and Willmott's famous study *Family and Kinship in East London*.

Stage 3 – the symmetrical family

By the early 1970s the stage 2 family had largely disappeared. The stage 3 family is nuclear and home-centred. Free time is spent doing chores and odd jobs, and leisure is mainly home-based. The conjugal bond between husband and wife is strong and they share work in the home. Young and Willmott use the term symmetrical family to describe the stage 3 nuclear family.

Reasons for the rise of the symmetrical family

1 A reduction in the need for kinship-based support because of rising wages and the welfare state.

2 Increased geographical mobility.

3 Reduction in the number of children per family.

4 More amenities and entertainment in the home, making it a more attractive place.

The 'Principle of Stratified Diffusion'

Young and Willmott believe that their theory of stratified diffusion explains many of the changes in family life. The theory states that what those at the top of the stratification system do today, those at the bottom will do tomorrow. The home-centred nuclear family began in the middle classes and eventually filtered down to the rest of society.

Families and kinship in the 1980s and 1990s

In a comparison of attitudes to the family in 1986 and 1995, McGlone *et al.* (1996) argue that families remain very important to people in contemporary Britain.

- Families remain an important source of help and support.
- Family contacts are still maintained even though family members tend to live farther apart than in the past.
- Differences between social classes remain significant, with the working class more likely to have frequent contact than the middle class.

Finch – family obligations and social change

Janet Finch (1989) has studied the changing nature of family obligations.

Finch rejects the view that there was a 'Golden Age' of the family which was undermined by the Industrial Revolution. She found no evidence, for example, that people automatically assumed responsibility for elderly relatives in pre-industrial times.

- Finch argues that kin relationships remain special to people and that people feel more sense of duty to their family than to anybody else.
- However, being independent is also important to family members, and reliance on kin is usually seen as a last resort.

The 'modified extended family'

In order to clear up confusion surrounding the term 'isolated nuclear family' a number of sociologists have used new terms to describe family structure today.

- Litwak uses the term 'modified extended family' to describe 'a coalition of nuclear families in a state of partial dependence'.
- Allan (1985) accepts Litwak's view that kin outside the nuclear family remain important, but he prefers the term 'modified elementary family'. The inner or 'elementary' family consists of wives and husbands, their parents, children, brothers and sisters, and within this unit there is a sense of obligation.
- Willmott (1988) claims that the dispersed extended family is becoming dominant in Britain. It consists of two or more related families who cooperate with each other even though they live some distance apart. Cars, public transport and telephones allow dispersed extended families to keep in touch.

Family diversity

Leach (1967) calls the image of the happily married couple – a male breadwinner and a female carer/housewife – with two children, the 'cereal packet image' of the family. This image is prominent in advertising.

However, recent research suggests that contemporary societies are characterized by a plurality of household and family types, and so the idea of a typical family is misleading.

Households in Britain

- There has been a steady decline in the proportion of British households consisting of married couples with dependent children, from 38% in 1961 to 23% in 1998.
- There has been a corresponding increase in single-person households.
- The proportion of single-parent households tripled from 2% in 1961 to 7% in 1998.

Types of diversity

Rhona and Robert Rapoport (1982) identify five types of family diversity in Britain:

1 Organizational diversity

There are variations in family structure, household type, patterns of kinship and differences in the division of labour in the household. There are also increasing numbers of reconstituted families – families formed after divorce and remarriage.

2 Cultural diversity

There are differences in the lifestyles of families of different ethnic origins and religious beliefs. (Ethnic diversity is discussed on pp. 81.)

3 Class diversity

There are differences between middle- and working-class families in relation to child-rearing and adult relationships.

4 Life-cycle diversity

Differences result from the stage in the life cycle of the family. Newly married couples without children may have a different family life from those with dependent children, for example.

5 Cohort diversity

This refers to the periods at which the family has passed through different stages of the family life cycle. High rates of unemployment during the 1980s, for example, may have increased the length of time children lived with their parents.

In addition to these five aspects of diversity, Eversley and Bonnerjea (1982) argue that there are distinctive patterns of family life in different areas of Britain: regional diversity. In the 'sun belt' of southern England, for example, two-parent upwardly mobile families are typical, whilst in rural areas strong kinship ties are more common.

Gay and lesbian families

Gay and lesbian households have become more common since the 1980s. Weeks, Donovan and Heaphey (1999) argue that gays and lesbians look on their households and even their friendship networks as 'chosen families'. They choose who to include in their families and negotiate their relationships.

New reproductive technologies

New reproductive technologies such as surrogate motherhood add an entirely new dimension to family diversity. The implication is that biology will no longer restrict the possibilities for forming and enlarging families by having children.

The increase in single-parent families

As mentioned earlier, single-parent families have become increasingly common in Britain. The figures must be interpreted with caution because they are only a snapshot and do not represent the changing family life of many individuals. Children may start their life in a single-parent family, but the single parent may well find a new partner, so the child will end up living with two parents.

The causes of single parenthood

People who are married can become single parents through:

- Divorce
- Separation
- Death of a spouse
  Single parents who have never married:
- May have been living with the parent of the child but subsequently separated.
- May not have been living with the parent of the child when the child was born.

The rise in lone motherhood (only 1 in 10 single-parent families are headed by a male) is closely linked to two factors:

1 Increases in the divorce rate (discussed on pp. 95–6).
2 Increases in births outside marriage – Brown (1995) suggests that in previous eras 'shotgun weddings' (couples getting married to legitimate a pregnancy) were common. Now partners may choose to cohabit rather than marry.

The Rapoports argue that the single-parent family is an important 'emerging form' of the family which is becoming accepted as a legitimate alternative to other family structures.

However, there is little evidence that a large number of single parents actively choose it as an alternative to dual parenthood. In a small-scale piece of research by Burghes and Brown (1995), all of the lone mothers in the sample aspired to forming a two-parent household.

The consequences of single parenthood
Some have argued that single parenthood has become a serious problem for society. Charles Murray, the New Right thinker, has gone so far as to claim that single parenthood has contributed to the creation of an anti-social underclass (see pp. 46–7).

Many sociologists disagree. McIntosh (1996) claims that lone mothers have been stigmatized and blamed for problems such as youth crime and unemployment.

However single parenthood is viewed, there is little doubt that it is associated with low living standards.

Effects on children
- McLanahan and Booth (1991) review the findings of American studies which seem to indicate that children are harmed by single parenthood. They are more likely to experience poverty, become delinquent and engage in drug abuse.
- However, as the authors themselves point out, these differences tend to stem from low income rather than the absence of a second parent.
- Burghes (1996) notes that some research indicates that children in families where parents divorce start to do poorly in education before the divorce takes place. This may reflect the quality of the family relationships, of which divorce is only one aspect.
- Cashmore (1985) argues that it is often preferable for a child to live with one caring parent than with one caring and one uncaring parent. Single parenthood can also give women greater independence than they have in other family situations.

Ethnicity and family diversity
Statistical evidence from the Policy Studies Institute survey (Modood *et al.*, 1997) suggests that there are differences in household types among different ethnic groups.
- Whites and Caribbeans had higher rates of divorce and cohabitation than other groups.
- Indians, Africans, Asians, Bangladeshis and Pakistanis were the ethnic groups most likely to be married.
- 90% of South Asian families with children had married parents, compared to 75% of white and 50% of Caribbean families.

- There had been a substantial increase in single parenthood in all of the above ethnic groups.

South Asian families
Ballard (1982, 1990) has examined South Asian families in Britain.
- Many children had the experience of two cultures. They behaved in ways that conformed to the culture of wider society for part of the time, but at home conformed to their ethnic subculture.
- Although children expected to have some say in their marriage partner, they did not reject the principle of arranged marriage.
- Despite the distance involved, most families retained links with their village of origin in Asia.
- In Britain, close family ties remained. By living close together, people were able to retain strong family links.

West Indian families in Britain
- Barrow (1982) found that mother-centred families could rely less on the support of female kin than they could in the West Indies. However, equivalent networks did build up in areas with high concentrations of West Indians.
- Berthoud and Beishon (1997) identified a low emphasis on long-term partnerships, especially formal marriage. British Afro-Caribbean families had high rates of divorce and separation and were more likely than other groups to have children outside marriage. Nevertheless, over half of Caribbean families with children were married or cohabiting in long-term relationships.

Ethnicity and family diversity – conclusion
The evidence suggests that immigrants and their descendants have adapted their family life to fit British circumstances but have not fundamentally altered the relationships on which their traditional family life was based.

Chester – the British neo-conventional family
In a strong attack on the idea that fundamental changes are taking place in British family life, Robert Chester (1985) argued that the changes have only been minor.
- If you look at the percentage of people rather than households, then nearly half the population still live in nuclear family households.
- It is inevitable that at any one time some people will not be members of nuclear family households. However, the vast majority of people still experience the parent–children household at some point.
- Chester accepts that many families are no longer 'conventional' in the sense that the husband is the sole breadwinner. He sees this type of family as a 'neo-conventional family' – little different from the conventional family apart from the increasing number of wives working for at least part of their married lives.

Family diversity – conclusion
Since Chester was writing, there has been a slow but steady drift away from nuclear families in Britain.

As Kiernan and Wicks point out (1990), the nuclear family is just one of several types people experience during their lives. And, as the Rapoports argued in 1982, the amount of family diversity indicates increasing acceptance of alternative households and families.

The changing functions of the family

The loss of functions
Many sociologists argue that the family has lost a number of its functions in modern industrial society. Institutions such as businesses, schools and welfare organizations now specialize in functions previously performed by the family.

Functionalist views
Parsons maintains that the family still has a vital role in preparing its members to meet the requirements of the social system (see pp. 89).

Fletcher (1966) disputes the claim that some of the family's functions have been lost. He argues that the family has retained its functions and that these have increased in importance. The family is no longer a unit of production, but the modern home-centred family is a vital economic unit of consumption – for washing machines, DVD players and so on.

Neo-Marxist views
Writers such as Marcuse (1972) argue that the capitalist-controlled media proclaim the virtues of family life and associate happy family life with the purchase of consumer products. This myth produces obedient, motivated workers and receptive consumers for capitalism.

Feminist views
Feminists disagree that the family has lost its economic function. They argue that much of the work that takes place in the family is not recognized as such because it is unpaid and usually done by women. (See pp. 89–90.)

Postmodernist and difference feminist views
These sociologists reject the view that there is any single type of family that always performs certain functions. With increasing diversity, some individual families and some types of family may be radical forces in society – for example, gay and lesbian families.

Conjugal roles

A major characteristic of the symmetrical family – which Young and Willmott claimed was developing when they were writing in the 1970s – was the sharing of domestic work and leisure activities between spouses (see p. 91). Relationships of this type are known as joint conjugal roles, as opposed to segregated conjugal roles.

Inequality within marriage
There is no generally accepted way of measuring inequality between husbands and wives. Different researchers have measured it in different ways. However, most find little evidence that inequality in marriage has been significantly reduced.

Conjugal roles, housework and childcare
- Oakley (1974) argues that Young and Willmott's claim of increasing symmetry is based on inadequate methodology. Their conclusions were based on only one interview question which was worded in a way that could exaggerate the amount of housework done by men.
- Small-scale research in the 1970s by Oakley (1974) and Edgell (1980) found little sharing of household tasks.
- The *British Social Attitudes Survey* (1992) found more sharing of child-rearing than household tasks, although there was some movement towards a more egalitarian division of labour over time.
- Ferri and Smith (1996) used survey data to focus on childcare. In almost every kind of household – even where the woman had paid employment outside the home and the man did not – it was more common for the woman to take the main responsibility for childcare.

Conjugal roles and hours worked
- Young and Willmott found that the differences between men's and women's work time in the home were not that great.
- Gershuny (1992) found that the husbands of working women continued to do less than half the total paid and unpaid work done by their spouses. However, although the 'dual burden' of paid and domestic work remained for women, men did seem to be making more effort to do housework when their wives were in paid work.
- Sullivan (1996) examined the allocation of leisure time. Although men did spend a little more time on socializing, sleeping, relaxing and eating than women, the difference was not great.

Conjugal roles and power
- Edgell (1980) interviewed husbands and wives about decision making. He found that women tended to dominate in areas such as domestic spending and children's clothes, but men dominated in areas that were considered more important, such as moving house and overall finance.
- A more recent study by Hardill, Green and Owen (1997) found that although males dominated decision-making in most households, this was not the case in a significant minority of households.

Conjugal roles – money management
- Pahl (1989, 1993) studied how couples manage their money. Just over a quarter of the couples in her study had a system of money management in which there was a fair degree of equality.
- Research by Vogler (1994) largely confirms Pahl's findings. She found an increase in the proportion of relationships with egalitarian financial arrangements but this proportion remained small.

Conjugal roles – invisible and emotion work
- DeVault (1991) conducted a qualitative study on 'feeding the family'. She found that this aspect of domestic work involves a great deal of 'invisible' work in planning and staging the meal. Again, it is women who are primarily responsible.
- Duncombe and Marsden (1995) identify another invisible element of women's domestic work, emotion

work. Many women in their study expressed dissatisfaction with their partner's emotional input into the relationship and the family. Most men did not acknowledge that emotion work needed to be done to make the relationship work. Women can end up doing a triple shift. Having completed their paid employment they not only have to do most of the housework, they also have to do the emotion work.

Inequality within marriage – conclusion
A study of lesbian households by Dunne (1999) suggests that an equitable domestic division of labour can be achieved. However, it is hard to achieve in a culture that still differentiates so clearly between masculinity and femininity. The evidence indicates that women are still a long way from achieving equality within marriage. Husbands of wives with full-time jobs seem to be taking over some of the burden of housework, but the change is slow.

Marriage and marital breakdown

A number of threats to marriage have been identified, and this has led some commentators to express concern about the future of the family.

The threats fall into two main categories:
1 Threats resulting from alternatives to marriage
2 Threats resulting from the breakdown of marriages

'Threats' from alternatives to marriage

Marriage rates
It is argued that marriage is becoming less popular because the marriage rate has declined. However, the decline seems to be due to people delaying marriages rather than not getting married at all, as the average age of marriage has been steadily increasing. As Bernades (1997) points out, most people do get married at some point in their life.

Cohabitation
Cohabitation is increasing. The percentage of non-married women who were cohabiting doubled between 1981 and 1996–7. However, Burgoyne and Clark (1984) found that a significant proportion of their sample thought that cohabitation was a good idea as a prelude to marriage but not as a permanent alternative to marriage.

Joan Chandler (1993) takes a different view. She notes that the time couples spend cohabiting is lengthening, and more of them appear to be choosing cohabitation as a long-term alternative to marriage.

Single-person households
Another alternative to marriage is to live on your own. Many single-person households may be formed as a result of divorce or separation but others may result from a deliberate choice to live alone. Single-person households are becoming more common in Britain.

Threats resulting from the breakdown of marriages
The second type of threat to contemporary marriage is the apparent rise in marital breakdowns.

Marital breakdown can be divided into three main categories:
1 Divorce – the legal termination of a marriage.
2 Separation, which refers to the physical separation of the spouses.
3 So-called empty-shell marriages where the spouses remain living together but their marriage exists in name only.

Marital breakdown statistics
There was a steady rise in divorce rates in modern societies throughout the twentieth century, although the rate appeared to stabilize during the 1990s. According to Chandler, approximately 40% of new marriages will end in divorce. The proportion of remarriages has also been rising.

Reliable figures for separation and empty-shell marriages are not available.

Explanations for marital breakdowns
The value of marriage
Functionalists such as Parsons and Fletcher argue that the rise in marital breakdown stems largely from the fact that marriage is increasingly valued. People expect more and demand more from marriage and are more likely to end a relationship which may have been tolerable in the past.

Conflict between spouses
The isolation of the nuclear family from wider kin places strain on the marital relationship. Leach (1967) suggests that the nuclear family suffers from an emotional overload which increases the level of conflict between its members.

Modernity, freedom and choice
Gibson (1994) claims that the development of modernity has put increasing emphasis on the desirability of individual achievement. The ideology of the market emphasizes consumer choice, and so, if you are not satisfied with your first choice of partner, you are more likely to leave and try an alternative in the hope of greater personal satisfaction.

The ease of divorce
It is generally agreed that the stigma attached to divorce has been considerably reduced. Gibson believes that secularization (the decline of religious beliefs and institutions) has weakened the degree to which religious beliefs can bind a couple together and make divorce less likely.

Changing attitudes to divorce have led to changes in the law which have made it easier to obtain a divorce. In Britain, before 1857, a private act of parliament was required to obtain a divorce.

Since 1857 the costs of obtaining a divorce have gone down and the grounds for divorce have been widened. By 1996 there was no need to show that either partner was at fault in order to prove that the marriage had broken down. Instead, the partners simply had to assert that the marriage had broken down and undergo a 'period of reflection', normally a year, to consider whether a reconciliation was possible.

The social distribution of marital breakdown
Marital breakdown is not spread evenly across the population. The changes that have influenced the rate

of marital breakdown do not affect all members of society in the same way.

Income, class and unemployment

A study by Haskey (1984) found that non-manual workers have considerably lower divorce rates than manual workers. The divorce rate is particularly high amongst the unskilled and unemployed, suggesting that material hardship may be an important factor in shaping divorce rates.

Age

The lower the age of marriage, the higher the rate of divorce. A number of reasons for this have been put forward:

1 Economic pressure on teenage marriages.
2 A high proportion of teenage marriages are undertaken to legitimate a pregnancy.
3 Teenagers are more likely to change their outlook and 'grow apart'.
4 Young people are less likely to have the experience to select a compatible partner and less likely to be aware of the responsibilities of marriage.
5 Working-class couples are more likely than the middle class to marry as teenagers, so class may be a factor.

The marital status of parents

If one or both spouses have parents who have been divorced, there is a greater possibility that their own marriage will end in divorce. Hart (1976) argues that the experience of having divorced parents may reduce the individual's aversion to divorce. In addition, divorced parents are not likely to oppose divorce as strongly as non-divorced parents.

Occupations

Various studies have indicated a link between particular occupations and high rates of divorce. Gibson (1994) argues that long separations between spouses are associated with high divorce rates. Time apart reduces dependence and provides opportunities for people to meet members of the opposite sex away from their spouse. Hart (1976) finds that long-distance lorry drivers and sales representatives, for example, have higher-than-average divorce rates.

Conclusion

It is easy to exaggerate the extent to which there has been a retreat from marriage. The socialist feminists Abbott and Wallace (1992) recognize the increasing diversity of family forms but see the alleged decline of the family and marriage as having been exaggerated for political ends by the New Right (see p. 93, for example).

The family, politics and social policy

Despite the traditional belief that politicians should not interfere in the family, state policies have always had an impact on family life. Taxation, welfare, housing and education policies all influence the way in which people organize their domestic life.

Feminists have argued that government policies tend to favour the traditional nuclear family with a male breadwinner. Allan (1985) argues that much state policy is based on an ideology of the 'normal' family. Such policies assume that one family member will put primary emphasis on childcare rather than work; that families will usually take care of the elderly; and that wives are economically dependent on their husbands.

Lorraine Fox Harding (1996) gives some examples of state policies that favour the traditional family:

- Few council or other public-funded houses have been built to accommodate groups larger than conventional nuclear families.
- Married women can only receive invalidity pensions if they can show that their physical condition prevents them from doing housework – a rule that does not apply to men and single women.
- Regulations relating to maternity leave and pay reinforce traditional gender roles (despite the introduction of paternity leave in 2001).

Not all policies reinforce traditional gender roles. Fox Harding points out that in 1991 the House of Lords ruled that men were no longer exempt from being charged with raping their wives.

New Labour and the family

In general the Blair government's policies have been based around strengthening traditional families. However, a number of measures have been taken to help parents combine paid work with domestic responsibilities.

Families and postmodernity

Stacey – the postmodern family

Judith Stacey (1996) believes that contemporary societies such as the USA have developed the postmodern family. She associates changes in the family with a movement away from a single dominant family type and with a greater variety in family relationships. Arrangements in the postmodern family are 'diverse, fluid and unresolved'.

The development of the postmodern family has destroyed the idea that the family progresses through a series of logical stages. There can be no assumption that any particular form will become accepted as the best, or normal, type of family. Diversity is here to stay.

Conclusion

Stacey acknowledges that the postmodern family can create unsettling instability but she generally welcomes it as an opportunity to develop more egalitarian family relationships.

However, it is questionable to what extent diversity and the postmodern family have become commonplace. It is possible that Stacey exaggerates the extent of change.

1 What term best describes the unit of a husband, wife and their dependent offspring?
   a Symmetrical family
   b Nuclear family
   c Universal family
   d Extended family

2 Three of the following form part of Murdock's definition of the family. Which is the odd one out?
   a Economic cooperation
   b Includes wider kin
   c Includes adults of both sexes
   d Common residence

3 Which one of the following questions is most likely to be asked by a functionalist?
   a Are family relationships based on equality?
   b How does the family benefit capitalism?
   c How does the family benefit society?
   d How does the family benefit men?

4 Three of the following are criticisms of Parsons's view of the family. Which is the odd one out?
   a Parsons fails to study the relationship between the family and society
   b Parsons fails to recognize negative aspects of the family
   c Parsons sees socialization as a one-way process
   d Parsons ignores variations in family types

5 Engels wrote about the development of the monogamous nuclear family. What is meant by the term 'monogamous'?
   a Male-dominated
   b Found in all societies
   c Men and women having different roles
   d A marriage system based on one partner

6 Which one of the following types of feminism takes into account the variations in women's experiences?
   a Marxist feminism
   b Radical feminism
   c Difference feminism
   d Socialist feminism

7 Which one of the following terms best describes a society based on male domination?
   a Patriarchal
   b Feminist
   c Hierarchical
   d Exploitative

8 Which one of the following perspectives is 'difference feminism' closest to?
   a Postmodernism
   b Functionalism
   c Marxism
   d Social action theory

9 Which one of the following writers is best categorized as a functionalist?
   a Laing
   b Benston
   c Murdock
   d Leach

10 Which type of family is thought of as typical of pre-industrial societies?
   a Nuclear family
   b Classic extended family

   c Symmetrical family
   d Agricultural family

11 Which of the following is a definition of structural differentiation?
   a Institutions evolve which specialize in fewer functions
   b Structures become more complex
   c Family forms become more diverse
   d Societies move towards achieved status

12 According to Young and Willmott, which stage of the development of the family was characterized by, first, the family moving away from being a unit of production and, second, the family including relatives beyond the nuclear family?
   a Stage 1
   b Stage 2
   c Stage 3
   d Stage 4

13 Which one of the following terms describes the tendency for trends to begin in the middle class and then 'filter' down to other sections of society?
   a Stratified diffusion
   b Structural differentiation
   c Class differentiation
   d Class structure

14 Three of the following are reasons given by Young and Willmott for the development of the symmetrical family. Which is the odd one out?
   a A reduction in the number of children
   b Increased geographical mobility
   c More amenities and entertainment in the home
   d The development of feminism

15 Which one of the following terms is used by Allan to describe the typical contemporary family structure in which there is an 'inner' unit consisting of wife, husband, their parents, children, and brothers and sisters?
   a Modified elementary family
   b Modified extended family
   c Dispersed extended family
   d Dispersed elementary family

16 Three of these are characteristics of the 'cereal-packet image' of the family. Which is the odd one out?
   a A male breadwinner
   b A female carer/housewife
   c Dependent children
   d Shared domestic roles

17 Which one of the following terms do the Rapoports use to describe family diversity based on the lifestyles of families of different ethnic origins and religious beliefs?
   a Cohort diversity
   b Organizational diversity
   c Cultural diversity
   d Life-cycle diversity

18 Which one of the following is **not** a cause of single parenthood?
   a Divorce
   b Separation
   c Remarriage
   d Death of a spouse

19 Which one of the following perspectives is most likely to see single-parent families as a problem for society?
   a Difference feminism
   b The New Right
   c Marxist feminism
   d Functionalism

20 Three of these statements about ethnic minority families are true. Which is the odd one out?
   a Most children from South Asian families reject arranged marriages
   b Most South Asian families retain links with their place of origin in Asia
   c There has been an increase in single parenthood among all ethnic groups
   d Whites and Caribbeans have higher rates of cohabitation than other groups

21 Chester would be likely to agree with three of these statements. Which is the odd one out?
   a The vast majority of people experience nuclear families at some point in their life
   b Nearly half of the population still live in a nuclear family
   c Changes in the family have been minimal
   d Britain is characterized by family diversity

22 Which one of the following sociologists is most likely to argue that the family is not important in modern society?
   a Parsons
   b Fletcher
   c Marcuse
   d None of the above

23 Which one of these terms is used to describe a domestic situation in which the roles of husband and wife are very different?
   a Conjugal roles
   b Segregated conjugal roles
   c Joint conjugal roles
   d Differentiated roles

24 In Pahl's research, what percentage of couples had a fairly egalitarian system of money management?
   a Just over 10%
   b Just over 25%
   c Just over 50%
   d Just over 75%

25 Which one of the following is **not** part of women's triple shift, according to Duncombe and Marsden?
   a Emotion work
   b Domestic work
   c Decision making
   d Paid employment

26 Three of the following are forms of marital breakdown. Which is the odd one out?
   a Divorce
   b Empty-shell marriages
   c Domestic violence
   d Separation

27 Three of the following have been suggested as reasons for the increase in the divorce rate. Which is the odd one out?
   a More is expected of marriage today
   b The isolation of the nuclear family increases levels of conflict between family members
   c The stigma attached to divorce has decreased
   d The rate of remarriage has increased

28 Identify the one correct statement about the social distribution of divorce.
   a The unemployed have higher rates of divorce than the employed
   b The middle class have higher rates of divorce than the working class
   c Skilled workers have higher rates of divorce than the unskilled
   d Older people have higher rates of divorce than younger people

29 What term do sociologists use to describe the idea that the traditional nuclear family is the 'normal' way of organizing domestic arrangements?
   a The ideology of the family
   b Joint conjugal roles
   c Social policy
   d Segregated conjugal roles

30 Three of the following reflect a postmodern view of the family. Which is the odd one out?
   a There is no single dominant family type
   b There is uncertainty about roles within the family today
   c The family is progressing through a series of logical stages
   d There is a lot more choice about how people live their personal lives today

Develop your analysis and evaluation skills   (see p. 202 for guidance notes)

For each of the following statements, identify which sociologists would argue in favour of and which against the view expressed. Explain the reasons for their view.

1 The family is a universal social institution.
2 Feminism has made the most significant contribution to the sociology of the family since the 1970s.
3 The family performs positive functions for society.
4 The isolated nuclear family is the dominant form in modern societies.
5 The divorce rate is increasing because divorce has become easier to obtain.
6 Conjugal roles are becoming more equal.

Answer all parts of this question

Total: 60 marks

Time allowed: 1 hour 15 minutes

1 mark = 1.25 minutes

ITEM A

As family size has become smaller and the family has seemed to lose its functions, some have argued that the family is dying out. As evidence they put forward the rising divorce rate. It is the increase in single-parent families that has caused most of the concern about the stability of the family. Single-parent families have a great social cost to individuals and financial cost to the state.

This idea might be useful when answering part [f]

Key term for parts [a] and [c]

Check your understanding of this term before answering part [d]

ITEM B

Increased opportunities for divorce have provided an escape route for many wives. It is not marriage that women resent, as many will re-marry. Rather it is a certain type of marriage they seek to leave. Despite all the so-called advances of recent years, women still work a triple shift.

Check your understanding of this term before answering part [b]

Comments on the question	Question	Advice on preparing your answer
• A statistical measure that expresses a number as a proportion of a specific population in a given time period	[a] What is meant by divorce rate? [Item A, line 4] [2 marks]	• The legal termination of a marriage • You should include the idea of a number per thousand of the **married** population per year
• This means three-part so you need to identify each aspect • Don't spend too long – about 5 minutes	[b] Explain what is meant by the triple shift. [Item B, line 6] [4 marks]	• The three elements of the term are explained on pp. 94–5 • Consider why the word 'shift' is used here. Think of other contexts where the word is used

Comments on the question	Question	Advice on preparing your answer
• Less and you can't score all the marks; more and you are wasting time. They should be made as discrete and separate points • This means what happens after divorce not what causes a divorce • This is not quite the same as asking about the effects of divorce, where the focus would be on the individual. The focus here is on the societal level	[c] Identify **three** effects of the rise in the divorce rate. [6 marks]	• You may pick up some ideas from pp. 95–6, although you may have to twist the ideas to fit the question • Think about the impact on society of increasing numbers of people divorcing. An individual child's low educational achievement becomes a social issue of under-achievement in education
• You must follow the instructions carefully to get full marks. Don't write about two social costs and no financial cost, or vice versa • Notice the focus of this question. It is **not** divorce	[d] Identify and explain **one** individual social cost and **one** financial cost to the state caused by single-parent families. [8 marks]	• Select an individual cost, see pp. 95–6 • Some of these costs can also be twisted and applied to cover a financial cost
• Consider these qualities in relation to what has been written: 1 How original or distinctive? 2 How useful? 3 How true and accurate? 4 How complete an account? 5 How much understanding is shown? • Plural suggests more than one sociologist • e.g. universality issue, family structure, roles and functions	[e] Examine the contribution of functionalist sociologists to the study of family life. [20 marks]	• You could organize your answer around either of these two parts of the question • For contributions made, pp. 88–9, 90–1 and 94 • For points against, p. 89, 91 and 94 should be used selectively to show up the weaknesses or inadequacy of functionalism in relation to the numbered points opposite
• This means within the last fifty years at most, so go no further back than 1952, and exclude historical material • You don't have to limit yourself to Britain • The best answers might question what this means	[f] Using material from the items and elsewhere, assess the view that the isolated nuclear family is typical of modern society. [20 marks]	• This is a functionalist concept, so there could be some overlap with the previous question • Spend more time on the points against, but still set out the argument for, briefly • pp. 92–3 are useful to show the diversity of family structures and hence lack of typicality of the nuclear family

OCR style Family and Households question, AS Unit 2533: Culture and Socialisation

Answer all parts of this question
Total: 45 marks 1 mark = 1 minute
Time allowed: 45 minutes

Comments on the question	Question	Advice on preparing your answer
• Make sure that the examiner can see that you have clearly identified two ways • No more, no less • Make sure that you develop explanations of why the two ways identified demonstrate differences across ethnic groups	[a] Identify and explain **two** ways in which household types differ across ethnic groups in the UK. [15 marks]	• Make sure that you know what is meant by this concept • You will find material on p. 93 that will assist you in your response to this question • Be specific in your identification of particular ethnic groups • Note that you must not use examples that do not apply to the UK
• Describe the view as fully as possible, using supporting evidence • Consider arguments and evidence that are specifically targeted at the view and/or alternative views on the role of the nuclear family	[b] Outline and assess the view that the nuclear family is in decline. [30 marks]	• Remember that this is only one view. You can challenge it • You should construct an introduction which sets the scene, i.e. identifies the key studies in this debate • You will find material that supports this view on pp. 92–4 • You should consider the following material as a critique

Chapter 9

Power, politics and the state

Specifications

Specification	Relevant module title	Place in module	Level	Assessment	Other relevant modules
AQA	4: **Power and Politics**; Religion; World Sociology	One of three options in this module.	A2	One compulsory short data-response question and one essay question from a choice of two.	Material from this chapter may be used in the A2 synoptic module 6.
OCR	Power and Control	**Protest and Social Movements** is one of six options in this module.	A2	One essay question from a choice of two.	Material from this chapter may be used in the A2 synoptic module.

Power, politics and the state: essential notes

Defining power

A broad distinction can be made between two types of power:
1 Authority is power that is accepted as legitimate – e.g. the power of Parliament to pass laws in a society where citizens accept the political system.
2 Coercion is based upon the imposition of power using force, or the threat of force, against people who do not accept it as legitimate.

Weber – power and types of authority
Max Weber defines power as the ability of people to get their own way despite the opposition of others.

He distinguishes three different types of authority:
1 Charismatic authority is based upon what are believed to be the special qualities of an individual.
2 Traditional authority is based upon a belief in the rightness of accepted customs.
3 Rational–legal authority is based upon the acceptance of an impersonal set of rules, e.g. an exam system or a legal system.

These are ideal types (idealized, pure forms of authority) which in reality will tend to be mixed together.

Lukes – a radical view of power
Steven Lukes (1974) provides an alternative, radical view of power.

He sees Weber's views as being largely based upon decision making (the first face of power).

The second face is non-decision making, where some issues are prevented from reaching the point where decisions are made.

The third face of power is ideological power, where people are persuaded to accept the exercise of power over them even when it is against their interests – e.g. women accepting patriarchal power.

A problem with this definition is determining what is for or against somebody's interests if it is not based on the opinion of the person concerned.

The state

Definitions
Weber defines the state as a body that successfully claims a monopoly of the legitimate use of force in a given territory.

Most sociologists see the state as embracing institutions such as state-run welfare services as well as the criminal justice system, the military and state bureaucracies.

By the twentieth century the world was dominated by nation-states, but in some pre-modern societies, such as the Nuer in Africa, there was no state.

Power – a functionalist perspective

- Talcott Parsons argued that all societies require a value consensus based on shared goals.
- To Parsons, power is used to achieve collective goals such as material prosperity.
- Everybody therefore benefits from the exercise of power (a variable-sum view of power). In more conventional views of power, some benefit at the expense of others (a constant-sum view of power).
- Authority in society is usually accepted as legitimate because it helps to achieve collective goals.

Critics argue that Parsons is wrong to see the exercise of power as benefiting everyone rather than being used to further sectional interests.

Power and the state – a pluralist perspective

Classical pluralists accept a Weberian (constant-sum) definition of power and, unlike Parsons, do not see society as having a value consensus.

They accept that there is some agreement in countries such as the USA about the basic features of the democratic system, but they believe that industrial society is differentiated into a plurality of social groups and sectional interests.

Divisions are based not only on class, occupation, age, gender, religion and ethnicity, but also on many other specific interests – e.g. whether you own a car, pay a mortgage, use public libraries or have children.

Societies need to prevent a tyranny of the majority in which a single interest group always outvotes minorities.

The state is seen as an honest broker mediating between different interests and ensuring that no one group becomes dominant. It makes decisions which favour different groups at different times, balancing their interests over extended periods.

Political parties are seen as broadly representative since they need to attract sufficient support to be elected. If the existing parties do not represent public interests, new ones emerge.

However, interest or pressure groups are needed:
- To influence governments in the long periods between elections.
- To represent minority interests and ensure that governments take account of all groups in society, not just their own supporters.
- To increase participation in politics.
- To represent views on new issues that arise.
- To respond to changing circumstances.

There are two different types of pressure group:

1 Protective groups defend the interests of a particular group in the population – e.g. the BMA and doctors.
2 Promotional groups are based on causes or issues rather than social groups – e.g. environmental groups. They may have more diverse membership than protective groups.

Pressure groups can try to influence the government in a variety of ways:
- By contributing to party funds – e.g. unions and the Labour Party.
- Through payments – e.g. Mohammed Al-Fayed paying cash to MPs to ask questions in the House of Commons.
- By appealing to public opinion – e.g. rock musicians campaigning for the cancellation of Third World debt.
- Civil disobedience or direct action – e.g. hunt saboteurs.
- By providing expert opinion to the government – e.g. by having seats on government committees or inquiries.

A number of studies have been used to support pluralist views. They have compared government decisions with the wishes of different interest groups. Classic studies by Dahl (1961) in the USA, and Hewitt (1974) and Grant and Marsh (1977) in the UK appear to show that no one sectional interest gets its own way all the time.

The 'New Labour' government of Tony Blair can be seen as balancing business interests (e.g. by allowing private involvement in public services) and worker/union interests (e.g. by introducing minimum wage legislation).

There have been many criticisms of classical pluralism:

1 Marxists argue that pluralists fail to take account of the second face of power. Radical questions such as real redistribution of wealth never reach the point of decision making.
2 Westergaard and Resler (1976) argue that power should be measured in terms of the consequences of decisions. Despite lots of legislation designed to help the poor, there has been little real redistribution of wealth in Britain.
3 Some studies – e.g. that of Marsh and Locksley (1983) – suggest that business interests have more influence than other groups.
4 Some promotional groups seem to have very little influence –e.g. Hugh Ward (1983) argues that anti-nuclear campaigners have had little success.
5 Some interests may be unrepresented – e.g. the unemployed lack a protective pressure group.

Some classical pluralists now admit that power may not be as equally distributed as the model originally suggested.

Elite pluralism

This approach modifies and tries to improve on classical pluralism. Unlike classical pluralists, elite pluralists believe that there are some inequalities in power, they acknowledge that there are other faces of power and they see elites – the leaders of interest groups – as more influential than ordinary members.

Richardson and Jordan (1979) argue that there is inequality between pressure groups:
- Insider groups are accepted by the government as legitimate representatives and are frequently consulted.
- Outsider groups are not recognized and have little influence.

Some groups – e.g. parents of children in the education system – are not represented by pressure groups.

Nevertheless Richardson and Jordan believe that pressure groups can force new issues on to the government's agenda – e.g. the success of environmental groups.

Wyn Grant (1999) believes that, despite changes in pressure group politics, Britain remains largely democratic. The changes include:
- The decline of the influence of the TUC and CBI.
- An increase in the number of pressure groups so that most interests are now represented.
- More campaigning directed away from Westminster – e.g. consumer boycotts to put pressure on companies and the increased importance of the European Union and devolved governments.

- Increased use of direct action – e.g. by anti-roads protestors.
- More consultation of pressure groups by government, although the insider/outsider distinction remains valid.

Although more realistic than classical pluralism, elite pluralism still ignores the third face of power and may underestimate the inequality of power in society and the possible use of power by elites to further their own interests.

Elite theory

Elite theory divides society into a ruling minority and the majority who are ruled. There are different versions of elite theory.

Classical elite theory was developed by the Italians – e.g. Pareto (1848–1923) – in opposition to Marxist theory.

Pareto emphasized the importance of the psychological characteristics of elites which made them superior to the mass and which allowed them to gain and retain power.

- Lions achieve power through incisive action and the use of force.
- Foxes rule by cunning.

Elites tend to circulate, with lions being replaced by foxes, and foxes then being replaced by lions, and so on.

Pareto can be criticized for simply assuming that elites are superior to the mass, ignoring the differences between political systems, ignoring the importance of wealth, and so on.

Modern elite theories offer more plausible views.

C. Wright Mills in the 1950s in the USA argued that there was a power elite which had power through holding key positions (command posts) in three institutions:

1 major corporations
2 the military
3 the federal government

The three elites were connected through intermarriage, movement of individuals between elites, a similar educational background and membership of the same prestige clubs.

As a unified group they were able to exercise power over a divided and passive mass of the population who took little interest in most political issues.

Elite self-recruitment in Britain

In Britain a number of studies have found high levels of elite self-recruitment – i.e. most people recruited into elites tend to come from elite backgrounds themselves. There is evidence of cohesion, with people having positions in more than one elite, and elite members having shared educational backgrounds.

George Borthwick et al. (1991) examined the educational backgrounds of Conservative MPs in the 1979, 1983 and 1987 elections and found that in 1987 over half had been to public school and 44% had been to Oxford or Cambridge University.

In the 1997 election, won by the Labour Party, MPs' backgrounds were more varied, but even a Labour government included members of the business elite such as Geoffrey Robinson and Lord Sainsbury.

Evaluation

Although many top positions in Britain and the USA are held by people from elite backgrounds, that does not actually prove that they act to further elite interests rather than those of the mass of the population. There is little attempt to measure power.

Marxists argue that elite theory neglects the importance of economic power as opposed to power based on positions held.

Fragmented elites

Fragmented elite theory, advocated by Budge, McKay and Marsh (1983), argues that elites do hold power, but elites are divided and fragmented and have different interests.

- MPs sometimes clash with ministers.
- Civil servants sometimes obstruct governments.
- Judges have the independence to make decisions that prevent governments from doing what they want.
- Organizations such as the BBC may be critical of governments despite being ultimately state-controlled.
- International elites such as the EC can limit British governments.

Criticisms

Fragmented elite theory may underestimate the amount of power exercised by central government and, from a Marxist point of view, it ignores the importance of wealth. However, it may be more realistic than conventional elite theory.

Power and the state – Marxist perspectives

- Like elite theory, Marxist theories see power as concentrated in the hands of a minority.
- Unlike elite theory, they see it as concentrated in the hands of a ruling class which derives its power from ownership of the means of production.

Marx and Engels argued that the ruling class used their power to exploit subordinate classes.

- It was in the interests of the subject classes to overthrow ruling-class power, but the ruling class used the superstructure to try to prevent this.
- The state, as part of the superstructure, was used to promote ruling-class interests.
- Engels argued that the first societies were primitive communist ones which did not have a state. In primitive communism no surplus was produced, so it was impossible for class power to develop through the accumulation of a surplus. As the purpose of the state is to maintain ruling-class power, no state was needed.
- As surplus was produced, wealth was accumulated, classes developed and states were born.
- Early states were oppressive (e.g. the use of slavery in Ancient Greece and Rome), but democratic states appear to be based on the will of the population.
- Engels believes that in democratic states power stays with the ruling class; such states only create the illusion of democracy.
- Corruption and the financial power of capitalists are used to shape state policies in capitalist democracies, ensuring that the state continues to further ruling-class interests.

- In future communist societies, based on communal ownership of the means of production, the proletariat would temporarily take control of the state to defeat the ruling class. Once this was completed, classes would disappear and the state would 'wither away'.

Marx and Engels describe the state as 'but a committee for managing the affairs of the whole bourgeoisie'. However, Engels accepted that the state could act independently – e.g. when two classes were competing for domination of a society. In some studies Marx showed an awareness of divisions within states – e.g. between industrial capitalists and financiers.

Modern Marxists have interpreted the Marxist view of the state in different ways.

Ralph Miliband (1969) argues that the state is often the direct tool of the ruling class.

- Many of those who occupy top positions in the state come from ruling-class backgrounds and are therefore likely to act to support ruling-class interests.
- Even those from other backgrounds will have to accept ruling-class values to gain positions in the state.
- The protection of private property (which serves ruling-class interests) is assumed to be a central role of the state.
- The way in which the state supports private enterprise is legitimated through advertising which celebrates the activities of large corporations.

Nicos Poulantzas (1969, 1976) criticizes Miliband, arguing that it is not direct interference from the ruling class that makes the state serve ruling-class interests, but the structure of society (a structuralist approach).

- As part of the superstructure, the state will automatically act to favour the ruling class.
- The state has relative autonomy – it has some independence from individual members of the ruling class.
- This allows the state to act in the overall interests of the ruling class rather than being dominated by a single capitalist faction (e.g. bankers).
- It also allows the state to make some concessions to the working class to defuse their protests and prevent an eventual revolution.
- This relative autonomy allows the state to promote the myth that it is acting in the interests of society as a whole.

Miliband (1972) criticizes Poulantzas for assuming that the state would act in ruling-class interests without showing how and why. The theory of relative autonomy makes it impossible to prove Poulantzas's theory wrong; whatever the state does can be taken as evidence of ruling-class domination or relative autonomy.

Evidence to support Marxism
- Westergaard and Resler (1976) argue that power can be measured in terms of effects rather than decision making. From this point of view, the continued concentration of wealth in the hands of capitalists provides evidence of this group's power.
- Westergaard and Resler argue that reforms such as the introduction of the welfare state, which appear to benefit the working class, have left the basic structures of inequality unchanged.
- Sociologists such as Urry (1973) put forward evidence of non-decision making – e.g. the way in which issues such as replacing capitalism are never considered.
- Marxists put forward evidence that ruling-class ideology makes use of the third (ideological) face of power to support its position.

Criticisms
Marxist views can be criticized:
1 For failing to explain why the state did not wither away in communist societies such as the Soviet Union.
2 For exaggerating the importance of economic power.
3 For failing to consider other possible sources of power.

Neo-Marxist approaches to power and the state

Neo-Marxist views retain elements of Marxist theory but diverge from orthodox Marxism in a number of ways.

Gramsci – hegemony and the state
- Gramsci (1891–1937) argued against economic determinism (the theory that the economy determined other aspects of society).
- He believed that the superstructure could influence the economic infrastructure as well as vice versa.
- He divided the superstructure into political society (essentially the state) and civil society (private institutions).
- To keep control over civil society, the ruling class needed to achieve hegemony, or domination, by gaining the consent of the mass of the population.
- To legitimate their rule, the ruling class might need to make concessions to win the support of other classes or class factions.
- Different sections of the capitalist class needed to be united.
- Ruling-class hegemony was never complete or total. A continuing process was needed to develop and maintain support and legitimate their position.
- An alliance of groups which dominated society was called a historic bloc.
- Opposition was always likely because people possessed dual consciousness. The experience of exploitation and oppression (e.g. at work) tended to make people radical, whereas the ideology promoted by the ruling class tended to make them more conservative.
- Control over ideas was as important in maintaining or overthrowing ruling-class hegemony as was control over the economy.

Coates – The Context of British Politics
David Coates (1984) applies Gramsci's ideas to Britain in the Thatcher era. He accepts that capitalists have considerable power.
- He discusses the power of multinational corporations to shape government policy.
- He describes how finance capital (banks, insurance companies, financial trusts) limits governments'

room for manoeuvre. If governments harm their interests, these institutions can move money abroad, undermining government policy.

However, Coates argues that this power is far from complete.

- Many individuals are critical of the power of the rich.
- Groups such as trade unions have some genuine power to change government policy.
- To maintain hegemony, governments have to make some real concessions to the working class, and they have to try to incorporate class factions (e.g. the petty bourgeoisie) outside the ruling class.

Evaluation

Neo-Marxist views avoid the mistake of seeing wealth as the only source of power. However, they provide a less clear theory about the nature of power and do not clearly explain which non-economic factors sometimes take on more importance.

State-centred theories of power

All the previous theories can be seen as society-centred: they examine the way in which society shapes the actions of the state.

State-centred theories see the state as an independent actor, able to exercise power in its own right and pursue its own interests.

Theda Skocpol (1985) argues that states have considerable autonomy, and their primary aim may be to increase their own power.

They have administrative control over a territory, the ability to raise taxes and the ability to recruit talented people to work for them.

States such as the communist regimes in China and Russia, and the Napoleonic regime in France, demonstrate the considerable power that states can possess.

Criticisms

Critics argue that such approaches may exaggerate state power. They also point out that some supposedly society-centred approaches recognize that the state has some independent power (e.g. Poulantzas's theory of relative autonomy).

Globalization and the power of the nation-state

The idea of globalization suggests that national boundaries are becoming less important, and that events throughout the world influence what happens in particular societies.

To some theorists of globalization this means that the nation-state is losing its power to non-governmental organizations.

Ohmae – *The Borderless World*

Ohmae (1994) argues that there is one giant inter-linked economy covering developed and rapidly developing societies.

- This inter-linked economy is dominated by giant corporations and is made possible by a rapid growth in world trade.

- Improved communications make national boundaries unimportant and allow individuals to buy products from anywhere in the world.
- Governments can no longer control economies within national boundaries because of the extent of trade across nations.
- Corporations can move production easily to cheaper countries; financiers can move money at will around the world.
- Corporations and consumers now have more power than governments.

Criticisms

Ohmae can be criticized for greatly exaggerating the loss of state power.

- States still have considerable control over access to their domestic markets from outside their immediate trading block (e.g. from outside the EC).
- States still largely monopolize military power.

Bonnett – globalization, power and politics

Kevin Bonnett (1994) takes a less extreme view but still believes that globalization is changing politics.

- Power no longer exists solely *within* nation-states; economic, military, political and ideological power is increasingly exercised *across* nation-states.
- Globalization can weaken power within nation-states. The lack of dominance by nation-states encourages the development of independence movements, such as those that led to the break-up of the Soviet Union.
- States are therefore threatened by internationalism from outside their borders and by nationalism from within.

Hirst and Thompson – questioning globalization

Paul Hirst and Grahame Thompson (1996) are more critical of the theory of globalization.

- They argue that most corporations are still largely based around their home nations and regions, generating most of their profits from the domestic market or the immediate region.
- They admit that states have lost some power, but the fact that states still control territory and regulate populations ensures that they retain much of their power.
- Most individuals still feel part of a particular state and this gives the state some power over them.

Giddens – globalization and high modernity

Giddens (1990) takes a more balanced approach.

- He sees globalization in terms of worldwide social relationships linking distant localities and shaping local events.
- Interaction is stretched across space and time in a process of time–space distanciation. This means that you no longer need to be present together to interact with somebody (e.g. by using the internet).
- There is increasing global competition in business and a world financial market producing a global economy.
- This restricts nation-state power since nations have to compete to attract inward investment from corporations.
- However, nation-states do not lose all their power.

They can sometimes mobilize nationalist sentiments and exercise some cultural influence over citizens, and they retain some economic power.

- However, nations need to cooperate together to maintain power against transnational corporations and other groups.

Evaluation

Giddens provides a more balanced view of globalization than Ohmae or Hirst and Thompson.

Mann – the sources of social power

Mann (1986, 1993) incorporates elements from different theories of power in his general theory.

He stresses that power has always operated across national boundaries through networks of power. Power cannot therefore be analysed in terms of its distribution within a particular society.

He argues that there are four main sources of power:

1 Economic power (which is important, but it is not the only source of power, as some Marxists believe).
2 Ideological power – power over ideas and beliefs.
3 Military power – based on physical coercion.
4 Political power – exercised by states over citizens.

Power is never monopolized entirely by one group, and changes in society – e.g. technological changes – make the distribution of power unstable.

Evaluation

Mann's approach shows the dangers of assuming that all power comes from one source and that power relationships are relatively fixed or stable.

Postmodernism, politics and new social movements

Postmodern approaches tend to broaden the definition of politics well beyond the activities of the state and pressure groups.

1 Jean Baudrillard (1983) argues that politics has become detached from reality.

- Rather than being concerned with the substance of policy, politics is more concerned with image.
- There is no real difference between the main parties – voters have little real choice.
- Politicians have no real power and simply try to maintain the illusion that they do.
- Politics is simply concerned with simulacra – signs that have no relationship to reality.

Critics suggest that politicians do make decisions that affect people's lives. Wars, for example, are real, and lead to real people being killed.

2 Lyotard (1984) argues that in the postmodern era metanarratives (big stories such as political ideologies) have declined in importance.

- People no longer believe in political ideologies.
- Politics becomes less about principles and more about local issues and the practicality of achieving things.
- Politics simply becomes a series of language-games about specialist topics.
- Power is more to do with knowledge than state activities.

Lyotard's approach ignores military power and may underestimate the continuing power of nation-states.

3 Nancy Fraser (1995) sees politics shifting away from the public sphere of the economy and the state, and moving more into the private sphere.

- Politics becomes more concerned with debate within groups rather than on a national level.
- This gives the relatively powerless (such as black women or lesbians) more involvement in politics.
- Politics is increasingly concerned with the definitions of issues rather than control over resources such as money.
- Issues such as gender, sexuality and ethnicity are increasingly important, and a greater plurality of groups now has a political voice.

Fraser may exaggerate the degree to which some of the issues she mentions are new on the political agenda. A plurality of groups and issues has had some role in politics for a considerable time.

New social movements and the new politics

Many commentators argue that, as conventional party politics has declined in importance, new social movements have become more important.

Hallsworth – 'Understanding new social movements'

- Hallsworth (1994) sees new social movements as political movements which have emerged since the 1960s which challenge the established order of capitalist society.
- Examples include feminism, environmentalism, anti-racism, anti-nuclear movements and so on.
- They are based around two types of issue:

1 The defence of the natural and social environment (e.g. the animal rights movement or environmentalism).
2 Furthering the rights of marginal groups (e.g. gay liberation).

- They have a number of novel features:

1 They try to extend the definition of what is political to include the private sphere (e.g. domestic violence and sexuality).
2 They tend not to develop bureaucratic organizations.
3 They tend to be diverse and fragmented (e.g. feminism).
4 They do not seek to hold political office themselves and, unlike conventional pressure groups, they are more likely to engage in direct action.
5 They are more concerned with culture than with material issues such as living standards.
6 They tend to be supported by the young, students and those who work in public services (or whose parents do).

To Hallsworth, they are mainly concerned with post-materialist values in societies where most people have already attained a reasonable basic living standard.

Crook, Pakulski and Waters – social movements and postmodernization

Crook, Pakulski and Waters (1992) associate the emergence of new social movements with a new politics of postmodernizing societies.

- Old politics was class-based and dominated by elites. It was focused on the state and seen as separate from everyday life.
- New politics involves a volatile electorate without strong class identities. There is a greater concern with moral issues than with sectional interests, a suspicion of leaders and elites, a move away from concentration on state activities and a politicization of culture and lifestyle.
- The move to the new politics is a result of class decomposition (members of the same class become increasingly dissimilar to one another) and social differentiation (those with similar backgrounds develop different lifestyles).
- The penetration of the media into all aspects of life results in a greater focus on the politics of words and images.

Evaluation
Crook *et al.* identify some important trends, but they may exaggerate them – e.g. many sociologists deny that there has been a decomposition of classes.

Giddens – social movements and high modernity
Giddens (1990) examines the relationship between social movements and high modernity (he does not believe that we have entered a postmodern age).
- Giddens sees modernity as characterized by four institutional dimensions each of which has corresponding social movements:
1 Capitalism produces labour movements such as unionism.
2 Military power produces peace movements opposed to destructive, industrialized warfare.
3 Surveillance (the control of information and monitoring of populations) produces free speech/democratic movements.
4 Industrialism produces ecological movements.
- Globalization produces increased risks in terms of ecological damage and military confrontation, and this leads to ecological and peace movements assuming a greater prominence.
- The emphasis in politics changes, but all these types of movement have existed throughout modernity.

Voting behaviour

Patterns of voting 1945–1974
From 1945 to the 1970s there were well-established and fairly predictable voting patterns, with a clear division between two main parties and two types of policy.
- The Labour Party was seen as left-wing. It was more likely to support: the redistribution of income and wealth from rich to poor through taxation; high levels of spending on welfare; and state intervention in the economy (e.g. through the nationalization of industries).
- The Conservative Party was seen as right-wing. It was more likely to support low taxation and the need for inequality and lower levels of spending on welfare, and to oppose nationalization of industries.
Butler and Stokes (1974) characterized voting patterns in this era in the following way:

- Class, as measured by a person's occupation, exercised a key influence on voting.
- Most voters had a strongly partisan self-image, thinking of themselves as Labour or Conservative.
- There were few floating voters; most voted consistently for the same party.
- There was a two-party system, with most of the working class voting Labour and most of the middle class voting Conservative.
- People were socialized by parents and the sorts of schools they attended into supporting particular parties.
- Third or minor parties attracted few votes.
Throughout the period there was a small number of deviant voters who failed to vote for the party associated with their class. This group influenced election outcomes.

A variety of factors were put forward to explain their deviant voting – e.g. the experience of social mobility, having a partner from a different class background or having parents who voted for different parties.

Patterns of voting since 1974

A number of commentators believe that voting patterns started to change in the 1970s.
- The influence of class on voting started to decline.
- The electorate became more volatile, switching votes more often.
- There was a big increase in the number of deviant voters.
- The third party in British politics (the Liberals, later the SDP/Liberal Alliance and finally the Liberal Democrats) began to attract more support.
- Many argued that the Labour Party was in decline, due to a shrinking proportion of the population in working-class, manual jobs.

Sarlvik and Crewe – partisan dealignment
Sarlvik and Crewe (1983) were leading advocates of the view that major changes were taking place.
- They argued that partisan dealignment was taking place. People's sense of attachment to a particular party was weakening rapidly.
- Class dealignment was taking place – class was exercising less influence on voting.
- These changes were produced by factors such as the working class buying their own houses and leaving trade unions, which weakened their working-class attachments.
- Sarlvik and Crewe believed that voting was increasingly shaped by policy preferences – people were voting for the parties whose policies they liked rather than the parties they had been brought up to support.
However, critics of Sarlvik and Crewe argued that they exaggerated their case.

Heath, Jowell and Curtice – the continuing importance of class
Heath, Jowell and Curtice (1985) argued that class continued to exercise a strong influence on voting.

- They supported their claims by adopting a sophisticated five-class model instead of what they saw as an over-simplified two-class model (working class and middle class).
- They argued that voters chose more on the basis of the ideological image of the party than on specific policies.
- The Labour Party was losing support because its ideological image was too left-wing for many voters, rather than because of changes in society.
- The Liberal/SDP Alliance was gaining support because its image (right-wing on economic issues but liberal on social issues) was close to the ideology supported by increasing numbers of voters.

The 1992 election
The Conservatives won the elections of 1979, 1983, 1987 and 1992. By 1992 some people were questioning whether Labour could ever win again.

Rose – Labour's 'shattering' defeat
Richard Rose (1992) argued that the 1992 election was fought under favourable conditions for Labour.
- The party was more united than in previous elections.
- The economy was in trouble, reflecting badly on the Conservative government.
- The Liberals seemed to be in decline; and Labour had abandoned what some voters saw as extreme left-wing policies (such as nationalization and big rises in income tax). It should have been well-placed to pick up voters with moderate views.

Despite this, Labour lost. This suggested that changes in society had made it unlikely that Labour would win future elections.
- The numbers of manual workers, unionists, inner-city residents and council tenants were all declining, reducing the core of people who normally supported Labour.
- Living standards and educational qualifications were rising, making people more inclined to vote Conservative.

Heath, Jowell and Curtice – 'Can Labour win?'
However, Heath, Jowell and Curtice (1994) thought that, although Labour faced serious problems, winning elections was not impossible.
- The electorate was increasingly volatile, making it possible that they might switch to Labour in large numbers.
- Opinion polls showed some support for Labour policies such as spending more money on welfare and redistributing wealth.
- Some social groups which tended to support Labour, such as ethnic minorities, were growing.

The 1997 election
In 1997 the Labour Party won a big majority, demonstrating that their task was not impossible. The *British Election Study* of the 1997 election, and other studies, have suggested a number of possible reasons for this.
1 Voters were indeed more volatile. This enabled Labour to take advantage of the short-term unpopularity of the Conservatives. The Conservatives were seen as divided, there were allegations of corruption or 'sleaze', and they were seen as incompetent when forced out of the ERM (the Exchange Rate Mechanism, which was supposed to control the value of British currency).
2 The Conservatives had moved ideologically to the right, and the Labour Party to the centre, making Labour's policies closer to those preferred by most people.
3 Evans, Heath and Payne (1999) admitted that class-based voting had declined, but argued that this had enabled Labour to attract many more middle-class voters than in previous elections.

There was research into non-class factors and voting in 1997.
- Saggar and Heath (1999) found that Labour continued to attract majority support from ethnic minority voters.
- Norris (1999b) found a shift in women's voting. In earlier elections women had been more likely to vote Conservative than men, but by 1997 they were more likely to vote Labour. Younger women were particularly likely to vote Labour, and Norris attributes this to the influence of the women's movement which has encouraged women to become more left-wing.

The 2001 election
In 2001 the Labour Party again won an overwhelming majority. A number of possible reasons might account for this.
1 The Conservatives continue to be seen as divided over European issues, particularly over whether to join a European currency.
2 Economic prosperity and the fact that the Labour Party has not raised taxes have cemented a reputation for economic competence.
3 The Conservatives continue to support policies which may be more right-wing than most of the electorate.
4 The Labour Party continues to be seen as following moderate policies.

Conclusion
Clearly social changes have not rendered the Labour Party unelectable, but with a volatile electorate without strong party identification future election results will be hard to predict.

1 Which **two** of the following are examples of rational–legal authority?
   a Football players accepting the decision of a referee because he was following the rules of football
   b Soldiers following a general's instructions because he made an inspiring speech to them
   c Women in a society doing most of the domestic work because their mothers had always been responsible for doing it
   d A motorist conforming to a 30 mph speed limit in a built-up area

2 Which one of these is an example of the second face of power?
   a A political party refusing to put a controversial motion, put forward by party activists, on to the agenda for a conference
   b The government deciding to pass a new law
   c A man persuading a woman that she should always obey his instructions
   d A school teacher placing a child in detention

3 Which one of these is an example of the third face of power?
   a A political party refusing to put a controversial motion, put forward by party activists, on to the agenda for a conference
   b The government deciding to pass a new law
   c A man persuading a woman that she should always obey his instructions
   d A school teacher placing a child in detention

4 Which one of these statements about Talcott Parsons's theory of power and the state is **untrue**?
   a According to Parsons, all societies require a value consensus
   b According to Parsons, power is used in the pursuit of collective goals
   c According to Parsons, authority is accepted as legitimate because it helps societies to achieve collective goals
   d According to Parsons, some members of society exercise power at the expense of other members

5 Which one of these statements about classical pluralism is true?
   a Classical pluralists believe that all members of society share similar interests
   b Classical pluralists believe that it is impossible to prevent a tyranny of the majority
   c Classical pluralists believe that different interests are effectively represented in a democracy
   d Classical pluralists believe that the state acts largely in its own interests

6 Classical pluralists see the state as:
   a An honest broker
   b A tool of ruling-class oppression
   c Controlled by unrepresentative elites
   d Essentially corrupt

7 Which one of these is an example of a protective pressure group?
   a Greenpeace
   b The National Union of Teachers
   c The RSPCA
   d The Campaign for Nuclear Disarmament

8 Which one of the following did **not** conduct a study to support pluralist theory?
   a Hewitt
   b Dahl
   c Borthwick
   d Grant and Marsh

9 Which one of these is a criticism of the pluralist view?
   a Pluralists ignore decision making
   b Pluralists assume that everybody in society shares the same interests
   c Pluralists underestimate the importance of pressure groups
   d Pluralists ignore the second face of power

10 Which one of these is **not** a change that has taken place in pressure-group politics, according to Wyn Grant?
   a Pressure-group politics has become increasingly dominated by class issues
   b Pressure-group campaigns have become increasingly focused outside Parliament
   c Pressure groups have begun to make more use of direct action
   d Governments are consulting pressure groups more than they did in the past

11 Which of these is **not** one of the three main elites identified by C. Wright Mills in the USA?
   a Directors of major corporations
   b Senior judges
   c Members of the federal government
   d Senior military officers

12 The process whereby the children of those from elites become members of elites themselves is usually referred to as:
   a Upward social mobility
   b Elite self-recruitment
   c Elite closure
   d Inequality of elite access

13 In Marx's theory, the state is seen as:
   a Part of the economic base
   b Part of the superstructure
   c Part of the infrastructure
   d Part of civil society

14 Marx thought that in communist society the state would ultimately:
   a Become democratic
   b Wither away
   c Become increasingly strong
   d Take on new functions

15 Which one of the following puts forward a Marxist view of the state, using a structuralist approach which emphasizes relative autonomy?
   a Poulantzas
   b Miliband
   c Westergaard and Resler
   d Gramsci

16 Which one of these concepts is **not** associated with Gramsci?
   a State-centred theory
   b Hegemony
   c Dual consciousness
   d Historic blocs

17 Which of these writers sees the state as having lost the most power as a result of globalization?
   a Bonnett   b Ohmae
   c Giddens   d Hirst and Thompson

18 Which of these writers is most sceptical about the theory of globalization?
   a Bonnett   b Ohmae
   c Giddens   d Hirst and Thompson

19 Which one of these statements about Giddens's discussion of globalization is **not** true?
   a Giddens sees globalization as destroying the power of the nation-state
   b Giddens sees globalization as involving better communications
   c Giddens sees globalization as partly caused by the increasing power of corporations
   d Giddens believes that globalization can sometimes increase nationalist sentiments

20 According to Michael Mann, the four main sources of power are:
   a Political, ideological, military and cultural
   b Cultural, political, economic and ideological
   c Ideological, economic, cultural and military
   d Ideological, military, economic and political

21 Which one of the following writers does **not** advocate a postmodern theory of power and politics?
   a Lyotard   b Baudrillard
   c Fraser   d Giddens

22 Which **two** of these statements would postmodernists tend to agree with?
   a Power is increasingly related to knowledge
   b Power is increasingly related to image
   c Power is increasingly about money
   d Voters have a real choice in democratic elections

23 Which **two** of the following does Hallsworth see as characteristic of new social movements?
   a They tend to be concerned with materialistic issues
   b They tend to have bureaucratic organizations
   c They tend to see private life as a political sphere
   d They tend to be concerned with culture

24 Which one of these statements would Crook, Pakulski and Waters agree with?
   a Those from the same background increasingly have similar lifestyles
   b Moral issues are of less concern to voters than they used to be

   c The media increasingly penetrate into all areas of social life
   d Politics is increasingly dominated by elites

25 Which **two** of the following are usually seen as left-wing policies?
   a Nationalization of industry
   b Low income tax
   c Cutting spending on welfare
   d Redistributing wealth from the rich to the poor

26 Which **two** of the following characteristics are associated with Butler and Stokes's analysis of voting from 1945 until the early 1970s?
   a Partisan alignment
   b A strong third party
   c Strong political socialization
   d A volatile electorate

27 Sarlvik and Crewe argued that:
   a By the 1980s class had no influence on voting behaviour
   b By the 1980s class was exercising less influence on voting behaviour
   c By the 1980s policies had little influence on people's voting behaviour
   d By the 1980s people were developing stronger attachments to particular parties

28 Which two of the following elections were won by the Labour Party?
   a 1983   b 1992   c 1997   d 2001

29 What was the name of the monetary system that the Conservative government was forced to leave?
   a The EU
   b The Common Currency
   c The ERM
   d The MSE

30 According to the *British Election Study*, in the 1997 election which one of the following had taken place in party ideology and policy?
   a The Conservatives had moved towards the centre and Labour had become more right-wing
   b The Conservatives had moved towards the centre and Labour had become more left-wing
   c The Conservatives had become more right-wing and Labour more left-wing
   d The Conservatives had become more right-wing and Labour had moved towards the centre

Develop your analysis and evaluation skills   (see p. 203 for guidance notes)

For each of the following statements, identify which sociologists would argue in favour of and which against the view expressed. Explain the reasons for their view.

1 In democratic societies the state balances the interests of all social groups.
2 In capitalist societies the bourgeoisie has most of the power, but its power is not complete.
3 A small elite exercises most of the power in countries such as Britain and the USA.
4 Although there is some evidence of globalization, the nation-state retains considerable power.

5 Economic power has always been more important than other sources of power.
6 Class is no longer important in conflicts over power in a postmodern society.
7 Voting behaviour is increasingly shaped by the policy preferences of the electorate.

Answer all the questions in Part One and one question from Part Two
Total: 60 marks   1 mark = 1.5 minute
Time allowed: 1 hour 30 minutes

Part One

ITEM A

The distribution of power (in Part Two) could be considered at these two levels

In 2000, research from the University of Durham (*Who Runs the North East Now?*), which focused on regional government, suggested that, despite new institutions, local politics was still the same old story – it was dominated by grey-haired, white men. ... The same sort of story emerges nationally.

This is the legislation that you have to consider for part [a]

New legislation in France now requires political parties to put up equal numbers of male and female candidates in all elections. The proportion of women in local councils leapt from 22% to 48% as a result.

Source: adapted from 'In focus: politics – for men', *Sociology Review*, vol. 11, no. 2, November 2001

Comments on the question	Question	Advice on preparing your answer
• Do exactly as the question asks • You need to interpret and apply this information • Just look at Britain • Don't spend too long on this – about 12 minutes at most	[a] Briefly examine two reasons why such legislation [Item A, line 8] might not work in Britain. [8 marks]	• You might consider the following points among others: 1 Legislation does not change attitudes 2 Marxist views on cultural hegemony 3 Those in control might wish to keep power
• Don't spend more than 15–20 minutes • Plural, so you must look at more than one, which could be organized around the following: 1 An age issue 2 Ethnicity issue 3 Sex/gender issues • Remember that these stratification issues may be found in any module as a core theme	[b] Briefly examine the reasons for the domination of politics by grey-haired, white men. [12 marks]	• The cynicism of youth and lack of political awareness are discussed in Chapter 12, p. 147 • Institutional racism (Chapter 4, p. 35) or cultural identity might be a good starting point for the ethnicity issue • Patriarchy (p. 23) might be a good starting point for considering the gender issue

Part Two
Answer **one** question from this part

Comments on the question	Question	Advice on preparing your answer
• Look at the strengths and weaknesses • Plural, so you need to consider more than one • This is one element of the question and refers to the form power takes • This must be looked at separately; it refers to who has the power • Usually taken to mean from the second half of the twentieth century • This section should take the bulk of your time – 50–55 minutes	Either: Assess sociological theories of the nature and distribution of power in modern society. [40 marks]	**Nature of power:** • Define, see p. 102 • Remember to look at different ways of measuring power (see p. 102 for ideas): 1 By decision making 2 By non-decision making 3 By ideology 4 By who benefits **Distribution of power:** 1 Role of the state, p. 102 2 Pluralist views, p. 103–4 3 Political parties and pressure groups, pp. 103–4 4 Elite theory, p. 104 5 Marxist theory, pp. 104–6 6 Role of globalization and transnational corporations, pp. 106–7 7 You could also consider the position of women, ethnic minorities and the underclass, p. 38 • You should look for empirical evidence to prove or refute the theories you have discussed
• Look critically at • Not necessarily political ones; plural, so more than one is expected • Focus is on changes, so do not lose sight of this • Only consider theories that suggest that class is less important than sex or ethnicity when you are evaluating • Ignore anywhere else • Keep to the time span, i.e. 1970s onwards	Or: Assess the sociological theories that explain the changes in the relationship between social class and voting behaviour in Britain in the last thirty years. [40 marks]	• Butler and Stokes (p. 108) could be the benchmark you use to look at the changes in class alignment • Reasons for de-alignment: 1 Policy preferences, p. 108 2 Volatility, p. 108 3 Role of ideology, pp. 108–9 • Theories that suggest that class alignment still exists: 1 Heath, Jowell and Curtice, pp. 108–9 2 Marxist theories about false consciousness • Consider theories that look at women and ethnic minorities as having different interests • Try to find empirical evidence to prove or refute the various arguments

Total: 60 marks

Time allowed: 1 hour

1 mark = 1 minute

Comments on the question	Question	Advice on preparing your answer
<ul><li>Make sure that you describe this view in a detailed way with supporting evidence</li><li>Look at a range of arguments for and against this point of view</li><li>Make sure that you have a balance, i.e. a similar number of arguments supporting the view and challenging the view</li></ul>	Outline and assess the view that the activities of new social movements aim to challenge the global capitalist order. [60 marks]	<ul><li>Remember that you don't have to accept this view. You can challenge it</li><li>An introduction is necessary to set the scene, i.e. which sociologist or theory takes this position</li><li>The section on pp. 107–8 should be useful in helping you to summarize the key arguments</li><li>Try to finish with an evaluative conclusion based on the evidence presented</li></ul>

Chapter 10

Work, unemployment and leisure *Textbook pp. 684–772*

Specifications

Specification	Relevant module title	Place in module	Level	Assessment	Other relevant modules
AQA	2: Education; Wealth, Poverty and Welfare; **Work and Leisure**	One of three topics in this module.	AS	One data-response question.	Material from Education may be used in the A2 synoptic module 6.
OCR	There is no module on this topic in the OCR specification.	n/a	n/a	n/a	The synoptic module **Social Inequality and Difference** considers inequality in the workplace.

Work, unemployment and leisure: essential notes

The nature of work

- Keith Grint (1991) argues that there is no single, universal definition of work that can be generally applied.
- Work is socially defined within particular societies. For example, although Grint defines housework as work, it is not always defined as such in male-dominated societies.
- In pre-industrial societies work was often regarded as an unfortunate necessity which should be kept to a minimum.
- Modern, industrial, capitalist societies tend to have more of a work ethic, seeing work as necessary and important, and unemployment or idleness as undesirable.
- Weber argued that the modern work ethic stemmed from the Protestant ethic, while E.P. Thompson (1967) attributed it to capitalist industrialization and the need to keep expensive machinery productive.

Work and leisure – conflict perspectives

Marx – alienated labour
- Marx argued that work was the means through which people fulfilled their potential as human beings.
- In capitalist societies people failed to gain true satisfaction from work.
- The products produced by workers were reduced to commodities to be sold in a market, rather than being an expression of the humanity of those who produced them.
- Workers were therefore alienated from the products they produced.
- Workers also became alienated from the act of production – the work itself – because they were forced to work for capitalists to earn a wage. They

no longer owned the means of production and had to work for those who owned the machinery etc.
- They were also alienated from fellow workers, since each individual was working purely for themselves rather than for the good of the community.
- Marx saw wage labour (work for a wage) as wage slavery. The worker was only given part of the value of the products they produced. The rest of it was stolen from them by capitalists, in the form of surplus value or profit.
- Marx thought that the problem of alienated labour could only be overcome through communism. In communism the means of production would be communally owned, and people would express their humanity through their work, working for the good of the community as a whole.

Critics have attacked Marx's views:
1. In communist countries such as the USSR people still felt alienated from their work.
2. Some Marxists have attacked Marx's work on alienation for being too abstract and philosophical and therefore unscientific.
3. Herbert Marcuse (1972) argued that people are increasingly alienated through consumption rather than production. Through advertising, people are encouraged to have false needs: they come to believe that they can only be fulfilled by purchasing and consuming unnecessary products.

Technology and work experience

Robert Blauner (1964) argued that alienation does not stem from the capitalist system but from the sort of technology employed at work.
  He defines alienation in terms of:
- The degree of control workers have over work.
- The amount of meaning they find in work.

115

- The degree of social integration within work.
- The degree of involvement in work.

In terms of these criteria, people who use craft technology – such as printers, who use their skill to produce a whole product from start to finish – are not alienated.

On the other hand, workers on assembly lines are highly alienated because their jobs are socially isolating and repetitive and require little use of skill or initiative.

However, Blauner believes that automation in industries such as the chemical industry will reduce alienation. Machines take over much of the routine work, and workers involved in monitoring, maintenance and repair of machinery have jobs which are not particularly alienating

Blauner has been criticized:

1 Marxists argue that he ignores the sources of alienation in the capitalist system.
2 The interpretation of the questionnaire data used by Blauner is open to question.
3 Grint (1998) argues that even in assembly-line systems much of the work is away from the assembly line itself, and this work is not alienating.
4 Grint sees Blauner as sexist, because Blauner suggested that women lacked the physical stamina to do certain types of work.
5 Nichols and Beynon (1977) found no evidence that levels of alienation had decreased in chemical plants. There was still much routine manual work, and many of those monitoring machines found the work tedious and unsatisfying.
6 Duncan Gallie (1978) studied oil refineries in England and France. The French workers were less satisfied than the British ones. This suggested that production technology on its own did not determine the degree of alienation. Instead management style was important. French managers were more autocratic than British ones.

Computers, technology and changes in work

There is a division between two main approaches in this area:

1 Technological determinism assumes that social life is determined by technology.
2 Social determinism assumes that cultural and social factors determine the development of technology and the uses to which it is put.

Many argue for an intermediate position between these two extremes.

Zuboff – In the Age of the Smart Machine

Shoshana Zuboff (1988) sees information technology as having a big impact on work, but she is not an extreme technological determinist.

She conducted a study of eight organizations, and found that:

- Manual skills were becoming less important where IT had been introduced.
- White-collar workers increasingly worked at computer terminals rather than interacting with one another, and they therefore felt more isolated.

- IT was also used to monitor the activities and performance of workers (the information panopticon).
- In some companies IT allowed greater participation by ordinary workers – e.g. in contributing ideas – which helped to break down hierarchies.

Zuboff concludes that managers use IT either to 'informate' a company (spread information to everybody to allow more participation) or to reassert hierarchical controls.

Clark, McLoughlin, Rose and King – The Process of Technological Change

Clark et al. (1988) argue that humans choose technology, but once chosen it has a strong influence on work.

From a study of telephone exchanges they found that the nature of the technology determined the type of skills needed to maintain the exchanges. However, there was considerable negotiation and decision making involved in determining who carried out the maintenance and how the work was organized.

Once working patterns were established, though, they became relatively fixed and hard to change, because they were constrained by the nature of the technology.

Kling – the consumption of technology

Rob Kling (1991, 1992) opposes theories that suggest that technology has a strong influence on work.

- He argues that technology can be used in many different ways and there is nothing inevitable about its influence on work.
- Using a series of case studies, he shows that technology can be used to increase efficiency, strengthen management control or expand the range of jobs carried out by individual employees.
- The impact of computers is largely shaped by the way in which companies organize access on information systems rather than by the nature of the technology.

Grint and Woolgar – discourse and computers

Keith Grint and Steve Woolgar (1992, 1997) argue that the use that is made of information technology is shaped by the discourse surrounding it – that is, the way people talk about the technology.

Those who have the power to shape the way the technology is talked about and interpreted, shape the sort of use to which it is put.

Critics argue that this view goes too far in attributing no importance to the nature of the technology itself. However people interpret technology, it retains certain objective capabilities which limit the uses to which it can be put.

The labour process and the degradation of work

The labour process concerns the way in which raw materials are transformed by human labour.

Harry Braverman (1974) puts forward a Marxist view of the labour process.

- He argues that automation results from attempts to change the labour process in order to increase the exploitation of workers.

- He believes that work has been progressively deskilled – the amount of skill needed to do jobs has been reduced.
- Deskilling is used so that employers can control workers more easily.
- Complex tasks are broken down into many simple operations, reducing the need for workers to use their initiative or skill, and allowing managers to control work more directly.
- Scientific management, developed by W. Taylor in the early twentieth century, was used to deskill work by analysing it and reducing the 'brain work' needed to carry out tasks.
- Management does make some concessions – such as higher wages for a few employees or human relations-style management – to make work more tolerable.
- Braverman claims that deskilling has not just affected manufacturing, but also clerical work, and professional work such as nursing and teaching. There have been many responses to Braverman.
- Andrew Zimbalist (1979) uses evidence from the printing industry to support Braverman.
- Paul Thompson (1983) argues that craft work was never as important as Braverman assumes, and the amount of deskilling has therefore been exaggerated by Braverman.
- Duncan Gallie (1994) argues that the expansion of the service class has led to an increase in workforce skill. He found that most British employees believe that the amount of skill required in their job has been increasing. Upskilling was more common than deskilling, although part-time female workers experienced more deskilling than other groups.
- Craig Littler (1983) believes that Braverman exaggerates the influence of scientific management.
- Some Marxists argue that methods other than deskilling (such as the use of technology to monitor workers) have become more important in controlling workers.
- Andy Friedman (1977) stresses that workers often resist management attempts to impose greater control.
- Braverman fails to define skill precisely. Some feminists argue that Braverman fails to recognize the amount of skill required in some female jobs.
- Sylvia Walby (1986) suggests that unions have protected skill levels in many male jobs, but they have failed to protect or gain proper wages for skilled female workers.

Flexibility and post-Fordism

Some sociologists argue that important changes have taken place in work which have led to increased skill requirements rather than deskilling.

Fordism (named after Henry Ford) involved the mass production of standardized products using relatively unskilled workers on machines dedicated to particular products. Fordist production techniques followed these assembly-line production methods.

Some people argue that there has been a shift to post-Fordism, or flexible production.

- Michael Piore (1986) argues that new computer technology makes production more flexible – it is easy to shift to making new products. This enables the production of small batches of specialized products. Flexible specialization requires more skilled and versatile workers.
- John Atkinson (1985) argues that, from the 1970s, the flexible firm developed as a response to economic recession. It involved:
1 Functional flexibility: the ability to shift core workers to different tasks.
2 Numerical flexibility: the facility to reduce or increase the size of the workforce. Workers were increasingly employed in subcontracted, part-time or temporary jobs rather than full-time permanent ones. These peripheral workers needed less skill and had less security than core workers.

There have been a number of responses to theories of post-Fordism:
1 Anna Pollert (1988) argues that Fordist production methods were never completely dominant in industry, and that Fordist production continues to be common today. She argues that flexibility does not necessarily increase the skills needed by workers, and she questions whether companies are shifting to peripheral rather than core, full-time workers.
2 Stephen Wood (1989), in a study of steel-rolling mills, found that flexibility did not increase skill requirements.
3 Dex and McCulloch (1997) studied statistical evidence on the British labour market and found some increase, but only a small one, in the proportions involved in flexible work.
4 Paul Thompson (1993) argues that there has been some move towards greater flexibility but the change should not be exaggerated. Workers are expected to perform a greater variety of tasks (multi-tasking) but in many workplaces (e.g. McDonald's) each task requires little skill. Often work is simply intensified rather than reskilled.

Conflict and cooperation at work

- Functionalists such as Talcott Parsons argue that workers and management share common goals – i.e. the success of their company. There should therefore be little conflict.
- Pluralists believe that there are some differences of interest between workers and employers (e.g. over wage levels), but there are some shared interests as well. For example, workers do not want to increase wages to the extent that they put their company out of business and lose their jobs. According to pluralists, different interests are represented in industrial societies. For example, workers have trade unions to represent them.
- Marxists argue that workers are exploited under capitalism, through the extraction of surplus value. This provides the potential for conflict at work.

The Marxists Littler and Salaman (1984) argue that employers tend to deskill and regulate work as much as possible in order to increase profits. However, they have to try to maintain a minimum level of cooperation.

Strikes

Strikes are one of the most obvious forms of industrial conflict.

- A strike is a stoppage of work by a group of employees.
- Strike statistics suggest that the strike rate was quite high from 1988 to 1992, but it declined in the later 1990s.
- Strike statistics may not be entirely accurate. They are based on employers' reports (which may underestimate the amount of striking). Definitions of strikes vary from country to country. In Britain, political strikes, strikes involving fewer than ten workers and strikes lasting less than one day are not included.

There appear to have been a number of phases of strike activity and trade union development in Britain.

- From the 1950s until the late 1970s there were several periods with high strike rates, and trade unions appeared to have considerable power.
- In 1979, Margaret Thatcher, leader of the Conservatives, was elected as prime minister, and she decided to undermine union power by introducing new laws which restricted the ability of unions to stage successful strikes.
- According to Hyman (1984), these changes led to considerable conflict with unions in the short term, but in the long term they weakened union power.
- Keith Grint (1991) argues that economic changes (such as high unemployment and low inflation), rather than government policies, are responsible for declining strike rates.
- Peter Ackers et al. (1996) argue that a variety of changes –e.g. the growth of subcontracting and part-time employment, new management techniques and information technology – have made it difficult for unions to retain the mass loyalty of workers, and this has led to them being more pragmatic.
- The Labour government elected in 1997 kept its distance from trade unions (unlike previous Labour governments), but it did introduce some laws that unions approved of (such as the minimum wage).

The causes of strikes

A variety of explanations for strikes have been put forward.

- In an early study, Kerr and Siegel (1954) argued that strikes were more common in jobs based in integrated communities (such as mining, dock work and shipbuilding). However, as coalmining and dock work have declined in importance and bargaining power, the strike rate has also declined.
- Writers such as Blauner (1964) argued that alienating mass production techniques (such as those used in car factories) led to a high strike rate. However, strike rates are much lower in the Japanese and German car industries than in Britain.
- Millward et al. (1992) found that strikes were most common in workplaces with a high proportion of manual workers, larger establishments, workplaces with a high level of unionization and workplaces with many different unions.

- Hyman argues that the workers' definition of the situation is more important than factors such as technology.
- Most strikes are over wages or redundancies, but Lane and Roberts (1971) argue that the underlying cause is always power.

Other forms of conflict

- Taylor and Walton (1971) have studied industrial sabotage, which involves deliberately damaging the work environment or interfering with production. This can have a number of motives:
1. It may be an attempt to reduce tension and frustration.
2. It could be an attempt to make work easier.
3. It can be used to assert workers' control.
- Edwards and Scullion (1982) examined the relationship between different forms of industrial conflict, including strikes, industrial sabotage, absenteeism, labour turnover, breaches of factory discipline and the withdrawal of cooperation and effort by workers.

They found conflict in all the workplaces they studied, but the nature of the conflict varied:

- Where the management had strong control, absenteeism and labour turnover tended to be high.
- Where workers had a stronger bargaining position, strikes were more common.

Unemployment

Unemployment statistics

- Between 1948 and 1966 the official unemployment rate in the UK averaged less than 2% of the workforce.
- In the period between 1975 and 1978 it rose to above 6%.
- Unemployment reached a peak in 1985 and 1986 when 11.8% of the workforce were unemployed.
- Rates then fell until 1992 when another peak of 10.8% was reached.
- Unemployment figures then steadily reduced to reach 4.5% in 1999.

Official statistics as an overestimation

Although most commentators would accept that official unemployment figures provide a general indication of trends in unemployment, such statistics need to be treated with great caution.

Some critics of the statistics have argued that they exaggerate the amount of unemployment. In the 1980s various Conservatives claimed that up to one million of the 'unemployed' were either working and claiming benefit illegally or not genuinely looking for work.

However, such claims may be exaggerated. Pahl (1984), for example, found that the unemployed were no more likely to engage in 'informal work' than those with paid employment.

Official statistics as an underestimation

Sociologists usually argue that official statistics underestimate the amount of unemployment rather than exaggerate it.

- Between 1979 and 1987, Margaret Thatcher's Conservative government changed the method of calculating unemployment statistics 19 times, and nearly all of these changes removed substantial numbers from the unemployment register.

- In 1996 unemployment benefit was replaced by the Jobseeker's Allowance. Sweeney and McMahon (1998) estimated that the associated set of changes removed about 60,000 claimants from the statistics.
- Unemployment figures have been further reduced by various training schemes, which remove young people in particular from the unemployment register.

The social distribution of unemployment
Unemployment is not evenly distributed among groups in the population. Despite the limitations of official figures, it is possible to identify overall patterns.

Class
The lower social classes are the most likely to experience unemployment. There was concern that the recession of the early 1990s was causing unemployment to spread to service-sector jobs, but upper middle-class workers continued to have much lower rates.

Gender
Official figures show higher unemployment rates for men than for women. According to recent figures, the unemployment rate for men was more than two-and-a-half times that for women. However, the female rate is likely to be an underestimate, as married women are sometimes ineligible for the benefits that would lead to them being registered.

Age
There are higher rates of unemployment for the young, though the unemployment rate for older men sometimes exceeds the national average. Although youth unemployment was seen as a serious issue in the 1980s and 1990s, unemployment is more likely to be a long-term problem for older members of the workforce.

Ethnicity
In general, ethnic minorities suffer from higher rates of unemployment. The rate for Indians is closest to the white rate. Unemployment is particularly common among younger members of ethnic minorities.

Region
Unemployment tends to be highest in regions that have traditionally relied on the heavier industries; these were badly hit in the recessions of the late 1970s and early 1980s. However, the gap between different regions narrowed in the 1990s, and there were some pockets of relatively high unemployment in areas of the south of England, including London.

Disability
Nearly 60% of those with a 'work-limiting' disability were economically inactive in 1998, with a further 6% unemployed.

Statistically, then, you are most likely to suffer from unemployment if you are a young, unskilled, male worker living in Northern Ireland, Wales or northern England, particularly if you are disabled.

The causes of unemployment, and government policy

Technological change and deindustrialization
Recent decades have seen a continuing decline in the importance of manufacturing industry, and some commentators have seen these changes as representing a deindustrialization of Britain, with serious implications for future unemployment.

Gill (1985) has suggested that new technology threatens to reduce the workforce in numerous occupations. The recession of the early 1990s seemed in line with this view, but recovery later in the decade seemed to suggest that a move towards a more service-based economy did not inevitably mean high levels of unemployment.

Theories of unemployment – market liberal theory
For much of the period since 1945 governments have accepted that they should take responsibility for maintaining low levels of unemployment – an approach based on the ideas of the British economist J.M. Keynes.

However, faced with rising inflation as well as rising unemployment, the Conservative government of Margaret Thatcher turned to market liberal economic theories which challenged the Keynesian view. These theories emphasized the importance of leaving market forces to determine the way the economy developed.

Taxation was reduced, nationalized industries were privatized and public support for 'lame duck' industries was withdrawn. It was hoped that unemployment would fall because:
- The costs of employing people would fall as unions lost power.
- Cutting welfare benefits would mean that there would be more incentive to accept low-paid work.

Evaluation of Conservative policies
MacInnes (1987) argues that market liberal policies actually caused unemployment to rise. However, it is possible to argue that some Conservative policies contributed to a fall in unemployment in the late 1990s.

Marxist theories of unemployment
Marx saw unemployment as resulting from the capitalist system itself. He believed that capitalist economies went through cycles. Periods of expansion in which there was full employment were followed by periods of crisis during which unemployment rose. Each successive crisis would be worse than the previous one until eventually the capitalist system would be destroyed.

Capitalism requires workers who can be hired during booms and fired during slumps. Marx refers to the part of the workforce who are used in this way as the reserve army of labour. The unemployed are the victims of the cyclical way in which the capitalist economy works.

Evaluation of Marxist views
Clearly Marx's predictions of the collapse of capitalism have not come true. Indeed the economic systems of some former communist countries came closer to collapse under communism than those of advanced capitalist countries. However, economic crises continue

to hit the capitalist system periodically – e.g. the problems experienced by Japan and other south-east Asian countries in the late 1990s.

The Labour government and unemployment policies
Despite the Labour Party's traditional commitment to full employment, Tony Blair's government only committed themselves to reducing unemployment rather than eradicating it. They introduced a number of policies, such as the 'New Deal', aimed at encouraging the unemployed back to work and giving employers incentives to take them on.

The effects of unemployment

The effects on society
The effects of unemployment are usually seen as damaging to society.
- Sinfield (1981) identifies four ways in which unemployment reduces quality of life in a society:
1 Those remaining in work feel less secure and may have their standard of living threatened.
2 Workers become less willing to leave an unsatisfactory job.
3 The unemployed and those in unsatisfying jobs may scapegoat weaker groups in society, such as married women or ethnic minorities, blaming them for their problems.
4 High unemployment reduces the chance of equality of opportunity being achieved. Employers no longer need to make an effort to recruit from disadvantaged groups.
- Lea and Young (1984) argue that unemployment amongst the young leads to their marginalization. This helped to create the subculture of despair which led to the urban riots of the 1980s.
- Allen and Watson (1986) point out that a range of social problems have been linked to unemployment but that such problems usually do not have one single, simple cause.

The personal effects of unemployment

Financial effects
Perhaps the most obvious effects of unemployment are financial. Gallie and Vogler's research for the Social Change and Economic Life Initiative (SCELI) (1994) found that many of the unemployed experienced considerable financial difficulties.

Social effects
Fagin and Little (1984) argue that the unemployed lose more than money when they lose their job.
- Work gives people a sense of identity and is a source of relationships outside the family.
- Work also provides obligatory activity. Fagin and Little's study of unemployed men in London revealed that many found it difficult to occupy themselves.
- Work helps to structure psychological time. The men in the study spent more of their time in bed, but their sleep was restless and they felt more tired than they did in paid employment.
- Work provides opportunities to develop skills and creativity, and it provides a sense of purpose. This sense of purpose is lost in times of unemployment.

- Fagin and Little argue that income from work provides freedom and control outside work. It creates the possibility of engaging in leisure activities that cost money.

Such effects can place strain on the personal relationships of the unemployed. Lampard (1994) found that marriages were more likely to break up during periods of unemployment.

Leisure and unemployment
One possible gain from unemployment is an increase in leisure time.
- Kelvin et al. (1989) found that only certain types of leisure increased with unemployment. Most of the leisure was solitary and passive and failed to compensate for the loss of social contacts at work.
- Gallie, Gershuny and Vogler (1994) found that men were slightly more likely to play and watch sport once they became unemployed, although women were less likely to take part in these activities. Expensive pastimes such as visiting the cinema decreased, while watching television and reading books increased.

Psychological reactions to unemployment
Research by Gershuny (1994) found that the unemployed had poorer psychological health than the employed. However, the psychological well-being of those of the unemployed who had wide social contacts and felt positive about how they spent their time was better than amongst the employed who did not have these advantages.

Physical health and unemployment
Perhaps the most dramatic claims about the effects of unemployment relate to health. In a review of research on this subject, Laurance (1986) notes the following conclusions:
1 Unemployed school leavers in Leeds were found to experience poorer mental health than those who got jobs.
2 A study based on 1971 census data (and confirmed by a 1997 Council of Churches report) identified higher mortality rates amongst unemployed men compared to the employed.
3 Researchers in Edinburgh in 1982 found that the suicide rate was 11 times higher for unemployed men than for employed men.
4 National studies of child development have found that the children of the unemployed are on average shorter than other children.

Youth and the effects of unemployment
British governments have devoted significant resources to dealing with youth unemployment. They identify unemployment as a particularly serious problem for the young.
- This view is supported by Willis (1984). He argues that unemployment disrupts the normal transition to adulthood. The young unemployed are denied the opportunity to be independent from parents, and often experience long periods of poverty.
- Not all researchers agree with this view. Roberts (1986) accepts that young people do not enjoy

unemployment, but he believes that they are better-equipped to deal with it than many older workers, as they have not yet established firm occupational identities.

Gender and the effects of unemployment

Most of the research on the effects of unemployment has focused on male unemployment.

- Writers such as Sinfield (1981) argued that women might be expected to suffer less from unemployment because domestic life offers them a sense of identity and purpose.
  This view was challenged during the 1980s.
- Henwood and Miles (1987) found that unemployment was at least as potentially damaging for women as it was for men, and that housewives suffer some of the problems – such as lack of social contact – associated with unemployment.
- It is sometimes assumed that working women suffer fewer financial hardships from unemployment. However, Coyle (1984) challenges this assumption. She found that wives' wages are usually a 'crucial component of family household income' and that unemployed married women resent returning to a state of financial dependence on men.

The effects on communities

Critcher, Dicks and Waddington (1992) studied two pit villages in Yorkshire which had experienced pit closures. The closures had significant effects on the local communities.

- The local economy suffered. Some local shops and services closed.
- The appearance of the villages declined, and community facilities started to decay.
- Informal mechanisms of social control began to break down. Drug-taking, burglary and other crimes increased.
- Marriages and family life came under increasing stress.

Leisure

The sociology of leisure has only been a major focus of study since the 1970s. Early contributions concentrated on the relationship between leisure and other areas of social life such as work and the family.

Parker – the influence of work on leisure

Stanley Parker (1976) defined leisure as the time left over once other obligations have been attended to. Parker argued that leisure activities were closely related to the freedom, autonomy (control) and satisfaction people experience at work. He saw the relationship between work and leisure as falling into three main patterns.

1 The extension pattern

In this pattern, work extends into leisure: there is no clear dividing line between the two. This pattern is associated with occupations providing high levels of involvement, autonomy and job satisfaction. Outside office hours, clients and colleagues are involved in leisure pursuits which allow business and pleasure to be combined.

2 The neutrality pattern

In the neutrality pattern, a clear distinction is made between work and leisure. Family life and leisure, rather than work, provide the central interest in life. Occupations typically associated with the neutrality pattern include clerical and semi-skilled manual work, where there are medium to low degrees of autonomy.

3 The opposition pattern

Here work is sharply differentiated from leisure. The opposition pattern is associated with jobs that often produce a feeling of hostility towards work. Hours of leisure are long and are used mainly to recover from and compensate for work. Activities include drinking in pubs and working men's clubs. This pattern is associated with traditional manual work such as mining and trawling.

Criticisms of Parker

1 Parker tends to ignore factors other than work which influence leisure patterns. The Rapoports (1975), for example, believe that family lifestyle is the most important influence on leisure. The leisure pursuits of adolescents tend to be different from those of middle-aged or retired people, for example.
2 Clarke and Critcher (1985) point out that Parker's analysis is rather deterministic: it does not allow for individual choice in leisure activities and does not account for the wide range of leisure activities engaged in by people who have the same job.
3 Clarke and Critcher also suggest that Parker's work does not deal successfully with the leisure patterns of women. He does not examine the influence of housework or the open-ended nature of domestic obligations for many women.

Roberts – a pluralist perspective on leisure

Ken Roberts (1978, 1986) stresses the variety of leisure patterns and the range of factors that influence those patterns. He sees leisure as involving individual freedom of choice.

Social factors and leisure

Unlike Parker, Roberts claims that work has relatively little influence on leisure. Many people do not have paid employment, and, even amongst those who do, television takes up the largest single block of leisure time for all occupational groups.

Roberts identifies other social factors that he believes are significant in leisure choices.

- Family life cycle is a significant factor. Unmarried people under 30 spend less time watching television and more time socializing than their married counterparts.
- Gender is important as women tend to have less leisure time than men.
- Those who stay longer in education watch less television and spend more time outside the home with friends.
- Married couples with joint conjugal roles tend to engage in home-centred leisure, while those with segregated conjugal roles tend to go out more. (See pp. 94–5 for a discussion of roles in marrriage.)

Clarke and Critcher – leisure in capitalist Britain

John Clarke and Chas Critcher (1985) have developed a neo-Marxist approach to leisure. They believe that writers such as Roberts exaggerate the degree of choice involved in leisure. Individual choices are limited by capitalism.

Capitalism and leisure

Clarke and Critcher claim that capitalism shapes the nature of work and leisure. The development of capitalism removed many of the opportunities for leisure that existed before the Industrial Revolution and created a clear distinction between work and leisure.

The state plays a key role in regulating leisure.

- It licenses certain leisure activities, such as pubs and clubs, and it censors films and videos.
- It is involved in the regulation of public space. The disadvantaged tend to use public spaces for leisure, and this means that the young, ethnic minorities and the working class in general have part of their recreation controlled by the police.
- The state is concerned to prevent disorderly leisure which might be a threat to social order. Middle-class tastes are promoted (e.g. the provision of subsidies to opera companies), and working-class leisure patterns are discouraged.

The commercialization of leisure

Perhaps the most important aspect of leisure under capitalism is the way it has become big business. Large corporations create new products and services and attempt to persuade consumers to purchase them.

However, despite their attempts to establish hegemony (or domination), big business has not always been successful. Clarke and Critcher give the example of CAMRA (the Campaign for Real Ale) which has resisted large brewers' attempts to replace natural with keg beers.

Evaluation of 'class domination' theories

Clarke and Critcher see leisure as being a far more restricted area of social life than Roberts. To Roberts, leisure choices in Britain are as free as can be expected in any society. Companies can only succeed if they provide what consumers want.

Both Roberts and Clarke and Critcher can be accused of generalizing about the role of leisure in society and paying too little attention to evidence that may contradict their theories.

Gender and leisure

Since the start of the 1980s, feminist sociologists have devoted increasing attention to the relationship between gender and leisure patterns.

Green, Hebron and Woodward – a feminist perspective

Green et al. (1990) studied 700 women in Sheffield, using a range of methods.

The definition of leisure

- Many of the women interviewed found it hard to separate leisure from other aspects of their lives, but often saw it as a state of mind.
- It is much harder for women to forget about work and put aside time for leisure because women tend to have open-ended domestic responsibilities.
- Some women with part-time jobs actually saw those jobs as a form of leisure – an opportunity to escape from domestic chores and a chance to socialize.

Patterns of work and leisure

- Overall, men have more time for leisure than women.
- Leisure for many married women is restricted by financial dependence on their husbands.
- Traditional male attitudes mean that women are often expected to choose their leisure activities from a restricted range of home- and family-based activities.

Leisure and social control

- Physical violence and sexual attacks outside the home make women afraid to venture out, particularly if they are on their own and it is dark.
- Many leisure venues are dominated by men, and women may feel uncomfortable in them. In Green et al.'s study, 80% of women said that they felt uncomfortable in a pub on their own.
- Ideology also limits women's behaviour. For example, many mothers feel guilty about leaving their children.
- Most married women took responsibility for the majority of housework, often in addition to paid employment. They thus had little time available for leisure.

Other influences on leisure

The Sheffield study found that a variety of other factors also affected leisure.

- Class – women from higher classes have more opportunity to engage in expensive leisure pursuits. They are more likely to participate in sport and keep-fit activities than working-class women.
- Age, work and domestic situation – single, young, employed women probably have the most freedom in leisure. They have more financial independence and fewer domestic responsibilities than married women. There are fewer ideological restrictions on their leisure outside the home, and there is no husband to frown on their behaviour.
- Ethnic group – ethnic-minority women are subject to racial as well as sexual harassment, and may be even more unwilling than other women to go out to leisure activities.

Different cultural traditions may affect leisure choices. Green et al. claim that Asian men are reluctant to encourage women to go out. Afro-Caribbean women are less restricted in their leisure, which is less home-based than for Asian women, and this encourages independence.

Conclusion

Although their emphasis is on the constraints on women, Green et al. are not entirely pessimistic. They found that women are able to develop and maintain friendships in many unlikely settings, such as outside the school gates and at the shops. They are also slightly more active than men in voluntary organizations and are more likely to attend night classes.

Modernity, postmodernity and leisure

A number of sociologists in recent years have argued that we are entering an era of postmodernity, and as a result the nature of leisure is changing.

Rojek – Decentring leisure

Chris Rojek (1995) argues that leisure needs to be decentred. By this he means that leisure should not be seen as a clearly demarcated area of social life which can be studied in its own right. This is because:

- Leisure can best be understood by examining it within the context of the society in which it exists.
- In postmodernity the meaning of leisure becomes less clear. Leisure overlaps with other areas of social life.

Rojek identifies some general differences between modern and postmodern leisure.

Modern leisure	Postmodern leisure
Work and leisure are two separate areas.	Work and leisure come together – for example, more people work in the leisure industries and experience fun and enjoyment at work.
Celebration of the authentic. For example, visiting the Tower of London is superior to visiting a model of it.	Virtual reality machines, models and representations are fully accepted as valid.
People have a strong sense of who they are and engage in leisure pursuits appropriate to their age-group identity.	Age-group identity is no longer a limitation to leisure. Older people might go to night-clubs and rock concerts, and younger people may engage in more sedate pursuits such as golf.
There are clear distinctions between different roles and areas of social life – for example, male and female, white and ethnic cultures.	People can pick and choose who they want to be, and leisure plays a central role in identity politics. Your leisure actually creates your identity.
There is a sharp distinction between the providers and consumers of leisure.	People cooperate to organize their own leisure.

Evaluation of Rojek

Rojek makes very general statements about leisure. As such he exaggerates and simplifies the changes in leisure that he claims have taken place. He provides little evidence to support his arguments.

Scraton and Bramham – leisure and postmodernity

Modernity and leisure

In the modern period, the state and voluntary groups became involved in organizing leisure activities that were supposed to benefit individuals and/or society. One focus of the policies was youth – particularly working-class males, who were seen as a potential social problem. Youth clubs and the Scouts were designed to keep young people occupied and out of trouble.

The idea of rational, planned leisure began to lose influence after the Second World War as society became more diverse and fragmented. These developments heralded changes which some refer to as postmodern leisure.

Postmodern leisure

Sheila Scraton and Peter Bramham identify a number of features of postmodern leisure.

1. Postmodern leisure is concerned with self-indulgence. You do what you want rather than what others tell you is good for you.
2. Elites can no longer dictate to the masses what is good for them. There is an enormous variety of subcultural groups pursuing their own leisure activities, from trainspotting to bungee jumping.
3. Leisure is an expression of the pursuit of a particular lifestyle. It is a means to express who you are, rather than a search for relaxation or self-improvement. People's identities become more wrapped up in the consumer goods they buy and their choice of pastimes, rather than in their jobs, families or communities.
4. Postmodernity blurs the distinction between work and leisure. Work increasingly intrudes into the home through emails and fax machines, while work sometimes becomes an extension of leisure activities.
5. Postmodern leisure involves an increasing concern with the body. 'Working-out' is all part of the attempt to develop a distinctive lifestyle, body shape and identity.
6. Nostalgia becomes important in postmodern leisure because people have lost faith in the future. The heritage industry grows and more people visit places that claim to recreate the past. However, this is often achieved through simulation and virtual reality – what the postmodern writer Baudrillard calls simulacra.

Evaluation of postmodern theories of leisure

Scraton and Bramham acknowledge that many of the changes described by postmodernists have taken place. However, they argue that these changes affect some groups more than others.

- Poorer sections of society do not have the time or the money to engage in postmodern leisure pursuits.
- Leisure remains gendered. Scraton and Bramham point out that video games and virtual reality technology are mostly enjoyed by men.
- Racism also restricts leisure activities. Scraton and Bramham quote research which suggests that racism is prevalent in many British sports.

1 According to Grint, work is:
   a Activity you get paid for
   b Activities other than leisure
   c Activities that involve effort
   d Activities that a society defines as work

2 According to Marx, work in capitalist societies produces:
   a Boredom   b Alienation
   c Anomie   d Egoism

3 According to Blauner, the degree of alienation experienced by workers is determined by:
   a The type of technology being used
   b The management techniques being used
   c The mental states of the workers
   d The nature of the capitalist system

4 Which of the following is not a criticism of Blauner?
   a Blauner made sexist comments about women's ability to do certain kinds of work
   b Blauner underestimated the alienation of assembly-line work
   c Blauner's questionnaire data could be interpreted in different ways
   d Management styles might determine the degree of alienation experienced by workers

5 Which of the following writers argues that the choice of technology is crucial in shaping work?
   a Zuboff
   b Clark, McLoughlin, Rose and King
   c Kling
   d Grint and Woolgar

6 Which of the following writers argues that the discourse surrounding technology shapes the way it influences work?
   a Zuboff
   b Clark, McLoughlin, Rose and King
   c Kling
   d Grint and Woolgar

7 What, according to Harry Braverman, has happened to work in capitalist societies?
   a It has been upskilled
   b It has been reskilled
   c It has become characterized by multi-tasking
   d It has been deskilled

8 The term Fordism refers to:
   a The manufacturing of motor cars
   b Manufacturing based on mass production
   c A management theory
   d The use of highly skilled workers

9 Which one of the following is not a characteristic of post-Fordism?
   a The production of small batches
   b A heavy reliance upon full-time, permanent workers
   c The use of flexible core workers
   d The ability to shift production to new products

10 Which of the following believe that management and workers have some different interests but also share some interests in common?
   a Pluralists   b Functionalists
   c Marxists   d Feminists

11 The highest point reached by the unemployment rate, since the Second World War, was in:
   a 1948
   b 1972
   c 1985
   d 1999

12 Which one of the following beliefs is not associated with a market liberal view?
   a Cutting welfare benefits will create more incentive to accept lower-paid jobs and will therefore reduce unemployment
   b If unions lose power, wage rates will decrease and employers will be able to take on more workers
   c Prospects for employment in the long term will be improved if market forces determine the way the economy develops
   d Government support for failing industries will reduce unemployment in the long term

13 Marxists refer to the part of the workforce that can be hired during booms and fired during slumps as:
   a The proletariat
   b The reserve army of labour
   c The bourgeoisie
   d Capitalism

14 Which of the following sociologists supports the view that young people are better-equipped to deal with unemployment than many older workers?
   a Willis
   b Sinfield
   c Roberts
   d Lea and Young

15 Which of the following sociologists suggests that women might be expected to suffer less from unemployment because domestic life offers them a sense of purpose and identity?
   a Sinfield
   b Henwood and Miles
   c Coyle
   d Roberts

16 Parker identified three patterns in the relationship between work and leisure. Which of the following is not one of those patterns?
   a The oppositional pattern
   b The marginal pattern
   c The neutrality pattern
   d The extension pattern

17 Which one of the following statements would be most likely to be supported by Roberts?
   a Leisure is a tool of the capitalist class
   b Leisure is central to creating identities in the postmodern world
   c There is considerable freedom of choice in the area of leisure activities
   d Leisure is a gendered activity

18 Which one of the following statements would be most likely to be supported by Clarke and Critcher?
   a Leisure is a tool of the capitalist class
   b Leisure is central to creating identities in the postmodern world
   c There is considerable freedom of choice in the area of leisure activities
   d Leisure is a gendered activity

19 Which one of the following statements would be most likely to be supported by Green et al.?
  a Leisure is a tool of the capitalist class
  b Leisure is central to creating identities in the postmodern world
  c There is considerable freedom of choice in the area of leisure activities
  d Leisure is a gendered activity

20 Which one of the following statements would be most likely to be supported by Rojek?
  a Leisure is a tool of the capitalist class
  b Leisure is central to creating identities in the postmodern world
  c There is considerable freedom of choice in the area of leisure activities
  d Leisure is a gendered activity

Develop your analysis and evaluation skills   (see p. 205 for guidance notes)

For each of the following statements, identify which sociologists would argue in favour of and which against the view expressed. Explain the reasons for their view.

1 Capitalism is the cause of alienation in capitalist societies.
2 Technology determines relationships at work.
3 Capitalist economies have shifted from Fordism to post-Fordism, and in the process most workers have been reskilled.
4 Industrial relations are increasingly characterized by peace and harmony.
5 Unemployment is caused by the capitalist system and has damaging effects on individuals and society.
6 Leisure patterns are determined to a large extent by the paid work people do.

AQA style Work and Leisure question, AS Unit 2

Answer all parts of this question
Total: 60 marks   1 mark = 1.25 minutes
Time allowed: 1 hour 15 minutes

ITEM A

Here is a clear statement of this view, use it to help you identify criticisms for part [b]

Technology affects work in a number of ways: the physical exertion required, the level of skill, the possibility of interaction with others. Technological determinism argues that machines and how they are organized lead directly to certain types of structures and specific attitudes held by workers.

Here is a specific type of determinism, which will help you to answer part [a]

ITEM B

There are two main responses to the question 'Why do people work?' The difference is often based on class, with the working class adopting an instrumental view and the middle class a self-actualizing view.

Here is information you need to interpret an answer to part [d]

An instrumental view sees work as a means to an end, and so focuses on the need to earn money to support a particular lifestyle. A self-actualizing view sees work as a means of fulfilling human potential and a source of personal satisfaction.

Use this material to help you answer part [c]

Comments on the question	Question	Advice on preparing your answer
• The item will help you to interpret the more general meaning of the word	[a] Explain the meaning of 'determinism'. [Item A, line 4] [2 marks]	• Read the section in Chapter 1 on positivism (p. 3) to help you • Make a general statement from the example in the item
• Do exactly this, just list them • You will not gain marks by saying 'it is too deterministic', as this is tautological. You have to say what this criticism means	[b] Identify two criticisms of technological determinism as a theory. [Item A, lines 3–4] [4 marks]	• You can apply the criticisms of Blauner's work (pp. 115–6) to answer this question
• No more, no less! • If you know more about factors that make work alienating, turn them round to answer the question set	[c] Suggest three characteristics of work in industrial societies that may make it fulfilling. [6 marks]	• Marx and Blauner (p. 115–6) describe alienation, which can be turned round to answer this question
• You must show both skills for both of the motivations in the item	[d] Identify and explain how the two motivations to work [Item B, lines 3–4] might be linked to patterns of leisure. [8 marks]	• An application of Parker's theory (p. 121) will provide an answer to this question
• An analysis of the relationship between two variables can be done in a number of ways: 1 Cause and effect, or effect to cause 2 A third variable could be the underlying cause of both 3 There may be an intervening variable that is more important 4 The relationship may have no causal association • You might want to define this term	[e] Examine the relationship between motivation to work and unemployment. [20 marks]	• Unemployment as cause of low motivation – Fagin and Little (p. 120) • Unemployment as effect – New Right/market liberal theory (p. 119) sought to increase incentives to work by cutting benefits • Physical and mental health may be an intervening variable (p. 119) • Marxists would see capitalism as the underlying problem that affects both (pp. 119–20)
• Discuss both sides of the argument • Bring in additional information • Refers to computerization, therefore the focus should be on more recent studies • This is the opposite of de-skilling • You could distinguish between white-collar and manual workers	[f] Using material from Item B and elsewhere, assess the claim that new technology has led to an upskilling of the workforce. [20 marks]	• Zuboff and Clarke et al. (p. 116) show that this is not a simple relationship • Kling argues that it is not the technology but how it is used (p. 116) • Older works, e.g. Braverman and Taylor, could be used selectively and more for the later studies they generated (pp. 116–7) • Post-Fordism and flexibility and their critics (p. 117) will provide further evidence

Answer all parts of this question
Total: 90 marks
Time allowed: 1 hour 30 minutes

1 mark = 1 minute

These might help in answering part (a)

> ## ITEM A
>
> The theory of proletarianization suggests that routine white-collar or clerical workers have become part of the proletariat (working class) and can no longer be considered middle-class. Marxist sociologists such as Braverman see such workers as little different from manual workers because they do not own the means of production nor do they perform important social control functions for capitalists. Braverman notes that clerical workers, like skilled manual workers, have been de-skilled, especially by computerization. Clerical work, like factory work, is highly regulated. Clerical tasks have been broken down into simple routines and the office has become like a production line for mental work.
>
> ## ITEM B
>
> *Skill characteristics by class (%)*
>
> | | Lower non-manual (routine clerical) | Skilled manual |
> |---|---|---|
> | GCSE only required | 61 | 51 |
> | No training necessary | 52 | 43 |
> | Learnt to do the job in less than a month | 21 | 17 |
> | Responsible for the work of others | 22 | 27 |
> | Consider job skilled | 68 | 86 |

Make sure you are clear about how the data is organised. Double-check any statistics that you use in answering part (b).

Comments on the question	Question	Advice on preparing your answer
• These characteristics should be extracted from Item A • There is no need to offer any explanation for these characteristics	[a] Using only Item A, identify two characteristics that routine non-manual workers have in common with manual workers. [6 marks]	• The item contains a possible four characteristics from which you only have to choose two

Comments on the question	Question	Advice on preparing your answer
• Do not go beyond the item for your answer • There is no need to offer any explanation for these differences	[b] Using Item B only, identify two differences in the skill characteristics of non-manual and manual workers. [6 marks]	• Look carefully at how the data are organized • If you use the data in your response, double-check that you have interpreted it correctly
• Don't just compile a list. You must explain how you have broken down the concept and how the questionnaire you have designed measures it • No more, no less	[c] Identify and explain two ways in which proletarianization might be quantitatively measured using a questionnaire. [12 marks]	• A synoptic question, which wants you to apply your knowledge of methodology to an inequality and difference problem. • Look at the definition and account of proletarianization on p. 10 for ideas on how you might break the concept down into measurable components
• A synoptic instruction. As well as using material from this unit for evidence, you should dip into two or three other topics you have covered • You only have to describe this evidence. There is no need to explain it	[d] Using your wider sociological knowledge, outline the evidence for the view that manual workers experience a greater range of inequalities compared with other social groups. [22 marks]	• Focus on statistics, trends and sociological studies • See p. 11 for evidence relating to this topic area • Other information can be found in the following topic areas
• Describe the main features of the argument and its supporting evidence • Examine specific criticism of this position and describe alternative views	[e] Outline and assess the view that the de-skilling of non-manual work has led to changes in class formation and identity. [44 marks]	• Item A might prove useful for your introduction • See pp. 116–7 for an account of the view

Chapter 11

Education

Textbook pp. 773–882

Specifications

Specification	Relevant module title	Place in module	Level	Assessment	Other relevant modules
AQA	2: Education; Wealth, Poverty and Welfare; Work and Leisure	One of three topics in this module.	AS	One data-response question.	Material from this chapter may be used in the A2 synoptic module 6.
OCR	Power and Control	**Education** is one of six options in this module	AS	One essay question from a choice of two.	Material from this chapter may be used in the A2 synoptic module.

Education: essential notes

Educational policy in Britain

Free state education began in 1870. By 1918 attendance was compulsory up to the age of 14, rising to 16 in 1972.

Since the Second World War the key concerns of educational policy have been:

1 Widening access and participation
- The gradual raising of the school-leaving age
- The expansion of higher education
2 Promoting equality of opportunity
- The introduction of comprehensive education

Under the previous tripartite system children were sent to different types of school according to their supposed aptitude at the age of 11. With comprehensive education the intention was that the old divisions between middle-class grammar schools and working-class secondary moderns would disappear.

The Conservative governments of 1979–97 moved the emphasis away from equality of opportunity. Their priorities were different:

1 Improving educational standards
Introducing competition into the system would give greater choice and drive up standards. Successful schools would thrive while the failures would close. This set of policies became known as the marketization of education (see pp. 131–2).
2 Ensuring that education met the needs of employers
There was an emphasis on basic skills and on vocational (related to jobs) education and training. These policies became known as new vocationalism (see p. 133).

The Labour government of 1997 retained some of the concerns of the previous government:
- The emphasis on literacy and numeracy in primary schools
- Key Skills at post-16

However, they also paid attention to equality of opportunity issues:

- The introduction of Education Action Zones where extra resources were provided to particularly deprived and difficult areas.

The British education system

Research by Benn and Chitty (1997) found that the British education system varied from locality to locality.

- Nearly all state secondary schools in Scotland and Wales were comprehensive but only 83% in England and none in Northern Ireland. Around 79% of secondary pupils were being educated in these schools.
- In England 9.6% of children were educated in private schools. These included both day and boarding schools. City Technology Colleges are also included in this category.
- Selective state schools also exist. Around 3% of secondary pupils are in grammar or secondary modern schools, and a further 4% are in selective 'foundation' schools (previously known as grant maintained schools).
- Voluntary and denominational schools account for 10% of pupils. These are funded by the state but in many cases retain control over finance and selection of pupils. Some denominational schools only allow access to pupils from their denomination (usually Church of England or Roman Catholic).
- There are also variations in the age ranges educated at various institutions. Some areas have middle schools for 9–13-year-olds, some have schools for 11–18-year-olds, while others cater for the 11–16 age range, with separate sixth-form colleges.
- Single-sex schools exist in some areas.

Education – a functionalist perspective

Functionalists ask two key questions about education:
1 What are the functions for society as a whole?

2 What are the functional relationships between education and other parts of the social system?

Functionalists tend to focus on the positive contribution education makes to society.

Durkheim – education and solidarity

Writing at the end of the nineteenth century, Durkheim saw the major function of education as the transmission of society's norms and values.

A vital task for all societies is the welding of a mass of individuals into a united whole – in other words, the creation of social solidarity. Education, and in particular the teaching of history, provides this link between the individual and society.

The school is a society in miniature. In school the child learns to interact with other members of the school community and to follow a fixed set of rules. This experience prepares the child for interacting with members of society as an adult and accepting social rules.

Education teaches individuals specific skills which are necessary for their future occupations.

Hargreaves – Durkheim and the modern school

Hargreaves (1982) has criticized the modern comprehensive school from a Durkheimian point of view. He claims that:

- Comprehensive schools place too much stress on developing the individual and not enough on the responsibility of the individual pupil to the school.
- If pupils do not achieve individual success they tend to rebel and form anti-school subcultures (see p. 131) which reject the values of wider society.

Criticisms of Durkheim

1 Durkheim assumes that the norms and values promoted in schools are those of society as a whole rather than those of powerful groups.
2 Most contemporary changes in education appear to be aimed at encouraging individual competition and training pupils for particular vocations. It could be argued that the sort of education favoured by Durkheim and Hargreaves is not the best preparation for future working life.

Unlike Durkheim and Hargreaves, other functionalists see competition as a vital aspect of modern societies.

Parsons – education and universalistic values

Parsons argues that school performs three major functions for society:

1 Education acts as a bridge between the family and wider society.

In the family particularistic standards apply: children are treated as individuals. In society, however, universalistic standards predominate. The individual is judged against standards which apply equally to all members of society.

In the family, status is fixed by birth – it is ascribed. However, in society, status is achieved (according to occupation, for example) – that is, it is based on meritocratic principles.

2 Education helps to ease these transitions. The exam system judges all pupils on merit, and school rules such as wearing uniform are applied to all pupils equally.

Family	Society
Particularistic standards	Universalistic standards
Ascribed status	Achieved status

Education helps to socialize young people into the basic values of society.

Schools instil two major values:

- The value of achievement
- The value of equality of opportunity

3 Education selects people for their future role in society.

The education system assesses students' abilities so that their talents can be matched to the job for which they are best suited.

Criticisms of Parsons

1 Parsons fails to consider the diversity of values in modern societies.
2 His view that education works on meritocratic principles is open to question.

Davis and Moore – education and role allocation

Like Parsons, Davis and Moore see education as a means of role allocation. The education system sifts people according to their abilities. The most talented gain high qualifications which lead to functionally important jobs with high rewards.

Criticisms of Davis and Moore

1 There is only a weak link between educational qualifications and income.
2 Intelligence and ability have only a limited influence on educational achievement.
3 The system of social stratification prevents the education system from grading individuals according to their ability.

Education – a conflict perspective

Bowles and Gintis – schooling in capitalist America

Bowles and Gintis (1976) argue that there is a close relationship between social relationships in the workplace and in education. This correspondence principle is the key to understanding the working of the education system. Work casts a 'long shadow' over the education system: education operates in the interests of those who control the workforce – the capitalist class.

The hidden curriculum

Capitalism requires a hard-working, obedient workforce which is too divided to challenge the authority of management. The education system helps to produce a workforce with these qualities through the hidden curriculum. The hidden curriculum consists of those things that pupils learn through the experience of attending school rather than through the stated aims of the school. It shapes the workforce in the following ways:

1 It helps to produce a subservient workforce. Bowles and Gintis found that students who were more conformist received higher grades than those who were creative and independent.

2 The hidden curriculum encourages an acceptance of hierarchy. Teachers give orders, pupils obey. Students have virtually no control over what and how they study. This prepares them for relationships at work where they will also need to defer to authority.

3 Pupils learn to be motivated by external rewards. Pupils work only for the qualifications they eventually hope to achieve. There is little satisfaction from school work as learning is based mostly on the 'jug and mug' principle, where teachers 'pour' their knowledge into students' empty 'mugs'. Work, too, is unsatisfying because it is organized to generate maximum profit rather than with the needs of the worker in mind. Workers, like pupils, are motivated only by external rewards: in their case, pay.

4 School subjects are fragmented. Knowledge in schools is packaged into separate subjects with little connection between them. In a similar way, most jobs are broken down into specific tasks carried out by separate individuals. Workers are kept unaware of all parts of the production process, so they remain divided.

The illusion of equality of opportunity

Bowles and Gintis reject the functionalist view that capitalist societies are meritocratic, providing genuine equality of opportunity. The children of the wealthy and powerful obtain high qualifications and well-rewarded jobs irrespective of their abilities. The education system disguises this with its myth of meritocracy. Those denied success blame themselves rather than the system. Inequality in society is thus legitimated: it is made to appear fair.

Evaluation of Bowles and Gintis

1 Bowles and Gintis have been accused of exaggerating the correspondence between work and education. Brown et al. (1997), for example, argue that much modern work requires teamwork, while the exam system still stresses individual competition. Reynolds (1984) claims that much of the curriculum in British schools is not designed to teach either the skills needed by employers or uncritical passive behaviour.

2 Numerous studies, such as that of Willis (1977) (see below), show that many pupils do not accept the hidden curriculum in schools. They have little respect for teachers or school rules.

Bowles and Gintis developed their theory in the 1970s and much has changed since then. However, some developments appear to support their theory:
● The freedom of teachers has been curtailed by the National Curriculum.
● Education has become more explicitly designed to meet the needs of employers (see p. 133).

Willis – Learning to Labour

Willis (1977) accepts the Marxist view that education is closely linked to the needs of capitalism, but he does not believe that there is a simple and direct relationship between education and the economy. Willis used a range of qualitative research methods, including observation, to study a group of 12 working-class boys during their last year at school and first months at work.

The 12 pupils – the 'lads' – formed a friendship group with a particular attitude to school. Willis refers to this as a counter-school culture. It had the following features:
● The lads felt superior to teachers and conformist pupils who they called 'ear'oles'.
● They saw no value in gaining qualifications.
● Their main objectives were to avoid going to lessons and to do as little work as possible. They entertained themselves by 'having a laff'. This usually involved misbehaviour.
● The 'lads' found school boring and tried to identify with the adult world by smoking, drinking alcohol and not wearing school uniform.
● The counter-culture was strongly sexist and racist. Traditional masculinity was valued and members of ethnic minorities were regarded as inferior.
● Manual labour was seen as more worthy than 'pen-pushing'.

These pupils did not defer to authority, nor were they obedient or docile. They rejected the belief that hard work would lead to success. The 'lads' have very little in common with the sort of conformist pupils described by Bowles and Gintis.

Shop-floor culture and counter-school culture

When Willis followed the 'lads' into their first jobs he found important similarities between the school counter-culture and the factory shop-floor culture:
● Both were racist and sexist.
● Both had no respect for authority.
● Both tried to minimize work and maximize 'having a laff'.
● Both cultures were ways of coping with tedium and oppression.

In their rejection of school the 'lads' partly see through the capitalist system. However, in the end rejecting school merely leads them into some of the most exploitative jobs capitalism has to offer.

Evaluation of Willis

1 Gordon (1984) believes that Willis's study has helped Marxists overcome a tendency to over-simplify the role of education in society.

2 Blackledge and Hunt (1985) put forward three criticisms of Willis:
● His sample is inadequate for generalizing about the role of education in society.
● Willis largely ignores the full range of subcultures within schools. Many pupils fall somewhere in between total conformity and total rejection.
● Willis may have misinterpreted some evidence to fit in with his own views.

3 With the decline in manual work since the period of Willis's research, male working-class attitudes to education may well have become more positive.

New Right perspectives influenced the policies introduced by governments throughout the 1980s and 1990s. The key themes of New Right policies were as follows.

1   Education and economic growth
    Education should largely be concerned with promoting economic growth. Many school-leavers were unemployable because of their lack of skills.
    A whole range of changes were introduced, such as YTS (Youth Training Scheme), a two-year course aimed at combining work experience with education. Training credits, first piloted in 1991, entitled school-leavers to spend a specified sum of money on training.
2   Competition, choice and standards
    The best method of raising standards in education was to introduce market forces and encourage competition between educational institutions. Schools that failed to attract students would lose funding and be forced to improve or close.
- The government laid down a National Curriculum which all state school pupils had to follow. Its aim was to ensure that pupils concentrated on what the government saw as key subjects.
- Parents were given the right to send their children to the school of their choice. A policy of open enrolment compelled every school to recruit the maximum number of pupils.
- Existing schools were allowed to opt out of local authority control and instead be funded directly from central government. Opting out created a new category of grant maintained schools. By 1996 these schools were educating about 20% of school pupils.
- Under the system of formula funding, the financing of schools was based on the number of enrolments. This was intended to reward the most successful schools.
3   Testing and examining
    Parents needed information in order to be able to make informed choices about schools. Increased testing and the publication of results were therefore necessary.
- League tables were introduced to enable easy comparisons between schools to be made.
- Testing and attainment targets were introduced for children of 7, 11, 14 and 16, in the hope that standards would rise as schools competed with each other to reach targets.
4   Curriculum content – the New Right and traditionalism
    A more business-oriented curriculum was favoured by the New Right, but at the same time, according to Ball (1990), there was an emphasis on retaining traditional values and traditional subjects such as Latin and Greek. Social education and multicultural approaches were frowned upon.
    Initiatives such as TVEI (Technical and Vocational Education Initiative) and courses such as GNVQ (General National Vocational Qualifications) were introduced to produce young people who had more understanding of work and the economy.

Critical evaluations of the educational reforms

Ball, Bowe and Gewirtz – competitive advantage and parental choice
    Ball et al.'s study attempted to discover the effects that parental choice and the encouragement of competition between schools were having on the education system and particularly on opportunities for different social groups.

The effects on schools

The study found that the changes were having significant effects on secondary schools.
- The publication of school league tables meant that schools were keen to attract academically able pupils who would boost their results.
- Some schools had reintroduced streaming and setting and were directing more resources at pupils who were likely to be successful in tests.
- As schools have concentrated on the more able pupils, they have paid less attention to those with special needs.
- In an effort to attract more pupils, some schools have taken to publishing glossy brochures, and some have brought in public relations firms. Staff are expected to devote more time and energy to marketing activities such as open evenings. More attention is devoted to the image of the school, particularly to making it seem to have a traditional academic focus – for example, by strictly enforcing rules about school uniform.
- Neighbouring schools have ceased to cooperate with each other, and instead there is 'suspicion and hostility'.
    These changes have led to a shift from comprehensive to market values in education.

The education market and degrees of choice

The study argues that three broad groups of parents can be distinguished in terms of their ability to choose between schools.
- Privileged/skilled choosers
    These parents spend a lot of time finding out about different schools and evaluating the claims made in their publicity. They often have the money to make choices that will assist their children's education, such as moving house or paying for private education. This group are usually middle-class and some – such as teachers – benefit from insider knowledge of the education system.
- Semi-skilled choosers
    Semi-skilled choosers are just as concerned to get the best possible education for their children but do not have the experience or skill of the privileged choosers. For example, they are more likely to accept rumours and local reputations at face value.
- Disconnected choosers
    These parents are not inclined to get involved in the education market. They tend to consider only the two schools closest to their home, often because they do not own a car or have easy access to public transport. They put more emphasis on the happiness of their child than on the academic reputation of the school. Disconnected choosers are likely to be working-class and are more likely to send their children to an under-subscribed school.
    Generally, the higher a person's social class, the more likely they are to benefit from the best schooling. According to Ball et al.'s study, the impression of choice is an illusion. In practice, people's choice is restricted by the limited number of schools available in any area and the class-based nature of the system of choosing.

The National Curriculum

Lawton (1989) identified a number of criticisms of the National Curriculum:

1. It was too bureaucratic. Many National Curriculum documents were more concerned with controlling teachers than improving standards.
2. It centralized power and undermined local democratic control of education.
3. Private schools were not subject to the National Curriculum. This meant that only the rich were provided with choice.
4. The content of the National Curriculum was accused of being traditional and unimaginative – for example, it was criticized for ignoring political and moral development.
5. Many objected to the publication of test results. Schools that did badly risked losing pupils and going into decline.
6. Some critics worried that all the testing would lead to the labelling of some children as failures.

The National Curriculum and ethnicity

MacNeil (1988) argued that the National Curriculum was based on white culture and that it excluded cultural input from ethnic minorities.

- In history the emphasis was on British history and the idea that British colonialism benefited those countries that were colonized.
- The language component of the National Curriculum placed the emphasis on European languages.
- In literature the works of distinguished black writers were ignored in favour of traditional English writers such as Shakespeare.

Troyna and Carrington (1990) also point out that religious education had to reflect the dominance of the Christian religion.

Youth training schemes

Finn – the hidden agenda of YTS

Finn (1987) has strongly attacked the new vocationalism involved in the various youth training schemes. He believes that its real objectives were different from those stated:

- The trainees could be used as a source of cheap labour.
- The small allowances paid to trainees would depress general wage levels.
- The scheme would reduce embarrassing unemployment statistics.
- The government hoped that the scheme would reduce crime by taking up the free time of young people.

Finn believed that there was no truth in the claim that school-leavers were unemployable. Many school pupils had experience of work through part-time jobs. The real problem was simply lack of jobs.

Cohen – social and life skills

Cohen (1994) looks at social and life skills training. Rather than teaching trainees skills, Cohen sees these courses as de-skilling the workforce. Individuals are persuaded that unemployment is a personal problem caused by trainees' failure to 'market' themselves to employers. The true nature of the labour market and the fact that unemployment is a structural feature of society are disguised.

'New Labour' and educational policies in Britain

'New Labour' and educational policies in Britain

The election of 'New Labour' in 1997 led to some changes in the direction of educational policy.

Some of the new policies were designed to improve standards. For example:

- The government promised to reduce primary school class sizes to 30.
- A literacy hour and a numeracy hour were introduced in primary schools to ensure that all pupils got a firm grounding in basic skills.
- Ambitious targets were set for pupil achievement.

A number of other policies were designed to reduce inequality of opportunity:

- Extra resources went into Education Action Zones. These were established in areas of high deprivation in an attempt to boost educational achievement.
- Social exclusion units were introduced to tackle the causes of social exclusion, such as truancy. (See p. 135 on compensatory education.)
- Grant maintained schools were abolished. They could no longer act as elite institutions, creaming off the brightest students.

Evaluation of New Labour policies

1. The 1997–2001 Labour government retained some New Right policies such as the importance of consumer choice and competition in raising standards. However, it also attempted to reduce inequalities of opportunity through initiatives such as Education Action Zones.
2. The introduction of tuition fees for higher education and the replacement of student grants with loans have been criticized for discouraging those from working-class backgrounds from staying on in education.
3. The New Right has attacked Labour policies by arguing that they have reduced diversity in schooling and are threatening academic excellence by trying to phase out selection. The 2001 Labour government has promised to increase diversity within the comprehensive system.

Differential educational achievement

Class and achievement

The children of parents in higher social classes are more likely to stay on in post-compulsory education, more likely to achieve examination passes when at school and more likely to gain university entrance. These differences were a feature of British education throughout the twentieth century and remain significant today.

- Bynner and Joshi (1999) found that class differences in educational achievement had persisted between the 1950s and 1990s.
- Participation in higher education has been increasing for all social classes. The proportion of those from lower classes participating has risen faster than the proportion of those from higher classes. However,

although the participation rate for the children of unskilled manual workers more than doubled during the 1990s, children from professional backgrounds still had a participation rate that was five times that of those from unskilled manual backgrounds.

Intelligence, class and educational achievement

The most obvious explanation for differences in educational achievement is the intelligence of the individual.

In Britain, the tripartite system (see p. 129) allocated an individual to one of three types of school largely on the basis of their performance in the eleven-plus intelligence test. There was a strong correlation between results and social class, with middle-class children gaining more places at grammar schools.

Culture and intelligence
- Many researchers argue that intelligence tests – IQ tests – are biased in favour of the white middle class, since they are largely constructed by members of this group.
- Different social groups have different subcultures and this affects their performance in IQ tests. This means that comparisons between such groups in terms of measured intelligence are invalid.

Genes and intelligence
There is general agreement that intelligence is due to:
1 The genes individuals inherit from their parents
2 The environment in which they grow up and live
Despite objections to their views, some social scientists still argue that genetically-based intelligence accounts for a large part of the difference in educational attainment between social groups.

According to Hernstein and Murray (1994), American society is increasingly meritocratic. People's class position is increasingly determined by their intelligence.

Environment and intelligence
- Research has indicated that a wide range of environmental factors – such as motivation, previous experience and education – can affect performance in IQ tests.
- Many researchers now conclude that it is impossible to estimate the proportions of intelligence due to heredity and environment.
- The debate about intelligence is only important if IQ affects educational attainment and level of income. Bowles and Gintis (1976) found that IQ was almost irrelevant to educational and economic success. Thus differences in IQ between different social groups may well have little significance.

Class subcultures and educational achievement

It has been argued that the distinctive norms and values of different social classes affect their educational performance.

Douglas – The Home and the School
Douglas's longitudinal study (1964) related educational attainment to a variety of factors, but the single most important factor was parental interest.

In general, middle-class parents:
- Visited the school more frequently to discuss their children's progress.
- Wanted their children to stay at school beyond the minimum leaving age.
- Gave their children greater attention and stimulus during their early years.

Douglas argued that many differences in educational performance could be traced back to primary socialization during the pre-school years.

Pre-school socialization
A large amount of psychological research has explored the relationship between child-rearing practices, social class and educational achievement.

In middle-class families:
- There is an emphasis on high achievement.
- Parents expect and demand more from their children.
- Parents encourage their children to constantly improve their performance in a wide range of areas, from games to talking and table manners.
- Rewards for success instil in children a pattern of high achievement motivation.

This kind of child-rearing lays the foundation for high attainment in the educational system.

Criticisms
The above views have been strongly criticized.
1 Blackstone and Mortimore (1994) make the following points:
- Working-class parents may have less time to visit the school because of the demands of their jobs
- Working-class parents may be put off visiting the school by the way teachers interact with them.
- More middle-class than working-class children attended a school where there was an established system of parent–school contacts.
2 Becker (1971) has challenged the view that behaviour patterns laid down in childhood have a lasting effect. Human action is not simply an expression of fixed patterns – it can change.

Bernstein – speech patterns
Since speech is an important medium of communication and learning, attainment levels in schools may be related to differences in speech patterns.

Bernstein (1961, 1970, 1972) distinguished two patterns of speech:
1 Restricted code
  This is a kind of shorthand speech, which uses short, simple and often unfinished sentences. Users of the code have so much in common that there is no need to make meanings explicit in speech. Meanings are more likely to be conveyed by gesture and tone of voice. Members of the working class are usually limited to the use of the restricted code.
  Example: 'She saw it'
2 Elaborated code
  This code is characteristic of the middle classes. It fills in the detail and provides the explanations omitted by restricted codes. Anyone can understand elaborated code users in any situation.

Example: 'The young girl saw the ball'

Bernstein explained the origins of these speech codes in terms of class differences in the family and work situations of the working and middle classes:

- In middle-class families and in non-manual work, relationships tend to be less rigid, people are treated as individuals and decisions are reached by negotiation.
- In working-class families and in manual work, relationships are based on a clear hierarchy and little discussion is needed.

Bernstein believed that the middle classes could switch from one code to the other but that the working classes were only able to use the restricted code. As formal education is conducted in terms of an elaborated code, working-class children are placed at a disadvantage.

Criticisms

Gaine and George (1999) attack Bernstein's arguments:

1 Bernstein's distinction between the classes is over-simplified. Even if there was a clear working class in the 1960s when Bernstein was writing, this is not the case today.
2 Bernstein produces little evidence for his assertions about working- and middle-class family life.

Cultural deprivation and compensatory education

From the kind of portrayal of working-class life described above, the theory of cultural deprivation was developed. This placed the blame for working-class educational failure on the culture of low-income groups.

This led to the idea of positive discrimination in favour of culturally deprived children: they must be given extra resources to help them compete on equal terms with other children. This policy is known as compensatory education.

Various schemes of compensatory education have been introduced. The most recent is the introduction of Education Action Zones by the Labour government in 1998. These provide extra educational resources in inner-city areas.

Criticisms of compensatory education

1 The theory of cultural deprivation has been attacked. By placing the blame for failure on the child and his or her background, attention is diverted from the deficiencies of the education system.
2 Morton and Watson (1973) argue that compensatory education cannot remove inequality of educational opportunity which is rooted in social inequality in society as a whole.

Bourdieu – cultural capital and differential achievement

The French sociologist Bourdieu is strongly influenced by Marxism. He argues that the education system is biased towards the culture of dominant social classes; it devalues the knowledge and skills of the working class.

Bourdieu refers to the dominant culture as cultural capital because it can be translated into wealth and power via the education system. Students with upper-class backgrounds have a built-in advantage because they have been socialized into the dominant culture.

The educational attainment of social groups is directly related to the amount of cultural capital they possess. Thus middle-class students have higher success rates than working-class students because middle-class culture is closer to the dominant culture.

Ball, Bowe and Gewirtz – cultural capital and educational choice

The study by Ball *et al.* (see p. 132) was influenced by Bourdieu. It discusses whether the increased emphasis on parental choice and market forces has led to greater equality of opportunity.

The educational market and middle-class parents

Ball argues that middle-class parents are in a better position than working-class parents to ensure that their children get to the school of their choice. There are a number of reasons for this:

1 Middle-class parents possess cultural capital, which means they have contacts and can 'play the system' to their advantage – for example, by making multiple applications.
2 Middle-class parents have the 'stamina' to research, visit schools, make appeals and so on.
3 Middle-class parents also possess material advantages. They can afford to pay for the transport necessary to send their children to more distant schools; they can move house if necessary to enter the catchment area of a desirable school; and they can afford extra tuition and childcare if necessary.

Working-class and ethnic minority parents

Ball *et al.* did not find that working-class parents were any less interested in their children's education than their middle-class counterparts. However, they did lack the cultural capital and material resources needed to use the system to their advantage.

- Many working-class parents preferred to send their children to the nearest school because of neighbourhood links, safety concerns and transport costs.
- Some ethnic minority parents have limited experience of the British educational system and do not feel confident enough about their English language skills to manipulate it.

Smith and Noble – material factors and British education

Smith and Noble (1995) reassert the importance of material factors in influencing class differences in educational achievement:

- Marketization is likely to lead to large differences between successful, well-resourced schools in affluent areas and under-subscribed poorly-resourced schools in poor areas.
- Having money allows parents to provide educational toys, books, a healthy diet, more space in the home to do homework, greater opportunities for travel and private tuition.
- To make ends meet, schools are increasingly charging for trips, material and equipment (technically parents are asked for 'voluntary

contributions'). Local education authorities are cutting back on free school meal provision and transport costs.

Cultural or material factors?
Halsey, Heath and Ridge (1980) attempted to measure the importance of cultural and material factors. They distinguished between:
- Family climate – measured in terms of levels of parental education and attitudes to education.
- Material circumstances – measured by family income.

The authors found both to be important. Family climate influenced the type of school attended but had little effect on later progress. Material circumstances determined how long children stayed at school.

Education – an interactionist perspective

Interactionists focus on processes *within* the education system which result in different levels of achievement. They have researched into the details of day-to-day life in schools.

Labelling and the self-fulfilling prophecy
The self-fulfilling prophecy theory argues that predictions made by teachers will tend to make themselves become true. The teacher defines or labels the pupil in a particular way, such as 'bright' or 'dull'. The teacher's interaction with pupils will be informed by their labelling of the pupils, and the pupils may respond accordingly, making the label become true: the prophecy is fulfilled.

Rosenthal and Jacobson (1968) selected a random sample of pupils in an elementary school in the USA and informed their teachers that these pupils could be expected to show rapid intellectual growth. They tested the IQ of all pupils and re-tested one year later. The sample population showed greater gains in IQ.

Rosenthal and Jacobson claim that the teachers' expectations significantly affected their pupils' performance. They speculate that the teachers' encouragement and positive feedback produced a self-fulfilling prophecy.

Criticisms
1 It has been suggested that the IQ tests used by Rosenthal and Jacobson were of dubious quality and were improperly administered.
2 Some interactionists have recognized that not all pupils will live up to their labels. Fuller (1984) found that black girls in a comprehensive school resented the negative stereotypes associated with being both black and female. They felt that people expected them to fail, but they tried to prove them wrong by devoting themselves to their work in order to achieve success. Fuller's work avoids some of the pitfalls of the deterministic versions of labelling theory which suggest that failure is inevitable for those with negative labels attached to them.

Ball – banding at Beachside Comprehensive
Ball's study (1981) examines the organization of a comprehensive school. Pupils were put into one of three bands according to information supplied from their primary schools. However, Ball found that, for pupils of similar measured ability, those whose fathers were non-manual workers had the greatest chance of being placed in the top band.

Ball identified the following effects of this banding:
- The behaviour of band two pupils deteriorated.
- Teachers had lower expectations of band two pupils. They were directed towards practical subjects and lower-level exams.

The interactionist approach – an evaluation

Advantages
1 It is based on far more detailed empirical evidence than functionalist or Marxist approaches.
2 It shows that educational experiences are not just determined by home background and IQ.
3 Woods (1983) claims that the interactionist approach has practical applications. Its insights could help schools to improve teaching and reduce deviance in schools.

Limitations
1 Many interactionists refer to class differences in education but fail to explain the origins of these differences.
2 Interactionists have been accused of failing to take account of factors outside the school which might influence what happens within education.

Gender and educational attainment

- By the late 1980s under-achievement by females was attracting more concern than working-class under-achievement.
- In the mid-1990s there was a sudden reversal. Changes in achievement statistics meant that attention switched to male under-achievement.
- There is disagreement over whether this change in emphasis is really justified.

Statistics on gender and differential achievement
- Girls have long been more successful than boys in the early years of education. However, in the past, boys tended to out-perform girls in most areas after the age of 16. This is no longer the case.
- In many areas at GCSE and A level, females are now marginally out-performing males.
- At some of the highest levels (such as postgraduate qualifications) men retain an advantage.
- Considerable differences remain in terms of the type of subjects studied by males and females. Males are more likely than females to be doing prestigious subjects and those that offer the best career prospects.

Explanations for under-achievement by females
Most of these explanations are based on the assumption that girls are less successful, and so are more relevant to explaining under-achievement in earlier decades. However, some of the processes described may still be preventing female pupils from achieving their full potential.

Innate ability
One possible explanation for female under-

achievement is that there are differences in innate ability between girls and boys.

However, girls actually out-perform boys in IQ tests at young ages. Some researchers have argued that this is because they mature earlier.

In a review of the available evidence, Trowler (1995) raises strong doubts about the usefulness of biological explanations of female under-achievement. He points out that:

- There is very little difference between the IQ scores of boys and girls.
- Differences in specific abilities might well be a product of social rather than biological differences.

Early socialization

Norman et al. (1988) point out that, before children start school, sex stereotyping has already begun.

- Playing with dolls and other types of toys that reinforce the stereotype of women as carers may affect girls' educational aspirations.
- Boys are more likely to be given constructional toys which help develop scientific and mathematical concepts.
- Gender stereotypes are further reinforced through the media.

Girls may come to value education less than boys, as a consequence of early socialization. Sharpe (1976) found that the concerns of her sample of working-class girls were 'love, marriage, husbands, children, jobs, and careers, more or less in that order'.

In the 1990s Sharpe (1994) repeated her research and found that girls' priorities had changed, and these changes may well help to explain why girls' educational attainment has improved.

Socialization in school

Abraham (1986) analysed textbooks used in a comprehensive school. He found maths textbooks to be especially male-dominated. Women tended to be shown in stereotypical roles such as shopping, while men were typically running businesses.

Behaviour in the classroom – self-confidence and criticism

Stanworth (1983) did a study of A level classes in a further education college. She found that classroom interaction disadvantaged girls in the following ways:

- Teachers found it difficult to remember the girls in their classes.
- Teachers held stereotypical views of what their female pupils would be doing in the future.
- Pupils felt that boys received more attention than girls. They were more likely to join in classroom discussion, seek help from the teacher and be asked questions.
- Girls underestimated their ability and placed themselves below their teacher's ranking.

Spender – Invisible Women

Spender (1983) claims that education is largely controlled by men, who use their power to further their own interests.

- The curriculum favours a male perspective. Women's contributions to human progress are often ignored.

- Girls receive less attention than boys in the classroom.
- Boys are often abusive to girls but are not told off.
- Male dominance in society is the cause of girls' difficulties in education but schools help to reinforce that dominance.

Criticisms of Stanworth and Spender

Randall (1987) criticizes the methods used by Stanworth and Spender. Stanworth's work, for example, was based on interviews rather than direct observation. Therefore it cannot actually establish that teachers are giving less attention to girls. Randall's own research failed to find such a clearcut bias.

Gender and subject choice

Although inequalities of educational achievement between males and females have declined, differences in the subjects studied remain considerable.

The National Curriculum limits these differences as school pupils have few options. When choices are available, however, distinct patterns arise.

Statistics on subject choice

A level:
- Males outnumbered females in all science and technical subjects apart from biology and related subjects.
- Females outnumbered males in all other subjects. English, modern languages and social studies had a particularly high proportion of female entries.

Degrees:
- Males were more likely to gain degrees in physical and mathematical sciences, engineering and technology, and architecture, building and planning.
- Equal numbers of males and females gained degrees in veterinary science and agriculture.
- In all other areas women predominated.

In some traditionally male areas, such as medicine, women have now made significant inroads. Male dominance in scientific and technical subjects remains. It could be argued that these are the subjects that often lead to well-paid and powerful jobs.

Socialization and subject choice

When choosing which subjects to study, females and males may well be influenced by what they have learned about femininity and masculinity. In her 1970s study Sharpe (1976) found that the girls she interviewed rejected jobs such as electricians and driving instructors because they felt that employers and society defined them as 'men's' work. It was therefore no surprise that girls saw little point in opting for typically 'male' subjects.

Schools and subject choice

Grafton (1987) studied a comprehensive school to examine the role of the education system itself in influencing subject choice.

- In the first year the school made it clear that there were only limited places available for members of either sex who wanted to study non-traditional craft subjects. The school made it clear what a 'normal' choice was.

- In the fourth year the timetable was organized in such a way as to limit pupils' choice of non-traditional subjects.
- Tutors were issued with guidelines which required them to discuss non-traditional choices with pupils before allowing them.

Grafton did, however, recognize that factors outside the school were also an important influence.

Science and gender

Kelly (1987) identifies two main reasons why science tends to be seen as masculine:

1. The way science subjects are packaged makes them appear to be boys' subjects. The examples used in textbooks and by teachers tend to be linked to boys' experiences, such as football and cars.
2. Pupils themselves make the greatest contribution to turning science into a boys' subject. Boys dominate classrooms, shouting out answers and grabbing apparatus first.

Colley – the persistence of gender inequalities in subject choice

Colley (1998) reviewed the reasons why gender differences in subject choice persisted in the late 1990s:

1. Perceptions of gender roles
   Despite all the social changes in recent decades, traditional definitions of masculinity and femininity are still widespread.
2. Subject preferences and choice
   Different subjects have different images. Computer studies involves working with machines rather than people, and this gives it a masculine image. The lack of opportunity for group activities and the rather formal way of teaching add to this.
3. The learning environment
   There is some evidence that girls are more comfortable with scientific and technical subjects when taught in single-sex schools or single-sex classes.

Reasons for the under-achievement of males

The educational achievement of both males and females has been increasing over recent decades. However, the performance of females has improved faster than that of males. These changes have been interpreted in a number of ways.

The improved achievement of women

Mitsos and Browne (1998) identify five main reasons for the improvement in girls' achievement:

1. The women's movement and feminism have raised the expectations and self-esteem of women.
2. Sociologists have drawn attention to some of the disadvantages faced by girls. As a result equal opportunities programmes have been developed.
3. The increase in service sector and part-time work has opened up employment opportunities for women. There is now more incentive for women to gain educational qualifications.
4. Evidence suggests that girls are more hard-working and motivated than boys. Girls' greater motivation

and organizational skills may give them a particular advantage in coursework.

5. Girls are estimated to be more mature than boys at the age of 16. Consequently they take exams more seriously than boys.

The moral panic about men

Weiner, Arnot and David (1997) are sceptical about the sudden discovery of male under-achievement. They make a number of important points:

1. The media see the under-achievement of black and working-class boys as a particular problem because it may lead to the creation of a potentially dangerous 'underclass'.
2. The differences in subject choice mean that female under-achievement is still characteristic of the higher levels of the education system.
3. The failure to celebrate girls' achievement is part of a 'backlash' against female success as men feel threatened by the possibility of women becoming equal.

Reasons for boys' under-achievement

Mitsos and Browne accept that boys are under-achieving and suggest the following reasons:

- Teachers may be less strict with boys, tolerating a lower standard of work and the missing of deadlines.
- Boys are more likely to disrupt classes. They are more likely to be sent out of the classroom and expelled from school.
- The culture of masculinity encourages boys to want to appear macho and tough. They are more likely to develop an anti-school subculture (see p. 131).
- The decline in manual work may result in working-class boys losing motivation. They see little point in working hard as it will not result in the sort of job they are seeking.
- Research suggests that boys tend to overestimate their ability. They may become over-confident and not work hard enough.
- Girls may spend their leisure time in ways that complement their education, such as reading and talking.

The ideas of Mitsos and Browne provide some initial suggestions to explain male under-achievement but, as they point out, more research needs to be done in this area.

New directions in the study of gender and schooling

Recent studies of gender and education have moved away from simply looking at differential achievement. They focus on:

- The wide range of processes related to gender within schools.
- The active role played by pupils in the creation of gender relationships.
- The way children form identities.
- The way class and/or ethnicity interact with gender in shaping school relationships.

Connolly – Racism, Gender Identities and Young Children

Connolly's study (1998) of young children in a multi-ethnic inner-city primary school emphasizes the diverse influences on gender in schools. In particular he examines how school relationships are also shaped by ethnicity.

Black boys

Teachers were more willing to criticize the behaviour of black boys than that of other groups. They felt that some of the black males in the school were in danger of growing up to be violent criminals, and they saw them as a threat to school discipline. However, they also took positive steps to encourage them to participate in school activities such as football.

The boys also brought their own values and attitudes to school, for example those relating to masculinity. These also contributed to their identity.

Black girls

Black girls were also perceived by teachers as potentially disruptive but likely to be good at sports, music and dancing.

South Asian boys

Some teachers contrasted what they saw as the close and supportive Asian families with the high rates of single parenthood amongst other groups in the area.

South Asian boys tended to be seen as immature rather than seriously deviant.

There was a tendency for other boys who wanted to assert their masculinity to pick on South Asian boys. The South Asian boys had difficulty in gaining status as males. This made it difficult for them to feel confident at school.

South Asian girls

South Asian girls were seen to be even more obedient and hard-working than South Asian boys, although Connolly's observations showed that their attitude to work was not significantly different from that of other female groups.

South Asian girls had a relatively low status among their peers. They were seen as feminine in terms of their passivity and obedience, but they were not seen as potential girlfriends by black and white boys because their culture was considered too alien.

Ethnicity and educational achievement

Ethnicity and levels of attainment

Most studies indicate that ethnic minorities tend to do less well than other members of the population. However, this hides important variations between and within ethnic groups, with some ethnic minorities being particularly successful.

The Policy Studies Institute (PSI) survey

The PSI *Fourth National Survey of Ethnic Minorities* (Modood *et al.*, 1997) found that the educational qualifications of ethnic minorities had improved considerably since the 1980s.

Men

- Chinese, African Asians and Indians were better qualified than whites.
- Caribbeans, Pakistanis and Bangladeshis were the least well qualified. However, a substantial number of Caribbean men had vocational qualifications.

Women

- Women of Indian, African Asian and Chinese origin all had high proportions of advanced qualifications.
- Caribbean women were more likely to have A level qualifications than white women.
- Bangladeshi women were the least well qualified, followed by Pakistani women.

The PSI study also compared the qualifications of those who had been born in Britain, or who were 15 or younger when they migrated, with the qualifications of migrants who came to Britain aged 16 or over:

- There were signs that considerable progress had been made in the educational achievement of Caribbeans.
- Overall, the qualifications of the second generation were much better than those of the migrants' generation.
- Bangladeshis and Pakistanis had made least progress and still achieved well below other ethnic groups.

Various attempts have been made to explain differences in educational attainment between ethnic groups.

Innate ability and attainment

As in the case of class and gender, some commentators have attributed differences in levels of achievement to IQ. Hernstein and Murray believe that there is a good case for arguing that differences are genetic. They found that, on average, blacks scored lower in IQ tests than whites.

Pilkington (1997) argues against the idea of a genetic basis for IQ differences, for the following reasons:

- It is questionable whether race is a biologically meaningful concept.
- It is also questionable whether IQ tests really measure intelligence.
- Differences in IQ can largely be explained by differences in socio-economic status.

Cultural and material factors and attainment

Language

In some Asian households English is not the first language used. The PSI study found that lack of fluency in English was a significant problem for some groups. Amongst men nearly everyone spoke English fluently. Amongst women about a fifth of Pakistanis and Bangladeshis were not fluent.

- Driver and Ballard (1981) found that Asian children for whom English was not their main home language were at least as competent as their classmates by the age of 16.
- The *Swann Report* (1985) found that language was not a significant factor in educational attainment.

Family life

A number of writers suggest that the nature of family life affects levels of attainment among ethnic minorities.

- It has been suggested that the West Indian population in Britain has a high proportion of one-parent families and working women who leave their children without close parental supervision in the early years of their life.
- Driver and Ballard (1981) found that South Asian parents have high aspirations for their children's education despite having little formal education themselves.

Pilkington (1997) argues that cultural explanations should be treated with caution:

- There are not clear boundaries between ethnic groups.
- There is a great deal of difference within ethnic minority groups.
- There is a danger of ethnocentrism, with white commentators criticizing ethnic minority cultures simply because they are different from their own cultures.

However, Pilkington does accept that there are real cultural differences between ethnic groups and that these can affect educational achievement. For example, the cohesiveness of some Asian families may assist in the high achievement of some Asian groups.

Social class and attainment

As we saw earlier, class is closely linked to educational attainment, with members of lower social classes gaining fewer qualifications and leaving the education system earlier than higher classes. Poor educational performance by ethnic minorities could be a result of their social class rather then their ethnicity.

Drew (1995) examined gender, class and ethnic differences in educational achievement. He found that class was easily the most important factor. However, some differences remain even when class is taken into account, with Afro-Caribbeans doing slightly less well than other groups.

Racism and the education system

Coard – racism and under-achievement

Perhaps the stongest attack on the British education system's treatment of ethnic minorities has been advanced by Bernard Coard (1971). He argues that black children are made to feel inferior because:

- West Indian children are told that their way of speaking is inferior.
- The word 'white' is associated with good, and the word 'black' with evil.
- The content of education tends to ignore black people.
- Attitudes in the classroom are reinforced by pupils in the playground where racial abuse and bullying may occur.

Coard believes that this leads to black children developing low self-esteem and low expectations.

Wright – racism in multi-racial primary schools

Wright (1992) studied four multi-racial inner-city primary schools. She found that, although the majority of staff were committed to equality of opportunity, there was still considerable discrimination.

Asians in primary schools

- Asian girls received less attention from teachers.
- Asian customs and traditions were sometimes disapproved of.

Afro-Caribbeans in primary schools

- Teachers expected Afro-Caribbean pupils to behave badly.
- Afro-Caribbean boys received much negative attention from teachers.

Racism reconsidered

The emphasis on faults in the education system should be treated with some caution.

- Teachers do not necessarily behave in ways that reflect negative stereotypes of ethnic minorities.
- Taylor (1981) points out that many teachers are actively concerned to develop a fair policy towards ethnic minority pupils.
- It has been questioned whether black pupils lack self-esteem. The *Swann Report* (1985) concluded that low self-esteem among ethnic minorities was not widespread.

Recent studies emphasize the variety of ways in which ethnic minorities respond to racism in the education system.

Mirza – Young, Female and Black

Mirza (1992) studied two comprehensive schools in south London.

- The black girls in Mirza's sample did better in exams than black boys and white pupils in the school. She believes that the educational achievements of black women are underestimated.
- Mirza also challenges the labelling theory of educational under-achievement. Although there was some evidence of racism among teachers, she denies that this undermined the self-confidence of the black girls. Most girls were concerned with academic success and prepared to work hard.
- Most teachers tried to meet the girls' needs but failed to do so by, for instance, failing to push black pupils hard enough or patronizing them.

Mac an Ghaill – ethnic minorities in the sixth form

Mac an Ghaill (1992) studied Afro-Caribbean and Asian students in a sixth-form college in the Midlands. He found that the way students responded to schooling varied considerably and was influenced by their ethnicity, gender and the class composition of their former secondary schools.

All of the ethnic minority students experienced problems in the education system, but they experienced them differently, depending on their gender and ethnic group. Nevertheless, they had all enjoyed some success. They had achieved this through adopting a variety of survival strategies.

- Some of the girls had banded together. They would help each other out with academic work but were less willing to conform to rules about dress, appearance and behaviour in class.

- Some of the other ethnic minority pupils were less hostile to their schools. They tried to become friendly with some teachers whilst avoiding others who they identified as racist.

The study is important because it shows how class, gender and ethnicity interact within the school system. Like Mirza's study, it also shows that negative labelling does not necessarily lead to academic failure. Although such labelling creates extra barriers, some students are able to overcome them.

Conclusion

It is probable that many of the factors outlined above work together in producing the lower levels of achievement found in some ethnic minority groups. The *Swann Report* concluded that racial discrimination inside and outside school, along with social deprivation, were probably the main factors.

Test your knowledge and understanding (answers on p. 216)

1 Which of the following is **not** a type of secondary school in Britain today?
   a City Technology College
   b Grammar school
   c Secondary modern school
   d Middle school

2 Durkheim would probably agree with three of the following statements about education. Which one would he disagree with?
   a The values promoted by education are the values of powerful groups
   b The school is a society in miniature
   c Education helps create and maintain social solidarity
   d Education makes a positive contribution to society

3 Which one of the following is an achieved status?
   a Son
   b Member of the royal family
   c Advanced level student
   d Female

4 Which of the following best describes Bowles and Gintis's 'correspondence principle'?
   a There is a close relationship between ability and achievement
   b There is a close relationship between relationships in the workplace and in education
   c There is a close relationship between relationships in education and in the family
   d There is a close relationship between education and society

5 Identify the concept used by Marxists that refers to inequality being made to appear fair.
   a Legitimation   b Ideology
   c Social reproduction   d Social class

6 Which of the following is **not** a similarity between shop-floor culture and counter-school culture, according to Willis?
   a Racism and sexism
   b Refusal to do homework
   c Lack of respect for authority
   d Minimizing work

7 Which one of the following is a criticism of Willis's work?
   a His sample is inadequate for making generalizations
   b He fails to put his research within a theoretical framework
   c His work is not based on empirical research
   d His work over-simplifies the role of education in society

8 During the 1980s and 1990s the New Right believed that the best way to raise standards in schools was through which one of the following methods?
   a Increasing teachers' pay
   b Making more resources available to schools
   c Introducing market forces into education
   d Abolishing private education

9 Three of the following are initiatives designed to produce young people who have more understanding of the world of work. Which is the odd one out?
   a GNVQ   b TVEI
   c SATS   d YTS

10 What term do Ball et al. use to refer to the group of parents who are least able to take advantage of the education market?
   a Disconnected choosers b Semi-skilled choosers
   c Skilled choosers   d Excluded choosers

11 Three of the following statements are criticisms of the National Curriculum. Which is the odd one out?
   a It is too bureaucratic
   b It centralizes power and undermines local control
   c The content is traditional and unimaginative
   d It allows girls to drop science subjects at an early age

12 What, according to Finn, was the key reason why so many young people were unemployed during the 1970s and 1980s?
   a They did not have the skills needed
   b Their expectations of pay were too high
   c There were not enough jobs available
   d They did not have enough qualifications

13 What is the name of the educational initiative introduced by the Labour government of 1997 to boost educational achievement in areas of high deprivation?
   a Educational Priority Areas
   b Compensatory education
   c Education Action Zones
   d Social exclusion units

14 Which one of the following statements is the most accurate summary of trends in social class and educational achievement since the 1950s?
   a Levels of achievement have remained stable for the middle classes but working-class achievement has increased, thus reducing inequalities
   b Levels of achievement have increased for all groups but inequalities of achievement between the classes remain broadly similar

c Levels of achievement have remained stable for all classes

d Levels of achievement have remained stable for the working classes but middle-class achievement has increased, thus increasing inequalities

15 Which one of the following statements reflects the views of Hernstein and Murray?

a Class position is increasingly determined by intelligence

b Class position is increasingly determined by an individual's own efforts

c Class position is increasingly determined by ethnic background

d Class position is increasingly determined by an individual's class of origin

16 Which one of the following terms was used by Bernstein to describe the language use of the working class?

a Restricted code   **b** Shorthand code
c Elaborated code   **d** Implicit code

17 Which one of the following is an example of the use of cultural capital?

a Parents buying a computer for their child to use for school work

b Parents sending their child to a private school

c Parents moving house to be near a popular school

d Parents writing an effective letter to a headteacher so that their child is moved to a set with the best teacher

18 What term do Halsey, Heath and Ridge use to describe parents' own educational achievements and attitudes to education?

a Cultural deprivation   **b** Cultural capital
c Family values   **d** Family climate

19 Which one of the following statements would be accepted by most interactionists?

a It is necessary to examine the day-to-day processes within schools in order to understand achievement patterns

b Patterns of educational achievement are simply a reflection of inequalities in society

c Patterns of educational achievement are closely linked to ability and effort

d It is necessary to examine a wide range of statistics in order to understand patterns of educational achievement

20 Which one of the following is a criticism of some interactionist approaches to educational achievement?

a They are not based on empirical research

b They are deterministic, assuming that pupils passively accept their labelling

c They ignore the interaction between teachers and pupils

d They do not take labelling and the self-fulfilling prophecy into account

21 Which one of the following statements best describes the changing relationship between gender and achievement?

a The achievement of girls has increased but boys' achievement has dropped

b The achievement of both boys and girls has increased, but girls have improved their educational performance more rapidly

c The achievement of both genders has remained stable

d The achievement of both genders has increased at a similar rate

22 Three of the following were identified by Stanworth as ways in which classroom interaction favoured boys. Which is the odd one out?

a Teachers held stereotypical views of what their female pupils would do in the future

b Boys received more attention than girls

c The exam system favoured boys

d Teachers found it difficult to remember girls' names

23 According to Colley, three of the following are factors in explaining why gender differences in subject choice still exist. Which is the odd one out?

a Subject preferences and choice

b The National Curriculum

c Perceptions of gender roles

d The learning environment

24 According to Mitsos and Browne, three of the following are reasons for the improvement in girls' achievement. Which is the odd one out?

a There is growing awareness of equal opportunities issues in schools

b Feminism has raised women's expectations and self-esteem

c The increase in service sector work has increased employment opportunities for women

d Girls' IQ scores are higher than boys'

25 In Connolly's study of young children in a multi-ethnic primary school, which group was seen by teachers as the most obedient and hard-working?

a Black boys   **b** Black girls
c South Asian boys   **d** South Asian girls

26 According to official statistics, which one of the following ethnic minority groups is better-qualified than white males?

a Pakistani males   **b** Caribbean males
c Indian males   **d** Bangladeshi males

27 Three of the following are arguments **against** the idea that there is a genetic basis for IQ differences between different races. Which is the odd one out?

a There is some evidence that race is linked to IQ

b It is questionable whether IQ tests really measure intelligence

c Differences in IQ can largely be explained by socio-economic factors

d It is questionable whether race is a biologically meaningful category

28 Which one of the following terms refers to the belief that your own culture is superior to others?

a Cultural capital   **b** Ethnocentrism
c Cultural deprivation   **d** Ethnography

29 According to Drew, which one of the following factors is crucial in explaining differences in educational achievement?

a Class   **b** Ethnicity
c Gender   **d** Age

30 What phrase does Mac an Ghaill use to describe the methods that ethnic minority students use to overcome the problems they face in the educational system?

a Equal opportunities policies

b Survival strategies

c Accommodations

d Anti-school subcultures

Develop your analysis and evaluation skills

(see p. 206 for guidance notes)

For each of the following statements, identify which sociologists would argue in favour of and which against the view expressed. Explain the reasons for their view.

1 Education systems simply reproduce inequality.
2 The marketization of education has raised educational standards.
3 The Labour government elected in 1997 made a significant contribution to improving equality of opportunity.
4 Social class differences in educational achievement are the result of factors within the home.
5 The under-achievement of boys is a major problem facing the education system today.
6 Racism remains common in schools and is a key factor in explaining ethnic minority under-achievement.

AQA style Education question, AS Unit 2

Answer all parts of this question
Total: 60 marks
Time allowed: 1 hour 15 minutes

1 mark = 1.25 minutes

ITEM A

The government tells us that educational league tables are not just to give parents more information but to spur on low-performing schools. However, some people argue that it is not fair or meaningful to judge a school's performance by its raw results. Research has consistently shown a link between educational achievement and socio-economic status; therefore you have to make allowance for the social circumstances and the language background of the pupils attending a particular school.

Check your understanding (see p. 132), as this gives you the context for part [a]

These are factors mentioned that cannot form an answer to part [b]

ITEM B

Bowles and Gintis argue that there is a correspondence between school and work. School trains people for work not so much through the formal curriculum of skills and knowledge but through the hidden curriculum which teaches norms, values and beliefs that have a strong influence on pupils' behaviour, making them docile and compliant workers.

Use these ideas to help you answer part [c] by giving an example of each that is taught incidentally or covertly in school

Interpret from here that this is a Marxist view of education. This will lead you into an answer to part [f]

Comments on the question	Question	Advice on preparing your answer
• Check that you understand the meaning of the phrase in the context of the passage	[a] Explain what is meant by 'raw results'. [Item A, line 5] [2 marks]	• Do not use the words you are being asked to explain • Always work backwards through the terms, i.e. find another term or phrase for 'results', then qualify this by giving a phrase to explain 'raw'

143

Comments on the question	Question	Advice on preparing your answer
• If you fail to read this part of the question you will be giving an answer that is the opposite of what is required • Your answer here will help you to form the basis of your answer to part [e], so it is a good idea to answer the questions in the examination paper order. This allows you to pick up on helpful clues left by the chief examiner	[b] Give **two** factors that affect educational attainment apart from those mentioned in Item A. [4 marks]	• This does not require any more than a list of two factors, so do not waste your time writing sentences • Do not use 'class', as this is too similar to socio-economic status • Gender (p. 136) and ethnicity (p. 137) are the obvious, but not the only, possible answers
• There will be 2 marks available for each way you suggest. You cannot make up for any lack of knowledge you might have by writing at length about only two ways	[c] Suggest **three** ways in which schools might prepare pupils for work through the hidden curriculum. [6 marks]	• The item will help to keep you focused if you apply the information given in Item B to actual examples • Make sure that you give ways that are part of the hidden curriculum (pp. 130–1)
• There are two skills to demonstrate here, so you will require a short paragraph for each of two separate ways • Make sure that your description relates to educational attainment and that it links to the way you have identified	[d] Identify and describe **two** ways in which language can affect educational attainment. [8 marks]	• You could refer to: 1 Bernstein, pp. 134–5 2 PSI study, p. 139
• The focus is on change, so don't give a static description at one point in time, although 'no change' is a relevant pattern • Note the time limit. Reference to patterns under the tripartite system may be inappropriate unless you show that you know this system is still in operation in certain localities (see Benn and Chitty, p. 129)	[e] Examine the patterns of differential educational attainment during the last 30 years. [20 marks]	• Socio-economic/class patterns (see pp. 133–4) • Use your answer to part [b] to alert you to other groups • Gender patterns, pp. 136–7, and subject choice, pp. 137–8 • Ethnicity, p. 139
• You must give knowledge beyond the item • This tells you to evaluate – if you do not do this you are unlikely to gain more than 7 or 8 marks • The best answers will pick up specific points of assessment on individual Marxist views as well as offering alternative perspectives as part of a critique • The plural tells you to write about more than one Marxist view	[f] Using material from Item B and elsewhere, assess Marxist views of the role of education in training people for work. [20 marks]	• Start by interpreting from the item that Bowles and Gintis are Marxist writers • Develop their analysis by using pp. 130–1 • Go beyond the item by using the work of Finn (p. 133) or Willis (p. 131), thus keeping a tight focus on this issue • Select ideas from the functionalists (pp. 129–30) as a critique of Marxism, but do not criticize this view as you will be going beyond the requirements of the question

Total: 60 marks   1 mark = 1 minute
Time allowed: 1 hour

Comments on the question	Question	Advice on preparing your answer
<ul><li>Make sure that you describe the view in a detailed way with supporting evidence</li><li>Look at a range of arguments for and against the point of view</li><li>Make sure that your response is balanced – attempt to minimize personal bias by presenting all sides of the argument objectively and with reasonably equal weight</li></ul>	Outline and assess the view that working-class under-achievement is the product of a hidden curriculum. [60 marks]	<ul><li>This is an essay question so spend at least 10 minutes planning your response</li><li>An introduction is necessary to set the scene, i.e. to make clear how the concept of the hidden curriculum is defined and which theoretical position is associated with it</li><li>See pp. 129–31 for theoretical accounts of the hidden curriculum</li><li>Criticisms are offered on p. 131</li><li>Try to finish with an evaluative conclusion based on the evidence</li></ul>

Chapter 12

Culture and identity

Textbook pp. 883–933

Specifications NB 'Socialization, Culture and Identity' is a core theme of both specifications.

Specification	Relevant module title	Place in module	Level	Assessment	Other relevant modules
AQA	There is no AQA module specifically on this topic.	n/a	AS/A2	n/a	Material from this chapter can be used in the A2 synoptic assessment.
OCR	The Individual and Society	**Culture and the formation of identities** is one of the topics in this module.	AS	One from a choice of two four-part structured questions.	Material from this chapter can be used in the A2 synoptic assessment.
	Culture and Socialization	**Youth and Culture** is one of four options in this module.	AS	One or two two-part structured questions from a choice of two.	
	Power and Control	**Popular Culture** is one of six options in this module.	A2	One essay question from a choice of two.	

Culture and identity: essential notes

The definition of culture

The word 'culture' has been used in different ways. Jencks (1993) distinguishes four main senses in which the word is now used:

1   Culture can be seen as a quality possessed by individuals who are able to gain the learning and achieve the qualities that are seen as desirable in a cultured human being.
2   The first definition is quite elitist as it sees some aspects of what is human as superior to others. The second definition is also elitist but sees certain societies rather than people as superior to others. Some societies are more cultured – in other words more civilized – than others.
3   The third definition sees culture as the sum total of all the arts and intellectual work in a society. This is quite a common definition, and culture in this sense is sometimes called high culture.
4   The final definition sees culture as the whole way of life of a people. As Linton (1945) puts it, 'The culture of a society is the way of life of its members; the collection of ideas and habits which they learn, share and transmit from generation to generation.'

Most contemporary sociologists adopt the fourth definition. Culture in this sense includes virtually all of the subject matter of sociology.

When the third definition is adopted it is easier to identify a distinct area of study, which includes the sociology of art, music and literature.

Types of culture

These definitions of culture can be developed by examining the different types of culture identified by sociologists.

High culture

High culture usually refers to cultural creations that have a particularly high status – for example, the products of long-established art forms such as opera, theatre and literature. For many who use the term, high culture is seen as superior to lesser forms of culture.

Folk culture

Folk culture refers to the culture of ordinary people, particularly those living in pre-industrial societies. Examples include traditional folk songs and stories that have been handed down from generation to generation.

Mass culture

For its critics, mass culture is seen as less worthy than high culture or folk culture. It is a product of the mass media and includes popular feature films, TV soap operas and pop music. Critics of mass culture (see pp. 149) see it as debasing for individuals and destructive for the fabric of society.

Popular culture
The term popular culture is often used in a similar way to the term 'mass culture'. Popular culture includes any cultural products appreciated by large numbers of ordinary people: for example, TV programmes, mass-market films, and popular fiction such as detective stories. While mass culture is usually used as a term of abuse, this is not the case with popular culture. While some do see popular culture as shallow and harmful, others, including some postmodernists, argue that it is just as valid and worthwhile as high culture.

Subculture
The term 'subculture' has been applied to a wide range of groups, including those who live close together and have a shared lifestyle, youth groups who share common musical tastes and enjoy the same leisure activities, ethnic groups, people who share the same religious beliefs, members of the same gang and so on.

Some theorists, particularly functionalists, emphasize the degree to which culture is shared by members of a society. Many other theorists emphasize cultural pluralism or subcultural variety in society.

Identity

The definition of identity
Identity refers to the sense that someone has of who they are, of what is most important about them. Important sources of identity are likely to include nationality, ethnicity, sexuality, gender and class.
- Personal identity refers to how a person thinks about themselves.
- Social identity refers to how they are perceived by others.
  Personal and social identity do not necessarily match. A person perceived by others to be male may see themselves as a woman trapped in a man's body.

The importance of identity
The concept of identity has become increasingly important in sociology. In the past, people's identities were seen as fairly stable, widely shared and based on one or two key variables such as class and nationality. More recent postmodern theories of identity have suggested that people's identities can frequently change and may contain considerable contradictions. For example, the meaning of 'masculine' and 'feminine' has become much less clearcut.

According to postmodernists:
- People actively create their own identities.
- People have a great deal of choice about what social groups to join.
- Through shopping and other forms of consumption people can shape and change their identities.
  To some writers, individuals no longer have a stable sense of identity at all – their identities are fragmented (see pp. 150–1).

Identity and culture

The concept of identity is closely related to the concept of culture. Identities can be formed through the cultures and subcultures to which people belong. However, different theories see the relationship between culture and identity in rather different ways.
- Theories such as functionalism and Marxism see identity as originating in a fairly straightforward way from involvement in particular cultures and subcultures, e.g. people living in Britain would be expected to have a strong sense of British identity.
- Theories influenced by postmodernism tend to stress the diversity of ways in which, for example, British people from different ethnic or national origins interpret British identity.

Culture – functionalist perspectives
Durkheim (1903) believed that a shared culture is necessary if a society is to run smoothly. This shared culture is passed down from generation to generation and exists over and above the wishes and choices of individuals. People must conform to the culture of their society if they are to avoid the risk of punishment.
- To Parsons (1951) society is not possible without a shared culture. It allows people to communicate and to work towards shared goals.
- Parsons and Bales (1955) argue that culture is passed on to children through socialization, particularly through primary socialization in the family (see p. 89).
- Parsons and Durkheim generally saw culture as slow to change although they believed that major changes in culture do occur as societies evolve.

Evaluation
Parsons has often been accused of exaggerating:
- The extent to which contemporary societies possess a common culture.
- The extent to which people conform to the culture into which they are socialized.
  Parsons did acknowledge that everybody did not share an identical culture. However, contemporary societies may possess such cultural diversity that they raise questions about how much culture needs to be shared. In Britain, for example, there is a great deal of ethnic, religious and regional diversity, yet British society continues to function. It may be that functionalist views are more applicable to traditional societies.

Marxist theories of culture and identity
Marx claimed that in class-stratified societies culture can be seen as little more than ruling-class ideology. It is simply an expression of the distorted view of the world advanced by the dominant class. Contemporary Marxists have developed theories of institutions such as the mass media along these lines (see p. 157).
- One interpretation of Marx sees the working class as suffering from false class consciousness – their beliefs and culture are shaped by the ruling class.
- Other interpretations see the working class and other cultures as possessing some independence from ruling-class domination.

Neo-Marxist theories of culture

Neo-Marxist approaches have been significantly influenced by Marxism, but all tend to argue that culture has considerable independence from economic influences, and that there is no straightforward correspondence between class and culture.

The Birmingham Centre for Contemporary Cultural Studies (CCCS) extended the study of culture to an examination of youth cultures. They draw extensively on the writings of the Italian Marxist, Antonio Gramsci (1971) who argued that dominant ideology could always be opposed and that ideological domination – what he called hegemony – is never complete.

Youth subcultures

To the CCCS, youth subcultures often represent creative attempts to win space from dominant cultures. Youth cultures create their own distinctive styles of dress and music and these represent an attempt to 'solve', in an imaginary way, the problems faced by youth.

The example of Teddy boys can illustrate these arguments.

Jefferson – Teddy boys

Jefferson (1976) argues that the youth culture of Teddy boys (or Teds) represented an attempt to recreate a sense of working-class community which came under threat in the post-war period from urban redevelopment and growing affluence (wealth) in some sections of the working class.

Some unskilled working-class youth responded by forming groups in which members had a strong sense of loyalty and were willing to fight over their territory. Their style of dress incorporated Edwardian-style jackets, bootlace ties and suede shoes. Jefferson sees aspects of this style as part of an attempt to buy status:

- Edwardian-style jackets were originally worn by upper-class 'dandies' in Edwardian times, and by wearing them the Teds hoped that some of the status of this group would rub off on them.
- Bootlace ties appeared to come from Western films where they were worn by the 'slick city gambler' who was forced to live by his wits. Like their counterparts in the Westerns, the Teddy boys felt themselves to be outsiders who needed to live by their wits.

By adopting these styles, working-class youth can at least feel that they are doing something to protect their territory, gain status and recreate community.

Evaluation

Neo-Marxist theories such as those of the CCCS tend to fall between two stools:

- To conventional Marxists they fail to fully acknowledge the importance of the economy in shaping culture.
- To postmodernists they fail to fully accept the freedom that people have to invent cultures.

Hebdige – Subculture: The Meaning of Style

Hebdige (1979) uses some Marxist ideas in his analysis of youth subcultures but is also influenced by semiotics – the study of the meaning of symbols and signs.

- Each subculture develops its own style by taking everyday objects and transforming their meaning. This new 'secret' meaning expresses, in code, a form of resistance to subordination. Punks, for instance, transformed the meaning of safety pins and ripped jeans.
- Each subculture is spectacular: it creates a spectacle and intends to get noticed.

Hebdige contrasts mod and skinhead subcultures. Skinheads' appearance was a kind of exaggerated version of the working-class manual labourer and expressed the image of the 'hard' working-class man. Mods, on the other hand, adopted a more respectable appearance which reflected aspirations to be upwardly mobile and join the middle class. However, despite their respectable suits, their style reflected a love of 'cellar clubs, discotheques, boutiques and record shops' which was outside the conventional middle-class world.

Hebdige also analyses black British subcultures. First-generation migrants adopted smart and conventional dress which reflected their aspirations to succeed in Britain. By the 1970s, the disappointments that stemmed from racism and high levels of unemployment began to be expressed in the style of Rastafarians. British Rastafarians expressed their alienation from British culture by adopting simple clothes with an African feel. The key themes of Rastafarian style were resistance to the dominance of white culture and the expression of black identity.

Evaluation

1 Hebdige's work is only as good as his interpretations. However, there is no evidence that members of the youth subcultures he writes about saw their own subculture in the same way as Hebdige. This lack of empirical evidence could be seen as a limitation of his work.
2 For postmodernists Hebdige is wrong to assume that it is possible to attribute any one meaning to a subculture. Rather, it is open to a variety of interpretations each of which is equally valid.

Grossberg – The Deconstruction of Youth

Grossberg's (1994) discussion of the changing meaning of youth is influenced by post-structuralism. This approach argues that our identity is created by our involvement with particular discourses – particular ways of thinking and talking about something.

To Grossberg, if people come to think of 'youth' in a particular way, then people who think of themselves as young will tend to act in ways that are consistent with this view.

Grossberg outlines three main phases in the development of youth discourses:

1 Following the Industrial Revolution, discourses about young people were concerned with the ideas of adulthood and childhood rather than youth. Childhood was seen as a time of innocence. Children were protected and kept away from work until they were deemed old enough to become adults and leave school.
2 After the Second World War the idea of youth as a transitional period between childhood and

adulthood became important. Youth was seen as 'on the one hand, a time of fun, a time in which one could take risks, and, on the other hand, a potential threat'. During this period youth created its own cultures, particularly those related to rock and roll. Young people took the new discourse of youth and used it to create their own culture.

3 From the late 1970s young people lost some of their rebellion and replaced it with cynicism. They lost the desire to celebrate youth in its own right and became more obsessed with becoming part of the adult world. Political activities were superseded by hanging around in shopping malls.

Grossberg attributes this change in the meaning of youth to the way in which adults have helped to shift the discourse of youth. Adults are increasingly unwilling to give up their idea of themselves as youthful, redefining it as an attitude of mind rather than simply an age. Also, many aspects of youth culture have become incorporated into adult-controlled institutions. Rock music is frequently used in advertising, for example.

Evaluation

The emphasis on language of post-structuralists such as Grossberg leads them to neglect material reality. Marxists would argue that material wealth has just as much influence on society as discourses or ways of talking about things. In the end it is capitalists who have the power to determine which records, clothes and so on are available to young people.

Mass culture

In 1950s America there was considerable concern about the impact of what was called mass culture. As individuals had more and more free time, the mass media stepped in to fill people's spare time with undemanding entertainment such as soap operas, popular films and magazines.

Macdonald (1957) saw no merit in mass culture. He believed it had nothing of significance to say and was designed to appeal to the lowest common denominator. He argued that mass culture was actually undermining the fabric of society because people were losing their involvement in social groups and becoming isolated individuals.

Strinati – a critique of mass culture theory

Strinati (1995) attacks mass culture theory on a number of grounds:

1 The consumers of mass culture are not a passive 'mass' of people. They are discriminating and reject many products which they find insufficiently interesting or entertaining.

2 It is not the case that all popular culture is homogeneous (the same). In reality there is a wide variety of styles. Popular music, for example, includes 'rap', jazz, heavy metal and so on.

3 It is not possible to distinguish a superior 'folk culture' from an inferior mass culture. Folk, blues and country music, for example, have all been influenced by a range of musical traditions.

4 There is no clear distinction between mass culture and high culture. Strinati gives the examples of jazz music, the films of Alfred Hitchcock and rock-and-roll records which have attained the status of classics.

Modernity, postmodernity and culture

Strinati – postmodernism and popular culture

Strinati (1995) describes how theories of postmodernism explain popular culture.

The main features of postmodernism

1 'The breakdown of the distinction between culture and society.' Society has become 'media-saturated' and this means that the media are extremely powerful. They become so all-consuming that they actually create our sense of reality.

2 'An emphasis on style at the expense of substance.' Products become popular because they have designer labels rather than because they are useful. Surface qualities assume more importance than anything deeper.

3 There is a 'breakdown of the distinction between art and popular culture'. Elements of what used to be thought of as 'high culture' become incorporated into popular culture – the pop artist Andy Warhol, for example, produced a print consisting of thirty representations of the *Mona Lisa*. Unlike the critics of mass culture (see above), postmodernists see no reason to be unhappy about this: they welcome the fun and variety of postmodern culture.

4 The development of 'confusions over time and space'. Rapid travel and instantaneous communications lead to confusions over time and space. The media make it possible to witness events on the other side of the globe almost as if you were there. Theme parks recreate the past and try to create the future; while some films and novels deliberately avoid following a storyline from start to finish.

5 Finally, postmodern culture involves 'the decline of metanarratives'. It involves a decline in faith in any absolute claim to knowledge, such as religion, science and Marxism. It denies that there is any sense of progress in history. Everything is equally valid and the search for truth is pointless and dangerous.

Reasons for the emergence of postmodernism

Strinati identifies three main reasons for the emergence of postmodernism:

1 Advanced capitalist societies emphasize consumerism. A more affluent population with more leisure time needs to be entertained and persuaded to spend money. The media is central to these processes and so media images come to dominate society.

2 New middle-class occupations such as design, marketing, advertising and creative jobs in the various media involve persuading people about the importance of taste. Once persuaded, people seek guidance on taste issues from the media. Other occupations – such as teaching and therapy – promote the idea that lifestyle is important, and so people are encouraged to consume the goods and services required for their favoured lifestyle.

3 There has been a gradual disappearance of identities based on such things as class, local communities and religion. People's identities become more personal and individual and constructed by the media.

An evaluation of postmodern theories of culture

Strinati raises a number of problems with postmodern theories:

1 Postmodernists exaggerate the importance of the mass media. There is no reason to think that people cannot distinguish between image and reality. Few people actually believe that characters in soap operas are real, for example.
2 People do not buy products just because of their image or the designer label attached to them; they also buy them because they are useful. What is more, not all members of society have a culture that attaches importance to the image of products.
3 Postmodernism is itself a 'metanarrative' so this undermines the claim that metanarratives are in decline.
4 Some people have less opportunity than others to experience changes in concepts of time and space. Poorer people do not have access to computer or satellite technology or jet travel. What is more, there are no studies that show that people actually are confused about space and time.
5 Generally people still find it possible to distinguish between what they consider art and what they see as popular culture. Strinati believes that postmodernists simply create their own hierarchy of taste, placing their own favourite cultural products at the top.
6 The impact of postmodernism on popular culture has been exaggerated. Strinati focuses on films and points out that many of the supposed postmodern aspects of contemporary cinema are nothing new. Also, many films regarded as postmodern still have strong narratives (storylines).

Identity

Stuart Hall

According to Hall (1992) contemporary societies are increasingly characterized by the existence of fractured identities. People no longer possess a single, unified concept of who they are. This fragmentation of identity has a number of sources.

Modernity and change

The pace of change has increased in 'late-modern' societies and this makes it difficult for people to retain a unified identity.

New social movements

In the past, social class provided something of a 'master identity'. However, in the 1960s and 1970s people began to organize around issues other than class. New social movements developed based around issues such as gender, ethnicity and the environment.

With the rise of new social movements, identity itself became a political issue. Identity politics emphasizes the importance of hearing the voices of oppressed groups such as gays and lesbians, black women, the disabled and so on.

Globalization

The ease with which people move around the world, improvements in communications and the global marketing of styles and images can lead to a 'cultural supermarket effect'. People can choose from a wide range of identities, adopting the values and lifestyles of any group they choose.

On the other hand, global consumerism can also lead to increased similarity as products such as Coca-Cola can be found anywhere.

Globalization and different sources of identity

In modern societies nationality was an important source of identity. National identity was used to create a sense of solidarity among citizens of different classes, ethnic origins and so on. With globalization this is not so easy. Hall identifies three responses:

1 In some places people have tried to reaffirm national identity as a defensive mechanism. They have perceived a threat to their national identity from immigration for example.
2 The first reaction is characteristic of ethnic majorities. But ethnic minorities sometimes react in defensive ways as well. In response to racism and exclusion, ethnic minorities have sometimes placed a renewed emphasis on their ethnic identities and culture.
3 A third reaction is the construction of new identities. A British example is the construction of a 'black' identity, embracing British Afro-Caribbeans and Asians. In this case identity becomes hybrid, mixing more than one existing identity into a new identity.

The first two responses to globalization have had the effect of reviving ethnicity as a source of identity, often in opposition to existing nationalism. In several parts of the world ethnic groups have demanded their own nation-states as bigger nation-states (such as the USSR and Yugoslavia) have broken up. This has led to considerable violence and even civil war.

Hall sees this nationalism as a worrying trend. He argues that the idea of ethnic purity is largely a myth as nearly all populations come from a variety of ethnic backgrounds.

Bradley – Fractured Identities

Bradley (1997) attempts to pull together classical and postmodern sociological approaches in understanding the relationship between identity and inequality.

Three levels of identity

Bradley believes that it is useful to think of identity as working at three levels:

1 Passive identities – these are identities which have the potential to become important but largely lie dormant. Bradley sees class identity in this way. Most British people accept that class inequalities exist but do not see themselves as a member of a class most of the time. However, circumstances could change.
2 Active identities – these are identities which individuals are conscious of and which provide a base for their actions.
3 Politicized identities – these are formed through campaigns highlighting the importance of a

particular identity and using it as a basis for organizing collective action. For example, feminists succeeded in turning gender into a politicized identity in the 1970s and 1980s.

Bradley accepts that postmodernists have a point in arguing that there is a good deal of choice over identity and that identities are becoming more fragmented. However, she still sees identities as rooted in membership of social groups.

Bradley examines four aspects of inequality: class, gender, 'race'/ethnicity and age, although she does recognize other important social divisions such as sexuality and disability.

Class and identity

Bradley does not see class as the strongest source of identity in contemporary Britain. She sees it as a passive form of identity, partly because it is less visible in the everyday world than age, 'race'/ethnicity and gender. However, she notes that inequality is increasing and that this creates the potential for class to be an increasingly important source of identity.

Gender and identity

Bradley notes the move away from theories such as radical feminism which saw women as a single group, towards theories which see women (and men) as being fragmented into different groups. She believes that both types of theory are important and that common experience of sexism provides a basis for a shared identity for women.

However, not all women experience disadvantage to the same extent or in the same ways. Black feminists, for example, have suggested that the family is experienced differently by white and black women.

To Bradley, gender is a very important source of identity in contemporary Britain. It is also an active, politicized identity for women as a result of feminism.

'Race'/ethnicity and identity

Like gender, 'race'/ethnicity has become a more important source of identity in Britain than class and is more likely to produce active and politicized identities. Sometimes this is due to the visibility of skin colour but this is not always the case. The violence in the former Yugoslavia occurred between white ethnic groups, for example.

The importance of 'race'/ethnicity depends on how it is used politically to mobilize groups and provide them with a sense of belonging. The identity of a British Muslim has assumed more importance than other potential identities as a result of the revival of Islam as a world religion.

For dominant ethnic groups, ethnic identity is rather less politicized but can become more politicized in certain situations. In Britain, Scottish and Welsh ethnic identities are more active and politicized than English identity, but an English identity can become important in some contexts (such as sporting events).

Age and identity

Age is an important source of identity for individuals but it is not usually a politicized identity. This is because people move through different age groups and know they will not stay in one group for ever. Also, the most disadvantaged groups are the young and the old, and they have little in common.

Some aspects of youth culture express a sense of conflict with adults and have helped age to become a more active identity. There are also some examples of age becoming a politicized identity, such as the coalition of youth groups that opposed the Criminal Justice Bill in the 1990s, and the activities of the Grey Panthers in America who have campaigned for the rights of the elderly.

Conclusion

Bradley concludes that stratification systems and identities are becoming both polarized and fragmented.

- Polarization – there are increasing differences between the rich and poor and young and old. There is also some polarization between ethnic groups, particularly with the re-emergence of nationalist and fascist organizations.
- Fragmentation – there is fragmentation and division in each of the categories above. As a result, people in contemporary societies tend to have fractured identities. They lack an identity that overrides all others.

1   Which one of the following definitions of culture is used by most sociologists?
   a   The sum total of all the arts and intellectual work in a society
   b   The whole way of life of a people
   c   A quality possessed by individuals who are particularly civilized
   d   A quality possessed by societies that are more civilized than others

2   Which term best describes the culture of ordinary people, particularly those living in traditional societies?
   a   Popular culture
   b   High culture
   c   Folk culture
   d   Subculture

3   Which perspective emphasizes the degree to which culture is shared?
   a   Functionalism
   b   Marxism
   c   Postmodernism
   d   Interactionism

4   Which one of the following concepts refers to how a person is perceived by others?
   a   Identity
   b   Social identity
   c   Identification
   d   Personal identity

5   Three of these statements would be supported by most postmodernists. Which is the odd one out?
   a   People shape and change their identities through shopping and other forms of consumption
   b   People have a great deal of choice about their identities
   c   People's identities are strongly shaped by their socialization
   d   People actively create their own identities

6   Three of these statements would be supported by most functionalists. Which is the odd one out?
   a   Cultural diversity is characteristic of all societies
   b   A shared culture is necessary for society to run smoothly
   c   Culture is passed on to children through socialization
   d   Culture is generally slow to change

7   Which Italian Marxist influenced the work of the Birmingham Centre for Contemporary Cultural Studies?
   a   Antonio Gramsci
   b   Friedrich Engels
   c   Louis Althusser
   d   Nicos Poulantzas

8   Which one of the following statements best describes the CCCS's analysis of youth subcultures?
   a   Youth subcultures represent an attempt to win space from dominant cultures
   b   Youth subcultures represent the diversity of young people's experience in contemporary societies
   c   Youth subcultures are little more than delinquency
   d   Youth subcultures are simply part of ruling-class ideology

9   Which one of the following terms is used to describe the method of analysing symbols and signs used by Hebdige in his study of youth subcultures?
   a   Postmodernism
   b   Semiotics
   c   Neo-Marxism
   d   Content analysis

10 Three of the following are criticisms of mass culture theory. Which is the odd one out?
   a   The consumers of mass culture are not a passive mass of people
   b   It is possible to distinguish between mass culture and high culture
   c   It is not the case that all popular culture is homogeneous
   d   It is not possible to distinguish between a superior folk culture and an inferior mass culture

11 What term do postmodernists use to describe theories that claim they have access to absolute knowledge about the world?
   a   Structuralism
   b   Metanarratives
   c   Social action theory
   d   Religions

12 Three of these statements are reasons given by Strinati for the growth of postmodernism. Which is the odd one out?
   a   There is a growing gap between the wealthy and the poor
   b   The more affluent population has more leisure time and so the media become more important
   c   People are encouraged to consume the goods and services required for their favoured lifestyle
   d   People's identities are less based on class, local communities and religion. They are now more personal and constructed by the media

13 Three of these statements are criticisms of postmodern theories of culture. Which is the odd one out?
   a   Postmodernists exaggerate the importance of the mass media
   b   People do not buy products just because of their label or image
   c   The majority of people can distinguish between art and popular culture
   d   Globalization is breaking down national boundaries

14 What sort of identities does Hall claim are characteristic of late-modern societies?
   a   Cultural identities
   b   Social identities
   c   Fractured identities
   d   National identities

15 Which one of the following can be described as a new social movement?
   a   The Conservative Party
   b   Environmental pressure groups
   c   The trade union movement
   d   Marxism

16 Which one of the following best describes the 'cultural supermarket effect'?
 a People can choose from a wide range of identities
 b Some positions in society earn more status and income than others
 c The media is dominated by large corporations
 d Popular culture appeals to less-educated people

17 According to Hall, what has been the most significant factor in causing national identity to decline in importance?
 a A decrease in the importance of social class
 b Globalization
 c English sports teams failing in recent years
 d The influence of ethnic minorities

18 What term best describes mixing more than one identity to create a new one?
 a Diversity
 b Hybridization
 c Globalization
 d Ethnic minority

19 Which one of the following is a definition of Bradley's 'active identities'?
 a Identities which have the potential to become important
 b Identities which are used as the basis for organizing collective action
 c Identities which have been created as a result of postmodernity
 d Identities which individuals are conscious of and which provide a basis for their actions

20 Which one of the following identities does Bradley see as being least politicized?
 a English
 b Scottish
 c Welsh
 d Irish

Develop your analysis and evaluation skills

(see p. 207 for guidance notes)

For each of the following statements, identify which sociologists would argue in favour of and which against the view expressed. Explain the reasons for their view.

1 Mass culture has had a dangerous effect on society.
2 Youth subcultures are ways of resisting dominant ideology.
3 Culture is shared by members of a society.
4 Postmodernism is the most effective perspective in understanding contemporary culture and identity.
5 Contemporary societies are characterized by fractured identities.

AQA style Culture and Identity questions (from a range of modules)

The AQA specification examines this area as a theme underlying all topics in sociology.
The questions that follow are taken from a variety of modules to show how the
information in this chapter can contribute to answers for the examination.

Comments on the question	Question	Advice on preparing your answer
Family and Households, AS Unit 1		
• Look at both sides and provide evidence where possible • This is about a stage in the life cycle; it is **not** a question about socialization	Examine the view that childhood is a social construction. [20 marks]	• This has a particular meaning, i.e. that 'childhood' means different things at different times and in different places • Grossberg (pp. 148–9) would be a useful starting point
Mass Media, AS Unit 1		
• You must look at both sides and come to a conclusion based on the evidence you use • This is a problematic concept • Do not repeat the question as an introduction; it is better to start by defining the key terms	Evaluate the claim that the mass media have created a mass culture society. [20 marks]	• Marxist theories, pp. 147–8 • Mass culture, p. 149 • Critiques of this approach, p. 149 • Pluralist theory as an alternative, Chapter 13, pp. 156–7 • The section on postmodernism (pp. 149–50) needs to be used selectively for its focus on the mass media
Crime and Deviance, A2 Unit 6 Synoptic Paper		
• This term can mean a variety of things: 1 Does it explain the cause? 2 Does it explain the effect? 3 Can it be operationalized? 4 Is it valid? 5 Is it reliable? 6 What are its strengths? 7 What are its weaknesses? 8 Does it provide policy solutions?	Assess the usefulness of the concept of subculture to an explanation of deviant groups. [40 marks]	• Choose the most appropriate issues from the list opposite to apply to this question • The term is explained on p. 142 • Neo-Marxist studies (p. 142) provide useful illustrative material • Other relevant material is in Chapter 6 on Crime and deviance
World Sociology, A2 Unit 4		
• Make sure that you understand this term • Use the three terms as the organizing principle for your answer • You will have to do additional reading on this topic to enable you to answer this question fully	'Globalization has changed the cultural, political and economic relationships between societies.' Explain and discuss this statement. [40 marks]	• The cultural supermarket effect, hybrid identities (p. 150) and popular culture (p. 147) can be applied to this part of the question • Ideas of consumerism could be used as a starting point • National identities and politicized identities (p. 150–1) can be applied here

OCR style Culture and Identity question, A2 Unit 2533: Culture and Socialisation: Youth and Culture

Answer both parts of the question

Total: 45 marks

1 mark = 1 minute

Time allowed: 45 minutes

Comments on the question	Question	Advice on preparing your answer
• Make sure that the examiner can see that you have clearly identified two characteristics • No more, no less • Make sure that you develop an explanation of why these two characteristics are unique to youth culture and not found in mainstream culture	[a] Identify and explain two characteristics of youth cultures that distinguish them from mainstream culture. [15 marks]	• You will find material on pp. 148–9 that will assist you in answering this question
• Describe the view as fully as possible, using supporting evidence • Make sure that you consider arguments and evidence against the view and/or alternative view(s) • Aim for balance –don't make the mistake of focusing on one theory or youth culture at the expense of others	[b] Outline and assess the view that deviant youth subcultures were formed in order to resist and shock dominant social groups. [30 marks]	• Remember that this is only one view. You can challenge it if you want • Your introduction should briefly define concepts such as youth culture and dominant groups, and terms such as 'resist' and 'shock' • Information about deviant youth subcultures can be found on pp. 148–9 • Some criticisms can also be found here

Chapter 13

Communication and the media

Textbook pp. 934–963

Specifications

Specification	Relevant module title	Place in module	Level	Assessment	Other relevant modules
AQA	1. Families and Households; Health; **Mass Media**	One of three options in this module.	AS	One data-response question.	Material from this chapter may be used in the A2 synoptic module 6.
OCR	Culture and Socialisation	**Mass Media** is one of four options in this module.	AS	One or two two-part structured questions from a choice of two.	Material from this chapter may be used in the A2 synoptic module 6.
	Power and Control	**Popular Culture** is one of six options in this module.	A2	One essay question from a choice of two.	

Communication and the media: essential notes

Introduction: defining the 'mass media'

The mass media can be seen as 'the methods and organizations used to convey messages to large, widely dispersed audiences'. It involves communication from a single point to many other points.

The mass media can utilize different modes of communication such as TV, radio, film and print.

However, these ways of defining the media may be becoming less relevant because:
- The media are becoming more interactive (audiences can respond – e.g. by casting votes).
- Networks (communication between many different points) are becoming more important – e.g. the internet.

The mass media are sometimes seen as having very powerful effects on their audiences, but remember:
- The audience should not necessarily be seen as one 'mass'. Audiences vary – e.g. according to class, gender, ethnicity and region.
- Postmodernists emphasize that media messages are polysemic – they can be interpreted in very different ways by different individuals.

Role and influence of the media: structure and content

Pluralist theories

Pluralists are sympathetic to the media and see them as acting in a responsible way and reflecting the wishes and interests of their audiences.
- To pluralists, society consists of many different groups with diverse interests.

- Each group has roughly equal access to power.
- The mass media reflect this diversity in what they cover.
- The media operate in the public interest.
- The media follow public opinion rather than shape it.

An illustration

In their book *Personal Influence*, Katz and Lazarsfeld (1955) studied the media's influence on political opinion in the USA in the 1940s. They found that:
- People had different amounts of exposure to the media.
- Different media had different degrees of influence (TV could be more powerful than newspapers when using images).
- The content of the messages determined whether they had much effect.
- People tended to accept messages that supported existing prejudices and reject those that contradicted them.
- Messages were mediated by opinion leaders and did not directly influence people's attitudes or how they voted.

There are a number of criticisms of pluralism:
1. Philo (1986) argues that pluralism may be an ideological justification for the media, put forward by those who work in the media industry.
2. Blumler and Gurevitch (1995) argue that journalists and politicians have a shared culture. Under the lobby system that operates, journalists rely on politicians for information and will tend to present the politicians' view of the world.

3 The pluralist model assumes that the content of the media is diverse, rather than providing evidence that it is.

Marxist theories

- Marxists see the ownership or control of the media by a capitalist ruling class as the key to understanding the mass media.
- The media transmit the ideas of the ruling class.
- The ruling class use the media to promote their products, to make a profit and to persuade people to accept the capitalist system.
- The ruling class largely own the means of production (e.g. TV stations, newspapers, publishers), and huge corporations dominate the media. For example, Rupert Murdoch's News Corporation owns BSkyB, the *Sun, The Times,* HarperCollins publishers, etc.

There is evidence of increased monopolization, as a few big companies gain monopoly control of the media.

According to Bagdikian (1997), the US media were controlled by 50 corporations in the 1980s, but just 10 in 1997. In 2000 Time Warner and the internet company America Online (AOL) merged, creating an enormous media corporation.

Boyd-Barrett and Rantanen (1998) point out that most media executives sit on the boards of several corporations. This allows capitalists to organize the media to support their collective interests. Media owners may directly interfere in media content – e.g. Rupert Murdoch has instructed newspaper editors on what to print.

Capitalism also influences the media in indirect ways. For example, the media need to attract rich readers for advertising revenue.

Bagdikian argues that news that is of interest to capitalists (e.g. stock market news) gets plenty of coverage. Negative news about capitalism (e.g. the living standards of the poor) gets little coverage. Left-wing newspapers get little financial support and do not last long.

Marxist perspectives have been criticized:

1 They may underestimate the importance of state regulation – e.g. of the BBC.
2 To pluralists, the media must respond to audience preferences if they are to survive. Capitalists need to serve audiences to make a profit.
3 Anti-establishment programmes do get made – e.g. *The Simpsons* with its negative portrayal of family life.
4 Postmodernists deny that power is concentrated in the hands of the rich.
5 The public can use the media to oppose the policies of giant corporations (e.g. public media pressure persuaded Shell not to dump the Brent Spar oil rig at sea).

Neo-Marxist theories: cultural hegemony

Neo-Marxist approaches put less emphasis than Marxism on direct control by capitalists, or the way in which the logic of capitalist competition shapes the media.

They argue that it is the dominance of ruling-class culture (cultural hegemony) that shapes the media.

There are competing views within the media, but ruling-class ideology becomes the main influence on how people understand and make sense of the social world.

A number of examples can illustrate this.

Hall and cultural hegemony

Stuart Hall (1995) argues that the way in which the media classify the world assumes a basic consensus about how the world works, and this dominant view is taken for granted.

For example, the media assume that wage demands cause inflation (rather than, say, profiteering by companies).

There is no conspiracy to manipulate the meanings of the media, simply a widespread acceptance of certain ways of seeing the world.

Discourse analysis

Discourse analysis examines the connections between power and how certain ways of thinking about certain types of event come to be accepted.

For example, Norman Fairclough (1995) argues that the television programme *Crimewatch* operates to legitimate the role of the police and to encourage the public to believe that they can work with the police in combating crime. It contradicts images of the police as corrupt, inept, etc.

However, discourse analysis represents only one person's analysis; other viewers might 'read' the message of *Crimewatch* differently.

The Glasgow Media Group and cultural hegemony

The Glasgow Media Group have done a variety of research supporting the cultural hegemony model.

They argue that connotative codes (which evoke attitudes and emotions) are used. For example, in industrial disputes, negative words (such as 'threat' and 'demand') are used to describe strikers, while more positive words (such as 'offer') are used to describe management. This evokes sympathy for managers and hostility towards strikers.

- Certain visual angles (e.g. filming from behind police lines in picket-line clashes) encourage identification with the police viewpoint.
- Media professionals set the agenda for news stories and take a pro-establishment stance (e.g. looking at effects rather than causes of strikes).
- 'Extremist' political views are treated unsympathetically.

Recent work by the Glasgow Media Group accepts that cultural hegemony is not complete.

- Some journalists (e.g. Jonathan Dimbleby) challenge establishment views.
- Audience research shows that audiences do not always believe media messages.
- There is an element of interaction between broadcasters and audiences, and audience reaction can change the views and actions of programme makers (as well as broadcasters influencing audiences). Audiences are not just passive. This process is called a circuit of communication.

Organizational factors

Media professions and organizations may have a direct effect on media content.

Galtung and Ruge (1965) identify criteria that journalists are taught to value in stories. These are:

- Frequency (short-lived events are preferred).
- Threshold (more intense events are preferred).
- Unambiguity (especially events that fit into an established story type).
- Meaningfulness (relevance to the audience).
- Unexpectedness (unexpected events are preferred).
- Elite nations in the story are preferred.
- Elite individuals in the story are preferred.
- Reference to individuals makes a story more newsworthy.
- Bad news is more newsworthy than good news.

Boyd-Barrett (1995) criticizes Galtung and Ruge, pointing out that they fail to explain where journalistic values come from, and they ignore structural factors and cultural hegemony (see above).

Grossberg et al. (1998) identify production processes as important (e.g. using official sources such as the police for information and comment). The use of such sources biases media content towards powerful social groups.

Role and influence of the media: audiences and their responses

1 The hypodermic model

The hypodermic model assumes that media messages are directly injected into audiences as if by a syringe.

The media can act like a drug or narcotic, directly changing behaviour.

This process was demonstrated by Bandura, Ross and Ross (1963), who conducted psychological experiments which showed that boys would imitate aggression in films they had watched (social learning theory).

The hypodermic model has been criticized:

1 Audiences are very diverse and react in different ways.
2 Long-term effects may not be the same as short-term ones.
3 It ignores the different uses audiences make of the media – e.g. TV programmes may only be used as background noise.
4 It ignores other media effects – e.g. watching violent films as an outlet for aggression rather than a cause of it.

Nevertheless many politicians and other commentators are still influenced by the hypodermic model

2 The two-step flow model

Merton (1946) and Katz and Lazarsfeld (1955) argued that media effects may not be direct, but that messages are interpreted by key individuals who then influence others.

- Step 1 – the media message reaches the audience.
- Step 2 – the message is interpreted by the audience and it influences them.

Social interaction is an important element of step 2. Opinion leaders interpret messages for others and shape what influence the messages might have.

Later the multi-step flow model was developed, which recognizes that there are several stages in the interpretation of media messages. For example, Dorothy Hobson (1990) shows how discussions about soap operas at work influence people's interpretation of them.

The two-step flow model has been criticized.

It is argued that there may be no dominant opinion leaders or consensus about the meaning of media messages.

3 The uses and gratifications model

This model is based on the idea that people use the media in a variety of ways.

McQuail (1972) suggests four possible uses:

1 Diversion or escape.
2 Personal relationships (e.g. feeling part of a soap opera community).
3 Personal identity (confirming or weakening the sense of who we are by using certain media messages).
4 Surveillance (finding out what is going on).

The uses made of the media may vary according to age, gender, etc.

This model has been criticized:

1 It fails to explain why people use the media in different ways.
2 It ignores the possibility that the media can create people's needs.
3 It focuses on individuals rather than social, cultural and structural factors.

4 The interpretative model

In the interpretative model, the audience filters messages, ignoring, rejecting, accepting or reinterpreting them.

Fiske (1988) uses the idea of intertexuality – relating different texts/contexts to one another, e.g. relating soap operas to your own life or relating interviews with actors to performance in a film.

Audience members can move between different levels of involvement in watching TV: engagement, detachment and referential (relating events to one's own experiences).

Buckingham (1993) uses the idea of media literacy. Degree of knowledge and understanding of the media affects the depth of people's interpretation of the media. The more sophisticated viewers can understand the codes or rhetoric of TV language and the meanings that can be inferred from the way programmes are produced.

There are criticisms of the interpretative model:

1 It may underestimate the power of media messages and how strongly they can be reinforced.
2 It is an individualistic approach, which neglects the role of subcultures in shaping interpretations.

5 The structured interpretation model

This model argues that audiences do interpret the meaning of the media, but there is a preferred reading, influenced by the way in which the message is encoded. However, researchers need to be aware that different subcultures (class, gender, ethnicity, age, religion, etc.) will tend to interpret the messages in different ways.

For example, David Morley (1980) showed how the audience of *Nationwide* interpreted a story differently:
- Trade unionists saw it as biased towards management.
- Managers accepted the news coverage as unbiased.
- Middle-class students saw the programme as superficial.
- Black, mainly working-class students saw it as boring.

Thus the media can be read/interpreted in many different ways (they are polysemic).

Different groups bring different languages, concepts and assumptions to interpreting messages.

There are a number of criticisms of this approach.

Some sociologists (e.g. postmodernists) deny that social groups have such a strong influence on interpretations of the media.

6 Audience reception and postmodernity

Postmodernists adopt views that question the idea of 'the audience' as conceived in other approaches.

Baudrillard (1988) argues that media-saturated societies have produced hyperreality, in which objectivity breaks down and images can be interpreted in many ways, even by the same people at different times.

Turkle (1996) sees TV as part of the postmodern culture of simulation – we identify more with the fictional life of TV than we do with real life.
- We treat media messages as if they were real – e.g. real *Cheers* bars have opened.
- The distinction between image and reality breaks down. People no longer search for the real meaning of media messages but use media images in the playful creation of different identities.
- The media become part of lifestyle rather than conveyors of information.

Critics have attacked postmodernism:
1 Webster (1999) argues that:
- The social context still influences the way in which the mass media are used and interpreted.
- You still need to look at *who* creates the media information and for what purposes (as Marxists, for example, would argue).
2 Lerner (1994) argues that postmodernism obscures inequality and prevents attempts to improve the world.

Role and influence of the media: images and social groups

Media messages can be seen as passing through four stages:
1 Formulation
2 Message content – the 'text'
3 Audience reception
4 Effects of message

These stages can be applied to different social groups.

Gender

Formulation
Most media workers are women, but Croteau and Hoynes (2000) found that in the USA in the mid-1990s

women made up only 6% of top newspaper managers and wrote 20% of TV news reports.

Radical feminists argue that patriarchal domination means that male perceptions of women dominate the media. 'Women's issues' – e.g. sexual harassment, police attitudes to rape, problems of childcare – get little attention.

Message content
Generally males outnumber females in all TV programme types – e.g. there is a ratio of seven males to three females in some soaps, there are few women in cartoons and there are three all-male ads for every one all-female ad.
- Bretl and Cantor (1988) found that males are more often shown in high-status jobs and away from home than women; and 90% of narrators are men.
- Meehan (1983) argues that women are portrayed in a small range of stereotypical roles in US drama – e.g. the 'Goodwife', the 'Bitch' (manipulative, dangerous), the 'Victim', the 'Courtesan', etc. She argues that women tend to be portrayed as extremes (e.g. good or evil).
- Saucier (1986) found that country music songs portray women exclusively in the housewife/mother/lover roles.
- Provenzo (1991) found that computer games normally portray women as passive, young and attractive, whereas men are 'macho'.
- Holland (1987) notes that there are more female than male news and weather presenters, but the women presenters tend to be young and attractive. Women are used to develop a more intimate style of presentation, as opposed to male, rationalistic, detached presentation.
- Ferguson (1983) sees women's magazines as encouraging a cult of femininity concerned with how to dress and act, how to be a super-cook, office boss or *femme fatale*. The growth in men's magazines only increases gender stereotyping.

Audience reception
Recent radical feminists argue that women are active interpreters of messages, and they may reject stereotypical and patriarchal messages.
- Ang (1985) argues that women may get pleasure from soap operas like *Dallas* and are not just the passive victims of stereotyping.
- Skirrow (1986) uses the concept of gender valence – the relationship between gender identities and technology. Women reject video games because they are part of a technology associated with male power.
- Turkle (1988) argues that women reject computers because they do not want a close relationship with a machine.
- Gray (1987) argues that telephones are a more female technology because they allow human contact.
- Lewis (1990) argues that music videos have a male gender valence because they are based on male adolescence – rebelliousness, sexual promiscuity and female conquest. However, girl bands, which

encourage female friendship and solidarity, may be changing this.

- The postmodernist Hermes (1995) argues that some women find women's magazines educative and relaxing. She stresses that the way in which these magazines are used by women can change.
(See also the discussion of class and audience reception, below.)

Media effects

To those using the hypodermic model (e.g. Provenzo), the media socialize women to be dependent and men to be dominant.

- Frueh and McGhee (in Tuchman, 1978) claimed that heavy TV viewing amongst US children correlated with traditional sex-role stereotyping.
- Beuf (1974) argues that children model themselves on TV role models, and this leads many girls to abandon their ambitions before they reach the age of 6. The media also make females concerned about their body image and the need to get and keep a man.
- To radical feminists, such as Kath Davies (1987), the media encourage women to accept patriarchal capitalism.
- Angela McRobbie (1991) uses a cultural hegemony approach, suggesting that an interest in make-up and appearance becomes taken for granted in girls' magazines.
- Liberal feminists find evidence of sex-role stereotyping in the media and then assume that it influences behaviour. However, Gaye Tuchman (1978) accepts that images may change with time, although media images tend to lag behind changes in society.

Ethnicity

Message content

Representations of ethnicity are varied. Some are very sympathetic to ethnic minority worldviews (e.g. Asian TV programmes and films), and some 'white establishment' programmes are quite sympathetic.
However, there is also evidence of stereotyping.

- Newspapers tend to portray ethnic minorities as a threat.
- TV tends to portray ethnic minorities in a restricted range of roles. The Broadcasting Standards Commission (1999) has found that black people tend to be portrayed in arts, media, entertainment, health and caring, sports and police roles, and Asians in arts, media, entertainment, health and caring and student roles. There are few portrayals of minorities in roles such as legal professionals.

Audience reception

Gillespie (1995) studied 14–18-year-old Punjabis in Southall, London.

- They used the media to define their own ethnicity, comparing themselves to characters in Indian 'soaps' such as the *Mahabharata* and non-Asian soaps such as *Neighbours*.
- They reflect on cultural differences between themselves and others, and dream of aspects of American culture, but recognize that their culture is different.

- They develop a hybrid national and cultural identity, combining elements of Islam and Westernization.
- This leads to some critical evaluation of their parents' culture.

Media effects

- Van Dijk (1991) argues that newspapers have a major impact in developing a perception of immigration as a problem. He uses a hypodermic model, arguing that this perception may lead to racist attacks etc.
- Hartmann and Husband (1974) studied the impact of media messages in different areas. In areas with a large Asian population (e.g. the West Midlands), race relations were seen as less of a threat than in areas with few Asians (e.g. Glasgow).
Factors such as class and gender also influence the degree to which media reporting of ethnicity will affect the audience.

Class

Formulation

Most people in senior positions in the media are of middle-class origin.

Message content

Glennon and Butsch (1982) studied class lifestyles in family contexts on US TV and found that:

- Working-class families are under-represented.
- Two-thirds of programmes had managers or proprietors as heads of household.
- Only 4% had blue-collar heads of household.
- Middle-class parents are usually portrayed as good at dealing with problems.
- Working-class fathers are often portrayed as figures of fun.
The Glasgow Media Group (see p. 157) have found that the working class are often associated with 'trouble'.

Audience reception

Ann Gray (1992) conducted a study of women from different classes and their use of TV and video.

- Lower social classes both used and accepted TV and video more than higher classes.
- Higher classes were more anxious about children using TV.
- Context (i.e. who you watched TV with) was important to viewing.
- Men enjoyed current affairs, documentaries and sport more than women.
- Men tended to control viewing more than women.
- In the highest classes, both men and women valued 'quality' 'classics' and disliked 'popular' 'trash' genres.
- In lower classes, women liked 'soppy', 'fantasy' and 'soft' genres; men preferred 'hard', 'tough' and 'factual' genres.
- In all classes, men preferred 'heroic', 'public', 'societal' and 'physical' programmes; women preferred 'romantic', 'domestic', 'familial' and 'emotional' programmes.

Age

Formulation

Media workers in senior positions tend to be older than those in junior ones.

Message content

- According to Pearson (1983), adolescents have long been portrayed as a problem by the media. There has been a long-standing myth of a golden age when youth was less troublesome (usually twenty years previously), but there have always been problem groups of youths (Victorian hooligans, Teds in the 1950s, Travellers today).
- Amongst older age groups, Sontag (1978) finds a double standard: women have to match up to a youthful ideal, men do not.
- Lambert *et al.* (1984) found that on British TV people over the age of 60 did appear – usually portrayed as politicians, business people, experts, etc. – but they were almost exclusively men.
- Biggs (1993) found that soap operas were dominated by middle-aged/older people. Sit-coms tended to present stereotypes of the old as enfeebled, forgetful or cantankerous. Biggs found that although there was little concern on TV about the problems of age, some more positive images of the elderly were coming through.
- Signorelli (1989) analysed 14,000 US TV characters and found that the very young and the very old were under-represented. Older characters were less likely to be represented as 'good' but also less likely to be involved in violence.
- There is some favourable treatment of older people. Dail (1988) claims that they often have a positive image in soap operas; and Featherstone and Hepworth (1995) show how, in a growing market, magazines like *Retirement Choice* generally present more positive images.

Audience reception

Gunter and McAleer (1997) found that the young (aged 4–24) watch less TV (2.8 hours per day) than older people.

- Those with access to more media watched less TV, and TV did not seem to displace other activities.
- For older viewers, TV was a comfort and company; and for those who did not get out much it offered 'virtual mobility'.

David Buckingham (1993) has examined whether children are less media literate and more 'taken in' by media messages than adults.

- He found that most children were aware of the purpose of advertising. They were sometimes critical of the quality of what was being sold and cynical about 'free' gifts.
- Some were 'wise consumers', trying out advertised toys before purchase. Less of a hypodermic effect and more of a uses and gratifications effect was found – e.g. they used adverts to generate lists of requests for Christmas presents, but were realistic about what parents could afford.

Buckingham found children to be active interpreters but he also notes that:

- They were enthusiastic about watching adverts.
- They did not always view adverts critically.
- The interviews may not have revealed the extent to which children accepted adverts.

Media effects

- Hebdige (1988) argues that the media structure the way in which the young perceive society. Youth subcultures are based partly on these perceptions but also on the reality of situations. Hebdige, as a neo-Marxist, sees the media as absorbing and neutralizing rebellious youth subcultures – e.g. by marketing signs of youth culture as mass-market products.
- Gillespie, as a postmodernist, sees youth as more empowered.

Disability

Formulation

Few senior people in the media are disabled.

Message content

The Broadcasting Standards Commission (1999) found that:

- Disabled people appeared in 7% of TV programmes but only accounted for 0.7% of all those who spoke.
- There were three disabled males to every disabled female.
- Only one in ten were both ethnic minority members and disabled.

Longmore (1987) found that disabled people/disability were commonly portrayed in the following ways:

- as an emblem of evil
- as monsters
- as the loss of one's humanity
- as compensated for by substitute gifts (e.g. the blind having special powers)
- as leading to courage or achievement against the odds
- as a sexual menace

Cumberbatch and Negrine (1992) suggest that the disabled are often seen as the objects of pity or charity, but rarely as a normal part of life. Disability is normally portrayed as their key characteristic.

Audience reception

Cumberbatch and Negrine found that people with disabilities, or those in close contact with disabled people, were less likely to accept media portrayal of disability.

Media effects

- Cumberbatch and Negrine found that for those without close contact with disabled people, disability is seen as a problem. This may make it difficult for disabled people to be integrated into everyday life. However, Cumberbatch and Negrine conclude that more than changes in media coverage are needed to improve the lot of the disabled.

1   Which one of these statements about pluralist theory is **not true**?
    a   Pluralists see society as consisting of many different groups
    b   Pluralists believe that the media tend to follow public opinion
    c   Pluralists believe that the most powerful social groups determine the content of the media
    d   Pluralists believe that there is considerable choice in the mass media

2   Which **two** of the following statements would be supported by pluralists?
    a   The media act in the public interest
    b   The media tend to produce stereotypical views of women
    c   The media tend to have a conservative bias
    d   Fairness and balance are important features of the media

3   Who conducted the study of political opinions in the USA entitled *Personal Influence*?
    a   Willmott and Young
    b   The Glasgow Media Group
    c   Merton
    d   Katz and Lazarsfeld

4   Which one of these statements could not be used as a criticism of pluralist theory?
    a   Pluralists fail to take account of the fact that consumers have choice in the media output they consume
    b   Pluralists ignore the influence of owners on the content of the media
    c   Pluralists fail to take account of how the lobby system shapes the content of the media
    d   Pluralism ignores the possibility that the state can shape the content of the media

5   According to Bagdikian's Marxist view of the media, which **two** of the following statements are true?
    a   The media are increasingly controlled by a few large capitalist companies
    b   News about capitalism (e.g. news about stock markets) gets more coverage than news about the harmful effects of capitalism
    c   The main feature of the media is that they are patriarchal
    d   Left-wing newspapers tend to thrive

6   From a Marxist point of view, the mass media can best be described as part of:
    a   The economic base
    b   The superstructure
    c   The means of production
    d   The forces of production

7   Which one of the following statements is **not** a valid criticism of Marxism?
    a   There are some anti-capitalist views in media output
    b   State regulation limits the power of media owners
    c   The audience has some influence on the content of the media
    d   The owners of the media have no influence on the content

8   Which one of these statements best describes the difference between Marxist and neo-Marxist views of the media?

a   Unlike Marxists, neo-Marxists think that the economy has no influence on the way capitalist societies are organized
b   Unlike Marxists, neo-Marxists believe that all social groups have their views fairly represented by the media
c   Unlike Marxists, neo-Marxists believe that capitalists conspire to ensure that all media views are pro-capitalist
d   Unlike Marxists, neo-Marxists believe that ruling-class ideology influences the media more than direct capitalist control

9   Which one of these statements best describes the neo-Marxist views of Stuart Hall?
    a   The media never include anti-establishment views
    b   The media tend to assume a basic consensus in society
    c   The media are shaped by a conspiracy against the working class
    d   The media are fair and balanced

10 Intertextuality can best be defined as:
    a   The tendency for people to use different types of media
    b   The fact that different texts are often similar
    c   The way in which people draw upon different types of text to interpret the meaning of texts
    d   The observation that texts do not have fixed meanings

11 According to Fairclough, *Crimewatch* can be read as:
    a   An attempt to strengthen the credibility of state institutions such as the police
    b   A programme that encourages crime
    c   A programme that tells the truth about crime
    d   An attempt to make people more afraid of crime

12 The Glasgow Media Group believe that coverage of industrial disputes:
    a   Is fair and balanced
    b   Favours the viewpoint of employers
    c   Favours the viewpoint of workers
    d   Provides a true account of industrial disputes

13 Which one of these is **not** a reason why cultural hegemony is never complete?
    a   Audiences do not always believe media messages
    b   Some journalists attack establishment views
    c   Audiences have some influence on programme makers
    d   The variety of messages conveyed by the media is always strictly limited

14 According to Galtung and Ruge, **three** of the criteria used by journalists when deciding whether to cover a news story are:
    a   Meaningfulness
    b   Frequency
    c   Articulation
    d   Inclusion of elite individuals

15 The idea that the media directly shape the behaviour of the audience is called:
    a   The hypothetical model
    b   The hypodermic model
    c   The injection model
    d   The drug model

16 In the two-step flow model, which one of the following intervenes between the audience and the interpretation of the message?
   a Opinion leaders
   b Gate-keepers
   c Audience preconceptions
   d Editors

17 The interpretative model can be criticized for which one of the following reasons?
   a It neglects the influence of membership of social groups on the audience
   b It exaggerates the power of the media
   c It puts too little emphasis on the differences between the ways in which individuals 'read' the media
   d It assumes that people copy what they see in the media

18 The structured interpretation model differs from the interpretative model because:
   a It suggests that the interpretation is predetermined by the content of the message
   b It is based on a clear model of the structure of society
   c It is adapted from Marxism
   d It suggests that there is a preferred reading of messages

19 According to postmodernists, media messages are increasingly used:
   a To access information
   b To create identities
   c To strengthen political ideologies
   d To help people make rational choices

20 Which one of the following is **not** a criticism that has been made of the postmodern view of the media?
   a It largely ignores inequality
   b It assumes that members of the audience interpret media messages in the same way
   c It says little about who has the power to shape the content of the media
   d It neglects the influence of factors such as class and ethnicity on the way messages are interpreted

21 Which one of these concepts is associated with the postmodern view of the media?
   a Hegemony   b Diversion
   c The public interest d Hyperreality

22 In his study of *Nationwide*, Morley showed that:
   a The audience all interpret the content of the programme in the same way
   b The interpretation is shaped by the social groups to which members of the audience belong
   c Each member of the audience interprets the message differently
   d The interpretation of the message largely depends upon the age of audience members

23 An example of gender valence is:
   a Women watching soap operas because they are interested in family life
   b Few women using video games because the technology is seen as masculine
   c Women discussing media programmes with other women
   d Women arguing with men over the content of the media

24 Which one of the following is a radical feminist who believes that the media encourage women to accept patriarchal capitalism?
   a Angela McRobbie   b Gaye Tuchman
   c Kath Davies   d Diana Meehan

25 According to the Broadcasting Standards Commission, which one of these is **not** a role in which ethnic minority groups are frequently seen in the media?
   a Legal professional
   b Sportsperson
   c Entertainer
   d Worker in the health and caring professions

26 According to Gillespie, young Asians use the media in a way that:
   a Encourages them to reject Asian culture and identity
   b Encourages them to accept Asian culture and identity
   c Encourages them to develop a hybrid culture and identity
   d Has no effect on their culture and identity

Develop your analysis and evaluation skills   (see p. 216 for guidance notes)

For each of the following statements, identify which sociologists would argue in favour of and which against the view expressed. Explain the reasons for their view.

1 The mass media perpetuate gender stereotypes.
2 The content of the mass media is fair and balanced and reflects the diverse interests of the population.
3 The mass media have little effect on people's behaviour.
4 We live in a media-saturated society in which people find it difficult to distinguish fantasy from reality.
5 The mass media promote racism.
6 The content of the mass media is largely determined by those who own the media.
7 Everybody interprets the media in their own way.

Answer all parts of this question
Total: 60 marks   1 mark = 1.25 minutes
Time allowed: 1 hour 15 minutes

ITEM A

We found that television and press reporting of mental illness often focused on violent incidents. People who worked in the area of mental health tended to discount this media view, yet we found some cases where the fear generated by media accounts overwhelmed direct experience. One young woman was afraid of her non-violent elderly patients because of what she had seen on television.

Source: adapted from Greg Philo, 'Media effects and the active audience', *Sociology Review*, vol. 10, no. 3, February 2001

This might help in answering part [c]

ITEM B

When strikes are reported, although both sides are usually presented, a system of agenda setting and gatekeeping tends to ensure that the views of the owners and managers are heard more clearly than those of the strikers. Thus cultural hegemony is maintained.

Look up these important terms if you do not know them

This can be interpreted for an answer to part [b]

Comments on the question	Question	Advice on preparing your answer
• Only 2 marks so keep this brief • This provides the context in which to locate your answer	[a] Explain what is meant by cultural hegemony. [Item B, line 5] [2 marks]	• See p. 157 for help if you do not understand this term
• No more, no less • See p. 944 of the textbook for a definition	[b] Suggest two ways in which journalists might act as gatekeepers. [Item B, line 3] [4 marks]	• Some of the criteria listed on p. 158 may help you to answer this

Comments on the question	Question	Advice on preparing your answer
• This requires only a list; you are not required to discuss them • Only do what you are asked to do • Item A can be interpreted to give one way	[c] Identify **three** ways in which people might be influenced by the output of the mass media. [6 marks]	• A selection from the following could be used: 1 Stereotyping of ethnic minorities, p. 150 2 Labelling of women, p. 159 3 Advertising 4 Behaviour changing/social learning theory, p. 158
• To demonstrate both skills you will need more than a list • It means what it says, so only do two	[d] Identify and briefly describe **two** criticisms of the view that the owners of the mass media control its output. [8 marks]	• The most obvious criticisms come from pluralists (p. 156) and postmodernists (p. 159)
• This means look at both sides of the argument • The best answers might distinguish between these two processes • Make sure that you know what these are – remember your culture and identity core theme	[e] Assess the view that the mass media create and perpetuate stereotypes. [20 marks]	• The section on gender, age and ethnicity (pp. 159–60) will be useful here • Look for empirical evidence to back up your arguments • You might use these processes to help you reach a conclusion; e.g. 'the media perpetuate but do not create the stereotypes'
• This means you need to look at arguments against the theory as well as at evidence that supports it • How far does it explain all or any aspects of the media's influence? • This is the focus of the question. Make sure that you apply your material to this issue	[f] Using material from the items and elsewhere, examine the usefulness of the uses and gratifications model as an explanation of the influence of the mass media on the audience. [20 marks]	• See p. 158 for an account of this model • Criticisms are offered on p. 158 • Alternative explanations can be found on pp. 158–9. These need to be used selectively and applied to the focus in a critical way

Answer both parts of this question

Total: 45 marks   1 mark = 1 minute

Time allowed: 45 minutes

Comments on the question	Question	Advice on preparing your answer
• No more, no less • Identify – do this clearly so that the examiner can see two points • Explain with reference to empirical studies, or illustrate with conceptual examples • Resist the temptation to be assertive or commonsensical	[a] Identify and explain two ways in which mass media representations of ethnic minorities may affect audiences. [15 marks]	• The way the media report on particular social groups • If possible, be specific about ethnic minority groups • Think about behaviour or attitudes • The section on ethnicity (p. 160) will be useful here
• This means describe the argument in the question • This means look at the critique of this view and if possible consider alternative points of view • This is the focus of the question – make sure that you apply your material (e.g. empirical studies, evidence, etc.) to it • Begin by outlining and discussing this particular theory	[b] Outline and assess the view that the relationship between the media and the audience is more complex than that indicated by the hypodermic syringe model of media effects. [30 marks]	• See p. 158 for an account of this model • A critique is offered on p. 158 • A selection of other models and empirical studies that focus on the relationship between the media and audiences could be used. Choose three or four from the following: 1 Two-step flow model, p. 158 2 Multi-step flow model, p. 158 3 Uses and gratifications model, p. 158 4 David Buckingham, p. 161 5 Interpretative model, p. 158 6 Structured interpretation model, pp. 158–9 7 Postmodernism, p. 159

Chapter 14

Methodology

Specifications

Specification	Relevant module title	Place in module	Level	Assessment	Other relevant modules
AQA	3: **Sociological Methods**	Sole topic of module.	AS	*Either:* One compulsory data-response question *or:* coursework task	Material from this chapter may be used in the A2 synoptic module.
	5: **Sociological Theory and Methods**	Major topic of module.	A2	*Either:* One compulsory data-response question **and** one essay question from a choice of two *or:* sociological study (coursework)	
OCR	Sociological Research Skills **or**	Sole topic of module.	AS	One four-part structured data-response question.	Material from this chapter may be used in the A2 synoptic module
	Research report	Sole topic of module.	AS	Research report (coursework).	
	Applied Sociological Research Skills **or**	Sole topic of module.	A2	One data-response question **and** one structured question on research design.	
	Personal study	Sole topic of module.	A2	Personal study (coursework).	

Methodology: essential notes

Introduction

Methodology is concerned both with research methods and with the philosophies underlying them. It tries to establish accepted ways of getting the best possible data about the social world.

Broadly some sociologists support using scientific methods and quantitative data, while others see such methods as inappropriate in the study of human society and prefer qualitative data.

Newer approaches include:

- Feminism – which is a branch of critical social science concerned with the liberation of women.

- Postmodernism – which rejects the idea that you can discover the truth about society.

'Scientific' quantitative methodology

Positivism

Positivism is an early influential approach, advocated by Auguste Comte (1986, first published 1840s) and Emile Durkheim (1897), which suggests that sociology can be scientific.

Positivism argues that:

1 There are objective social facts about the social world.

2 These facts can be expressed in statistics.
3 You can look for correlations (patterns in which two or more things tend to occur together).
4 Correlations may represent causal relationships (one thing causing another).
5 Multivariate analysis (analysing the importance of many different possible causes) can help you to find what the true causes of things are.
6 It is possible to discover laws of human behaviour – causes of behaviour which are true for all humans everywhere and throughout history.
7 Human behaviour is shaped by external stimuli (things that happen to us) rather than internal stimuli (what goes on in the human mind).
8 To be scientific you should only study what you can observe. It is therefore unscientific to study people's emotions, meanings or motives, which are internal to the unobservable mind.

Popper – falsification and deduction
An alternative approach which says that sociology can be scientific is put forward by Popper (1959).

Popper argues that you cannot ever be sure that you have found the truth. What is considered true today may be disproved tomorrow.

A scientific theory is one that can be tested. From the theory you can deduce hypotheses and make precise predictions. If repeatedly tested and found to be correct, a theory may be provisionally accepted, but there is always the possibility that it will be proved wrong (or falsified) in the future.

Scientific theories are ones that make precise predictions. Popper regards some sociology (such as Marxism) as unscientific because the predictions are not precise enough.

Popper uses a deductive approach: you deduce hypotheses from a theory and check that they are correct.

Experiments
Many sciences make use of experiments. In experiments theories can be tested in precise conditions controlled by the researcher.

Experiments involve trying to isolate the effects of independent variables (possible causes) on a dependent variable (the thing to be explained).

A control (in which everything is held constant) and an experiment (in which one independent variable is changed) are compared, allowing scientists to find precise causes.

Experiments can be replicated (reproduced exactly) to test the reliability of findings.

However, sociologists rarely use laboratory experiments because:
● Laboratories are unnatural settings and people may not behave normally.
● It is impractical to conduct laboratory experiments on large numbers of people or over long periods.

Field experiments
Field experiments take place outside the laboratory in natural settings.

Examples include Rosenthal and Jacobson (1968) on labelling in education (see pp. 136 and Brown and Gay (1985) on racial discrimination by employers (pp. 37–8)

Field experiments avoid unnatural laboratory situations, but it is difficult to control variables, and if those being studied are aware of the experiment, this may alter their behaviour (the Hawthorne Effect). If subjects are unaware that they are being studied, this raises ethical issues.

The comparative method
This involves using the same logic as the experiment, but using events that have already taken place rather than creating artificial situations. Social groups, times or places are systematically compared to try to isolate variables.

The comparative method has been very widely used. Examples include Durkheim on suicide (see p. 169), Weber on the Protestant ethic (see pp. 75–7) and Marx on social change (see pp. 185–6).

It is more difficult to isolate variables than in controlled experiments, but the comparative method is based upon real social events and is the only systematic way to study long-term or wide-scale social change. It is central to sociology.

Interpretive and qualitative methodology

Qualitative data usually take the form of words.

Compared to statistics, qualitative data tend to be richer and to have more depth.

The interpretive approach
● Interpretivists usually advocate the use of qualitative data to interpret social action, with an emphasis on the meanings and motives of actors.
● Interpretivists often see sociology as different from the natural sciences in that it requires the understanding of meaningful behaviour by humans.
● From this viewpoint, people do not simply react to external stimuli but interpret the meaning of stimuli before reacting. An understanding is therefore required of people's unobservable subjective states, which cannot be reduced to statistical data.

There are several different interpretivist approaches.
1 Weber
● Weber (1948) sees sociology as the study of social action (or meaningful behaviour).
● This requires understanding or verstehen.
● You need to understand why people behave in particular ways. For example, in The Protestant Ethic and the Spirit of Capitalism (1958) Weber tries to understand why Calvinists reinvested their money and became early capitalists.
2 Symbolic interactionism
● Symbolic interactionists see individuals as possessing a self-concept or image of themselves.
● This is largely shaped through the reactions of others to the person.
● Herbert Blumer (1962) argues that sociologists need to understand the viewpoint of the people whose behaviour they are trying to understand. They cannot do this simply by using statistical data.
● Interactionists prefer methods such as in-depth interviews and participant observation.
● Labelling theory is the best-known version of interactionism.

3 Phenomenology
- Phenomenologists go further than other interpretivist approaches, rejecting the idea that causal explanations are possible.
- To them the social world has to be classified before it can be measured. Classifications (e.g. whether an act is suicide, or whether somebody is a criminal) depend upon the judgements of individuals.
- These judgements reflect the common sense and stereotypes of individuals rather than some objective system.
- Since there is no way of choosing between classification systems, no hard facts can be produced, so causal explanations are not possible.
- Phenomenologists try to understand the classifications people use to give order and meaning to the social world.
- Cicourel's (1976) study of juvenile justice is an example.

The sociology of suicide

This topic provides a good illustration of different research strategies.

Durkheim

Durkheim (1897) tried to show that suicide was not just a product of individual psychology and that positivist methods could be used to study it and explain the suicide rate.

He showed that suicide rates varied fairly consistently. High suicide rates were correlated with:
- Protestants rather than Catholics or Jews.
- Married people rather than single people.
- Parents rather than the childless.
- Political stability and peace rather than political upheaval and war.

From the statistical patterns, Durkheim claimed to have found four types of suicide:
1 Egoistic suicide was caused by insufficient integration into social groups (e.g. Protestants had less connection to their church than Catholics).
2 Anomic suicide resulted from too little regulation in industrial societies at times when rapid social change disrupted traditional norms (e.g. both economic booms and depression led to a rise in suicide rates).
3 Altruistic suicide resulted from too much integration in non-industrial societies (e.g. the practice of suttee – Hindu widows throwing themselves on their husband's funeral pyre).
4 Fatalistic suicide resulted from too much regulation in non-industrial societies (e.g. the suicide of slaves).

Despite his association with positivism, Durkheim used elements of a realist approach in looking for unobservable structures underlying suicide rates.

Responses to Durkheim
- Positivists have generally supported the principles on which his work was based but have modified details.
- Halbwachs (1930) argued that Durkheim overestimated the importance of religion. Halbwachs himself found that living in urban areas was an important factor correlated with high suicide rates.
- Gibbs and Martin (1964) tried to define integration in a more precise way than Durkheim, by using the concept of status integration.

Interpretive theories of suicide

J.D. Douglas
Douglas (1967) points out that suicide statistics are based on coroners' interpretations and negotiations between the parties involved. The relatives/friends of an individual might persuade the coroner not to record a death as suicide.

Douglas believes that there are different types of suicide based on their social meanings. There are different meanings in different societies – e.g. in Innuit society, elderly Eskimos were expected to kill themselves in times of food shortage.

Case studies are needed to find the different social meanings of suicide, such as transformation of the soul, transformation of the self, a search for sympathy or a means of revenge.

Jean Baechler
Baechler (1979) develops Douglas's approach, defining suicides in terms of the types of solution they offer to different types of situation:
1 Escapist suicides involve fleeing from an intolerable situation.
2 Aggressive suicides are used to harm others.
3 Oblative suicides are used to obtain something that is desired (e.g. saving another or getting to heaven).
4 Ludic suicides involve taking risks for excitement or as an ordeal.

Criticisms of interpretive theories
A problem with interpretive theories is that the categories used to classify suicides are simply a matter of the researcher's judgement.

J. Maxwell Atkinson
Atkinson (1978) develops a phenomenological view. He believes that it is impossible for coroners or researchers to objectively classify suicides. The facts are simply a social construction.

From studies of coroners' courts he finds that four factors shape the commonsense theories of coroners:
1 The presence of a suicide note is taken to indicate suicidal intent.
2 Some types of death (e.g. hanging) are seen as more likely to be suicide.
3 Location and circumstances are important.
4 Evidence of depression or particular difficulties tends to encourage suicide verdicts.

When positivists study suicide statistics, all they uncover are the commonsense theories of coroners – for example, a tendency to record the deaths of depressed or lonely people as suicides.

Critics of phenomenology, such as Barry Hindess (1973), point out that the logic of this view can be turned against phenomenologists' own theories of how deaths are categorized as suicides – i.e. they are no more than their own interpretations and cannot be supported by objective data.

Steve Taylor

Taylor (1982, 1989, 1990) tries to move beyond positivism and phenomenology using a realist approach.

He agrees with phenomenologists that certain factors influence coroners. From a study of deaths on the London underground he found that evidence of social failure or social disgrace tended to lead to suicide verdicts.

However, Taylor claimed that evidence from case studies revealed underlying patterns of suicide.

Suicides could be seen as one of four types, based on a person's certainty or uncertainty about themselves or others:

1 Submissive suicide involves certainty that your life is over, e.g. a terminal illness.
2 Thanatation involves uncertainty about yourself and whether you should live, e.g. playing Russian roulette.
3 Sacrifice involves certainty that others have made your life unbearable, e.g. rejection by a lover.
4 Appeal suicide involves uncertainty about others, e.g. suicidal behaviour which may win back a lover if they save you from death.

Taylor explains some variations in suicide – for example, why some suicide attempts are more serious than others – but his theory is hard to test and relies upon the interpretation of sometimes limited secondary data.

Quantitative and qualitative methodology

Ray Pawson (1989) points out that in practice most sociologists use both qualitative and quantitative data:

- Most positivists use some interpretation in their research (e.g. Durkheim), and most interpretivists use some numbers (e.g. Cicourel).
- Disputes between positivists and anti-positivists have become less common in sociology.
- New philosophies of science (e.g. realism) move beyond old approaches.

Feminist methodology

Feminists such as Abbott and Wallace (1997) criticize 'malestream research' (male-dominated mainstream research) for:

1 Researching only men and using male-only samples.
2 Ignoring 'women's issues' such as housework.
3 Neglecting sex and gender as variables.

However, there is increasing attention to women and gender in sociology, and research is becoming less dominated by the 'malestream'.

Feminist research methods

Ann Oakley (1981) argues that in a masculine approach to interviewing:

- There is an emphasis on objectivity and detachment.
- Interviewees are manipulated as sources of data and have an entirely passive role.
- The emphasis is on reliability.

Oakley believes that in a feminist approach to interviewing:

- The interviewer should be willing to answer questions and provide helpful information to respondents.

- Research should be collaborative. You should always gain consent and even help out those being interviewed.
- Interviewees can help improve the validity of the results by becoming increasingly reflective about their own lives.

Oakley uses this approach in her study of childbirth.

Pawson (1992) has criticized Oakley for simply adopting the techniques of unstructured interviewing. However, Oakley's approach has novel features, such as advising and helping the interviewees (which other theorists see as unduly influencing those being studied).

Feminist standpoint epistemology

Feminist standpoint epistemology argues that women have a unique insight into the social world by virtue of being an oppressed group.

Some standpoint feminists, such as Stanley and Wise (1990), believe that you should examine a plurality of women's viewpoints (e.g. women of different ethnic groups).

Critics such as Pawson suggest that:

1 Some feminist researchers will not accept the viewpoints of women they disagree with (such as those who don't think they are oppressed).
2 Standpoint epistemology neglects the oppressors (usually men) and therefore makes it difficult to understand how oppression comes about.
3 It can be relativistic, i.e. accepting a variety of women's viewpoints as valid without any way of distinguishing between more and less useful ones.

Postmodern methodology

- Epistemological postmodernists reject the idea that any research procedure can produce a single 'true' description of the world.
- Lyotard (1984) sees all knowledge as story-telling, with no way of distinguishing between true and untrue stories.
- Postmodern ethnography allows us to collect different people's stories.
- Some postmodernists are simply concerned to reveal the contradictions in other sociological theories, using the technique of deconstruction.

Evaluation

Many critics regard postmodernism as too relativistic (knowledge simply depends on your point of view). They point out that postmodern 'stories' about the social world cannot be shown to be better than any other stories.

The research process

To start research, sociologists have to select an area to study. This may be influenced by:

- The values and beliefs of the researcher (e.g. Townsend saw poverty as a problem, see pp. 44–5).
- Developments in the subject and the desire to follow fashion or advance your career.
- Developments in the social world (e.g. the emergence of fundamentalist religion).
- Government policies (e.g. research into the new vocationalism in education).

- The availability of research funds.
- Practicalities such as time, money and access.

- Primary sources are data collected by sociologists themselves.
- Secondary sources are pre-existing sources of data.

Choosing a primary research method

Like choosing a topic, the choice of method may be influenced by factors such as funding (it is usually easier to get funding for quantitative studies).

The nature of the topic may make particular methods more appropriate, and the approach of the researcher (e.g. positivist or interpretivist) will influence the choice.

Also important are questions of:

- Reliability – whether another researcher using the same procedure would obtain the same results. Quantitative methods are sometimes seen as more reliable.
- Validity – whether the data produce a true reflection of social reality. Some see qualitative data as offering a more valid picture of social reality.
- Practicality – particularly issues of time, money, sample size and access.

Choosing a sample

A sample is a part of a larger population, often chosen as a cross-section of the larger group.

Sampling is used in order to generalize about the larger population (to make statements about a group bigger than the one you have actually studied).

- The population is the total group you are interested in.
- The sampling unit is the individual thing or person in that population.
- The sampling frame is a list of all those in the population (e.g. the electoral register is a sampling frame of those eligible to vote). There is no comprehensive sampling frame of everyone in Britain, but the Postcode Address File is often used (e.g. it is used by the *British Crime Survey*).
  There are a variety of ways to produce a sample.

Random sampling

In this approach every sampling unit has an equal chance of being chosen. It relies upon statistical probability to ensure a representative sample, so a large sample is needed to give a high chance of representativeness.

Stratified random sampling

To ensure representativeness, the population is divided into groups according to important variables such as class, gender and ethnicity, and the sample is then chosen in the same proportions as their preponderance in the population. This method ensures a good cross-section and requires a smaller sample than random sampling, but it is only possible with a sampling frame containing all the relevant information about members of the population.

Quota sampling

In this method quotas are established which determine how many people with particular characteristics are studied. Once a quota is filled no more people in that category are studied. It is useful if the proportions of different types of people in a population are known and if there is no suitable sampling frame. It is often used in opinion polls and it is generally quicker and cheaper than random sampling.

However, the results may be distorted if, for example, the researcher questions people in one particular place at a particular time, since the sample will not then be representative. Also, people may be unwilling to reveal personal details to see if they fit into a quota category, and there may be practical difficulties finding members of particular quota groups.

Multi-stage sampling

This involves getting a sample of a sample – e.g. a sample of voters in a sample of constituencies. It can save time and money but it makes a sample less genuinely representative.

Snowballing

In snowballing, a member of a sample puts the researcher in touch with other potential members of the sample. It is useful for studying groups who cannot be easily located, but the networks connecting them make it less than representative.

Non-representative sampling

This occurs when members of a sample are picked because they are untypical or have specific characteristics. It is used:

- To falsify a general theory by looking for exceptions to a rule (e.g. Oakley on gender roles, see pp. 22–3).
- To find the key informants who can tell you most about an area of social life.

Case studies

Case studies involve the study of a single example of something. They can be used:

- To develop a comprehensive understanding of something by studying it in depth (e.g. Pryce's study of St Paul's, Bristol, see p. 34
- To develop a general theoretical approach by falsifying a theory (e.g. Gough's study of the Nayar, falsifying Murdock's theory that the family is universal, see p. 88).
- To develop typologies (e.g. Douglas's typology of the social meanings of suicide, see pp. 169).
- To generate new hypotheses (e.g. Willis's study of education, producing hypotheses about capitalism, education and work, see pp. 131).

A problem with case studies is that you cannot generalize from them. Bryman (1988) suggests that this can be overcome through multiple case studies (e.g. Edwards and Scullion compared industrial relations in several British factories (1982)). However, it can be difficult to compare the findings of case studies carried out by different researchers.

Life histories

A life history is a case study of one person's life. An example is Thomas and Znaniecki's (1919) study of Jenny, an ageing woman.

Plummer (1982) suggests that they are useful for helping you to understand the world from an individual's point of view. They provide rich detail and can help to generate hypotheses.

Some feminists, such as Mies (1993), think that life histories can be used to help women understand their own situation and perhaps change their life – e.g. life histories discussing domestic violence may help women decide to leave a violent partner.

Pilot studies

Pilot studies are small-scale preliminary studies carried out before a bigger study to improve, help to design or test the feasibility of proposed research.

They can be used:
- To test how useful and unambiguous interview questions are (e.g. Young and Willmott, see p. 91).
- To develop ways to gain the cooperation of respondents.
- To develop research skills.
- To decide whether or not to proceed with research.

Social surveys

Social surveys are large-scale studies which collect standardized data about large groups, often using questionnaires.
- Factual surveys collect descriptive information (e.g. Mack and Lansley on poverty (1985, 1992)).
- Attitude surveys examine subjective opinions (e.g. opinion polls).
- Explanatory surveys test theories or produce hypotheses (e.g. Marshall et al.'s study of class (1988)).

Questionnaires

Questionnaires consist of written questions.
- When administered by an interviewer, a questionnaire becomes a structured interview. This allows clarification of questions but introduces the possibility of interviewer bias.
- Postal questionnaires avoid interviewer bias but have low response rates.
- Telephone questionnaires tend to result in unrepresentative samples.

Questionnaires involve operationalizing concepts, i.e. turning concepts – such as alienation and class consciousness – into questions.

Questions may be open-ended or fixed-choice:
- Open-ended questions may give more valid data, as respondents can say what is important to them and express it in their own words. However, the data are difficult to quantify, and interpretation is required when using the data. Coding of the answers (putting them into categories) distorts the actual replies given by respondents by linking responses that are not identical.
- Fixed-choice questions are easy to classify and quantify, but respondents are limited to using the concepts and categories predetermined by researchers. The answers may be reliable but lack some validity.

Questionnaire data are often analysed using multivariate analysis and statistical techniques.

The advantages of questionnaires

1. Large amounts of data can be collected quickly.
2. There is little personal involvement by researchers.
3. Access to subjects is easy.
4. It is easy to quantify the results, find correlations and use multivariate analysis to look for causes.
5. Positivists see differences in answers as reflecting real differences since everyone responds to the same stimuli.
6. Comparative analysis and replication (repeating the questionnaire) are easy, making the results reliable.
7. A large, geographically dispersed sample can be used, increasing the representativeness of the data and the ability to generalize.
8. To positivists, the statistical patterns revealed can be used to develop new theories; and questionnaires can be devised to test existing theories.
9. Non-positivists see questionnaires as useful for collecting straightforward, descriptive data.

The disadvantages of questionnaires

Interpretive sociologists question the use of questionnaires, while phenomenologists reject them altogether.

1. Different answers may not reflect real differences between respondents since they may interpret questions differently.
2. In designing questionnaires, researchers assume they know what is important, and therefore it is difficult to develop novel hypotheses.
3. The operationalization of concepts distorts the social world by shaping concepts in line with researchers' rather than respondents' meanings.
4. The validity of the data may be undermined by deliberate lying, faulty memory or respondents not fully understanding their own motivations. People may not act in line with questionnaire answers. For example, La Pierre (1934) found that US hoteliers were racist when replying to questionnaires but not when faced with real situations.
5. Researchers are distant from their subjects, making it difficult to understand the social world from their viewpoint. Interaction cannot be understood through questionnaires. To feminist researchers, questionnaires preclude the possibility of subjects evaluating the research.
6. The coding of open-ended data distorts the distinct answers given by individuals.

Most sociologists accept that surveys are useful for collecting factual or descriptive data, but there is more controversy over their use in explanatory studies.

Interviews

- Structured interviews are questionnaires administered by a researcher.
- Unstructured interviews do not have preset questions but are more like a conversation.
- Many interviews are partly structured, with some preset questions, or the researcher has a list of

topics to cover. Some interviews allow prompts where interviewers can clarify questions or stimulate responses.

There are different interviewing styles:

- Most interviews are non-directive – they try to avoid influencing the interviewee, in order to increase the objectivity of the research.
- Becker (1970) suggests that more aggressive interviewing is useful for some topics, e.g. hidden racist feelings may be revealed through confrontation.
- Some feminists believe that interviewees should be collaborators in the research.
- Group interviews are sometimes used to put respondents at ease or to make respondents more reflective and more likely to open up as a result of interaction between interviewees.

Advantages of interviews

A variety of sociologists use interviews. They may not be ideal for positivists or interpretivists, but interviews are useful to both.

- Quantitative researchers prefer interviews to participant observation because you can use larger samples, produce statistical data with the coding of questions, replicate the research to increase reliability, etc.
- Qualitative researchers prefer interviews to questionnaires because concepts can be clarified, and there is more opportunity for respondents to express ideas in their own way, say what is important to them and explore issues in depth.
- However, the main advantages are practicality and flexibility. Interviews can examine past, present or future behaviour, subjective states, opinions, attitudes or simple factual information. They can be as in-depth or as superficial as the researcher wants.
- Interviews are useful for studying groups who would not return questionnaires or consent to participant observation (e.g. Laurie Taylor's study of professional criminals (1984)).
- To feminists, interviews have theoretical advantages since they provide space for critical reflection and interaction between interviewer and interviewee.

The disadvantages of interviews

1 As with questionnaires, the validity of the data may be affected by respondents being untruthful, having faulty memory or not fully understanding their own behaviour. People may have reinterpreted past events in the light of later experience (e.g. David Matza's delinquents disapproved of delinquent behaviour (1964)).
2 The presence of the researcher may influence answers (interviewer bias). Labov (1973) found that the 'race' of the interviewer affected young black children in speech tests. Interviewers might consciously or unconsciously lead respondents towards preferred answers.
3 Social factors such as ethnicity may influence the sort of answers members of different social groups are willing to give.

Conclusion

Despite their imperfections, the practicality and flexibility of interviews make them attractive to researchers using different theoretical perspectives, and they are widely used.

Observation and participant observation

Observation is used by a variety of sociologists.

- Positivists see observation as essential.
- Interpretive sociologists tend to particularly support participant observation, in which the researcher becomes part of the social life being studied.
- Ethnography is the study of a way of life and often uses participant observation

Joining the group, collecting and recording the data

Overt participant observers are open about doing research. This is advocated because:

- It is regarded as unethical to mislead subjects.
- It allows you to ask questions.
- You can retain some detachment.
  However:
- You may influence the subjects' behaviour if they know they are being observed.

In covert participant observation, the researcher does not reveal that they are doing research. This is advocated because:

- Respondents may act more naturally.
- Some groups would not allow an overt observer.
- You become fully engaged with the group.
  However:
- Some regard it as unethical to lie.
- It may be difficult to opt out of illegal/immoral activities.
- You may 'go native' and lose objectivity.
  Recording data from participant observation can be a problem, as the use of cameras/tape recorders may not be possible. Researchers usually write up field notes when they can, but they may forget things or be highly selective about what they do record.

The advantages of participant observation

1 Researchers are less likely than in other methods to impose their own concepts, structures and preconceptions on the data.
2 You may gain answers to questions which you hadn't anticipated (e.g. Whyte, 1955).
3 It is difficult for respondents to lie or mislead.
4 For these reasons many see participant observation as having a high degree of validity.
5 Symbolic interactionists support participant observation because it allows an understanding of the subjective viewpoints of individuals and the processes of interaction in which people's meanings, motives and self-concepts constantly change. It therefore avoids a static picture of social life.
6 The researcher understands subjects better because they experience some of the same things.
7 It provides in-depth studies which can be useful both for developing new theories and for falsifying existing ones.

The limitations and disadvantages of participant observation

1. It can be time-consuming and expensive for the researcher.
2. You are limited to studying a small number of people in a single place.
3. It will be impossible to join some groups to carry out observation.
4. Researchers' lives may be disrupted, they may need to do illegal/immoral things or they may face dangers.
5. Samples may be too small for generalizations.
6. You can't replicate studies, so the results may be unreliable, and comparisons are difficult.
7. The interpretations are rather subjective as the researcher has to be very selective about what is reported.
8. The presence of the researcher will change group behaviour and affect the validity of the data.
9. To positivists it is an unsystematic, subjective and unscientific method.

Conclusion

Participant observation is the only research method that gets very close to real social life, but it is rather subjective. It is strong on validity but weak on reliability.

Postmodern ethnography

Postmodern ethnographers do not believe that an objective description of social life is possible.

Tyler (1986) sees postmodern ethnography as designed to stimulate the imagination, like a work of literature. He believes that ethnography should simply be used to record the viewpoints of the many different groups in society. The researcher has no special ability to interpret the accounts of subjects.

Critics argue that this approach is too relativistic – ethnography becomes similar to fiction with no special claim to describe a real world.

Longitudinal research

Longitudinal research or panel studies follow a group of people over an extended period, using periodic data collection.

Examples include J.W.B. Douglas's (1964) study of home life and education and the *Child Health and Education Survey*.

They are usually large-scale quantitative studies, but participant observation can also be longitudinal.

Advantages of longitudinal research

1. People don't have to report on events retrospectively so problems of faulty memory or reinterpretation of events are reduced.
2. It can be used to examine a large number of variables.

Disadvantages of longitudinal research

1. The size of the participating sample may drop over time, affecting the reliability of findings.
2. Whatever method is used will have limitations.
3. Taking part in the study might affect subjects' behaviour.

Secondary sources

Secondary sources are data that have already been produced – by, for example, the government, companies, or individuals (personal documents).

Existing sociological studies become secondary sources when used by other sociologists.

- They can be quantitative (e.g. government statistics) or qualitative (e.g. letters and diaries).
- They can be historical or contemporary.

Secondary sources are used for practical reasons. They save time and money and may include data that are beyond the scope of sociologists to collect (e.g. census data). They allow the study of societies in the past for which it is impossible to produce primary sources.

Official statistics

Government statistics cover a wide range of topics including demography (census statistics), crime, employment and unemployment, industrial relations, educational achievement, family life (e.g. divorce statistics), household composition data, and so on. The government conducts statistical surveys such as the *General Household Survey* and the *British Crime Survey*, and since 1801 it has carried out a census every decade.

Such sources are invaluable because they are easily accessible and much more thorough than any data sociologists could produce. The census is the only survey that tries to include the whole of the population, and participation is legally compulsory.

However there are different views on statistics.

Some positivists such as Durkheim (1970) have seen official statistics as both valid and reliable (e.g. his study of suicide).

However, many official statistics are highly unreliable – for example, many crimes are not reported to or recorded by the police (see pp. 59–60).

Some sociologists believe that it is possible to produce valid and reliable statistics. For example, they believe that reliable crime statistics can be produced using surveys.

- Self-report studies are questionnaires which ask people if they have committed crimes (e.g. West and Farrington's study of delinquency (1973)).
- Victim studies ask people if they have been the victims of crime (e.g. the government's *British Crime Survey*).

However, such studies may not be entirely reliable, due to factors such as non-response and the limitations of sampling.

Some argue that the results are invalid. Box (1981) argues that in self-report studies people may lie, hide or exaggerate crimes. The total number of crimes recorded in studies depends on the willingness and ability of respondents to be honest and the interpretation of the researcher as to whether a crime has taken place.

A phenomenological view

Phenomenologists regard all crime statistics as invalid. They are simply the product of the categorization procedures used to produce them. For example, Maxwell

Atkinson (1978) sees suicide statistics as the product of coroners' taken-for-granted assumptions about the sort of people who commit suicide. To Cicourel (1976), all statistics are based on subjective classifications.

A conflict view

Conflict theorists see statistics as the product of inequalities in power. To Miles and Irvine (1979), government statistics are not lies, but the collection procedures and definitions used are manipulated by governments. Examples include frequent redefinitions of unemployment which reduce official unemployment figures and the manipulation of data on NHS hospital waiting lists by removing people who have missed appointments for an operation. Some poverty statistics are no longer published.

Some conflict theorists question the categories used in statistics. For example, the Marxist Theo Nichols (1996) argues that official definitions of social class ignore the existence of wealth inequalities. From this point of view, statistics reflect ideological frameworks which in turn reflect power inequalities rather than individuals' assumptions.

Historical sources

These are vital for studying long-term social changes.

Peter Laslett (1972, 1977) used parish records and Michael Anderson (1971) used census data to show that industrialization led to an increase in extended family households in Britain (see p. 91).

Parliamentary investigations, diaries, letters, autobiographies, speeches and mass media reports are all useful sources.

However, statistical sources suffer from the same possible problems of reliability and validity as contemporary statistics. Qualitative sources reflect the subjective views of those who produced them. Sometimes this is nevertheless useful – for example, Weber (1958) used qualitative documents to study the effects of religious beliefs on the development of capitalism (see pp. 76–7).

Life documents

These are documents created by individuals which record subjective states. They include diaries, letters, photos, biographies, memoirs, suicide notes, films, pictures, etc.

Thomas and Znaniecki (1919) used letters and statements to study Polish peasants who emigrated to the USA. However, Plummer (1982) argues that personal documents are rarely used by contemporary sociologists because:

- Surviving documents may not be representative.
- They are open to differing interpretations.
- They are highly subjective – the same events discussed in a document such as a diary might be described very differently by someone else involved.
- The content may be influenced by the identity of the person or people intended to read the document.
- Private diaries, not intended to be read by others, overcome the above problem, but few are available to researchers.

However, Plummer believes that life documents are still very useful because:

- They allow insights into people's subjective states.

- Symbolic interactionists see them as revealing the personal meanings and self-concepts which they see as shaping behaviour.

The mass media and content analysis

The mass media may be unreliable for providing factual information, but they may be the objects of study. Some researchers see such studies as useful for revealing the ideological frameworks of those who produce the mass media. This is important because of the influence of the media.

Pawson (1995) describes different ways of analysing the content of the mass media:

1 Formal content analysis involves classifying and counting content. For example, Lobban (1974) and later Best (1993) counted the appearances of girls and boys in different gender roles in children's books.

   This technique is reliable but it involves inferring the meaning of the text from numbers alone.

2 Thematic analysis examines a topic and looks for the messages that lie behind the coverage. For example, Soothill and Walby (1991) found that newspaper coverage of rape emphasized the pathological nature of individual rapists and largely ignored rapes by partners and friends.

   However, such studies rarely use representative samples and don't examine the impact of the messages on the audience.

3 Textual analysis involves the detailed analysis of small pieces of text. For example, the Glasgow Media Group looked at the words used to describe managers and strikers.

   However, this relies heavily on the researcher's interpretation and may therefore be unreliable.

4 Audience analysis examines how the audience interprets the messages of the media – e.g. Morley's (1980) study of responses to *Nationwide*.

   However, the honesty and openness of respondents may be questionable, and such studies cannot reveal long-term effects of media messages.

Assessing secondary sources

John Scott (1990a, 1990b) argues that the following criteria can be used to assess secondary sources:

Authenticity

- Soundness concerns whether the document is complete and reliable.
- Authorship concerns whether it was written by the claimed author.

Credibility

Sincerity concerns whether the author intended to provide a true account or was trying to mislead the readers.

Accuracy concerns whether the author is able to be truthful, e.g. whether faulty memory might affect accuracy.

Representativeness

This concerns whether the documents are typical or representative of what is being studied.

- Survival, or lack of it, may mean that representative documents do not exist.

- **Availability**, or lack of it, may mean that researchers cannot gain access to representative samples even where they have survived.

Meaning
- **Literal understanding** involves being able to read, decipher or translate the content.
- **Interpretative understanding** involves interpreting what the document signifies, and there may be very different possible interpretations.

Triangulation

Bryman (1988) argues that most sociologists use a mixture of quantitative and qualitative sources. Sociologists as far back as Weber have combined methods.

Triangulation means looking at the subject from a variety of angles using different methods. It can be useful, according to Bryman, because:

1 Different types of data can be used to cross-check each other's accuracy.
2 Qualitative data can produce hypotheses which can then be checked using quantitative data.
3 Combining methods produces a more complete picture.
4 Qualitative research helps to explain statistical links. Examples include:
- Eileen Barker's (1984) study of the Moonies which used observation, questionnaires and interviews.
- The use of statistical computer programmes to analyse ethnography.
- Delamont's (1976) use of interaction categories to quantify classroom interaction.

Bryman sees quantitative data as useful for finding overall patterns and structures, and qualitative data as useful for studying processes.

Sociology and science

Scientific methodology

Positivists see sociology as a science based on the use of objective observation, statistics, a search for correlations, causal relationships and laws (see pp. 167–8).

Popper (1959) sees science as based on falsifiable theories which make precise predictions. He regards some sociology, such as Marxism, as non-scientific (see p. 168).

Both see a scientific methodology as desirable. Positivists see science as producing objective truth, while Popper sees science as *getting as close as possible* to the truth, since it is always possible that a theory will be falsified in the future.

Phenomenologists reject the idea of a scientific sociology because:

1 The social world cannot be objectively classified and measured; classification reflects the subjective categories and interpretations of individuals.
2 Sociologists can only study the way classifications are made; they cannot discover some underlying objective truth.

The social context of science

Some sociologists argue that science does not follow any single methodology. It takes place in a social context and often does not involve an objective search for truth.

Kaplan (1964) distinguishes:
1 Reconstructed logics (the methods scientists claim to use).
2 Logics in use (the actual methods they use).

Michael Lynch (1983) illustrates this by showing how scientists studying rats' brains ignored slides that contradicted their theories, dismissing them as artefacts (or mistakes produced during the laboratory procedures). Scientists look for evidence to confirm theories, ignoring evidence that might falsify them.

Roger Gomm (1982) argues that Darwin's theory of evolution was accepted because the social context of Victorian Britain, with its *laissez-faire* capitalism, welcomed the ideas of natural selection and survival of the fittest. Opposition to revolution encouraged acceptance of evolutionary theory, and evolutionary thinking allowed Victorian Britons to see themselves as superior to the people in conquered colonies. Lack of fossil evidence of evolution was ignored because of the social context.

Kuhn – paradigms and scientific revolutions

Kuhn (1962) argues that scientific communities develop a commitment to a particular paradigm – a set of shared beliefs about some aspect of the physical world: how it works, how to study it and how to interpret evidence. A paradigm provides the complete framework within which scientists operate. Ideas from outside the paradigm are normally dismissed.

During a scientific revolution, however, anomalies, which the paradigm cannot explain, come to the fore. One paradigm is rejected and replaced by another, and science returns to its normal state in which the paradigm is not open to question. An example is the move from Newtonian to Einsteinian physics.

From this point of view, sociology can be seen as pre-scientific because there are a variety of paradigms (or perspectives), such as feminism, Marxism, postmodernism, etc.

It may not be desirable for sociology to become scientific, in Kuhn's sense, because the conflict between perspectives is a critical element of sociology. Anderson, Hughes and Sharrock (1986) criticize Kuhn for underestimating the extent of disagreement between scientists and question whether his approach has much relevance to sociology.

The realist view of science

Realists such as Roy Bhaskar (1979) and Andrew Sayer (1984) believe that it is both possible and desirable for sociology to be scientific. They see physical and social sciences as similar.

Sayer argues that some sciences have closed systems in which all variables can be measured. However, many sciences are open – all variables cannot be measured and precise predictions cannot be made (e.g. seismology and meteorology). Sayer therefore rejects Popper's view that a scientific theory must make precise predictions.

Sayer believes that sociology is scientific but societies are complex open systems, making it impossible to make precise predictions.

Keat and Urry (1982) argue that some sciences deal which things that cannot be directly observed – e.g.

sub-atomic particles, continental drift and magnetic fields. They therefore reject the positivist view that science confines itself to studying the observable. They argue that sociology can still be seen as scientific if it studies unobservable meanings and motives.

Realists believe that scientists try to discover the underlying structures and processes that cause observable events (e.g. evolution). Sociologists try to do exactly the same, looking for social structures (e.g. in Marxism the economic base and superstructure and social classes) and processes (e.g. capital accumulation). Realists therefore argue that much sociology is scientific.

Methodology and values

There are different views on whether sociology is or can be objective or value-free.
- Bierstedt (1963) defines objectivity in terms of the investigator not being influenced by their own beliefs.
- Comte, Durkheim and Marx all thought they were objective and scientific.
- Weber argued that the actual selection of a topic for research was bound to be influenced by values, but that the research itself could be value-free.
However, many sociologists who considered their work value-free have been accused of being value-laden:
- Functionalists have been seen as having a conservative bias in stressing the usefulness of institutions.
- Durkheim's values are revealed in his opposition to inherited wealth.
- Marx was committed to revolutionary politics.
- Weber's values influenced his view that bureaucracy could stifle human freedom.

Can values be eradicated from sociology?
- As Weber suggested, values are bound to influence what topics sociologists think are important enough to study.
- Sociologists' values may also influence which aspects of a topic they study. Gouldner (1971) argues that all sociologists make domain assumptions – e.g. about whether humans are rational or irrational, whether society is essentially stable or unstable, etc.

- All research is selective – e.g. what questions are included in a questionnaire or what aspects of a social setting an observer takes note of – and values may influence the selection process.
- All research involves some degree of interpretation which may be influenced by values. For example, interpretive sociologists see questionnaires as distorting the real nature of the social world in line with the researcher's assumptions and values. Positivists see participant observation research as based on the subjective and value-laden perceptions of interpretive researchers.

Phillips (1973) concludes that values influence the choice of topic and the methods and sources of data used in research.

In 'Anti-minotaur', Gouldner argues that fact and value cannot be separated in sociology, just as the bull and human in a minotaur cannot be separated. Gouldner thinks that sociologists should bring their values into the open so that others are aware of any possible bias.

To many postmodernists, knowledge is simply the reflection of the values of the social groups that create the knowledge.

However, other sociologists argue that sociology is not simply an expression of people's values. Carspecken (1996) argues that there is a real, objective social world, and this makes it possible to reject some claims about the truth which do not fit reality. Thus, while values will always influence sociology, research can show that some theories are more supported by evidence than others.

This view is also supported by the realist theory of science.

1 Which **two** of these statements would positivists agree with?
   a Human behaviour is shaped by external stimuli
   b Human behaviour is unpredictable
   c There are no such things as social facts
   d Sociology should be scientific

2 Which **one** of these statements would Popper agree with?
   a No theory can be seen as definitively true as it may be proved wrong in the future
   b Scientists can discover the absolute truth
   c All sociology is scientific
   d It is not desirable for sociology to be scientific

3 Which **one** of the following is a description of a dependent variable?
   a The possible cause of something you are trying to explain
   b A comparative group
   c The researcher carrying out an experiment
   d The thing you are trying to explain in an experiment

4 Which **two** of these statements about field experiments are true?
   a Field experiments allow you to control all the variables
   b Field experiments can be easily replicated
   c Field experiments take place in a more naturalistic setting than laboratory experiments
   d Rosenthal and Jacobson's study of labelling is an example of a field experiment

5 Which **one** of these is **not** associated with interpretive and qualitative methodology?
   a Max Weber
   b Experimentation
   c Symbolic interactionism
   d *Verstehen*

6 Which **one** of these statements is true?
   a Phenomenologists do not believe it is possible to objectively classify the social world
   b Symbolic interactionists believe it is impossible to explain human behaviour
   c Weber believes there are no facts about social life
   d Herbert Blumer does not believe that you can understand the viewpoint of other human beings

7 Which of Durkheim's types of suicide results from a lack of regulation in a rapidly changing society?
   a Altruistic suicide   b Anomic suicide
   c Fatalistic suicide   d Egoistic suicide

8 According to Maxwell Atkinson's theory of suicide, which **one** of the following statements is **not** true?
   a Suicide statistics reflect the commonsense opinions of coroners
   b The location of a death influences coroners' decisions
   c Evidence of depression influences coroners' decisions
   d Coroners usually reach the right verdict in determining whether a suicide has taken place

9 Steve Taylor's theory of suicide can best be described as:
   a A positivist theory
   b A social action theory

c A realist theory
d A phenomenological theory

10 Which **one** of these approaches does Oakley advocate in feminist research?
    a Researchers should be objective
    b Researchers should be collaborative
    c Researchers should keep their distance from subjects
    d Researchers should put reliability before validity

11 The type of sampling in which every member of the relevant population has an equal chance of being selected is called:
    a Random sampling
    b Snowball sampling
    c Quota sampling
    d Stratified sampling

12 A list from which a sample is drawn is called:
    a A sampling unit   b The population
    c A sampling frame   d A quota

13 Which **one** of these is a strength of case studies?
    a They produce reliable data
    b They can be easily replicated
    c They can be used to falsify existing theories
    d It is easy to generalize from them

14 Which **one** of these statements is false?
    a Telephone surveys tend not to be representative of the whole population
    b Postal questionnaires avoid interviewer bias
    c Postal questionnaires usually have a high response rate
    d Fixed-choice questions make it easy to quantify data from questionnaires

15 Questionnaire research is most likely to be used by:
    a Interactionists
    b Feminists
    c Phenomenologists
    d Positivists

16 Which **one** of these descriptions does **not** usually apply to questionnaires?
    a They allow the use of large samples
    b They are quite reliable
    c They allow you to collect in-depth data
    d They are often used in social surveys

17 Which **one** of the following would **not** be an example of interviewer bias?
    a The interviewee forgets some information
    b The interviewee is influenced by the gender of the interviewer
    c The interviewee gives the answer they believe the interviewer would most like to hear
    d The interviewer unintentionally puts ideas into the interviewee's head

18 Which **two** of these statements are correct?
    a Interviews are one of the most flexible research methods
    b Positivists believe that unstructured interviews provide the most reliable data
    c Interviews are only used by interpretivist sociologists
    d Interviews generally use larger samples than participant observation

19 'Going native' involves:
  a Conducting participant observation in a foreign country
  b Keeping field notes during participant observation
  c Becoming too involved with the group being studied and losing your objectivity
  d Blending in to the group being studied

20 Participant observation is most likely to be used by:
  a Feminists
  b Functionalists
  c Marxists
  d Symbolic interactionists

21 Postmodern ethnography can be criticized because:
  a It cannot be used to study historical societies
  b It is too relativistic
  c It doesn't allow you to understand the world from the viewpoint of those being studied
  d It requires specialist training for researchers

22 Which **two** of the following statements are criticisms of longitudinal research?
  a Faulty memory is particularly likely to produce unreliable data in longitudinal research
  b The sample size may decline with time
  c Awareness of being studied may affect subjects' behaviour
  d It is not possible to study a large number of variables

23 Which of these is **not** a secondary source?
  a Official statistics
  b A personal diary
  c An interview
  d A government report

24 The *British Crime Survey* is an example of:
  a A self-report study
  b A victim study
  c Police statistics
  d An in-depth study

25 Conflict theorists tend to see official statistics as:
  a A reliable and valid representation of social life
  b Based on the personal opinions of officials
  c Reflecting ideological frameworks
  d Of little interest to sociologists

26 Triangulation refers to:
  a Research where three respondents are used
  b A type of longitudinal study
  c The process of interpreting qualitative data
  d The use of several research methods in one study

27 Karl Popper believes that:
  a All scientific theories are false
  b All scientific theories should be falsifiable
  c Marxism is the most scientific theory of society
  d Scientific methods should not be used in sociology

28 Thomas Kuhn believes that:
  a A scientific theory may always be superseded by a new theory
  b Scientific theories never change
  c Sociology is dominated by a single paradigm
  d Scientists are always objective

29 Realists believe that:
  a It is possible and desirable for sociology to be scientific
  b It is possible but undesirable for sociology to be scientific
  c It is impossible but desirable for sociology to be scientific
  d Sociologists have nothing to learn from scientists

30 Which one of these perspectives has often been seen as reflecting conservative values?
  a Feminism
  b Weberian sociology
  c Functionalism
  d Interactionism

Develop your analysis and evaluation skills

(see p. 209 for guidance notes)

For each of the following statements, identify which sociologists would argue in favour of and which against the view expressed. Explain the reasons for their view.

1 Sociology cannot be a scientific subject because humans possess consciousness.
2 Participant observation makes up in validity what it lacks in reliability.
3 Interviews may be practical, but they are unlikely to provide reliable or valid data.
4 Official statistics always provide a misleading picture of the social world.
5 All research methods have their uses, especially when combined together.
6 The theoretical approach influences the choice of method more than practical constraints.

Answer all parts of this question
Total: 60 marks
Time allowed: 1 hour

1 mark = 1 minute

ITEM A

Official Statistics
Governmental

If you don't know what any of these are, check them in your notes, or textbook, before answering the questions

Be sure to find out about these before answering part [b]

SURVEYS *Snapshots of society*	REGISTRATION DATA *Continuous collection of data*
● Population census	● Births, marriages & deaths
● General Household Survey	● Divorces
● Mortality & Morbidity	● Business accounts
● British Crime Survey	● Unemployment
● Family Expenditure Survey	● Crime
	● Child abuse

The column headings can help you with your answer to part [b]

Source: adapted from Lawson, Jones and Moores, *Advanced Sociology through Diagrams*, Oxford University Press, 2000

ITEM B

Insert your meaning of the phrase here to check it makes sense for part [a]

This raises questions about the usefulness for part [e]

After long years of rejection, happy days are here again for researchers in the social sciences. In Whitehall the search is for 'evidence', but Government largesse does not come free. 'Too often in the past, policy has not been informed by good research, but too many academics want to address issues other than those that are central to the political and policy debate.' But academic social scientists worry that 'evidence led' may mean, 'what we want for our own political purposes'. What was that adage about pipers and tunes?

This is a use for research and can help you to answer part [f]

Answer: 'He who pays calls the tune.' This can be interpreted to give you a practical factor for [f]

Source: adapted from David Walker, 'You find the evidence, we'll pick the policy', *Guardian*, 15 February 2000

Comments on the question	Question	Advice on preparing your answer
● Interpret the meaning from the item ● Check its appropriateness by testing it in the original context	[a] What do sociologists mean by 'evidence led'? [Item B, line 8] [2 marks]	● Basing conclusions on the evidence, or facts found after investigation or research

Comments on the question	Question	Advice on preparing your answer
• You should pick out features that distinguish these sources • Note: in this context they are both secondary sources, so this cannot be used as a difference	[b] Explain the difference between Crime Statistics and the British Crime Survey. [4 marks]	• Use the information from the item to help you • See p. 174 for more detail
• Concentrate on the statistics mentioned. Think about how and why births are registered, compared to crime or child abuse which may never be uncovered	[c] Explain why the statistics for births are likely to be more accurate than for crime or child abuse. [6 marks]	• Think of the legal obligation to register births. Look at pp. 174–5 and see if you can twist this to make an answer here
• Just two! • Notice the negative here. Give reasons for not using opinion polls • This should take you no longer than 8 minutes	[d] Identify and explain two objections that could be made to the use of opinion polls in sociological research. [8 marks]	• Look at the section on surveys and questionnaires, p. 172, and see if you can use this material in answering parts of this question
• Look at the advantages and disadvantages • Concentrate on the ones in Item A • You should consider issues of reliability and validity • i.e. not to those people who collected them in the first place	[e] Using material with which you are familiar, examine the usefulness of Governmental Official Statistics to sociologists doing research. [20 marks]	• This is the positivist/anti-positivist, quantitative versus qualitative debate • Look at pp. 167–8, 174 and 168–9 for the positivist points and p. 176 for the anti-positivist points
• This means that you do not have to limit your answer to secondary sources • Look at both sides and come to a conclusion • The planning rather than the actual carrying out of the research	[f] Using material from the items and elsewhere, assess the importance of various factors that might affect research design. [20 marks]	• Use the three types of factors – practical, theoretical and ethical – as your organizing principle. This will help you to make an assessment • See pp. 170–1 for help

Answer all parts of this question

Total: 60 marks   1 mark = 1 minute

Time allowed: 1 hour 30 minutes

ITEM A

Mac An Ghaill's methodology

The Making of Men by Mac an Ghaill was an ethnographic study of 'Parnell School', an 11–18 comprehensive school in an inner-city area of the Midlands characterized by high unemployment and poverty. Mac an Ghaill collected research data over a four-year period whilst employed as a teacher at the school. He mainly observed school life and wrote down his observations on a daily basis. He also encouraged some students to keep diaries and to design questionnaires focused on issues that they thought were important. Moreover he carried out formal and informal group and individual interviews with both pupils and teachers.

Part of his research focused on a group of lads he labelled the 'Macho Lads', who belonged to an anti-school subculture which actively resisted the authority of the school and teachers in an exaggerated masculine way. Mac an Ghaill concluded that their resistance was understandable and rational because the lads realized that they were likely to face a future of unemployment, youth training and social exclusion. As Mac an Ghaill says of these lads, 'they're more straightforward than those half hippie middle-class kids. You can be sure that none of them with all their connections will end up on a training scheme or on the dole.'

ITEM B

His research findings

The National Union of Teachers requires quantitative and qualitative data to discover the levels of stress that teachers in secondary schools face. You have been asked, as a sociological researcher, to design a proposal which will target a representative sample of 500 secondary school teachers across a dozen schools of similar size in one inner-city area and one suburban area.

Comments on the question	Question	Advice on preparing your answer
• No more, no less • There is no need to explain why particular types of method are used	[a] Using only Item A, identify **one** quantitative and **one** qualitative method used in this study. [6 marks]	• The item identifies six methods but you only need to mention two

Comments on the question	Question	Advice on preparing your answer
• Make sure that the examiner can clearly see two separate strengths identified with explanations	[b] Identify and explain two strengths of triangulation. [8 marks]	• See p. 176 for an account of this approach
• Describe only, don't offer an explanation. • There is no need to use material outside of this item • Note that the focus is on the research findings, not the research methods	[c] Summarize what the research findings in Item A tell us about some working-class boys' attitudes towards education. [10 marks]	• Don't copy the item word for word. Attempt to put it into your own words
• Note the focus on the process of the research • Describe all stages of the research – e.g. choice of method, access issues, sampling, operationalization, ethical issues, etc. • You must link the research process to the research context outlined in Item B	[d] Outline and explain the research process you would adopt in collecting quantitative and qualitative data on the experiences of secondary school teachers. [Item B] [14 marks]	• Think carefully about your choice of method. It has got to be practical • The sample size is going to rule out straight away some methods • The fact that the research is sponsored by the NUT means that there is access to a sampling frame, which should bring to mind the possibility of using a questionnaire • The design should incorporate both open and closed questions in order to generate both quantitative and qualitative data • See the section on questionnaires on p. 172, and think about which of the strengths of questionnaires are appropriate to this research context • Similarly, see the section on sampling techniques on p. 171. Which is the most appropriate and why?
• You need to anticipate certain types of problems relating to all aspects of the research process • You must suggest some possible ways of dealing with these problems	[e] Assess the potential weaknesses of your research proposal, briefly explaining how you intend to overcome them. [22 marks]	• For example, look at the weaknesses of questionnaires (see p. 172). Which of these could be related to this research context? • Look through this section for ideas on how you might deal with potential problems. In particular, you should examine the section on triangulation and methodological pluralism (p. 176)

Chapter 15

Sociological theory

Specifications

Specification	Relevant module title	Place in module	Level	Assessment	Other relevant modules
AQA	5: **Sociological Theory** and Methods	Major topic of module	A2	*Either:* One compulsory data-response question and one essay question from a choice of two *or:* sociological study (coursework).	Sociological theory is intrinsic to all modules but especially in A2 and the synoptic module 6.
OCR	There is no module on this topic in the OCR specification (see last column).	n/a	n/a	n/a	This topic is intrinsic to the whole specification, especially at A2. Material from this chapter may be used in the A2 synoptic module.

Sociological theory: essential notes

Introduction

Structural versus social action theories

There are two main types of sociological theory:

1 Structural or macro perspectives examine the way in which society as a whole fits together. Examples include Marxism and functionalism. They tend to see human activity as a product of social structure.

2 Social action, interpretive or micro perspectives examine smaller groups of people in society and are concerned with the subjective states of individuals. They tend to see society as a product of human activity. Examples include symbolic interactionism and Weber's theory of social action.

   However, many theories do not fit neatly into one category or the other, there are variations within perspectives and some perspectives and individual studies combine elements of both approaches. For example, Weber used both structural and social action perspectives in his general approach, and postmodernism cannot be readily categorized in terms of these concepts.

Functionalism

- Functionalism views society as a system with interconnected parts.
- Early functionalists used a biological analogy, comparing parts of society to parts of the human body (e.g. the government was compared to the brain).

- In terms of this analogy, both humans and societies have certain basic needs (or functional prerequisites) that must be met if they are to survive.
- Social institutions are held to meet these basic needs (e.g. families provide socialization which helps meet a basic need for a common culture).
- Institutions are studied by identifying the way in which they contribute to meeting needs.
- The function of an institution is seen in terms of its contribution to the survival of the whole (i.e. society).
- Some functionalists accept that there may be aspects of society which are dysfunctional – which prevent it from operating smoothly – but they generally pay little attention to them.
- Functionalism has been accused of having a conservative ideology. It tends to support preservation of the status quo, since anything that persists in society is seen as providing a useful function.

Emile Durkheim

- Durkheim believed that people were constrained by social facts: ways of acting, thinking and feeling in a society.
- Shared moral codes shaped individual consciousnesses.
- Social facts were caused by other social facts (e.g. the influence of religion on suicide rates) but could

also be explained in terms of the functions they performed for society.

- Parts of society would only persist if they served useful functions.
- Societies needed a collective conscience, or shared morality, in order to function successfully.
- Modern industrial societies could be disrupted by the existence of anomie (normlessness) and egoism (where individuals are not integrated into social groups). Both of these stemmed from a complex division of labour. People did specialist jobs, and this weakened solidarity in society.

Talcott Parsons

- Parsons believed that all societies needed a value consensus based upon shared goals.
- Societies developed rules based upon this value consensus and norms about how people should behave, which fitted in with the overall goals.
- When individuals are socialized to accept the values, goals and norms, and where this works smoothly, social equilibrium is achieved.
- Parsons saw society as a system with four basic needs or functional prerequisites:
1 Adaptation – the need for an economic system to ensure the survival of members of society.
2 Goal attainment – the need to set goals, a function primarily carried out by the government.
3 Integration – the need to control conflict, a function carried out by the legal system.
4 Pattern maintenance – the maintenance of values, achieved largely through education, religion and family life.
- Parsons saw change in terms of a shift in values from pattern variables A to pattern variables B. Under the former, status was based on ascription, and people were treated as specific individuals. Under the latter, in modern societies status is based upon achievement, and individuals are judged according to impartial universalistic standards (e.g. exam systems).
- Social change also involves the development of specialist institutions, such as those of the welfare state – a process called structural differentiation.

Robert K. Merton

- Merton was a functionalist, but he accepted that societies did not always work smoothly.
- He argued that parts of society could be dysfunctional and might prevent society from running smoothly.

Functionalism – a critique

1 Functionalism has been accused of being teleological – that is, it confuses cause and effect. The functions of an institution are the effects it has rather than the reasons why it exists.
2 Functionalism assumes, without putting forward evidence, that a value consensus exists, and it ignores conflict and diversity in society.
3 Functionalism is too deterministic. It sees human behaviour as shaped by the needs of the social system, and makes no allowance for the fact that

individuals have choices about how they behave.
4 Alvin Gouldner (1971) argues that functionalism ignores the extent to which people are coerced in society to do things they do not wish to do.
5 Lockwood (1970) argues that functionalism ignores conflicts of interest between groups, which tend to destabilize social systems.
6 Jonathon Turner and Alexandra Maryanski (1979) argue that functionalism remains useful for understanding social structures and how they influence behaviour, although it does have many flaws.

Conflict perspectives

Conflict perspectives take many forms – e.g. Marxism, feminism, anti-racism – but all agree that there are different groups in society with conflicting interests.

Marxism

- Karl Marx saw history in terms of conflict between social classes.
- Marxism is based upon a philosophy of dialectical materialism: the idea that history proceeds through the clash of material forces, particularly classes.
- Marx saw human society as based upon work and the production of goods. Hence he argued that society had a material base.
- In the earliest stages of history, under primitive communism, there was no economic surplus and no private wealth, so classes did not exist.
- As some individuals began to accumulate wealth (e.g. herds of animals), and passed it down to their children, classes emerged.
- Power tended to be monopolized by a ruling-class minority (those who owned the means of production) who dominated a subject-class majority.
- This caused tension and provided the potential for conflict.
- The ruling class used their control over institutions such as religion to justify or legitimate their position and persuade the subject class that they were not being exploited.
- Humans became increasingly alienated from their true selves and their true interests. Religion was a form of alienation, since people created in their minds a non-existent alien being which then controlled their behaviour.
- In capitalist societies, where people worked for wages and companies made profits, workers were alienated from their work. They were alienated because they worked for other people, lacked control over their work and did not own the products they produced.
- An end to alienation and exploitation could only be achieved in a communist society in which there was no private property. Instead there would be communal ownership of the means of production. There would be no classes and therefore no exploitation. Instead of working for others to make a profit, people would work for the good of the society as a whole.

- All societies apart from communist ones have two main classes: the owners of the means of production (the ruling class) and the non-owners of the means of production (the subject class).
- The means of production are those things that are necessary to produce other things, such as land, capital, raw materials, machinery and labour power.
- In capitalist societies, the ruling class or bourgeoisie owned capital (money used to finance production), whereas the subject class, or proletariat, owned only their own labour power which they had to sell to the bourgeoisie.
- The bourgeoisie used the superstructure – the non-economic parts of society such as education, religion and the state – to stabilize society.
- They encouraged the development of false class consciousness whereby people saw society as fair and just.
- Eventually the proletariat (or working class) would become aware that they were being exploited, and they would develop class consciousness (an awareness of their true class interests).
- The proletariat would be increasingly exploited, they would suffer from slumps in the capitalist system and they would become aware of increasing inequality between themselves and the bourgeoisie.
- They would organize themselves into trade unions, political parties and revolutionary movements, overthrow capitalism and establish a communist society.

Marxism – a critique

1 Critics have argued that as capitalism has developed, class consciousness has reduced rather than increased.
2 Communist societies did not end inequality and exploitation, and they tended to be unpopular and to restrict individual liberty. By the early 1990s most communist regimes had collapsed.
3 Marxism seems to exaggerate the importance of economic factors, ignoring the influence of ideas and culture (e.g. Weber's Protestant ethic theory).
4 Marxism has been accused of economic determinism – seeing individuals' behaviour as determined by the economic system and neglecting the extent to which individuals have free choice.
5 Marxism emphasizes class differences and pays too little attention to gender, ethnicity, sexuality, age, lifestyle, etc.
6 Defenders of Marxism argue that it is not truly an economically deterministic theory. Marx emphasized that individuals and groups had to make their own history, but the economic structure determined the context in which that process took place.

Neo-Marxism

Neo-Marxists are new Marxists who are strongly influenced by Marx but reject one or more aspects of his work.

Antonio Gramsci is one example. Gramsci suggested that ownership of the means of production was not enough to win ruling-class control. It needed to make alliances with other classes and make some real concessions in order to attain hegemony (political domination).

Gramsci saw aspects of the superstructure as having some independence from the ruling class. (See p. 105 for a detailed description of Gramsci.)

Neo-Marxists tend to place more emphasis on cultural and ideological factors than Marx himself did. In doing so they rather water down the ability of Marxism to explain how society works in economic terms.

Conflict theory

Conflict theories emphasize the importance of conflict between different groups in society, but they do not place emphasis on class alone.

Conflict may take place between occupational groupings, men and women, ethnic or religious groups, age groups, heterosexuals and homosexuals, the disabled and able-bodied, and so on.

Weber's views on class, status and parties (see p. 7) illustrate aspects of conflict theory.

Social action and interpretive perspectives

- Some of these approaches deny the existence of a clear social structure that tends to direct individual behaviour.
- Some accept the existence of a structure but see it as shaped by individuals.

Max Weber

Weber combined a consideration of social structure (e.g. classes, status groups and bureaucracies) with a concern with social action.

He described sociology as the study of social action – which he defines as any intentional, meaningful behaviour which takes account of the existence of other people.

Explaining social action requires *Verstehen*, or understanding. You need to understand what actions mean to people – e.g. it is possible to understand that a woodcutter with a piece of wood and an axe is chopping wood. But you also need to understand the motive behind an action.

An example is the Protestant ethic study, in which Weber discusses the meaning of Protestantism to some of its followers and their motives for working hard to reinvest money.

Weber accepts the existence of institutions such as bureaucracies, but he sees them as consisting of individuals carrying out social actions.

- Bureaucracies are organizations with sets of rules and hierarchical relationships (e.g. the civil service or large corporations).
- In bureaucracies individuals carry out rational social action: social action intended to achieve particular goals, such as increasing the profits of a company.

Weber saw the modern world as increasingly governed by rational social action (or the process of rationalization). Pre-modern societies were regulated more by traditional social action: people behaved in certain ways because people had long behaved in those ways.

In modern societies governed by rational social action there was far more scope for innovation, but to some extent bureaucracies with strict rules stifled individual creativity.

Weber was neither a materialist (like Marx) who believed that material forces shaped history, nor an idealist who believed that ideas shaped history. Instead, Weber believed that both materialism and idealism played a part in explaining human history. For example, the development of capitalism required both the right material conditions and the religious ideas of Protestantism.

Weber – a critique

1 Weber has been criticized by Lee and Newby (1983) as a methodological individualist – somebody who reduces everything to the actions of individuals and ignores how social structure shapes society.
2 To the extent that Weber does deal with social structure, what he says seems to contradict some of his ideas on the importance of individual social action.
3 Postmodernists deny that the contemporary social world is increasingly characterized by rationalization.

Symbolic interactionism

George Herbert Mead

- Mead is usually seen as the founder of symbolic interactionism.
- Human behaviour is social because people interact in terms of symbols.
- Symbols (e.g. words or flags) stand for other objects and imply certain behaviour – e.g. the symbol 'chair' implies an object that you can sit on.
- Humans do not have instincts, and thus they need symbols in order to survive and interact. For example, they need symbols for different plants which indicate whether they are edible or poisonous.
- Meanings and symbols are largely shared by members of society.
- In order to understand the behaviour of others, it is necessary to take the role of the other: i.e. imagine that you are them in order to try to understand the reasons for their behaviour.
- Individuals have a self – an image of what sort of person they are. This largely reflects how other people react to them. By taking the role of the other (imagining how others see us) we build up a self-concept. For example, we come to see ourselves as brave or cowardly, hard or soft.
- Society has a culture and a plurality of social roles – e.g. the roles of husband and wife. These roles imply certain behaviours, but the roles are flexible and can change. For example, there is considerable leeway in how people carry out different family roles.

Herbert Blumer

Other interactionists, such as Herbert Blumer, have developed Mead's approach.

- Blumer emphasizes that people do not react automatically to external stimuli but interpret their meaning before reacting (e.g. they interpret the meaning of a stimulus such as a red light before deciding how to react to it).
- Meanings develop during interaction and are not fixed.
- Rules and structures restrict social action and shape the interpretation of meaning to some extent, but they are never absolutely rigid and fixed.

Symbolic interactionism – a critique

1 Interactionists fail to explain where the norms which partly shape behaviour come from.
2 They may underestimate the degree to which human behaviour is constrained.
3 They neglect the role of structural factors – such as the unequal distribution of power and the existence of inequality – in shaping human societies.

Phenomenology

Phenomenology is a European philosophy. Like other social action approaches it is concerned with subjective meanings, but unlike them it denies that you can produce causal explanations of human behaviour.

- According to its founder, Husserl, individuals organize chaotic sensory experience into phenomena.
- Phenomena are things which are held to have characteristics in common – e.g. the category 'dog' includes a range of animals with particular characteristics.
- The emphasis is on the subjective nature of the categorization. Although a real world exists, how it is categorized is a matter of human choice rather than an objective process.
- The purpose of phenomenology is to understand the essence of phenomena – the essential characteristics which lead to something being placed in a particular category.
- An example of phenomenology is Atkinson's work on suicide, which looks at why certain events are categorized as suicides, rather than looking at the causes of suicide (see p. 169).

Uniting structural and social action approaches

As discussed, there are two main approaches in sociology:

1 Structural approaches (which emphasize how social structures shape social action).
2 Social action approaches (which emphasize how social groups produce society through their actions).
Sociologists have increasingly tried to combine these two approaches.

In *The Sociological Imagination*, C. Wright Mills (1959) suggested that you needed to understand how the larger historical scene affected individuals.

Giddens – the theory of structuration

Anthony Giddens advocates structuration theory. He sees structure and action as two sides of the same coin.

- Structures make social action possible, but social actions create the structures.

- Giddens calls this the duality of structure.
- This can be illustrated by language. Grammar is the structure of language, but individuals create the structure by talking and writing in ways that follow grammatical rules. If people start to use language in a different way, then grammatical rules will change. However, people can only use language and understand each other because there is some grammatical structure.
- In the same way, societal structures and institutions are reproduced through people's actions, but if their actions change, the structures and institutions change.

Critics of Giddens, such as Margaret Archer (1982), argue that he puts too much emphasis on people's ability to change society by acting differently, and he underestimates the constraints under which people operate.

Modernity, postmodernity and postmodernism

It is possible to distinguish two types of theoretical approach within sociology:

1 Modern theories – such as those of Durkheim, Marx and Weber – argue that the objective truth about society can be discovered.
2 Postmodernism, on the other hand, argues against the idea of objective truth.

Some sociologists distinguish different eras in human development and argue that there has been a move from modernity to postmodernity, although others dispute this.

Modernity

Many sociologists have distinguished between pre-modern and modern societies. The change is often associated with industrialization.

- Marx, Weber, Durkheim and most classic sociologists saw the development of modernity as progress.
- The Enlightenment (an eighteenth-century intellectual movement) is often seen as the starting point of modernity. The Enlightenment rejected the idea that thinking should be limited by religious beliefs and tradition and argued that humans could work out the best way to organize societies for themselves.
- Weber in particular saw the change to modernity in terms of the triumph of scientific rationality over superstition, tradition and religious faith.

Postmodern theories

Postmodern theorists reject the idea that human society can be perfected through rational thought; they reject the idea that grand theories can discover the truth.

Postmodernism first developed in architecture. It rejected modern concrete, steel and glass tower blocks, which some modern architects saw as the solution to the problem of accommodating people.

Postmodern architecture uses a greater variety of styles and uses the architecture of earlier eras rather than just using modern materials and designs.

There are two particularly influential postmodern theorists: Lyotard and Baudrillard.

Lyotard – postmodernism and knowledge

Jean-François Lyotard is a French social theorist.

- Lyotard argues that the move to postmodern culture started in the 1950s.
- It involves changes in language-games.
- Pre-industrial societies had a language-game based on narrative. The narrator of stories has legitimacy because of who they are (e.g. their position within a tribe).
- With the Enlightenment, denotative language-games became dominant. In these, statements are judged in terms of abstract standards of proof, deriving from science.
- Science itself is based upon metanarratives – big stories which give meaning to other narratives. Metanarratives behind science see progress through science and conquering nature as possible. Such metanarratives influenced events such as the French Revolution and helped to make Marxism popular in the twentieth century.
- Postmodernism leads to 'incredulity towards metanarratives'. The metanarratives of the twentieth century failed to solve the world's problems and in fact made things worse. For example, Marxism led to tyranny in the communist USSR. People no longer believe in a simple recipe for progress.
- In postmodernism, denotative language-games are replaced by technical language-games. These are not judged by standards of truth, but by standards of usefulness.
- Postmodern society is based upon producing saleable, useful knowledge rather than searching for eternal truths.
- Postmodern society is more diverse, pluralistic and tolerant than modern societies in which doctrinaire metanarratives dominated.

Lyotard – a critique

1 Critics argue that Lyotard's theory is itself a sweeping metanarrative about the development of society.
2 He advances little evidence to support his theory.
3 The Marxist Terry Eagleton sees Lyotard's theory as justification for uncontrolled capitalism which puts profit before human well-being.

Baudrillard – Simulations

Like Lyotard, Baudrillard sees society as moving through several stages.

He argues that Marxists are wrong to see contemporary society as based on the production of material goods. The economy is increasingly based on the production and sale of signs and images – e.g. the image of pop stars is what sells rather than the content of their records.

Signs have developed through four stages:

1 Signs are a reflection of a basic reality.
2 Signs become a distortion of reality.
3 Signs disguise the absence of reality (e.g. images of a non-existent God).

4 Signs bear no relation to any reality – signs become simulacra.

Examples of simulacra are:

- Disneyland, which reproduces imaginary worlds such as 'Future World'.
- The mummy of Rameses II, which was transformed by attempts to preserve it.
- Los Angeles, which Baudrillard sees as an 'immense script ... a perpetual motion picture'.

Baudrillard believes that politics has imploded into a meaningless exchange of signs in which politicians have no real power.

People become trapped in a situation where image and reality cannot be separated, particularly through watching TV.

Baudrillard – a critique

1 Baudrillard's arguments are highly abstract and not based on systematic research.
2 David Harvey (1990) suggests that the decisions made by politicians make a real difference to people's lives.
3 Baudrillard makes absurd statements such as claiming that the Gulf War was simply a series of images on TV screens.

Harvey – Marxism and postmodernity

Harvey accepts that we are moving towards a postmodern era, but he rejects postmodern theory. He believes that modern theories such as Marxism can be used to understand and explain postmodernity.

- He emphasizes the role of the economy in changing society.
- He accepts that images have become more important but sees this as part of capitalists' attempts to maintain and increase profit.
- He argues that the economic crisis of the 1970s (which followed a rise in oil prices) made it difficult to make profits out of mass production.
- Firms moved towards a system of flexible accumulation, in which there are frequent shifts in consumer demand and the products produced by firms.

- Capitalism increasingly turns cultural products (such as fashion, music and art) into commodities to be bought and sold.
- Time and space become compressed, as people can travel and communicate more easily, and products from around the world become available in local stores.
- This produces unsettled, rapidly changing cultures.
- There is a process of globalization in which governments lose some power to control events in their own territory.

Harvey therefore accepts that there is a move towards postmodernity but believes that this can be understood in terms of modern social theory. He also believes that the planned improvement of society is still possible.

Modern theories of society and the sociology of modernity

There are numerous sociologists who reject postmodern theories and still argue that societies can be understood, explained and improved.

Anthony Giddens is one example.

- Giddens believes that societies have entered an era of high modernity.
- Despite important changes, such as globalization, key features of modern societies remain.
- In particular, societies are still based upon the modern characteristic of reflexivity.
- Reflexivity involves people reflecting upon the world and thinking about acting differently in the future to improve things.
- People increasingly reflect upon all aspects of their lives and consider changing them.
- This makes contemporary culture increasingly unsettled and changeable. This is not, however, a feature of postmodernity but an extension and development of a key feature of modernity.

(answers on p. 216)

1 Which **two** of the following are structural perspectives?
   a Functionalism
   b Marxism
   c Symbolic interactionism
   d Weber's theory of social action

2 Another term for a structural perspective is:
   a A micro perspective
   b An interpretive perspective
   c A postmodern perspective
   d A macro perspective

3 Parsons calls a basic need of society:
   a A functional prerequisite
   b Structural differentiation
   c The infrastructure
   d Biological analogy

4 Functionalism is often seen as having:
   a A conservative ideology
   b A liberal ideology
   c A radical ideology
   d An anarchistic ideology

5 According to Durkheim, which **two** of the following are problems of societies with a complex division of labour?
   a Fatalism   b Anomie
   c Egoism   d Social facts

6 Dialectical materialism means:
   a The existence of conflict
   b The study of socialization
   c The clash of material forces such as classes
   d The economic foundations of society

7 In capitalism, Marx calls the ruling class:
   a The proletariat   b The petty bourgeoisie
   c The bourgeoisie   d Serfs

8 A communist society is a society in which:
   a Everybody is completely equal
   b Everybody has the same income
   c The means of production are communally owned
   d All classes share power

9 According to Gramsci, hegemony means:
   a Conflict   b A democratic system
   c Equality   d Political dominance

10 In Weber's sociology, *Verstehen* means:
    a Social action   b Structure
    c Meaning   d Understanding

11 Weber thought that modern societies were dominated by:
    a Traditional social action
    b Charisma
    c Rational social action
    d Idealism

12 Herbert Blumer believes that:
    a There are no rules in society
    b Rules are fixed and inflexible
    c Rules exist but are flexible
    d Modern societies are increasingly dominated by rules

13 In phenomenology, phenomena are:
    a Things which belong in the same category
    b Amazing social events
    c The basic rules of society
    d Causal explanations

14 The founder of symbolic interactionism was:
    a Max Weber   b George Herbert Mead
    c Howard Becker   d Edmund Husserl

15 Lee and Newby criticize Weber as:
    a A determinist
    b A methodological individualist
    c An idealist
    d A materialist

16 In interaction, when you try to understand the viewpoint of somebody else, you:
    a Take the role of the other
    b Step into somebody's shoes
    c Engage in empathy
    d Use telepathy

17 Which one of the following is a functionalist who emphasized that societies could be dysfunctional?
    a Parsons   b Comte
    c Merton   d Weber

18 What term does Giddens use to describe the unity of structure and social action?
    a Structuralism   b Unityism
    c Reproduction   d Structuration

19 The intellectual movement which gave rise to modernity is known as:
    a The Awakening   b The Rebirth
    c The Illumination   d The Enlightenment

20 Postmodernism first developed in:
    a Art   b Architecture
    c Sociology   d Economics

21 The term metanarratives is used by:
    a Lyotard   b Baudrillard
    c Harvey   d Giddens

22 According to Baudrillard, postmodern society is based on:
    a Materialism
    b The production and sale of signs
    c Art
    d Language-games

23 Simulacra are:
    a Postmodern games
    b A type of narrative
    c Signs which distort reality
    d Signs which bear no relation to reality

24 Which one of the following conflicts did Baudrillard argue was not real?
    a The Vietnam War   b The Falklands War
    c The Gulf War   d The war in Kosovo

25 David Harvey believes that time and space have become:
    a Distorted   b Compressed
    c Squashed   d The same thing

26 David Harvey:
    a Accepts that truth about society cannot be found
    b Rejects the idea that postmodernity has arrived
    c Advocates a theory of high modernity
    d Thinks that postmodernity can be understood using a modern theory

27 According to Giddens, reflexivity means:
  a Greater flexibility
  b Automatic reaction
  c Reflection and planning future actions
  d Insensitivity to other cultures

28 The sociological theory that puts most emphasis on materialism is:
  a Interactionism   **b** Marxism
  c Functionalism   **d** Postmodernism

29 The sociological theory that denies the existence of facts about society is:
  a Marxism   **b** Weberian theory
  c Phenomenology   **d** Giddens's theory

30 Which one of the following developed a theory of bureaucracy?
  a Marx   **b** Weber
  c Durkheim   **d** Parsons

Develop your analysis and evaluation skills (see p. 211 for guidance notes)

For each of the following statements, identify which sociologists
would argue in favour of and which against the view expressed.
Explain the reasons for their view.

1 Marxists place too much emphasis on classes and material factors.
2 Functionalism is an outdated theory.
3 Both structural and social action theories are useful for understanding society.
4 We may have entered a period of postmodernity but that does not mean we should accept postmodernism.
5 Interpretive approaches tend to ignore constraints in social life.
6 No single sociological theory can explain all aspects of society.
7 There are both similarities and differences between Marxism and functionalism.

Total: 60 marks   1 mark = 1.5 minutes
Time allowed: 1 hour 30 minutes

SECTION A
Answer all parts of this question

This is the variable that has to be operationalized for part [a]. The graph cannot be plotted without doing this

These are official statistics which can be used as a secondary source (see Chapter 14)

Compare this hypothesis with the results, for your answer to part [b]

You have to decide on the type, based on the research context that is given, before answering part [c]

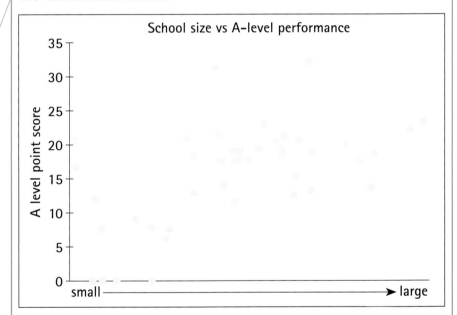

ITEM A

For her coursework project, an A level sociology student decided to investigate the relationship between school size and pupil performance. She hypothesized that smaller schools would gain better A level results than larger schools. She took her data from the Department of Education school league tables published annually in a national newspaper. When she saw how many schools there were, she decided to limit her analysis to one local authority area.

The results looked like this:

School size vs A-level performance

As part of the evaluation of the project, the student wrote that she would have liked to follow up her study by interviewing two headteachers, of a small and a large secondary school, to explore with them the associations she was investigating.

Comments on the question	Question	Advice on preparing your answer
• Check that you understand this term which is an important concept when carrying out quantitative research	[a] Suggest one way that school size might be operationalized in the project in Item A. [2 marks]	• The meaning can be found in Chapter 14 (p. 172). Apply this understanding to your own knowledge of schools

Comments on the question	Question	Advice on preparing your answer
• This is the prediction she made at the beginning of the study about what she was expecting to find (see Popper, Chapter 14, p. 168) • Do not forget to answer this part of the question. It will carry most marks	[b] Was her hypothesis confirmed or rejected by the findings? Explain the reason for your answer. [4 marks]	• Before you interpret the results in the item, look at causality (Chapter 14, p. 168). This will help you to understand the different types of relationships that might exist
• You need to select one (see Chapter 14, pp. 172–3) • The marks will be awarded here, not for your selection of a type of interview	[c] What type of interview would you use for the follow-up study? Give three reasons for your choice. [6 marks]	• To help you make a logical analysis that you can apply to this research problem, read Chapter 14, pp. 172–3 on interviewing, and p. 176 on triangulation
• This is an important distinction that you should be able to make and use appropriately: 1 Practical problems will apply to all researchers regardless of their perspective 2 Theoretical problems will be specific to one group of sociologists	[d] Identify and explain one practical and one theoretical problem of using official statistics reported in the press as a source of data for the research project in Item A. [8 marks]	• Distinguish the theoretical from the practical problems, which are discussed in Chapter 14, pp. 175–6 • Choose only one of each and explain the problem in the context of the research described in the item

SECTION B
Answer one question from this section

Comments on the question	Question	Advice on preparing your answer
• A balanced response is required that recognizes that this is not the only or necessarily the best approach to sociology • This tells you to explore the link between methods and theory	Either: Assess the view that the 'social world has to be studied and explained from the actor's point of view'. [40 marks]	• Identify the theoretical position in the question as interactionist • Develop and explain this theory using p. 187 • Offer a critique of the theory (p. 187) • Alternative theoretical perspectives can offer a different view: functionalism (pp. 184–5); Marxism (pp. 185–6) • A conclusion could be drawn from the work of Giddens (p. 187–8)
• You will need to distinguish between these two terms • Your answer should be reasonably balanced between the two elements of the question	Or: Examine the concepts of modernity and postmodernity in relation to sociological theory. [40 marks]	• Explain the meaning of the terms (p. 188) • Describe the essential features of each (pp. 188–9), using at least one named writer for each concept • Make appropriate critical comments throughout your answer (p. 189)

Total: 60 marks
Time allowed: 1 hour

1 mark = 1 minute

Comments on the question	Question	Advice on preparing your answer
• Make sure that you describe both views in a detailed way with supporting evidence • Look at a range of arguments for and against both theoretical positions • It is important to be balanced. Try to give equal weighting to both theoretical positions	Outline and assess modernist and postmodernist theories of culture and consumption. [60 marks]	• This is an essay question so spend at least 10 minutes planning your response • Construct an introduction which briefly and clearly explains the concepts used in the question • The sections on pp. 188–9 offer accounts of both the modernist and postmodernist positions • Try to finish with an evaluative conclusion based on the available evidence

Guidance Notes

Chapter 1

Sociological perspectives

1 **In Britain today we live in a modern society**

This statement appears, at first sight, to obviously be true. However, sociologists don't use the term 'modern society' simply to refer to contemporary society. Modern society or modernity is used to describe a particular phase in the development of society (see p. 2). It is usually seen as having been preceded by a premodern or pre-industrial society (see p. 1). Some of the main features of the change from premodern to modern society include: an increasing proportion of people working in industry; the development of a capitalist system; increased proportions of the population living in urban areas; and the development of liberal democracy. Also important is a belief in the idea of progress and a belief in science and rational planning, rather than putting faith in religion (see p. 2).

However, this does not mean that all sociologists believe that modern Britain is a modern society. Some sociologists argue that modernity has been superseded by postmodernity (see p. 2). Features of postmodernity include: a lack of faith in science; pessimism about the prospect of progress; and a revival of non-rational beliefs.

2 **All societies are characterized by a structure in which people cooperate on the basis of shared norms and values**

This is the view advocated by functionalists (see p. 2). Values are general guidelines about what society considers good and desirable or bad and undesirable (see p. 1). Norms are specific guidelines defining acceptable behaviour in different situations (see p. 1). Functionalists believe that there are shared values which provide the basis for norms which allow people to cooperate together.

However, other sociologists dispute this. Marxists deny that all social groups cooperate together. Instead they emphasize the conflict between classes which have different interests (see p. 2). Feminists also believe that there is conflict in society and differences of interest. In their case the conflict is between males and females (see p. 2). Interactionists would accept that there are some shared norms and values, but they would see these as flexible and constantly changing rather than rigid (see p. 3). They also deny that society has any fixed structure, adopting a micro theory which looks at society in terms of interaction in small groups. Many postmodernists emphasize that people no longer behave in ways determined by socialization which might provide shared norms and values (see p. 3). Instead they argue that people are increasingly free to construct their own identities, meaning that no rigid social structure exists.

3 **Sociology is a scientific subject which should use scientific methods**

This is the view of positivists (see p. 3). They believe that sociology can be based on objective, statistical data which record social facts. Causal relationships can be established and even laws of human behaviour.

This view is rejected by social action perspectives (see p. 3). They argue that society can only be understood by taking account of the unobservable meanings and motives that shape people's social actions. Since these are subjective, they cannot be studied in a scientific way.

Phenomenologists also reject the idea that sociology can be scientific (see p. 3). To them, the main problem is that the social world cannot be objectively classified, so there are no objective, hard facts on which to base a scientific sociology.

Chapter 2

Social stratification

1 **Stratification is an inevitable and desirable feature of human societies**

This view is particularly associated with functionalists, especially Davis and Moore. They see stratification as inevitable, due to the functional prerequisite of role allocation and the need for a rewards system to match the most able to the most functionally important jobs. Stratification is desirable because it ensures that important jobs are done by able and motivated people (see p. 6).

Talcott Parsons would also agree with this statement. He sees stratification as inevitable because people are bound to be evaluated in terms of a value consensus, and all societies have values which form the basis of judgements about people (see p. 6).

Melvin Tumin attacks a number of aspects of Davis and Moore's argument. Marxists see stratification as undesirable because it is exploitative. They do not believe it is inevitable because it did not exist under primitive communism, and they believe it will disappear in a future communist society (see p. 7). Weber and Weberians stress the damaging effects of stratification (such as conflict) although they see no prospect of it disappearing.

2 **Britain is now a meritocratic society**

The idea of meritocracy suggests that your place in society is based on merit: a combination of effort and ability. Functionalists such as Davis and Moore believed that modern industrial societies were meritocratic (see p. 6). This view has been questioned by Melvin Tumin (pp. 5–6), Marxists

(p. 7) and Weberians (p. 7).

More recently, Peter Saunders has put forward evidence – particularly relating to the amount of upward social mobility and its relationship to intelligence – to suggest that Britain is a meritocracy (pp. 13–14). However, critics have pointed to inequalities in opportunities for upward mobility, and limitations in Saunders's evidence relating to intelligence and mobility (see p. 14). Studies of social mobility (see p. 13) show that class background still influences mobility chances.

3 The British class system is now dominated by a homogeneous middle class

There is evidence of the growth of the middle class in the British occupational structure (pp. 7–8). This goes against Marx's view that the middle class would become proletarianized (p. 9). Giddens argues that the middle class forms a single group based on having educational qualifications (p. 10). However, there are many who question whether the middle class is homogeneous. Goldthorpe sees the middle class as split in two, Roberts *et al.* see it as fragmented, and Abercrombie and Urry see it as polarized (see p. 10). Savage *et al.* see the middle class as divided into those with property, organizational and cultural assets (see pp. 10–11).

A number of Marxists question the view that there is a dominant middle class. The theory of proletarianization suggests that many supposedly middle-class clerical workers are really working-class (see p. 10). Westergaard argues that the central division is still between an increasingly rich ruling class, and the comparatively poor mass of workers (see pp. 8 and 14–15).

4 The working class is an increasingly small and unimportant group

This view is opposed to Marx's view that the working class would grow, become class conscious and become the dominant group in society (see p. 7). It is supported by evidence that manual workers make up a declining proportion of the population (see p. 8), and by the apparent decline in class identification and class consciousness, and increased divisions, in the working class (see Dahrendorf, p. 12, Crewe, p. 12, and Goldthorpe *et al.*, p. 11). The growth of a separate underclass could also be seen as evidence of a declining working class (pp. 12–13).

However, opponents of the proletarianization thesis question the idea that the working class is shrinking (pp. 11–12). Beynon denies that we are witnessing 'the end of the industrial worker' (pp. 11). Marshall *et al.*, Devine, and Warwick and Littlejohn all question the decline of class consciousness and the extent of divisions in the working class. Blackburn and Mann and Marshall *et al.* see the potential for class consciousness. There are also many opponents of the idea of an underclass (see p. 13).

5 Class is dead

This view is most strongly supported by the postmodernists Pakulski and Waters (p. 14). They see new cleavages emerging, declining class consciousness and an increasingly fluid stratification system. They link these to globalization, the growing importance of educational qualifications, and the growth of new politics.

This view is strongly opposed by critics such as Bradley and Marshall (p. 14). The research of Marshall *et al.* suggests the persistence of class (p. 12). Westergaard argues that objective data show that class inequalities are hardening rather than disappearing. Most of the evidence and arguments in the chapter suggest that class remains important even if some changes in the class system are taking place.

6 Marxism contributes little to an understanding of class in modern Britain

This view would obviously not be supported by Marx or Marxists. Possible reasons for questioning the usefulness of the Marxist view include: the decline in class consciousness and the fragmentation of the working class (see note 4 above); the death of class (see note 5 above); and the growth of the middle class (see note 3 above).

There are many sociologists who adopt a Weberian approach to class, such as Weber himself, Lockwood, Goldthorpe and Marshall *et al.* (see pp. 7, 10 and 12). They all argue that there are important divisions within classes as well as between a ruling and working class. However, some sociologists continue to support a Marxist view. These include Westergaard and Resler (see pp. 8 and 14–15). They argue that class inequalities are hardening and that Britain continues to have a ruling class.

Chapter 3

Sex and gender

1 Gender roles are shaped as much by biology as by culture

Stoller defines gender in terms of psychological and cultural differences between masculinity and femininity (see p. 22). This implies that physical, sex differences are not the only reason for differences in gender roles – they are also shaped by culture. There are a number of sex differences that might account for male and female behaviour. These include hormones and brain lateralization. Critics question the validity and reliability of research in this area (see pp. 22–3).

Sociobiologists explain behaviour in terms of differences in male and female reproductive strategies. Critics point to the existence of celibacy and homosexuality (see pp. 22). Murdock argues that all societies have a sexual division of labour along traditional lines. Parsons argues that women are better psychologically adjusted to bring up children; and Bowlby argues that children suffer if they experience maternal deprivation. However, Oakley points to examples of societies where there is an unconventional division of labour and/or men play a major part in child-rearing.

Oakley and others point to the importance of gender role socialization in creating gender differences (pp. 23). Most feminists (Firestone is an exception) do not see biology as particularly significant in creating gender differences and inequalities (see pp. 23–4).

2 **Gender inequalities originated with and are maintained by economic inequalities**

This view is supported by Marxist and socialist feminists. Engels saw gender inequalities as originating in the emergence of private property, and Coontz and Henderson in the way men controlled female labour (see p. 23). Ann Oakley, although not a Marxist or socialist, argues that the Industrial Revolution played a part in tying women to domestic life.

Marxists and feminists also explain the persistence of inequalities in economic terms. Engels argued that lack of access to paid work kept women subservient. Benston argues that women are used as a reserve army of labour. Hartmann sees this as important but argues that patriarchy plays a part too (p. 24). There is plenty of evidence that women continue to be economically unequal to men (see p. 25).

Other feminists see the origins of gender inequality differently. Firestone sees biology as important, while Ortner argues that cultural factors are more important (see p. 23). Millett argues that a wide variety of factors, including psychology and violence, play a part in women continuing to be unequal, but economics plays some part (see p. 24). Sylvia Walby sees paid employment as just one of six structures of patriarchy (pp. 24–5). Biological theories reject the view that economics are important, but they have been heavily criticized (see pp. 22–3).

3 **British society continues to be patriarchal**

First you need to define patriarchy as dominance by men over women and children. Millett can be used to illustrate what is seen as a patriarchal society (see pp. 24). Walby is useful for suggesting that patriarchy remains but it has changed from private patriarchy to public patriarchy.

The idea that patriarchy remains can be backed up with evidence of inequality in the labour market (p. 25) and in the home (pp. 94–5). However, Anna Pollert attacks the use of the term patriarchy and stresses the interrelationship between class, ethnicity and gender (see p. 24). Postmodernists emphasize the importance of differences between women as well as any shared experience of patriarchy. Walby

suggests some ways in which patriarchy has decreased (pp. 24–5), and there is some evidence that women have made gains in the workplace and in the home. Postfeminists see traditional feminism with its emphasis on patriarchy as outdated, but Faludi insists it is still relevant (see pp. 26–7).

4 **Patriarchy is no longer a useful concept for feminists**

This has some similarities to note 3, but you can't include the data on contemporary Britain as this is a more theoretical issue. Again start off by defining patriarchy, and examine the ideas of Millett, Walby and Pollert (see note 3). Focus particularly on the arguments surrounding Pollert's criticisms of the concept. You should look at why postmodernists are suspicious of the idea of patriarchy. You might conclude that patriarchy is still a useful concept so long as it is not seen as the only source of inequality in society.

5 **Family responsibilities are largely to blame for women's low wages**

This statement concerns gender and the labour market. It is useful to start by identifying the extent of low wages (see p. 25). Those who would agree with the statement include human capital theorists (see p. 25). They argue that career breaks and raising children make employers less likely to invest in women's training.

However, many other factors have been suggested as being important. Dual labour market theory stresses employer sexism and lack of female unionization (see p. 25). Braverman's theory emphasizes deskilling. The reserve army of labour theory sees the capitalist economy as a whole as the underlying factor, but it does recognize that women's domestic role makes it easier to throw them out of work (see p. 25). Feminists such as Walby look at the role of male trade unionists in keeping women's wages low. Radical feminists look at workplace harassment and the sexualization of work, while Crompton and Sanderson examine the role of different sorts of labour markets (see pp. 26). Thus family responsibilities might play some part in keeping women's wages low, but a range of other factors are important as well.

6 **Masculinity continues to be characterized by competitiveness, rationality and the use of violence**

Seidler sees masculinity as characterized by rationality (see p. 27). Gilmore's research suggests that in most societies men, as impregnators, providers and protectors, are likely to be competitive and perhaps violent (see p. 27). However, he finds that men's roles vary and in some societies men are not violent.

A number of feminists associate elements of patriarchy and masculinity with violence (such as Millett, p. 24), and the existence of domestic violence could support this. Rutherford argues that masculinity tends to be associated with science and reason but the possibility of the emergence of 'new men' might undermine this. Bob Connell stresses the plurality of masculinities in contemporary societies. Some masculinities, particularly hegemonic masculinity, might be associated with competitiveness, rationality and violence, but this is not true of other masculinities such as the environmental movement (see p. 27). Thus you should avoid assuming that any characteristics are associated with all men.

Chapter 4

Race, ethnicity and nationality

1 **There are biologically distinct races some of which are superior to others**

This view is typical of polygenetic theories of 'race' which suggest that racial groups have distinct origins. It was supported by Herbert Spencer who saw some groups as higher on the evolutionary scale than others (see p. 32). There have been many examples of political movements that have given support to the idea that some 'races' are superior to others – e.g. Nazi Germany.

However, Steve Jones argues that from a genetic viewpoint there are no distinct 'races'. Race is simply a social definition (p. 32). Richardson and Lambert argue that history shows that different 'races' have been dominant at different times in history, showing that no 'race' is innately superior to any other (p. 32).

2 **Racism explains the main inequalities and differences between ethnic groups in Britain**

First you should establish that there are differences and inequalities between ethnic groups – for example, in terms of employment and housing (see pp. 35–6). The racism approach generally attributes this to racism. There are a number of studies that show that racism still exists (see pp. 35–6); there are racially motivated attacks (p. 35); and experiments by Brown and Gay show that employers sometimes discriminate on racial grounds (see pp. 37–8). The idea of institutional racism (see p. 35) sees racism as an important factor holding back ethnic minorities; and theorists such as Oliver Cox and the Birmingham Centre for Contemporary Cultural Studies attribute much importance to racism (see pp. 36).

However, the idea of institutional racism has been criticized by Robert Miles for ignoring the possibility that factors other than racism cause inequality (see p. 35). Studies of employment, such as those of the PSI, show that there are important differences between ethnic groups who would be likely to experience racism. For example, British Bangladeshis tend to get poorer jobs than British Indians, suggesting that cultural and class factors play a role in inequality (see p. 38). There are also gender differences between males and females from the same ethnic group (e.g. female British Afro-Caribbeans tend to be more successful than male British Afro-Caribbeans in some areas).

3 **Ethnicity is a more useful concept than racism in understanding ethnic groups**

The idea of ethnicity stresses the importance of cultural differences between groups (see p. 33). Studies of ethnicity tend to look at the lifestyle of the group being studied (p. 34). They are better at examining the viewpoint of minorities, rather than seeing them as the passive victims of racism. They help to produce an understanding of the identity of ethnic minorities and how they adapt to changing circumstances. Sociologists such as Michael Brown use the concept of ethnicity to help in understanding conflict between ethnic groups (see p. 34). However, critics point out that this approach tends to ignore the effects of racism, which are beyond the control of ethnic groups (see p. 34). Racism, in itself, may play an important part in creating ethnic identity. It could therefore be argued that both ethnicity and racism are important concepts that need to be taken into account when trying to understand the position of minorities.

4 **Both racism and inequalities between ethnic groups are dying out in Britain**

There is some evidence of a reduction in racism (see the results of British Social Attitudes Surveys, p. 35) and in inequalities between ethnic groups (see PSI studies, p. 35). However, the same studies show that substantial racism and inequality remain. An ICM opinion poll in 1995 found that two-thirds of the sample admitted to being racist (p. 35); and some ethnic minorities continue to be disadvantaged in employment, housing (see pp. 35–6) and education (pp. 139–40). However, some groups, such as the Chinese and East African Asians, are enjoying considerable success and doing better than whites in some areas, so it is dangerous to generalize about ethnic groups as a whole.

5 **Nationalism and ethnic conflict are both becoming more common, and there are a variety of reasons for this change**

There are certainly many examples of nationalism and ethnic conflict in the contemporary world (see p. 36). While it is hard to measure whether they are more common than in the past, this may be the case, with factors such as the break-up of the Soviet Union, globalization and the revival of Islam playing a part. Michael Brown looks at ethnic conflict in terms of systemic, domestic and perceptual explanations (see p. 34). David McCrone examines nationalism in terms of different forms that nationalism can take (see p. 36). Both emphasize the variety of types and causes of these phenomena. Stuart Hall stresses the importance of globalization and migration in causing increased tension, but he sees hybridization as one factor which might counteract this (pp. 37).

6 Ethnic minorities in Britain constitute an underclass

This view is supported by Anthony Giddens and by Rex and Tomlinson (see p. 38). Charles Murray supports the idea of an underclass, but only sees it as being constituted by ethnic minorities in the USA (see p. 38). Some writers deny that an underclass exists, but do see ethnic minorities as disadvantaged (e.g. Castles and Kosack, and Phizaklea and Miles, p. 38). However, Andrew Pilkington specifically rejects the idea that ethnic minorities form an underclass in Britain, pointing out that some ethnic minority groups have been very successful in getting non-manual jobs (see p. 38).

7 Racism is a product of modernity

This view is supported by Zygmunt Bauman, a postmodernist, who sees the Holocaust as a product of features of modernity such as bureaucratic planning, organizational discipline, nation-states and scientific rationalism (see p. 37). Goldberg believes that modernity created the conditions in which some people saw themselves as superior to 'others' (see p. 37). Bauman, Goldberg and Rattansi all believe that postmodernism might undermine racism – for example, by creating more fluid identities (see p. 37).

However, Malik attacks these views. He points out that the Enlightenment encouraged a view of people as equal, and he sees capitalism as responsible for racism rather than modernity.

Chapter 5

Poverty and social exclusion

1 Poverty is best understood in terms of relative deprivation

Poverty is a very elusive concept which has been the subject of fierce debate over the last century and beyond. The reason why its definition is controversial lies in the fact that how you define poverty affects how you measure it, and its measurement affects the numbers of people considered to be in poverty at any one time. In the past, poverty was often defined in absolute terms (see p. 43) but due to the problems of using this sort of definition (see p. 45) more relative measures came into use which took into account the fact that ideas of poverty will change from society to society and from time to time.

Relative definitions have provided the basis for much important research into poverty, such as that of Townsend (see p. 44) and Mack and Lansley (see p. 45) More recently, definitions of poverty have begun to move beyond a consideration of only material resources to see it in terms of multiple deprivation and social exclusion (see p. 45).

New Right approaches tend to prefer an absolute definition so that advocates can demonstrate how capitalism has benefited all sections of society (see p. 46); while Marxist and other more left-wing approaches prefer relative definitions which link poverty to levels of inequality in society (see pp. 47–8).

2 Constructing a 'poverty line' is an impossible task

The lack of a clear and uncontested definition of poverty makes its measurement extremely difficult. A major problem lies in the fact that 'acceptable' standards of living vary across societies, times and social groups (see p. 44). These problems have not, however, prevented sociologists from attempting to draw a line below which individuals and households can be said to be in 'poverty', although each attempt has been met with serious criticisms. The budget standards approach (see p. 44) involves costing a list of essential purchases and using the resulting cost to draw a poverty line. This method of measuring poverty was used by Rowntree as far back as 1901 (see p. 44) and was still influential in the 'deprivation indices' used by Townsend (p. 44) and Mack and Lansley (p. 45). The latter studies have tried to broaden their measurement of poverty to include social deprivation and social exclusion.

3 The welfare state produces a culture of dependency

This view represents a New Right approach which sees over-generous welfare benefits acting as a disincentive to individuals being self-sufficient. Marsland (p. 46) is a particular proponent of this approach, although he has been heavily criticized by those who dispute this view of the welfare state (p. 46). The idea of a culture of dependency is closely linked to Murray's views on the underclass (pp. 46–7?) which have also been extensively challenged (see p. 47).

4 The existence of an underclass is crucial in understanding poverty in Britain today

The idea of an 'underclass' has been used in different ways and there is no clear definition of this group. The most controversial view is that of the leading New Right thinker, Charles Murray (pp. 46–7). He sees the existence of an underclass in Britain as a major social problem as this group has developed values and lifestyles which pose a major threat to society. Murray blames the welfare state in part for creating this group. Murray's work has caused much controversy and been subject to serious attack.

Field (p. 47) has also used the idea of an underclass but in a rather more sympathetic way. He believes that certain groups such as the long-term unemployed are forced to live off benefits and have little chance of escaping their poverty.

Conflict theorists tend to reject the idea that an 'underclass' exists (see pp. 47–8). They see the poor as simply the most disadvantaged section of the working class, and evidence from Blackman (see p. 47) supports their view that the values of the poor are not substantially different from those of the rest of society.

5 **Poverty cannot be abolished without major changes to social and economic structures**

The view expressed in this quotation represents a conflict perspective on poverty (see pp. 47–8). Conflict approaches see the causes of poverty as lying in the way society is organized. They reject individualistic and cultural explanations which see poverty as arising from the inadequacies of the poor themselves (see p. 46). The conflict view implies that poverty can only be solved if society distributes resources more fairly. The most extreme version of the view comes from Marxists such as Westergaard and Resler (see pp. 48) who see poverty as functional for capitalism. Its elimination is dependent on the replacement of the capitalist system by socialism.

Less extreme conflict theorists, such as Mack and Lansley and Townsend (see pp. 44–5), accept that the welfare state has never previously redistributed resources (see pp. 47–8) but still believe that improving welfare provision can help in the fight against poverty.

For the New Right the view expressed above is ridiculous (see pp. 46). They believe that rising living standards have all but abolished poverty. The small numbers left in absolute poverty are in that situation due to their own inadequacies and they need to be encouraged to be self-sufficient by reducing welfare benefits.

Chapter 6

Crime and deviance

1 **The origins of deviance lie in the individual's position in society**

The first major sociologist to propose this structural view was the functionalist Robert Merton (p. 57). He argued that deviance was the result of individuals being prevented from achieving shared goals such as wealth and status by their position in society. His theory was adapted by later writers such as Albert Cohen (p. 57) and Cloward and Ohlin (p. 58) who introduced the idea that deviance was not simply an individual response but the result of the development of deviant values in subcultures. Marxist and neo-Marxist approaches also emphasize the importance of the structure of society in explaining deviance (pp. 62–3). More recently, the concept of relative deprivation used by left realists (pp. 63–4) has its origins in the work of Merton.

Biological and psychological theories of deviance (p. 56) reject the link between deviance and social position. They see the causes of deviance as lying within the individual. Labelling theorists (pp 60–1) see the origins of deviance in the labelling of acts as deviant, but they accept that the power to label depends on an individual's or group's position in society.

2 **Official statistics of crime are completely unreliable**

Many of the earlier theories of deviance were based on the assumption that official statistics gave an accurate picture of patterns of crime (p. 59). However, the reliability of these statistics is subject to serious doubt as many crimes go unreported and unrecorded. Alternative methods of collecting information about crime, such as victimization and self-report studies (pp. 59–60), go some way to revealing the 'dark figure' of hidden crime.

Marxists are particularly critical of the amount of white-collar and corporate crime that goes unnoticed (p. 60); and feminists have brought the issue of domestic and sexual violence to public attention. Left realists, however (pp. 62), accept that there have been increases in serious and violent crime, as revealed by official statistics, and argue that crime is a 'real' problem, particularly for more vulnerable groups in the community.

3 **Deviance is simply a label attached to some people's behaviour**

This statement is the basis of the labelling theory approach to deviance (pp. 60–1). Labelling theory is closely associated with the interactionist perspective. Key writers are Becker, Lemert and Goffman. Labelling theory has been subject to much criticism, particularly from more radical perspectives such as Marxism. Gouldner, for example, argues that labelling theory fails to take into account the wider distribution of power in society and attributes too much influence to agents of social control such as the police (p. 68).

4 **Deviance can best be understood by looking at the workings of capitalism**

The use of the word 'capitalism' indicates the Marxist perspective here (p. 62). Marxist approaches see the law and its enforcement as part of the exploitation of the working class. They suggest that the immoral acts of the powerful are ignored while the working class are effectively criminalized.

Traditional Marxist views on crime and deviance have been subject to criticism (p. 62), and the theory has been updated in the form of neo-Marxist approaches such as The New Criminology (p. 63). The most influential study here is Policing the Crisis (p. 63), which attempts to use both labelling theory and Marxism to understand the moral panic over mugging in the 1970s. More recently, Marxism has influenced writers, such as Taylor, who have studied the impact of marketization and globalization on crime and deviance (p. 66).

5 **'Zero tolerance' policing is an effective approach to reducing crime**

The idea of zero tolerance is that the police clamp down on minor offences in order to discourage people from moving on to more serious crime. This method of policing is heavily influenced by American right realist sociologists, such as James Q.

Wilson (p. 65), who see maintaining the character of communities as crucial in fighting crime.

Left realists, however, argue that the police can only win the support of the public by becoming more democratic and focusing their attention on investigating the more serious crimes which are of most concern to the public (pp. 64–5). For these sociologists, such as Jock Young, it is vital to tackle the wider social causes of crime such as inequality, poverty and lack of job opportunities.

6   The police and courts treat women more leniently than men

Official statistics give a clear indication that crime rates among women are far lower than those among men (p. 66). Some sociologists believe that one reason for this difference is a 'chivalry factor' which means that agents of social control (mostly male) treat women more leniently than men. Evidence for the chivalry factor comes from Pollack in the 1950s, and from more recent self-report studies such as Allen's (p. 66).

Many feminists, however, have been critical of the idea of the chivalry factor. Studies of sentencing indicate that women are often treated more severely than men for the same offence; and writers such as Walklate point out the many problems women face from the criminal justice system as victims of sexual crimes (pp. 66–7).

Chapter 7

Religion

1   The functionalist perspective on religion ignores the role of religion in causing conflict in society

Functionalist views emphasize the role of religion in creating and maintaining shared values, therefore reducing conflict. Durkheim, Parsons and Malinowski (see pp. 74–5) all show how religion functions to hold society together and prevent conflict and disruption.

Marxist views are quite different as they locate religion within the Marxist model of class conflict. However, they do not really argue that religion creates conflict, more that religion makes it appear that conflict does not exist. In this sense religion is an ideological tool which creates false class consciousness among the working class (see p. 75).

It is possible to give a number of examples of close relationships between religion and conflict in contemporary societies. These appear to undermine the functionalist case (see p. 74–5). Perhaps functionalism is at its most convincing when analysing small-scale traditional societies. The contemporary world is characterized by diversity and, as postmodernists point out, it is increasingly difficult to make general statements about the role of religion.

2   Religion is a conservative force in society

The term 'conservative' is quite confusing as it can be used in two different ways: first, in terms of conserving society as it is; and second, in terms of causing societies to revert to more conservative or traditional culture and values (see p. 76). The first meaning reflects a functionalist or Marxist perspective, seeing religion as playing a key role in maintaining social order and control (see pp. 74–5). The second meaning sees religion as having a possible role in social change, and can be illustrated by the example of the Islamic overthrow of the rule of the Shah in Iran (see p. 76).

Some sociologists see religion as having quite a powerful part to play in social change. Weber's classic book The Protestant Ethic and the Spirit of Capitalism shows how it was possible to argue that religion had a role in the creation of capitalism back in the seventeenth and eighteenth centuries (see p. 77). Although this book has provoked much debate, examples of the relationship between religion and social change can be seen around the world (see p. 77), leading many sociologists to accept that religion can play a variety of roles, depending on a number of factors relating to the particular society and religion in question (see p. 77).

3   The growth of new religious movements since the 1960s is due to rapid social change

There is a need to discuss the term 'new religious movements' here, so that it is clear what sort of religious organizations are being discussed (see p. 78). Although sects have been around for many hundred years, there was a rapid increase in their number and membership in the 1960s and 1970s, particularly in the USA. The emergence of a small number of world-rejecting new religious movements has become a source of particular public concern, with allegations of brainwashing and members being forced to reject their families.

A number of reasons have been put forward to explain the appeal of sects. The earliest came from Weber who focused on their appeal to the marginalized in society (see p. 79). However, this does not apply directly to the period beginning in the 1960s. A number of sociologists, such as Bruce and Wallis, have put forward explanations that refer explicitly to the phenomenon of new religious movements, and their views will need to be discussed here (see pp. 78–9). A key point to bear in mind is that, although the numbers involved in these groups have grown, they are still very small, especially the number involved in world-rejecting movements (see p. 78).

4   Church membership and attendance statistics indicate a clear decline in religiosity

This is a very general statement. What particular churches are being referred to and where? If you take Britain as an example then there has been a clear decline in the major churches (see p. 80). However, this is not the case in the USA, where attendance remains high (see p. 80).

The statement suggests that there is a clear link between participation in churches and the level of people's religious involvement and commitment. But is this the case? The reliability and validity of church statistics from the nineteenth century and before have been questioned, and Martin has argued that people may have gone to church in Victorian England more as a sign of middle-class respectability than out of religious commitment (see p. 80). What is more, people may express their religious beliefs in different ways today. Opinion poll data suggest that belief in God is still widespread (see p. 80); and the number of people participating in non-Christian religious organizations and 'New Age' activities, such as yoga and aromatherapy, is growing (see p. 76).

5   Secularization is occurring in modern societies

This is a complex question as there is no agreement on how to actually operationalize (define and measure) the concept of secularization. To make matters even more tricky, there are very different patterns of religious belief and participation in different countries, often providing what appears to be quite contradictory evidence (see pp. 80 and 82).

One starting point is the definition of secularization provided by Wilson (see p. 79). This allows the debate to be separated into three different parts: religious practices, religious institutions and religious thinking.

The area of religious practices concerns participation in organized religion. Changes in patterns of membership of religious organizations and attendance at religious services and events need to be considered here, as well as the different ways in which these patterns have been interpreted (see p. 80).

In many countries, religious institutions are less influential in wider society than they were in the past. This leads into the debate about disengagement and differentiation (see pp. 80–1), as well as the different interpretations of increasing religious pluralism (see p. 81).

Finally, religious thinking will need to be considered. Many sociologists believe that the growth of science and rational thought has undermined religious explanations of events. People look to science rather than religion to explain, say, natural disasters. Weber referred to this process as desacrilization (see p. 82). Some contemporary sociologists, such as Bruce, broadly accept this view, while others, including many postmodernists, question the degree of faith people have in scientific and technological advancement (see p. 82).

It is very difficult to reach firm conclusions about secularization as there is so little agreement among sociologists. Kepel goes so far as to suggest that there is evidence of a religious revival around the world, while others, such as Bruce, believe that religion remains strong only in certain very specific social situations. The last word might go to Martin who suggests that the debate has become so confusing that sociologists should actually stop using the word 'secularization'.

Chapter 8

Families and households

1   **The family is a universal social institution**

Murdock argued that the nuclear family is universal – it is found in all societies (p. 88). This view represents a functionalist perspective as Murdock goes on to identify key functions that the family performs in all societies (pp. 88–9).

Some cross-cultural and historical evidence questions Murdock's view, identifying cultures in which alternatives to the conventional nuclear family have developed (pp. 88–9). From a feminist angle, Sheeran argues that it is the 'female-carer core which is the most basic family unit' (p. 88). Postmodern approaches to the family stress diversity and reject the sort of general claims about the family reflected in the statement above (p. 96). They believe that relationships are increasingly about personal choices – they use the phrase 'chosen families' to refer to gay and lesbian families, for example. In the end, your view about the universality of the family will depend on how broadly or narrowly you define a 'family'.

2   **Feminism has made the most significant contribution to the sociology of the family since the 1970s**

It is hard to deny that feminism has been the most significant sociological perspective in understanding families and households in recent years. It has introduced a far more critical way of viewing the family than was the case when functionalist approaches (see pp. 88–9) dominated, and it has opened up new areas of study such as housework (see pp. 89–90). In general, feminism has focused on the ways in which the family benefits men and exploits women.

It is important to realize that feminism is a very broad term which in fact includes quite a wide variety of views. Marxist feminists focus on the benefits to capitalism of female subordination (p. 90), whilst radical feminists use the concept of patriarchy as their central tool in understanding the role of the family in society (p. 90). Difference feminism is a more contemporary approach which stresses the diversity of female experience.

In terms of practical research, feminists have highlighted inequalities in conjugal roles (pp. 94–5), celebrated family diversity (p. 92), and identified male bias in social policy on the family (p. 96).

New Right thinkers do not deny the influence of feminism, but they believe it has had a really damaging effect on the family, undermining traditional values and causing many of today's social problems, which, they believe, are rooted in the decline of the conventional family (pp. 46–7).

3 **The family performs positive functions for society**

This view of the family represents a functionalist perspective. Writers such as Parsons (p. 89) and Murdock (pp. 88–9) have identified the functions of the family. There has been some debate about how these functions are changing. Parsons argues that the family is losing functions as the process of structural differentiation occurs, but it retains its importance as it specializes in a limited number of key functions. Fletcher argues that the family still retains a number of vital functions (p. 94).

Other perspectives do not take such a rosy view of the family. Marxists such as Zaretsky (p. 89), Marxist feminists such as Benston (p. 90), and radical feminists such as Delphy and Leonard (p. 90) see the family as functioning for the benefit of men and the capitalist system rather than society as a whole. Leach and Laing take a very critical view of the family, arguing that it is actually psychologically damaging for many of its members.

4 **The isolated nuclear family is the dominant form in modern societies**

The 'classic' functionalist view is that the nuclear family is a flexible and streamlined family structure which uniquely meets the needs of industrial societies (pp. 90–1). It came to replace the larger extended family which was characteristic of pre-industrial societies (p. 90).

This view is open to question when detailed historical evidence is considered. Laslett, for example, identifies the nuclear family as a common family form in pre-industrial England (p. 91), while Anderson finds the extended family thriving after industrialization (p. 91). Young and Willmott accept that there has been a gradual move towards the nuclear family but see the development of the family as more complex than functionalists such as Parsons suggest (pp. 91).

Statistically the nuclear family is becoming less common in Britain today, although the extent of its decline is disputed. Writers such as the Rapoports identify a range of family types and emphasize diversity in family structures (pp. 92). However, Chester reads the figures in a rather different way and argues that the nuclear family is still common (pp. 93).

5 **The divorce rate is increasing because divorce has become easier to obtain**

There were huge increases in the divorce rate during the twentieth century, and some commentators have seen this as a major threat to the institution of the family. Sociologists have pointed out that divorce is only one way of measuring unhappiness within a relationship – separation and 'empty-shell' marriages also occur (p. 95). These, however, are much harder to measure than divorce.

Functionalists tend to argue that the rise in divorce reflects the high value placed on marriage today: people expect a lot and will end the marriage if the relationship does not meet their expectations (p. 95). More critical sociologists, such as Leach, focus on the emotional pressures placed on the nuclear family today; while a postmodern outlook emphasizes increasing choice in all areas of life (p. 95).

Divorce has certainly become easier to obtain, but the legal changes that have led to this are themselves the result of changes in social attitudes to divorce. The stigma attached to divorce has considerably reduced as society has become more secular and personal freedom and choice have increased.

6 **Conjugal roles are becoming more equal**

The idea that the roles of husband and wife were becoming more equal was suggested by Young and Willmott in their book The Symmetrical Family (p. 94). This view has subsequently been questioned by a wide variety of sociologists, particularly feminists, who point out the continuing inequalities between husbands and wives.

Different research has looked at different aspects of the conjugal relationship. Writers such as Ferri and Smith and Gershuny have looked at the domestic division of labour in terms of housework and childcare, whilst Edgell focused on decision making in the family, and Pahl on money management (pp. 94–5).

Recent research has revealed 'hidden' aspects of the conjugal relationship such as 'emotion work'. Duncombe and Marsden use the term 'triple shift' to refer to women's responsibilities in paid employment, domestic tasks and emotion work (pp. 94–5). Overall, the balance of research indicates little movement towards greater equality.

Chapter 9

Power, politics and the state

1 **In democratic societies the state balances the interests of all social groups**

The state should be defined before answering this question (see p. 102). Weber's definition is useful, but note that it is controversial. The statement expresses the view of classical pluralists (see p. 103), so you will need to outline their views and the evidence supporting them. Use the concept of the state as an 'honest broker'. You should examine specific criticisms of the classical pluralist view (p. 103) before examining a variety of competing views. Elite pluralists (see pp. 103–4) accept that the state might not balance the interests of all groups exactly equally, although all major sections of society have some influence. Elite theory, on the other hand, thinks that elites in command positions ensure that the state favours them (see p. 104).

Marxists see the state as reflecting the interests of a ruling class (see pp. 104–7), although some neo-Marxists accept that the state can take some account of interests other than those of the ruling class (see pp. 105–6).

2 **In capitalist societies the bourgeoisie has most of the power, but its power is not complete**

Define the terms bourgeoisie and power (see p. 102), pointing out that the definition of power is controversial. The view expressed here is supported by neo-Marxists such as Coates and Gramsci (see pp. 105–6), so their views should be explored. Make some specific evaluative points (see p. 106) before examining alternative views. Pluralists generally argue that power is much more widely distributed than neo-Marxists suggest (see pp. 103–4), while conventional Marxists see power as monopolized by the bourgeoisie (see pp. 104–5), and elite theorists believe that it is monopolized by a ruling elite (see p. 104). State-centred theories argue that the state itself has considerable power rather than the bourgeoisie (see p. 105).

3 **A small elite exercises most of the power in countries such as Britain and the USA**

Define power and elite, and describe the elite theories that support this statement (see p. 104). Examine some specific criticisms of elite theory (see p. 104), and then go on to examine alternative views. These should include Marxism (pp. 104–5) and neo-Marxism (pp. 105–6), both of which emphasize the importance of economic power. Pluralism suggests that power is not concentrated (pp. 103–4). You might mention Michael Mann's four sources of power (see p. 107), and suggest that elite theory concentrates on political power and neglects other sources of power.

4 **Although there is some evidence of globalization, the nation-state retains considerable power**

Define globalization (pointing out that it is used in different ways (p. 106)), nation-state (see p. 102) and power (see p. 102). The view expressed here is somewhat critical of the more extreme views on globalization, and would perhaps be supported most by Anthony Giddens (see pp. 106–7). Ohmae would strongly reject the statement on the grounds that the state has lost most of its power, while Bonnett (p. 106) would also believe that the power of the nation-state has declined more than the statement implies. Hirst and Thompson would attack the statement from a different viewpoint, arguing that the state has lost little power (p. 106), while state-centred theories generally insist that the state retains substantial power.

5 **Economic power has always been more important than other sources of power**

This is the Marxist view of power (see pp. 104–5). You should define power (see p. 102) and point out alternative sources of power (see Mann's arguments on the four sources of power (p. 107)). Describe the Marxist/neo-Marxist view – you could use the work of Coates which might illustrate some of the ways in which wealth can provide power (see pp. 105–6).

Other theories emphasize alternative sources of power. Pluralists see power as stemming from decision-making political processes in democracies (see pp. 103–4), while elite theorists believe that power comes from occupying senior political and other positions in society. Even neo-Marxists recognize that ideology is an important source of power, which can be to a certain degree independent of economic control (see pp. 105–6). All of these theories tend to neglect military power which is of more interest to state-centred theories (see p. 106).

6 **Class is no longer important in conflicts over power in a postmodern society**

You need to start off by explaining what postmodernism is, perhaps using the work of Lyotard. This view is supported by Nancy Fraser (p. 107) and Crook, Pakulski and Waters (see pp. 107–8). The idea of new social movements can suggest that non-class issues are becoming more important (see p. 107). However, writers such as Westergaard argue that class differences remain real, are hardening and are still politically important. Giddens sees capitalism and class conflicts as retaining some importance alongside other political issues (see p. 108). You could briefly discuss theories of voting, and competing views about the importance of class in British voting behaviour (pp. 108–9).

7 **Voting behaviour is increasingly shaped by the policy preferences of the electorate**

The policy preference theory is associated with Sarlvik and Crewe (see p. 108). You will need to describe their theory and explain that they believed that there was a shift away from class-based voting in the 1980s. Heath, Jowell and Curtice are amongst the strongest critics of this view (see pp. 108–9), and they see ideological image as more important than detailed policies. Increased volatility might suggest that people are more interested in policies than before, but you can question how far people are familiar with the details of party policy. Party image is probably more important – for example, in explaining the Conservatives' loss of the 1997 election (see p. 109) – although the movement of the Labour Party towards more moderate policies might also be an important factor (see p. 109). Social factors may retain a substantial influence, and a range of factors, rather than a single factor, could be seen as influencing voting.

Chapter 10

1 **Capitalism is the cause of alienation in capitalist societies**

You need to define alienation and capitalism, and outline the Marxist view, which agrees with the statement (see p. 115). Discuss the main ways in which Marx saw workers as alienated, and discuss the ways in which critics have attacked Marx (see p. 115).

Blauner disagrees with Marx, arguing that production technology determines the degree of alienation (pp. 115–6), but there have been extensive criticisms of Blauner (p. 116). The debate about deskilling and post-Fordism (pp. 116–7) is partly about whether the experience of work has deteriorated for workers, and this could be used to bring the debate more up to date. For example, if work has been deskilled, it is likely to have become more alienating, depending on how you define alienation.

2 **Technology determines relationships at work**

Leading on from the alienation debate, Blauner does believes that technology influences relationships at work, whereas Marx does not (see pp. 115–6). More directly relevant is the debate on computers, technology and work. Start by distinguishing technological determinism, which would agree with the statement, and social determinism, which would not agree (see p. 116). Zuboff would support the statement, as would Clark *et al.* (p. 116). Kling and Grint and Woolgar would strongly reject it (p. 116), although critics argue that Grint and Woolgar go too far in minimizing the influence that technology has.

3 **Capitalist economies have shifted from Fordism to post-Fordism, and in the process most workers have been reskilled**

You will need to define Fordism and post-Fordism (p. 117). This statement would clearly be supported by advocates of post-Fordism, such as Piore and Atkinson (p. 117). However, Atkinson would suggest that only core workers have been reskilled, not peripheral ones. There are a number of criticisms of their views (see p. 117). Braverman's ideas on deskilling clearly oppose the view expressed in the statement, although Braverman has also been heavily criticized (pp. 116–7). You might conclude that the picture is mixed, with evidence of post-Fordism in some areas of employment, but not in others, and a mixture of deskilling and reskilling. Paul Thompson makes useful comments to conclude with (see p. 117).

4 **Industrial relations are increasingly characterized by peace and harmony**

You could begin by discussing the nature of industrial relations using different theories such as functionalism, pluralism and Marxism (see p. 117). Functionalists suggest that there has always been a degree of peace and harmony based on shared interests, while Marxists argue that capitalism inevitably produces differences of interest. Evidence does suggest a decline in strikes over recent years (see p. 118), but this may be due to weakened union power rather than harmony. Edwards and Scullion point out that industrial conflict can take a number of forms (see p. 118), and a reduction in the number of strikes does not necessarily show that there is peace and harmony in industrial relations.

5 **Unemployment is caused by the capitalist system and has damaging effects on individuals and society**

There is a range of views about the underlying causes of unemployment. The statement above represents a Marxist viewpoint because it sees unemployment as rooted in the capitalist economic system. Capitalism proceeds in a series of booms and slumps, and requires a disposable pool of workers – known as a reserve army of labour – who can move in and out of work as needed (see p. 119). Another viewpoint emphasizes the impact of technological change (p. 119), while market liberal theory (favoured by Margaret Thatcher) represents a 'New Right' position which totally rejects Marxism and links unemployment to powerful unions and unfeasibly high pay rates.

Sociologists have identified a number of effects of unemployment, much of the research being conducted in the 1980s when the unemployment rate was at a historically high level (see pp. 118–9). A range of effects have been identified, which relate to people's financial, personal, psychological and social states (see pp. 120–1). Particularly alarming is the evidence linking unemployment with ill-health and premature death. Sociologists have also noted how the effects of unemployment vary according to age, gender and ethnicity. A slightly different angle is taken by Critcher, Dicks and Waddington (see p. 121) who examine the effects of pit closures on local communities.

6 **Leisure patterns are determined to a large extent by the paid work people do**

Parker's research in the 1970s focused on the link between work and leisure by showing how different types of job encouraged different kinds of leisure activities (see p. 121). However, his work has been subjected to a number of criticisms, which have focused largely on his failure to consider the issue of gender, and the range of other factors that influence leisure patterns (see pp. 121–2).

Roberts's research identifies a range of factors other than work that may influence leisure, such as family life cycle, gender, education and type of marital relationship (see pp. 121–2). Green *et al.* show how women have been ignored in the study of leisure. They demonstrate the different ways in which men and women experience leisure in a patriarchal society, and they show how a careful consideration of gender issues makes definitions and explanations of leisure more complex (see p. 122).

Postmodern theories of leisure reject any clear link between work and leisure. They see distinctions between work and leisure as becoming increasingly blurred, and emphasize the ways in which leisure is used to construct identity in the postmodern world (see pp. 123).

Parker's work, although influential in its time, now appears very dated.

Chapter 11

Education

1 Education systems simply reproduce inequality

This statement represents a Marxist point of view. It suggests that your class background determines your educational achievement and that equality of opportunity is merely an illusion which disguises social reproduction. Bowles and Gintis are key writers here (see pp. 130–1). Willis also believes that the education system reproduces class differences, but not in the straightforward manner proposed by Bowles and Gintis. His research shows working-class 'lads' actively rejecting the school's values and developing their own 'counter-school culture'. But their rebellion leads them into poorly paid manual jobs where they seek exactly the same sort of 'laffs' as they had at school.

Functionalist writers, such as Parsons and Davis and Moore (see p. 130), propose a different view. They believe that education performs the function of role allocation. Education assesses individuals so that they can be allocated to the jobs most suited to them. To have an accurate idea of people's talents, society needs to be based on meritocratic principles.

Statistics on the relationship between achievement and social factors such as class, gender and ethnicity indicate that members of certain groups face real disadvantages in education. There is a close link, for example, between wealth and achievement (see pp. 133–4). This rather undermines functionalist views.

2 The marketization of education has raised educational standards

New Right ideas exerted a decisive influence on the Conservative governments between 1979 and 1997. They believed that the most effective method of raising educational standards was to bring market principles into education (see pp. 131–3). A series of measures was introduced to encourage schools to compete with each other for pupils, and to give parents more information about school performance so that they could make effective school choices (see p. 132).

The Conservative reforms were evaluated in research by Ball, Bowe and Gewirtz (see p. 132). They identify a wide range of problems associated with marketization, and show how the reforms tend to benefit the middle classes and disadvantage those without cultural capital.

3 The Labour government elected in 1997 made a significant contribution to improving equality of opportunity

The educational measures introduced by the Blair government are outlined on p. 133. Some of these measures, such as the introduction of Education Action Zones, can be seen to be a form of positive discrimination aimed at improving the achievement of less privileged pupils. However, in other ways there has been continuity with the market-oriented policies of the previous Conservative administrations (see pp. 129 and 133). The replacement of student grants with loans, for example, may have had the effect of discouraging those from working-class backgrounds from applying to university. See p. 133 for an evaluation of New Labour policies.

4 Social class differences in educational achievement are the result of factors within the home

The relationship between social class and educational achievement is spelled out on p. 133–4. A variety of sociologists have proposed that the link between class and achievement is caused by home background. In the 1960s Douglas (see p. 134) identified primary socialization and parental interest as key factors, while Bernstein pointed to class differences in the use of language (see pp. 134–5). These views, which seem to point the finger of blame at working-class culture, have been heavily criticized (see p. 135), but they still led to the theory of cultural deprivation (see p. 135) and resulting policies of compensatory education.

Ball et al. (see p. 135) focus on the role of cultural capital in creating and maintaining class inequalities in education; while others such as Smith and Noble (see pp. 135–6) focus on material inequality between the classes. Halsey, Heath and Ridge (see p. 136) stress the importance of both material and cultural factors.

Interactionist sociologists have focused their attention away from the home and have instead looked closely at the role of interaction in schools in reproducing class inequality. Ball's research (see p. 136) shows how working-class pupils can be negatively 'labelled' and directed into lower bands, and the effect this can have on both their own and teachers' behaviour and expectations.

5 The under-achievement of boys is a major problem facing the education system today

Statistics on gender and education show that the educational performance of both sexes has been increasing but that girls' attainment has been improving particularly rapidly, to the point where they are now slightly ahead of boys in most areas (see p. 136). It is not clear, therefore, that boys are actually under-achieving. Weiner, Arnot and David (see p. 138) are sceptical about the claim, seeing it as a 'moral panic' and part of the 'backlash' against feminism. They believe that the 'moral panic' about boys takes attention away from a celebration of female educational success (see p. 138 for an explanation of the reasons for this).

Mitsos and Browne (see p. 138) accept that boys are under-achieving and offer a range of possible reasons. However, recent work, such as that of Connolly (see p. 139), points to a more complex picture in which it is necessary to look at the relationships between class, gender and ethnicity.

6 **Racism remains common in schools and is a key factor in explaining ethnic minority under-achievement**

There is considerable variation in the educational achievement of ethnic minority groups (see p. 139), so the phrase 'under-achievement' has to be used very carefully in this context. Nevertheless a variety of explanations have been put forward to explain patterns of ethnic minority achievement, many of which focus on racism (usually unconscious) in schools.

Coard (see p. 140) identifies a significant degree of racism in schools. He argues that both the formal curriculum and the hidden curriculum disadvantage black pupils; while Wright (see p. 140) discovers a worrying level of racism among teachers in her research. Recent studies, such as those by Mirza (see p. 140) and Mac an Ghaill (see pp. 140–1), suggest that many ethnic minority pupils are able to overcome the negative labelling and discrimination they face in British schools.

A range of other explanations have also been put forward to explain ethnic minority under-achievement. Hernstein and Murray have gone so far as to suggest the possibility of genetic differences in the intelligence of different races, although this view has been heavily criticized (see p. 139). Other writers have looked at aspects of home background, in particular language (see p. 139) and family life (see p. 140).

Chapter 12

Culture and identity

1 **Mass culture has had a dangerous effect on society**

A definition of mass culture can be found on p. 149. Note its similarity to the term popular culture. The view expressed in the statement above derives from the concern of writers such as Macdonald, during the 1950s, about the impact of the mass media on society (see p. 149). These ideas have been heavily criticized by Strinati (see pp. 149). Postmodernists take a very different view of culture, celebrating mass (or popular) culture and denying any distinction between high and popular culture.

2 **Youth subcultures are ways of resisting dominant ideology**

A definition of the term 'subculture' can be found on p. 147. The view in the statement above

represents the starting point of analyses of youth subcultures by the Birmingham Centre for Contemporary Cultural Studies (see pp. 148). Jefferson's analysis of Teddy boys, for example, argues that the style and behaviour of the Teddy boys were an attempt to recreate a sense of working-class community in the face of growing affluence (see p. 148). Hebdige is also influenced by Marxist ideas and his approach is not dissimilar (see p. 148). He uses the techniques of semiology to analyse the 'hidden' meanings of youth styles. The work of the CCCS and Hebdige is evaluated on p. 148.

3 **Culture is shared by members of a society**

This view represents a functionalist perspective. Functionalists such as Parsons and Durkheim argue that the sharing of culture is crucial to the successful functioning of any society. This shared culture is passed from generation to generation through the process of socialization.

Functionalist views and their idea that culture is totally shared have been questioned by a number of other perspectives (see pp. 147–8). Marxists claim that what may appear to be shared culture is, in fact, ruling-class ideology (see p. 147), although recently some neo-Marxists have claimed that aspects of culture such as youth subcultures can act as ways of symbolically resisting ruling-class domination (see pp. 148). Postmodernists reject the view that any one culture is dominant. They stress cultural diversity and analyse the effects of a media-saturated society (see pp. 149–50).

4 **Postmodernism is the most effective perspective in understanding contemporary culture and identity**

A variety of perspectives – such as functionalism and Marxism (see pp. 147) – offer explanations of culture and identity. However, both functionalism and Marxism originated many years ago and some sociologists have questioned their ability to relate to societies at the beginning of the twenty-first century. Postmodernism grew up far more recently and its advocates argue that it offers a more convincing explanation of the nature of culture and identity today.

Postmodern views of identity (see p. 147) stress the changing, unstable and contradictory nature of identity today, and argue that people have a great deal of choice about what social groups they identify with. Strinati (see pp. 149–50) offers a clear explanation of the key features of postmodernist analysis of culture and the reasons for the growth of postmodernism, and a number of evaluative points.

5 **Contemporary societies are characterized by fractured identities**

Functionalists believed that the construction of identity was a fairly straightforward process. Through socialization people learnt what was expected of them as a man, woman, member of the family and local community, and so on (see p. 147). Writers such as Hall (see p. 150) and Bradley (see pp. 150–1) argue that people no longer possess a single, unified concept of who they are. Instead, their identity is broken up into a number of diverse and unstable parts, hence the use of the term, 'fractured identities'.

Hall identifies a number of processes – globalization, for example – which have led to this new situation. Bradley explains how identities based on class, gender, 'race'/ethnicity and age have 'fractured' in recent years. Both writers use some ideas drawn from postmodernism but hold back from claiming that societies have changed completely.

Chapter 13

Communication and the media

1 **The mass media perpetuate gender stereotypes**

This view is supported by most, if not all, feminists. Radical feminists in particular would support it (see p. 159).

Many sociologists have used content analysis to show that the portrayal of women tends to be stereotypical. Examples include the work of Bretl and Cantor, Meehan, Saucier, Provenzo, and Holland and Ferguson (see p. 159). These claim, variously, that women are under-represented in certain areas of the media, that they are portrayed in conventional gender roles, that they are seen as passive in computer games, that they are included in serious programmes only if they are young and attractive, that magazines encourage a cult of femininity, etc.

Some sociologists assume that such content does perpetuate gender stereotypes (e.g. Provenzo, who uses a hypodermic model). Frueh and McGhee have evidence that heavy TV viewing encourages acceptance of traditional roles amongst young children. Beuf claims that it leads to young girls abandoning ambitions by the age of 6 (see p. 160).

However, you need to be cautious about assuming that the media perpetuate gender stereotypes, for three main reasons:

1 The degree to which the media portray traditional stereotypes may be decreasing.
2 Even where stereotypes exist, you cannot assume that they are necessarily accepted by women. The hypodermic model of media effects has been heavily criticized, and it is this model that is used in some studies (e.g. Provenzo). Some radical feminists emphasize that women are active interpreters of media messages and may well be critical of stereotypical images of women (see p. 159).
3 Where stereotypical views of gender are perpetuated, the media may not be the cause. Other factors (such as sexual discrimination in the labour market or lack of childcare facilities)

may be responsible, rather than media stereotypes.

2 **The content of the mass media is fair and balanced and reflects the diverse interests of the population**

This view is supported by pluralists (see p. 156) see the media as reflecting the public interest. However, pluralists are criticized: by Marxists who argue that owners influence the media (p. 157); by the neo-Marxist cultural hegemony model which stresses the influence of ruling-class culture; and by those who stress the influence of organizational factors on media content. There are numerous studies which suggest that the content of the mass media is not fair and balanced with respect to gender, class, ethnicity, age and disability.

3 **The mass media have little effect on people's behaviour**

Models of media effects generally disagree with this statement. The hypodermic model and the two-step flow model suggest strong effects, but both have been criticized (see p. 158). The uses and gratifications model sees the effects as influenced by the use made of the media by the audience (p. 158). The interpretative model probably agrees most closely with the statement, since it stresses that any effects are mediated by the way in which people interpret the media, and people reject many messages (see p. 158). However, the structured interpretation model suggests that particular social groups will interpret media messages in certain ways. More recent approaches, such as the last two models and postmodernism (p. 158–9), move away from seeing the media as directly affecting behaviour, and see the effects more in terms of influencing the way in which people see the social world.

4 **We live in a media-saturated society in which people find it difficult to distinguish fantasy from reality**

This view is strongly supported by postmodernists, particularly in the work of Baudrillard on hyperreality and Turkle on simulation (see p. 159). The media may be prevalent in modern societies, but the idea of saturation may be an exaggeration. People may also be influenced by friends (as in the two-step flow model) (see p. 158) and by social position (as in the structured interpretation model) (see pp. 158–9). People can still reject media messages where they do not accord with personal experience (see Morley's study of Nationwide, pp. 158–9). There is little evidence that people fail to distinguish fantasy from reality, and there are a number of specific criticisms of postmodernism (see p. 159).

5 **The mass media promote racism**

There are some studies which might support this view, such as that by the Broadcasting Standards Commission (see p. 160). Studies by Van Dijk and

Hartmann and Husband (see p. 160) also support the statement. However, these studies are quite old and there is evidence that representations of ethnic minorities are becoming more diverse and sympathetic (see p. 160). Furthermore, ethnic minorities are active interpreters of media messages (as in Gillespie's study, p. 160), and there is no guarantee that audiences will interpret media representations of ethnic minorities in a racist way.

6 **The content of the mass media is largely determined by those who own the media**

This view is supported by Marxists, such as Bagdikian, and Boyd-Barrett and Rantanen (see p. 157). There is plenty of evidence that ownership of the media is concentrated, and that owners sometimes interfere in content. However, there are a number of specific criticisms of Marxism (see p. 157). State regulation, audience preferences and radical journalists can all influence content. Neo-Marxists argue that ruling-class culture has more influence than direct interference by owners (p. 157), and organizational factors also have an impact on content (see pp. 157–8).

7 **Everybody interprets the media in their own way**

This view tends to be supported by the interpretative model and writers such as Buckingham (see p. 158). However, it neglects the influence of opinion leaders (see the two-step flow model, p. 158) and subcultures (as in the structured interpretation model, pp. 158–9), and it ignores the possibility that people might sometimes be directly influenced by the media (the hypodermic model, p. 158). Neo-Marxists argue that certain messages become dominant in a cultural hegemony of the ruling class, as illustrated in the work of the Glasgow Media Group (see p. 157). People do interpret the media differently, but the interpretations are not random and may be strongly influenced by social factors.

Chapter 14

Methodology

1 **Sociology cannot be a scientific subject because humans possess consciousness**

This viewpoint would be supported by phenomenologists and some interpretive sociologists. Phenomenologists argue that the possession of consciousness means that humans classify the world in terms of their taken-for-granted assumptions. These classifications are shaped by human consciousness and cannot be objective. Sociology therefore lacks the factual data on which to base a scientific sociology. Studies by Atkinson (suicide) and Cicourel (juvenile justice) can illustrate this point. In addition, humans are, by their nature, somewhat unpredictable, and sociology cannot therefore produce the sort of universal

theories advanced by scientists.

Interpretive sociologists generally argue that the possession of consciousness makes scientific methods inappropriate for the study of humans. Humans interpret the meaning of events before reacting to them, so internal factors shape behaviour as much as external stimuli. Internal meanings and motives cannot be directly observed in a scientific way. Experimentation cannot produce reliable data about humans since humans react to the fact that they are being studied, not just to the variables controlled by sociologists.

Positivists, however, believe that humans can be studied scientifically. Although they accept that humans possess consciousness, this does not prevent sociologists from collecting social facts about human beings, expressing them in a statistical form, looking for correlations, identifying causal relationships and even finding laws of human behaviour. An example of this is Durkheim's study of suicide. Positivists believe that human behaviour can be explained in terms of observable external stimuli. Humans may not be aware of the influence of external factors upon them, but positivists can discover this using statistical analysis.

Realists would disagree with part of this statement. They accept that humans possess consciousness, and that this shapes behaviour, but they do not believe that this prevents sociology from being scientific. According to realists, scientists often study unobservable phenomena in the natural world (e.g. magnetic fields), but they can see the effects of those phenomena. Similarly sociologists can see the effects of internal stimuli on people's behaviour. Furthermore, scientists often study unpredictable aspects of the natural world (e.g. weather systems). The unpredictable nature of humans because of their consciousness does not prevent scientific study of them. To realists both science and sociology can study unpredictable things in complex open systems. According to this point of view, social and physical sciences are concerned with studying the underlying and often unobservable structures and processes that shape observable events. These structures and processes can include elements of human consciousness.

2 **Participant observation makes up in validity what it lacks in reliability**

Participant observation lacks reliability according to positivists (and others) because it is impossible to repeat the research and check the findings. Each study is unique because it relates to a specific place and time. It involves interaction between the particular researcher and those being studied, and the presence of any other researcher would change the interaction. Furthermore, the interpretation of what happens depends very much on the personal preconceptions and interests of the researcher. A different participant observer would not note and take account of exactly the same aspects of the interaction. A different participant observer might well interpret particular events differently.

However, advocates of participant observation argue that it is more valid. It is closer to real social life than other methods. The researcher's interpretations are likely to be more valid than they would be using other methods because the researcher has some of the same experiences as those being studied. The researcher does not impose questions, or categories, on those being studied, and may therefore find out what is important in the process of the research. Hypotheses can emerge from the research rather than being devised before it commences.

However, it should not be assumed that the research will be entirely valid. To some extent the presence of a researcher will change the interaction, even if the researcher is covert and tries to blend into the background. The research is bound to rely upon the researcher's subjective interpretations, which may be wide of the mark. Without the use of interviews, it is difficult to check whether the researcher's interpretations match those of the subjects. Nevertheless, overall, its closeness to social life does support the claims of interactionists (and others) that it remain perhaps the most valid of methods.

3   Interviews may be practical, but they are unlikely to provide reliable or valid data

It is possible to agree with the first part of this statement, that interviews are practical. In particular they can be used to produce a very wide range of data, from simple facts to data on internal processes, meanings, motives, feelings, emotions, etc. You can ask people about their past or current lives and future aspirations, about their feelings and attitudes and their reasons for behaving in particular ways. Interviews are not usually especially expensive, and unstructured interviews may require little preparation. They allow access to groups who might not admit an observer, and they require little in terms of personal commitment from the researcher. However, they are less practical than questionnaires if you want to conduct a large-scale survey with a geographically dispersed population.

The second part of the statement can also be supported. The validity of the data may be affected by faulty memory, deliberate lies, people's inability to fully understand their own behaviour, and the effects of interviewer bias. People may not act in accordance with what they say in interviews. (Expand on all these points.) Nevertheless, unstructured interviews are less shaped by the researcher than questionnaires are. Unlike participant observation, you can ask people to reflect upon your interpretations, and you can ask people what is going on in their heads rather than inferring it from their behaviour. Given that no research method is entirely valid, interviews are not particularly lacking in validity. They are certainly fairly practical.

4   Official statistics always provide a misleading picture of the social world

Sociologists of different theoretical persuasions would agree with this statement. Phenomenologists, such as Atkinson and Cicourel, argue that official statistics reflect the taken-for-granted assumptions of those who produce them. They are based upon the categorization procedures used and cannot describe reality objectively.

Conflict theorists argue that statistics reflect power structures and are always therefore liable to be distorted. Miles and Irvine see statistics as manipulated by governments – e.g. the redefinitions of unemployment or the distortions in NHS figures. Marxists argue that statistics neglect key features of society – e.g. Nichols on the lack of wealth statistics. Statistics can be seen as representing ideological frameworks.

However, positivists see official statistics as offering reliable and valid data based upon social facts. They can be used to uncover correlations and to discover causal relationships and even laws of behaviour.

All these positions are somewhat extreme. Certain types of statistics may be highly unreliable – e.g. statistics on the numbers of crimes committed. Others (such as the statistics on criminal convictions) are rather more reliable. The validity of some statistics is not particularly open to question – e.g. court and prison statistics, or basic statistics from the census. Therefore whether statistics are misleading or not may depend on the type of statistics, and so it is dangerous to generalize.

5   All research methods have their uses, especially when combined together

Positivists tend to dismiss qualitative research methods as being unreliable because they are hard to replicate, and they criticize them for being unscientific. Such methods do not confine themselves to studying measurable, objectively quantifiable phenomena. On the other hand, interpretive sociologists dismiss some quantitative techniques because they see them as invalid. In their view, such methods are distant from real social life, they impose the researcher's own concepts and ignore the meanings and motives that shape behaviour.

Both these positions are rather exaggerated, and in practice most sociologists use a variety of methods. Phenomenologists sometimes produce statistical data (e.g. Cicourel). Positivists often discuss meanings (e.g. Durkheim discussed different types of suicide). Different research methods may be useful for collecting different types of data. Questionnaires are useful for collecting simple factual data, for their reliability, and for their ability to use large samples which can form the basis for generalizations. Interviews allow the exploration of what people think in depth, while participant observation gets you close to actual social life.

It is increasingly accepted that there are benefits in using a range of methods, especially if used together. Bryman identifies the advantages of triangulation, such as using different types of data to check accuracy, qualitative data generating hypotheses to be checked using qualitative data, combining methods to produce a more complete picture and using qualitative data to explain statistical links.

6 **The theoretical approach influences the choice of method more than practical constraints**

Some sociologists are strongly committed to particular theoretical approaches to sociological methodology. On the surface you would expect positivists to confine themselves to using statistical data and interpretivists to use exclusively qualitative data. To positivists only quantitative data can be objective. Such data can record observable social facts and allow the researcher to look for correlations, causal relationships and laws. Positivists should therefore favour the use of questionnaires and official statistics.

Phenomenologists see the social world as made up of the interpretations of individuals, such as coroners deciding whether a suicide has taken place or police deciding whether an incident is criminal. You would therefore expect phenomenologists to use more qualitative methods, such as in-depth interviews (Atkinson interviewed coroners' officers) or participant observation (used by Cicourel). Symbolic interactionists are interested in the way in which interaction takes place and the way in which people's self-concepts change during the course of interaction. They should therefore favour participant observation.

Although sociologists of particular persuasions do often stick to the methods suggested by their approaches, this is not always the case. For example, Cicourel (a phenomenologist) made extensive use of statistics in his study of juvenile justice; Atkinson (a phenomenologist) used observation in his study of coroners' courts; Becker (a symbolic interactionist) used interviews in his study of marijuana smokers. Durkheim (often seen as a positivist) attempted to interpret the meaning of different types of suicide as well as using statistics.

Part of the reason for such anomalies is certainly that practicalities sometimes make the preferred research method impossible. For example, Becker could hardly have hung around with groups of young people in the hope that they might start using marijuana – it would have been too time-consuming. Similarly, Atkinson would have found it impossible to find a role as a participant observer in a coroner's court. Problems of access, time, money and funding often mean that researchers compromise on their ideals.

However, it is not simply a matter of practicality.

As Bryman points out, it is very difficult for interpretive researchers to avoid any reference to numbers in a study, and very difficult for quantitative researchers to avoid interpreting people's meanings and motives when analysing statistics. Furthermore, many sociologists have followed Weber in arguing that all research methods have their uses, depending on the nature of the subject being studied and the sort of data required. Many sociologists do not adhere rigidly to a particular theoretical approach and can therefore use a range of methods without compromising their beliefs. As Bryman points out, there are good theoretical reasons for using the triangulation of different methods.

The choice of research method tends to be shaped by a variety of factors. The theoretical approach is one such consideration, but practicalities and the nature of the subject being studied are probably at least as important as theoretical preferences.

Chapter 15

Sociological theory

1 **Marxists place too much emphasis on classes and material factors**

A number of sociological approaches would agree with this. Conflict theorists argue that class is only one of the important social divisions, along with gender, ethnicity and age (see p. 186). Weber is a particular critic of Marx. He argues that ideas as well as material factors shape history (see pp. 186-7). His views can be illustrated by referring to his work on the Protestant ethic (see pp. 76-7). Feminists argue that Marxists neglect or ignore gender differences (see p. 23), while some sociologists stress the importance of racism (see pp. 34-5). Some postmodernists believe that the significance of class has been greatly reduced (see p. 14).

However, there are still Marxists who see class as of paramount importance (for example, John Westergaard, pp. 14-15). Marxism has been adapted to explain gender inequality (see pp. 23 and 24) and racism (see p. 36), which have been portrayed as developing from class inequality. Many Marxists do not place exclusive emphasis on material factors, and neo-Marxists such as Gramsci stress the importance of ideology and culture (see p. 105).

2 **Functionalism is an outdated theory**

Functionalism developed in the nineteenth century and reached the peak of its popularity in the middle of the twentieth century. Since the 1960s it has certainly declined in popularity in comparison with interactionism (p. 187), Marxism (pp. 185-6), feminism (pp. 23-4), and more recently postmodernism (pp. 188-90). There are numerous criticisms that have been directed against functionalism (see p. 185), and it does not seem to provide an explanation for the operation of multicultural societies in which there is conflict. Nevertheless the work of Durkheim (see pp. 184–5) continues to influence contemporary sociologists, particularly in terms of identifying problems of modern societies such as anomie and egoism. Functionalism may not, therefore, be entirely outdated.

3 **Both structural and social action theories are useful for understanding society**

Structural theories include Marxism (pp. 185–6) and functionalism (pp. 184–5), while social action theories include symbolic interactionism (p. 187). Structural theories tend to stress the way in which society shapes human behaviour, whereas social action theories stress the way in which human behaviour shapes society. It is increasingly accepted that the two approaches need to be combined. Weber examined both social structure and social action (pp. 186–7); and more recently Anthony Giddens has tried to combine the two approaches, using the concept of structuration (see pp. 187–8).

4 **We may have entered a period of postmodernity but that does not mean we should accept postmodernism**

The concept of postmodernity refers to changes in society, whereas postmodernism is a new theoretical approach to understanding society. The idea of postmodernity does not entail rejecting traditional sociological approaches to studying society, and it is embraced by theorists of postmodernity such as David Harvey (see p. 189). On the other hand, writers such as Baudrillard (pp. 188–9) and Lyotard (p. 188) support the idea of postmodernism. Lyotard argues that all metanarratives (including modern sociological theories) should be rejected, while Baudrillard believes that fact and fiction have become confused as a result of the development of simulacra. However, both Lyotard and Baudrillard have been criticized (see pp. 186 and 187), and many sociologists believe that it is still possible to understand the way in which society works. Anthony Giddens even denies that we have yet entered a period of postmodernity, and believes that a modern sociology, which can develop an objective understanding of society, is possible (see p. 189).

5 **Interpretive approaches tend to ignore constraints in social life**

Interpretive approaches include phenomenology (p. 187), symbolic interactionism (p. 187), and Weber's approach to social action (pp. 186–7). All emphasize the extent to which humans possess consciousness, and the idea that consciousness shapes how people interpret the world or how they

behave. These approaches have been criticized by structural sociologists for neglecting the way in which factors such as power constrain people's choices. For example, Marxists argue that class inequality means that subject classes have less economic power than ruling classes to shape their own lives (see pp. 185–6). Similarly many feminists argue that women are constrained by patriarchy (see pp. 23–4). On the other hand, some interpretive approaches take some account of the existence of constraints. For example, symbolic interactionists accept that the existence of social roles places some limits on human action (even though those roles are flexible). Weber was well aware of constraints on social action, as exemplified in concepts such as class and status (see p. 7) and bureaucracy (pp. 186–7).

6 **No single sociological theory can explain all aspects of society**

A number of sociological theories have claimed to be able to explain all aspects of society, but arguably each is better at explaining certain things. For example, Marxism is useful for explaining class inequality and conflict and for highlighting the influence of material factors in social life (see pp. 185–6). Functionalism is better for explaining how societies cohere and remain stable (pp. 184–5). Feminism is useful for understanding gender inequality (see pp. 23–4), and conflict theories emphasize the variety of sources of conflict and inequality (see p. 186). Weber too recognizes that there is a range of social divisions, and he shows that ideas as well as material factors can shape social life (see pp. 186–7). Symbolic interactionism is useful for studying how people interact in small groups (p. 187), while phenomenology and ethnomethodology stress the importance of the way in which people interpret and make sense of the world (p. 187). Postmodernists highlight important changes in the contemporary world, but some reject modern sociological approaches altogether and so their theory cannot really be combined with previous sociological theories.

7 **There are both similarities and differences between Marxism and functionalism**

It is possible to agree with this statement. The differences are more obvious and more numerous, but there are some similarities.
The differences include:
- Marxists emphasize conflict whereas functionalists emphasize consensus.
- Marxists see inequality as undesirable; functionalists see it as functional (see Davis and Moore, pp. 6–7).
- Marxists stress revolutionary change whereas functionalists stress evolutionary change.
- Marxists see the economy as the most important part of society, whereas functionalists see all parts of society as interrelated.

- Marxists explain institutions in terms of economic infrastructure, whereas functionalists explain them in terms of functional prerequisites.
- Marxists expect a communist revolution; functionalists do not.

However, there are some similarities. For example:

- Both functionalism and Marxism are structural approaches which stress the way in which the structure of society tends to shape behaviour.
- Both are modern approaches which are optimistic about the future.
- Both believe that an objective science of society is possible.
- Both see religion as a conservative force (see pp. 74–5).

Test your knowledge and understanding: Answers

Chapter 1

1 c	4 d	7 a	10 c	13 d	16 b	19 d
2 a	5 a	8 a, c	11 b	14 c	17 b	20 c
3 b	6 d	9 a	12 d	15 d	18 b	

Chapter 2

1 c	5 c	9 a, d	13 d	17 b, c	21 c	25 c	29 b
2 c	6 c	10 a	14 c, d	18 b	22 c, d	26 a	30 b, c
3 b	7 a	11 c	15 b, c	19 c	23 a	27 d	
4 d	8 b	12 b	16 b	20 a, c	24 c	28 d	

Chapter 3

1 a, b	5 c, d	9 c	13 b, c	17 c	21 c	25 b	29 d
2 c, d	6 c	10 c	14 c	18 b	22 d	26 b	30 b
3 c	7 a	11 c	15 c	19 c	23 b	27 d	
4 b	8 b	12 c	16 c	20 a	24 a	28 c	

Chapter 4

1 a	5 b	9 a	13 b	17 c	21 d	25 b	29 c
2 b	6 a	10 c	14 c	18 b	22 a	26 d	30 a
3 d	7 a	11 b	15 c	19 b	23 c	27 d	31 a
4 c	8 d	12 c, d	16 a	20 d	24 b	28 b	32 d

Chapter 5

1 a	4 d	7 a	10 c	13 b	16 c	19 d
2 b	5 c	8 b	11 b	14 d	17 c	20 a, c
3 a	6 c	9 d	12 c	15 a, c	18 b	

Chapter 6

1 a	5 d	9 c	13 a	17 c	21 c	25 d	29 c
2 c	6 b	10 b	14 b	18 a, d	22 a	26 b	30 c
3 c	7 a	11 b	15 c	19 c	23 c	27 b	
4 c	8 a	12	16 d	20 b, c	24 b	28 a	

Chapter 7

1 c	5 a	9 a	13 d	17 c	21 b	25 b	29 b
2 d	6 c	10 c	14 a	18 b	22 a	26 a	30 d
3 c	7 b	11 a	15 c	19 a	23 d	27 a	
4 c	8 a	12 b	16 c	20 c	24 b	28 b	

Chapter 8

1 b	5 d	9 c	13 a	17 c	21 d	25 c	29 a
2 b	6 c	10 b	14 d	18 c	22 d	26 c	30 c
3 c	7 a	11 a	15 a	19 b	23 b	27 d	
4 a	8 a	12 b	16 d	20 a	24 b	28 a	

Chapter 9

1 a, d	5 c	9 d	13 b	17 b	21 d	25 a, d	29 c
2 a	6 a	10 a	14 b	18 d	22 a, b	26 a, c	30 d
3 c	7 b	11 b	15 a	19 a	23 c, d	27 b	
4 d	8 c	12 b	16 a	20 d	24 c	28 c, d	

Chapter 10

1 d	4 b	7 d	10 a	13 b	16 b	19 d
2 b	5 d	8 b	11 c	14 c	17 c	20 b
3 a	6 b	9 b	12 d	15 a	18 a	

Chapter 11

1	d	5	a	9	c	13	c	17	d	21	b	25	d	29	a
2	a	6	b	10	a	14	b	18	d	22	c	26	c	30	b
3	c	7	a	11	d	15	a	19	a	23	b	27	a		
4	b	8	c	12	c	16	a	20	b	24	d	28	b		

Chapter 12

1	b	4	b	7	a	10	b	13	d	16	a	19	d
2	c	5	c	8	a	11	b	14	c	17	b	20	a
3	a	6	a	9	b	12	a	15	b	18	b		

Chapter 13

1	c	5	a, b	9	b	13	d	17	a	21	d	25	a
2	a, d	6	b	10	c	14	a, b, d	18	d	22	b	26	c
3	d	7	d	11	a	15	b	19	b	23	b		
4	a	8	d	12	b	16	a	20	b	24	c		

Chapter 14

1	a, d	5	b	9	c	13	c	17	a	21	b	25	c	29	a
2	a	6	a	10	b	14	c	18	a, d	22	b, c	26	d	30	c
3	d	7	b	11	a	15	d	19	c	23	c	27	b		
4	c, d	8	d	12	c	16	c	20	d	24	b	28	a		

Chapter 15

1	a, b	5	b, c	9	d	13	a	17	c	21	a	25	b	29	c
2	d	6	c	10	d	14	b	18	d	22	b	26	d	30	b
3	a	7	c	11	c	15	b	19	d	23	d	27	c		
4	a	8	c	12	c	16	a	20	b	24	c	28	b		